Roger II of Sicily

Although many recent studies have a⌐   ⌐pects of medieval
southern Italy, this is the first w⌐   ⌐ to be devoted
specifically to the life and⌐   ⌐under of the
kingdom of Sicily.

 The book provi⌐'   ⌐of the reign,
and a clear, scho⌐   ⌐e and of the development of roya⌐   ⌐ated by the Norman
Roger of Hautville 1.⌐   ⌐ century was a monarchy
with highly develope⌐   ⌐ elaborate bureaucracy, a reasonably well-filled treasu⌐   ⌐d cultural heritage reflected by the
presence of Arabs and Gre⌐   ⌐ourt. Based on many years of research in
archives and libraries across ⌐urope, the book offers a valuable overview
of one of the most striking periods in south Italian and European history.

HUBERT HOUBEN is Professor of Medieval History, Università degli
Studi di Lecce, Italy.

Cambridge medieval textbooks

This is a series of specially commissioned textbooks for teachers and students, designed to complement the monograph series Cambridge Studies in Medieval Life and Thought by providing introductions to a range of topics in medieval history. This series combines both chronological and thematic approaches, and will deal with British and European topics. All volumes in the series will be published in hard covers and in paperback. For a list of titles in the series, see end of book.

ROGER II OF SICILY

A ruler between east and west

HUBERT HOUBEN

Translated by
Graham A. Loud and Diane Milburn

CAMBRIDGE
UNIVERSITY PRESS

PUBLISHED BY THE PRESS SYNDICATE OF THE UNIVERSITY OF CAMBRIDGE
The Pitt Building, Trumpington Street, Cambridge CB2 1RP, United Kingdom

CAMBRIDGE UNIVERSITY PRESS
The Edinburgh Building, Cambridge, CB2 2RU, UK
40 West 20th Street, New York, NY 10011-4211, USA
477 Williamstown Road, Port Melbourne, VIC 3207, Australia
Ruiz de Alarcón 13, 28014 Madrid, Spain
Dock House, The Waterfront, Cape Town 8001, South Africa

http://www.cambridge.org

Originally published in German as *Roger II. von Sizilien*
by Wissenschaftliche Buchgesellschaft, Darmstadt, 1997
and © Wissenschaftliche Buchgesellschaft, Darmstadt, 1997

First published in English by Cambridge University Press 2002 as *Roger II of Sicily*
English translation © Cambridge University Press 2002

Printed in the United Kingdom at the University Press, Cambridge

Typeface Bembo 10/11.5 pt.   *System* LATEX 2ε [TB]

A catalogue record for this book is available from the British Library

Library of Congress Cataloguing in Publication data
Houben, Hubert.
[Roger II. von Sizilien. English]
Roger II of Sicily: a ruler between east and west / Hubert Houben; translated by
Graham A. Loud and Diane Milburn.
p.   cm.
Translation of: Roger II. von Sizilien.
Includes bibliographical references and index.
ISBN 0 521 65208 1 (hardback) ISBN 0 521 65573 0 (paperback)
1. Roger II, King of Sicily, d. 1154.   2. Sicily (Italy) – Kings and rulers –
Biography.   3. Sicily (Italy) – History – Roger II, 1105–1154.   I. Title: Roger
the second of Sicily.   II. Title
DG867.25 .H6813   2002
945′.704′090–dc21
[B]   2001043669

ISBN 0 521 65208 1 hardback
ISBN 0 521 65573 0 paperback

CONTENTS

——————— • ———————

ILLUSTRATIONS

———— · ————

FOREWORD TO THE GERMAN EDITION

———————— • ————————

King Roger II of Sicily is undoubtedly one of the most important, but also most controversial, rulers of the twelfth century. For many years we have relied upon the monograph of the then twenty-five-year-old Erich Caspar (1879-1935), an excellent work comprising some 651 pages, including a calendar of documents, on which the high reputation of this famous German medievalist was founded. This work, which originally appeared in 1904, was republished as a photomechanical reprint in 1963 by the Darmstadt Wissenschaftliche Buchgesellschaft, as part of its highly commendable programme of reprints, because of its closeness to the sources, which to this day has never been surpassed, even though the book had been out of print for a long time. Despite the high quality of this work a new account of this ruler and his sphere was called for, which had to evaluate the results of the extensive international research which had taken place since 1904 – work not just by Italians, but by French, English, American and now once again German scholars as well. Caspar published his book while he was a collaborator (between 1903 and 1908) on the *Italia Pontificia* of Paul Kehr, the director of the Prussian (after 1937: German) Historical Institute in Rome. It was from members of this Institute that the most important German contributions to the history of southern Italy in the high Middle Ages came. After the Second World War, above all Walther Holtzmann was outstanding as director of this research. In 1982 Raoul Manselli could of course talk of 'the rearguard action of a great army retreating' with regard to the German contingent. There is no question that since then this rearguard has grown into a more powerful German contingent within the international troops again. It is to this contingent that the author of the present volume belongs, having researched his doctorate and *Habilitationsschrift* in Germany. He has been employed as professor of Medieval History at the universities of Bologna and Lecce for many years and through his numerous contributions to the history of southern Italy in the high Middle Ages has himself become part of an intensive Italian research effort. He is therefore more suited than anyone else to be the first to write about Roger II in the series of continuing synthesis in the German language. The limitation to about a third of the length of Caspar's work, necessary for economic reasons, prevents the epic breadth of that account; but it is also in its conciseness and precision that this book, firmly based upon modern research, including the author's own investigations, will definitely stimulate further work in this field. To the non-specialists, both students and educated general readers, it offers a scholarly account of an important aspect of European history in the twelfth century.

Peter Herde
Würzburg, February 1997

PREFACE TO THE GERMAN EDITION

——————— · ———————

It was at an international conference at Potenza in April 1989 that Peter Herde, the editor of the series 'Figures of the Middle Ages and the Renaissance' which was then in the planning stage, prompted me to write this book. This conference was organized by the Universities of Lecce and Potenza, and run by myself together with my colleagues Cosimo Damiano Fonseca (Potenza) and Benedetto Vetere (Lecce) on the subject of 'Political Unity and Regional Differences in the Kingdom of Sicily' ('Unità politica e differenze regionali nel Regno di Sicilia'). The reason, or the pretext, was the 800th anniversary of the death of King William II of Sicily, the grandson of Roger II. The papers delivered at this conference showed what progress had been made in research on the foundation of the Norman state in Sicily since the publication of the pioneering works of Erich Caspar (1904) and Ferdinand Chalandon (1907). When it was suggested that I write a new biography of Roger II, based on modern scholarship, to replace Caspar's now outdated youthful work, I was absolutely delighted.

I am indebted to many friends and colleagues. First to the series editor, who checked through the manuscript carefully. Individual sections were read by Martin Bertram (Rome), Reinhard Elze (Munich), Vera von Falkenhausen (Rome), Thomas Frank (Berlin/Rome), Jörg Jarnut (Paderborn), Theo Kölzer (Bonn), Michael Marsch (Berlin/Rome), Bernd Schneidmüller (Bamberg), Wolfgang Stürner (Stuttgart) and Loris Sturlese (Lecce). Adalgisa De Simone (Palermo) assisted me with Arabic questions. A research visit to Oxford in 1992 was necessary for my work; in the incomparable collegiate atmosphere of St John's I had the good fortune to meet the Emeritus Laudian Professor of Arabic A. F. L. ('Freddie') Beeston (1911–95). Jeremy Johns (Oxford) and Graham Loud (Leeds) gave me advice on a number of matters, as did Guglielmo Cavallo (Rome), Jean-Marie Martin (Paris/Rome), Norbert Kamp (Göttingen) and Lucinia Speciale (Rome/Lecce). The often difficult task of finding relevant literature was made considerably easier by my annual, repeated, albeit brief visits to the German Historical Institute in Rome, where the director Arnold Esch, the library director Hermann Goldbrunner and their colleagues did their utmost to accommodate me in every way. It only remains for me to express my gratitude to the Vatican Library, the Bibliotheca Hertziana and the Library of the Ecole Française.

My wife and my daughter tolerated my frequent absences with the greatest patience and understanding. I am indebted to Gianfranco Madonna (Lecce) for drawing the tables and maps and to Marit Borchering (Darmstadt) for taking care of the printing.

Hubert Houben
Lecce, January 1997

PREFACE TO THE ENGLISH EDITION

———————— • ————————

The English translation of my book on Roger II gives me the opportunity to undertake a few corrections and supplements to the text, particularly in the section concerning the regency of Adelaide and in those about culture and administration.

After I had completed the manuscript in January 1997 some important publications appeared which I have taken into account in the present English edition. These include Richard Bünemann's biography of Robert Guiscard, essays by Vera von Falkenhausen on Adelaide's regency and the Greek charters of the Norman kings of Sicily, William Tronzo's monograph on the Palatine Chapel in Palermo, and Errico Cuozzo and Jean Marie Martin's anthology in memory of Léon-Robert Ménager. I have also taken into account a recent contribution from Adalgisa De Simone. This refers to an Arabic biographical sketch of George of Antioch (al-Maqrīzī, *Kitāb al-Muqaffā*) which has hitherto been ignored, but which contains important new information.

For the benefit of the English readers and students I have made particular reference to the English translation of the history of so-called 'Hugo Falcandus' by Graham A. Loud and Thomas Wiedemann, which also contains a selection of other primary sources in English translation which are important for the history of the kingdom of Sicily in the twelfth century. Some reference has also been made in the footnotes to Graham A. Loud's *The Age of Robert Guiscard* (2000), but this was published too recently for its findings to be incorporated fully into the text. Other footnotes have been shortened with respect to the original text.

I am indebted to Vera von Falkenhausen and Francesco Panarelli for invaluable advice, to Graham Loud and Diane Milburn for making this translation, and to Dr Loud for allowing me to quote his unpublished English translations of the Latin sources. I take full responsibility for any errors which remain.

I dedicate this English version to my daughter Sofia for her eighteenth birthday.

H.H.
Lecce, November 2000

ABBREVIATIONS

———————— • ————————

Al. Tel.	*Alexandri Telesini abbatis Ystoria Rogerii regis Sicilie Calabrie atque Apulie*, ed. L. De Nava and D. Clementi (*FSI*, Rome 1991)
Amatus	*Storia de' Normanni di Amato di Montecassino*, ed. V. De Bartholomaeis (*FSI*, Rome 1935)
BAS	M. Amari, *Biblioteca Arabo-Sicula* (2 vols., Turin 1880)
Ca.	Caspar (1904), Calendar no.
CDB	*Codice Diplomatico Barese* (19 vols., Bari 1897–1950)
CDCaiet.	*Codex Diplomaticus Caietanus* (2 vols., Montecassino 1887–92)
CDP	*Codice Diplomatico Pugliese* (13 vols., Bari 1975–94)
Chron. Cas	*Chronica Monasterii Casinensis*, ed. H. Hoffmann (*MGH Scriptores* xxxiv, Hanover 1980)
Cusa, *Diplomi*	*I Diplomi greci ed arabi di Sicilia*, ed. S. Cusa (2 vols., Palermo 1868–82)
DA	*Deutsches Archiv für Erforschung des Mittelalters*
DBI	*Dizionario biografico degli Italiani*
Falcandus	*La historia o liber de regno Sicilie e la epistola ad Petrum Panormitane ecclesiae thesaurarium di Ugo Falcando*, ed. G. B. Siragusa (*FSI*, Rome 1897)
Falco	*Falcone di Benevento, Chronicon Beneventanum*, ed. E. D'Angelo (Florence 1998)
FSI	*Fonti per la storia d'Italia*
It. Pont.	*Italia Pontificia*
JL	*Regesta pontificum Romanorum*, ed. P. Jaffé and J. Loewenfeld

LdM	*Lexikon des Mittelalters*
Malaterra	*De rebus gestis Rogerii Calabriae et Siciliae comitis auctore Gaufredo Malaterra*, ed. E. Pontieri (*RIS*, Bologna 1925–8)
MGH	*Monumenta Germaniae Historica* (following the usual conventions, *SS* = *Scriptores*, *SRG* = *Scriptores Rerum Germanicarum* etc.)
NA	*Neues Archiv der Gesellschaft für ältere deutsche Geschichtskunde*
PG	Migne, *Patrologia Graeca*
PL	Migne, *Patrologia Latina*
QFIAB	*Quellen und Forschungen aus italienischen Archiven und Bibliotheken*
Reg. Imp.	*Regesta Imperii*
RIS	*Rerum italicarum scriptores* (Muratori)
Roger II, *Diplomata*	*Rogerii II. Regis Diplomata latina*, ed. C. Brühl (Codex Diplomaticus Regni Siciliae, Ser. 1.ii(1), Cologne 1987)
Romuald	*Romualdi Salernitani Chronicon*, ed. C. A. Garufi (*RIS*, Città di Castello 1935)
Tyrants	*The History of the Tyrants of Sicily by 'Hugo Falcandus' 1154–69*, trans. G. A. Loud and T. E. J. Wiedemann (Manchester 1998)
W. Ap.	*La geste de Robert Guiscard de Guillaume de Pouille*, ed. M. Mathieu (Palermo 1961)

CHRONOLOGY

———— • ————

1060	Roger I of Hauteville, Count of Sicily
1095	Birth of Roger II
1101	Death of Roger I; regency of Adelaide del Vasto
1112	The start of Roger II's independent rule
1113	Marriage of Adelaide to King Baldwin I of Jerusalem
1117	Expulsion of Adelaide, return to Sicily
1117 (?)	Marriage of Roger II to Elvira, daughter of King Alfonso VI of Castille-León
1122	Duke William of Apulia transfers all of Sicily and Calabria to Roger II
1124	Roger II reaches the Basilicata (Montescaglioso)
1127	Childless death of Duke William of Apulia; Roger, Prince of Salerno, Duke of Apulia, Calabria and Sicily
1128	Pope Honorius II invests Roger II with the duchy of Apulia, Calabria and Sicily
1129	Quelling of revolts in Apulia, and Peace of Melfi
1130	Schism of Anacletus II and Innocent II; Anacletus raises Roger II to be king; his coronation in Palermo (25 December).
1131–39	Campaigns against rebellions in southern Italy
1135	Roger II enfeoffs his son Alfonso with the principality of Capua; before he had enfeoffed Roger with the duchy of Apulia and Tancred with the principality of Bari
1137	Campaign by Emperor Lothar III and Innocent II against Roger II; they invest Rainulf of Alife with the duchy of Apulia

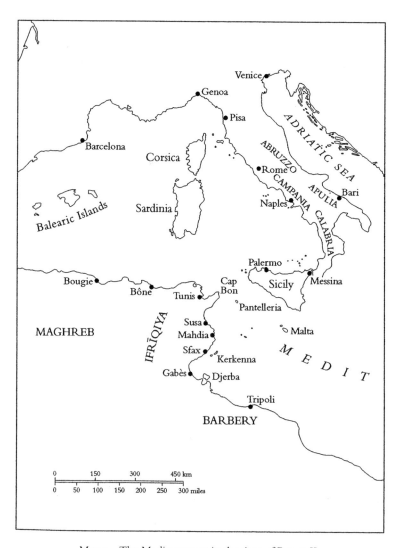

Map 1   The Mediterranean in the time of Roger II

Map 1 *(cont.)*

Map 2   The Norman kingdom of Sicily

Table 1. Roger II of Sicily

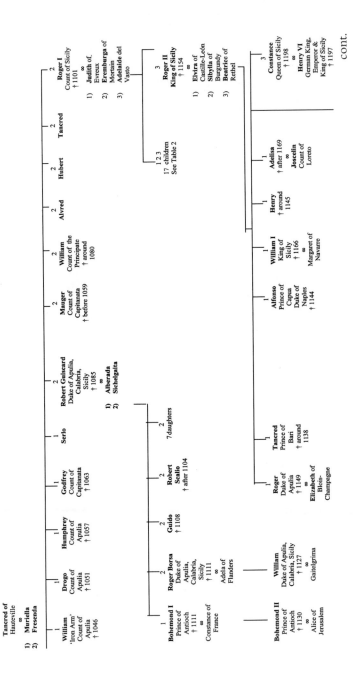

cont.

Table 1. (*cont.*)

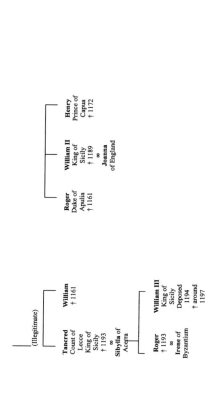

(Illegitimate)

William
† 1161

Tancred
Count of
Lecce
King of
Sicily
† 1193
∞
Sibylla of
Acerra

Roger
† 1193
∞
Irene of
Byzantium

William III
King of
Sicily
Deposed
1194
† around
1197

Roger
Duke of
Apulia
† 1161

William II
King of
Sicily
† 1189
∞
Joanna
of England

Henry
Prince of
Capua
† 1172

Several
illegitimate
children

Frederick II
King of
Sicily,
German
King,
Emperor
† 1250

Sketch: H. Houben   **Drawing: G. Madonna**

Table 2. The children of Roger I of Sicily

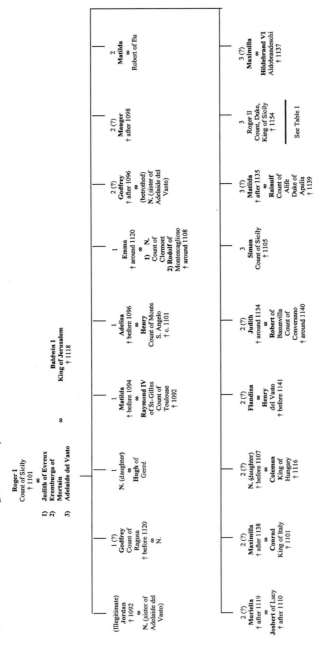

Sketch: H. Houben   Drawing: D. B. Milburn   Source: Houben (1996a), 107–13

INTRODUCTION. ROGER II: A CONTROVERSIAL RULER

———————— • ————————

The period from 1050 to 1200 has been described as a 'turning point in European and German history'.[1] In terms of German history we think mainly of the Investiture Contest and its consequences, and the struggle between empire and papacy. From the European perspective we think of the development of the urban communes, the schism between the eastern and the western Church, the Crusades, and the development of the universities. In the early Middle Ages the Christian west was put on the defensive mainly by the expansion of the Arabs, but also by the attacks of the Vikings and Hungarians (Magyars). It was only by making a great effort that the Christian west was able to fend off an invasion by these peoples. Since the eleventh century it had prepared for a kind of 'counter attack'. A number of different factors, not least the massive growth in population, contributed to the western borders starting to expand. The most important change was the reconquest of the Mediterranean, hitherto ruled by the Arabs, the *mare nostrum* ('our sea') of the Romans, the birthplace of western culture.

The Normans played a decisive role in this development. Coming from Scandinavia, they had settled in Normandy in the tenth century and had been subsumed by the Frankish–Christian culture. They took part in the Crusades, and in southern Italy and in Sicily they founded a new and novel state. At the same time they conquered England where a Norman kingdom also emerged. The circumstances in which this kingdom was created were very different from those in southern Italy, even though certain similarities can be established. The same is true of the principality

[1] Fuhrmann (1986), 39. See also Violante and Fried (1993).

of Antioch, founded by the Norman Bohemond in 1098, which was to last for just as long as did the much better-known Latin kingdom of Jerusalem. Whilst the Norman principality of Antioch has only occasionally attracted the interest of scholars, the Norman foundation of the state in southern Italy has benefited from a long history of scholarly study.

What is important from the German point of view is the fact that the kingdom of Sicily was united with the Romano-German empire by the emperors of the Staufen dynasty. As a result of Henry VI marrying Constance of Sicily in 1186, Roger II became the grandfather of Frederick II on his mother's side, alongside Frederick I Barbarossa on his father's side. The monarchy created by Roger II has been viewed by British scholars as part of a Norman 'commonwealth', by the French as 'an astonishing chapter in the history of the French aristocracy outside of France', ('un curieux chapitre de l'histoire de la noblesse française hors de France'), while for the Italians it has appeared as a precursor of the Italian national state. As a point of intersection of the Latin-western European, Byzantine-eastern and the Islamic-oriental culture, Norman Sicily has even recently aroused the interest of a Japanese historian.[2]

By the beginning of the twentieth century the Norman state in southern Italy and its founder Roger II were already proving extremely interesting to European historians. According to Erich Caspar in his 1904 monograph about Roger II – in many ways still the leading work on the subject – Roger II was 'the strong man whom strife-torn Sicily needed'. This historian from Berlin saw in the foundation of the Norman–Sicilian monarchy 'the historically appealing spectacle of a young, strong, rapidly rising power: it rose quickly from the ruins of decayed states, first conquered its immediate neighbours, then it encountered increasingly greater opposition, exerted a growing influence over a wider area, finally it asserted itself after dangerous battles against a world of enemies, and entered the circle of the established powers as a recognized equal member'. Here, an implicit comparison was made between the Norman kingdom and the Hohenzollern monarchy, the new German empire, which wanted to secure for itself 'amidst a world of enemies' a place amongst the European great powers.[3]

Three years later (1907) Ferdinand Chalandon published his two-volume history of Norman rule in southern Italy, which was also based on thorough knowledge of both primary sources and modern scholarship. For

---

[2] Douglas (1969, 1976), Brown (1984), especially 6–8, Chalandon (1907), I.1. Fonseca (1979), 16–18, reprinted in Fonseca (1987), 289–91. Takayama (1993), based on his Yale PhD thesis of 1990.

[3] Caspar (1904), vii, 236. Caspar described Roger as 'the first statesman in the modern sense', 'the first medieval prince who was not a knight', and as 'this first absolute monarch of the medieval west', *ibid.*, 436, 438.

the French the Norman period was 'par sa grandeur inouïe' ('because this period was so extraordinary') the most brilliant phase in the history of southern Italy. In 1912 a biography of Roger was included in the British series 'Heroes of the Nations'. This book by Edmund Curtis was written *Bib.* for the general public, and it met with little response amongst academics since it was largely limited to a summary of the findings of Chalandon and Caspar. A study of the Norman administration of southern Italy by Evelyn Jamison (1877–1972), which appeared in 1913, was quite different, providing new source material, and the author remained faithful to this subject throughout her life. Apart from that, interest in Roger and his kingdom seemed largely exhausted after the First World War.[4]

There was no new impetus until 1954 when a conference was organized in Palermo to commemorate the 800th anniversary of the death of Roger II. Important progress came in 1966 with a study of legal history by Mario Caravale, as well as in a series of conferences: in 1972 in Palermo on the 900th anniversary of the Norman capture of the city; and from 1973 onwards with the bi-annual 'Giornate normanno-sveve' which take place in Bari. Meanwhile, an interested layman, the Englishman John Julius Norwich, published a two-volume history of the Normans in southern Italy (1967–70), which was aimed at the general reader. It was soon translated into other languages and went through several editions.[5]

Judgements on Roger II have varied considerably. The right-wing historian Antonio Marongiu credited him with creating a medieval 'model state', a forerunner of the early modern state. He referred specifically to Jacob Burckhardt, who had seen in the Sicilian kingdom of Frederick II a 'model' for the Italian Renaissance states. Another right-wing historian, Léon-Robert Ménager, arrived at a diametrically opposed judgement. He believed that Roger's state did not have any original characteristics; he also disputed its dependence on the Byzantine model, as emphasized for instance by Josef Deér.[6]

The most recent assessments are also controversial. In 1989 Errico Cuozzo endorsed Marongiu's opinion and spoke of the 'conception of an absolute monarchy based on bureaucracy'; he argued that even more so than Frederick II, Roger regarded his kingdom as a 'work of art'. However, in 1992 Donald Matthew was largely in agreement with Ménager's

---

[4] Chalandon (1907), II.742. See the bibliography for full details of these other works.

[5] Fonseca (1979) assesses the historiography up to 1977. Cf. Norwich (1967), xi: 'Why is it that one of the most extraordinary and fascinating epics of European history between the ages of Julius Caesar and Napoleon should be so little known to the world at large?'

[6] Marongiu (1964, 1973), Ménager (1959, 1969), criticized by Elze (1964). Cf. Deér (1972), 169: 'a rare synthesis of ancient Norman traditions... with the Byzantine ideas, that is with East Roman political and ecclesiastical concepts'.

argument that the kingdom of Sicily was not an original creation. Roger
did not have a definite concept as his starting point when he founded the
state – he largely improvised, following available structures and models.
Jean-Marie Martin (1994) regarded it as a state with an ambivalent structure: on the one hand western and 'feudal', on the other hand eastern
and bureaucratic; a monarchy which was western in its structure, but in
its heart was eastern, that is its court was oriental.[7]

Roger was controversial even amongst his contemporaries. For the so-
called Saxon annalist, who is identified with the abbot Arnold of Berge
and Nienburg (d. 1166), he was 'Rokker, a certain tyrant of Sicily' and
'a semi-pagan'. He was viewed in similar terms in Magdeburg as 'the
tyrant Ruoker'. However, another German monk, from Pöhlde in Saxony, painted a more positive picture. He called Roger (*Rozierus*) 'King
of Apulia' and praised his piety. The great religious reformer Bernard of
Clairvaux (d. 1153) regarded him as an upstart whose support had been
bought by the antipope Anacletus II 'for the ridiculous price of a usurped
crown'. In a letter to the emperor Lothar III this influential Cistercian
abbot called Roger 'the Sicilian usurper' and 'an intruder in the empire'.
Bishop Otto of Freising (d. 1158) expressed similar views a few years
later. It is true that after Roger's kingdom had been recognized by the
pope, Bernard of Clairvaux did change his opinion. He hoped that its
ruler would support his order in southern Italy: 'Your Royal Highness has
spread far and wide across the earth. In fact, where has the renown of your
name not spread?... Oh King! You have the light of my eyes, my heart
and my soul.'[8]

Although John of Salisbury (d. 1180) did not describe this ruler directly
as a tyrant, he nevertheless considered him to be one: 'In the manner of

[7] Cuozzo (1989a), 639, 655, with reference to Mazzarese Fardella (1966), 22. However,
Tramontana (1983), like Caravale (1966), stresses that 'feudal' jurisdictions still continued
even under Roger II; cf. Matthew (1992), 208–9, Martin (1994), 78, 287. Giunta (1982),
provides a biographical sketch, without footnotes, while neither Tessitore (1995) nor
Musca and Iorio (1997) have much claim to scholarship.
[8] *Annalista Saxo, MGH SS* VI. 770–4; cf. Schmale (1978). *Annales Magdeburgenses, MGH
SS* XVI.185. *Annales Palidenses, MGH SS* XVI. 77, 83, 88–9. In the Middle High German
poem *König Rother* the protagonist, like Roger II, 'thanks to his force and intelligence
shows himself superior to the Byzantine emperor', Schreiner (1992), 573. However,
the model here was probably not Roger II but the Lombard king Rothari (636–52),
see Störmer (1992), 592. Bernard of Clairvaux, 'Lettere', *Opere di S. Bernardo*, ed.
F. Gastardelli (Milan 1986–7), VI, no. 127, to Duke William X of Aquitaine, c. April 1131;
no. 130, to Pisa c. 1134–5, 'the evil of the Sicilian tyrant'; nos. 139–40, c. 1135–6; nos.
207–8, to Roger, after c. 1142. [English translations of all but the first of these letters in
The Letters of St Bernard of Clairvaux, ed. B. Scott James (London 1953), 201–2, 210–11,
348–9.] Otto of Freising, *Chronica* II.19, p. 90, '*invasor imperii*'. Cf. Wieruszowski (1963),
64–6.

other tyrants' Roger had oppressed his country's church. The judge Falco of Benevento was a critical opponent of the 'Godless king'. He described in his chronicle, amongst Roger's other misdeeds, the destruction of the vineyards around his home town and the starving out of his fellow citizens: 'We call on the eternal king and judge of all as a witness that to our knowledge not even the cruellest pagan emperor Nero committed such slaughter amongst the Christians.' Nor did the Byzantines have a high opinion of Roger. The historian John Kinnamos did not refer to him as a king at all, only as the tyrant of the Sicilians or of Sicily. Another writer, Theodore Prodromos, denounced him as the 'tyrant of a small toparchy of apes'.[9]

However, the 'History' of Abbot Alexander of Telese, a work commissioned by one of the Roger's sisters, gave a positive picture the king. His rise from count to duke and finally king was depicted as an act of divine Providence. His rule was justified by the necessity of restoring law and order in the political chaos of southern Italy. It was to the king's credit that he brought anarchy to an end there. In a letter to Roger, Peter the Venerable, abbot of Cluny, is of the same opinion: 'Where once Saracens, robbers and thieves wreaked havoc, there is now peace and tranquillity', in short 'a peaceful and very pleasant kingdom like that of the peacemaker Solomon'. It is with good reason that the ruler can be counted amongst the 'great kings'. For the so-called 'Hugo Falcandus', author of the history of the kingdom of Sicily in the years after the death of Roger II (1154–69), the king was the embodiment of a model which his incompetent successors should have taken as their example. He represented the virtues of the ideal ruler: intelligence, wisdom, energy and justness.[10]

However, in the Middle Ages Roger was mainly painted in dark colours, particularly his deviation from the knightly canon of virtue which was the European ideal of a good ruler. On the other hand, a great deal of what his contemporaries viewed in the most negative light is regarded as positive by modern historians: his relentless ability to assert himself, his independent stance against the papacy, his receptiveness to Arab culture, and his innovations in legislation and administration.

[9] *The Historia Pontificalis of John of Salisbury*, trans. M. Chibnall (London 1956), c. 32, p. 66. *Falco*, 158, *rex nefandus*. For Falco, Loud (1993), D'Angelo (1994), and the introduction to the edition. John Kinnamos, *Epitome rerum ab Ioanne et Manuelo Comnenis gestarum*, ed. C. Meineke (Bonn 1836), II.4, 12; III.5, 12; IV.2; = *Deeds of John and Manuel Komnenus by John Kinnamos*, trans. C. M. Brand (New York 1986), 38, 58, 80, 94, 107. For the citation from Theodore Prodromos, see Mathieu (1954), 65, cf. Pertusi (1977), 93–5, Bernardinello (1975), 53–5. Cf. also Theodoros Prodromos, *Historische Gedichte*, ed. W. Hörandner (Vienna 1974), 21ff.

[10] For Alexander, see Oldoni (1979), 269, Cilento (1981), 172ff. Delogu (1981), 186ff. *The Letters of Peter the Venerable*, no. 131, pp. 300–1 (1142), cf. *ibid.* no. 90, p. 231 (1139). *Falcandus*, 57–8; cf. Cantarella (1994).

In order to achieve a balanced judgement on the historical significance of Roger II we must reconsider the sources used in research up to now. The foundations for this enterprise are now reasonably good. Thus, in the course of his work on the collected charters of the Kings of Sicily (*Codex diplomaticus regni Siciliae*), which he founded with Francesco Giunta and André Guillou, Carlrichard Brühl has examined and edited Roger's Latin documents. Jeremy Johns has undertaken a revision of the Arab sources. It is regrettable that we do not yet have a critical edition of the Greek charters, which probably account for about half of the entire production of the royal chancery. We suspect that Roger II issued more diplomas than his contemporary western European monarchs. Nevertheless, only around 150 of his charters from forty-one years of independent rule are preserved, making an annual average of 3.6. We must therefore assume exceptionally high losses in transmission.[11]

The narrative sources are fairly well edited, this of course includes not only the Latin but the Greek and Arab as well. In the last few decades Roger's legislation and the ecclesiastical, economic and social history of the kingdom have been the subject of intensive research. The art and architectural evidence of multicultural Sicily have also repeatedly attracted the interest of scholars of a variety of nationalities.[12]

It goes without saying that this book is not in the true sense a biography. The personality of Roger II is reflected only in his deeds and statements, as they are transmitted to us by contemporary or later sources. We can only suspect what he felt, what he thought, and what he wanted. However, it is possible to put him into his historical context. This is important because recent research has increasingly accepted the view that the rulers of the Middle Ages were not 'the men who made the history', but were enmeshed 'in a complex network of relationships with political and social forces' and hence had only limited scope for independent action.[13]

Modern research therefore shows the development of the relationships which Roger found when he came to rule. The Norman conquest of

---

[11] Brühl (1978), 17–18, 22. Falkenhausen (1980a), Brühl (1983a), 18. Brühl estimated the proportion of Greek charters as 75–80 per cent of the total, Enzensberger (1995a), as 'more than 50 per cent'. Brühl (1994) 378 estimates the number of Roger II's diplomas that have been lost as about 1,350. For the Greek charters, see most recently Falkenhausen (1998b).

[12] See the primary sources and bibliography of secondary works at the end of this volume. On legal issues see especially the works by Caravale, Dilcher and Zecchino; on the Church, those by Fonseca, Houben, Kamp and Loud; on economic and social history, Abulafia, Bresc, Falkenhausen, Johns, Martin and Takayama; on art and architecture, Brenk, Deér, Kitzinger, Meier and Tronzo.

[13] Quote from Beumann (1985), 7. For the 'margins of manoeuvre' [*Handlungsspielräume*] and 'modalities of action' [*Wirkungsweisen*] of a sovereign, see also Haverkamp (1992), 11ff.

Sicily was mainly the work of his father, Roger I, whilst he owed the preservation of his inheritance to his mother, Adelaide, who after the death of her husband held the regency until Roger II came of age. After the extinction of the dynasty of the Dukes of Apulia, founded by his uncle Robert Guiscard and whose vassal the Count of Sicily was, Roger II was able to succeed to their inheritance, against the wishes of his papal overlords, and then unite the whole of southern Italy, including the old Lombard principalities of Salerno and Capua, under his rule.

The papal schism of 1130 prepared the way for the creation of the kingdom, something which was regarded by many contemporaries as a violation of the traditional, divinely willed order. By prudent action and as a result of a series of fortunate circumstances Roger managed to secure his kingdom despite the opposition of the pope, the Roman and Byzantine emperors, many of the nobility, and the towns. He was also able to bring under his rule the north African coast lying directly opposite to Sicily, bringing him the (unofficial title of) a 'King of Africa'. However, in the eyes of the Roman and the Byzantine emperors, as well as those of the European kings, Roger remained an upstart; and his attempt to use the Second Crusade to integrate his kingdom into the society of the established monarchs of the west met with only limited success. Nevertheless, by the end of Roger's lifetime the kingdom of Sicily had become a reality which could no longer be ignored.

This study will examine the nature of this new monarchy, including its cultural aspects, representations of its ruler, its legislation, administration and economy. It will then address the question of the later destiny of the kingdom, which fell to the Staufen by a dynastic accident, namely the childless death of Roger's grandson William II. It was then linked by Henry VI in a personal union with the Romano-German empire. Under Frederick II, a grandson of Roger II through his mother Constance, the kingdom of Sicily would continue play a central role in the history of Europe for several decades.

I

THE INHERITANCE

·

ROGER I, THE CONQUEROR

Roger II was left a considerable inheritance by his parents. His father, Roger I (c. 1040–1101) had created a comital lordship in Calabria and Sicily, which allowed him to become a desirable ally to the ruling houses of Europe. As the youngest of twelve sons of a minor Norman nobleman, Tancred of Hauteville, Roger I could not count on any inheritance. In 1055 he followed his brothers who had sought and found their fortune in southern Italy. In the 1090s Geoffrey Malaterra, a Norman monk, who had settled in the cathedral monastery of Catania, wrote a history of the Norman conquest of Sicily, in which Roger I stood at the centre. He reported that the future count had come to the south at a young age.[1]

   The first Normans had arrived in southern Italy about the year 1000. When returning from a pilgrimage to Jerusalem they had helped Prince Guaimar III of Salerno (989–1027) to defend that town against the Saracens. This Lombard prince rewarded them handsomely and invited them to stay. Around 1016 other Normans undertook a pilgrimage to the

---

[1] *Amatus* III.43, p. 159, suggests that Roger came to Italy after the battle of Civitate (1053), although according to *Malaterra* I.19, p. 18, this was only after the death of his brother Humphrey (1057). This latter claim cannot be accepted insofar as, according to the letters of Jewish merchants from Sicily, the conquest of the Island, undertaken by Roger some time after his arrival in the peninsula, was already under way by 1057; see Gil (1995), 120ff. One should therefore correct the chronology, based on Malaterra, in Chalandon (1907), I.150–2. Malaterra suggests that Roger came to Italy while of *juvenilis aetas*, for which cf. Hofmeister (1926), 315ff, suggesting that he was born c. 1040. The notice in *Romuald*, 202, that he was aged fifty-one when he died in 1101 (and thus was born c. 1050) cannot therefore be accurate. Cf. also Matthew (1981), 266.

shrine of St Michael on Monte Gargano in northern Apulia. There they met Melus, also called Ishmael, the leader of an anti-Byzantine rebellion in Bari, who asked them for help as he tried to free his native town from the rule of the Byzantine emperor. Nor did the Normans have any hesitation in making their military skills available to him. At first they met with some minor success, but at the battlefield of Cannae, which had once witnessed the victory of Hannibal over the Romans, they were defeated by Byzantine troops in 1018. Melus fled to Germany and requested help from Henry II (1002–24). It is possible that the emperor enfeoffed Melus with the duchy of Apulia. However, before Henry was able to set off for the south with an army, Melus died at Bamberg in 1020.[2]

The first Norman to achieve rank and reputation in southern Italy was Rainulf I Drengot (d. 1045). In 1030 the Duke of Naples, Sergius IV, gave him his sister, the widow of the Duke of Gaeta, in marriage and enfeoffed him with the newly created county of Aversa. Aversa, lying half way between Capua and Naples, was the only town in southern Italy to be founded by the Normans. Otherwise they settled in already existing communities. After the death of his wife in 1034 Rainulf changed sides. He married a niece of the Duke of Naples's enemy, Prince Pandulf IV of Capua (1026–49), and became his vassal. However, he soon changed sides once more; now he supported Prince Guaimar IV of Salerno (d. 1052). In May 1038 Guaimar's rule was recognized by the emperor Conrad II (1024–39), who enfeoffed him in Capua with the county of Aversa. Later, in 1041, he also received the duchy of Gaeta from Guaimar IV. Around this time the brothers William, known as 'the Iron Arm', and Drogo de Hauteville came to the south and entered the service of the Prince of Salerno.[3]

Both brothers appear to have soon become a nuisance to Guaimar IV. In 1038 he sent them to Sicily – they were supposed to help the Byzantines

[2] *Amatus* I.16–21, pp. 21–8. *W. Ap.* I.1–34, pp. 98–100. Cf. Hoffmann (1969), and with a different, but far from convincing interpretation, France (1991). The whole issue has recently been re-examined by Loud (2000b), 60–6. *Notae sepulchrales Babenbergenses, MGH SS* XVII.640. On Melus, Chalandon (1907) I.42–4, Deér (1972), 44ff; for the Armenian origin of his family, Falkenhausen (1982a), 67. Although, as Martin (1993), 520, notes, the name Melus was widely used at Bari, the fact that his son carried the Greek name of Argyros undoubtedly suggests that he belonged to the Byzantine governing class. The gold-embroidered cloak – the so-called 'starred cloak' – given by Melus appears not to have come from southern Italy, as was once thought, but from southern Germany (perhaps Regensburg), Baumgärtel-Fleischmann (1990). The 'description of the world' (*descriptio totius orbis*) embroidered on the cloak, with its characterization of Henry II as the 'honour of Europe' (*decus Europae*) and the wish that his empire would increase, may perhaps reflect the ideas of the donor.

[3] *Amatus* I.41ff, pp. 52ff; II.6, pp. 63ff. Cf. Chalandon (1907), I.82ff. Houben (1987), 75ff [reprinted in Houben (1989), 46ff]. Cuozzo (1992), 689–92. Taviani-Carozzi (1991), 930ff, (1996), 145ff. Loud (2000b), 74–80.

reconquer the island which had now been under Arab rule for two centuries. But there disputes arose over the way the booty was shared out. As a result the Hauteville brothers left the island, along with the other Normans and Arduin, a northern Italian who had led their contingent of troops, and made themselves independent. They settled on the border between the Basilicata and Apulia, in an area that had been under Byzantine rule. The town of Melfi became their 'capital'. Mercenaries started to become conquerors. The twelve most powerful amongst the Normans acquired the title of count. In 1042 they elected William 'the Iron Arm' as their leader, the 'Count of Apulia' – his pre-eminent position was also reflected in his marriage to a niece of Guaimar IV of Salerno.[4]

All this was an affront both to Byzantium and to the German king (and Roman emperor). As the successor to Charlemagne, who had incorporated the Lombard kingdom into his empire, he laid claim to rule the whole of Italy. However, Henry III (1039–56) was forced to grin and bear it. When he arrived in the south in 1047 he could not avoid recognizing the status quo which had been created in the meantime. Drogo of Hauteville (d. 1051), the successor of William 'the Iron Arm' (d. 1046), was enfeoffed with the county of Apulia, and Rainulf II 'Trincanocte' (d. 1048) with the county of Aversa.[5]

The pope wanted to play a role in southern Italy as well. When the population of Apulia appealed to Leo IX (1049–54) for help against the invaders, the latter attempted to drive the Normans out of southern Italy with the aid of German and Byzantine troops. However, in 1053 he suffered a crushing defeat at Civitate in the north of Apulia. As a result papal policy towards the Normans changed. Nicholas II (1058–61) concluded an alliance with the invaders. At the synod of Melfi (1059) he enfeoffed the Count of Aversa, Richard I Quarrel (1050–78), with the principality of Capua, which had been conquered by this Norman leader in 1058 and which had previously been under the lordship of the emperor. At the same time he granted investiture to Robert Guiscard, who had succeeded his brother Humphrey (d. 1057) as Count of Apulia, of the duchy 'of Apulia, Calabria, and in the future, with the help of God and St Peter, of Sicily'. The pope did not make clear from where he derived this right. Probably he drew implicitly on the Donation of Constantine, and perhaps also on Carolingian and Ottonian privileges which had allowed the Roman pontiffs lordship over southern Italy and Sicily. The papal–Norman alliance

---

[4] *Amatus* II.8, pp. 66–8; II.14, pp. 72ff; II.29, p. 93. Cf. Chalandon (1907), I.91ff. Jahn (1989), 24, 42ff. Houben (1993b), 314ff [reprinted in Houben (1996a), 321ff]. Taviani-Carozzi (1996), 168ff. Loud (2000b), 92–9.

[5] *Amatus* III.2, p. 117. Cf. Chalandon (1907), I.113. Kehr (1934), 7ff. Deér (1972), 46ff. Loud (2000b), 106–7.

was though not only a consequence of the battle of Civitate, but also an indirect result of the Lateran synod held a few months previously. It could be predicted that the decrees there about the election of a pope and lay investiture would provoke an adverse reaction from the Roman nobility and the emperor. But for the Normans the investiture by the papacy was a tremendous success – their reputation rose, and their conquests received a new legitimacy.[6]

The Normans had hitherto distinguished themselves by using brutal force and not even stopping at seizing church property. In despair the population turned to the pope for help. In the 'Life of Pope Leo IX' we read that many people came to Rome from southern Italy with their eyes gouged out or their noses, feet and hands cut off. Confronted with this wretched sight, the pope decided to fight the Normans, 'certainly with much love of God, but perhaps with less wisdom', according to this author alluding to the close of the battle of Civitate. After they had become the pope's vassals the doers of wrong transformed themselves into doers of good. They gave to churches and monasteries, where prayers were henceforth said for their spiritual salvation. They also founded new abbeys which attracted Norman monks. Soon it was possible in some south Italian monasteries to hear monastic choral music according to the liturgy of Saint-Evroult.[7]

However, the Normans were and remained upstarts. Bishop Benzo of Alba (d. circa 1090) was particularly caustic in his remarks. As a supporter of Henry IV he could not forgive them for having supported Gregory VII (1073–85): 'Instead of Normans it would be better to call them non-persons (*nullimani*), the most foul-smelling rubbish in the world . . . , sons of filth, tyrants who have risen from the rabble.' This reputation stuck to them. Incidentally, by no means all these 'Normans' came from Normandy – and those that did were mainly men and only a few thousand at that. Probably about a third of the newcomers came from other regions of France, particularly Brittany. For many young nobles there was no place for them at home. They had to seek their fortune abroad. It was their horses and equipment – light chain mail and long almond-shaped shields – that made them superior to their Byzantine and Moslem opponents. They quickly adopted new methods of war such as building mobile wooden towers which facilitated the approach to town walls. Disunity amongst

---

[6] *Vita Leonis IX*, in J. M. Watterich, *Pontificum Romanorum Vitae* I (Leipzig 1862), 98. Deér (1972), 61ff, 78ff. For the battle of Civitate, see also Bünemann (1997), 20–4, Loud (2000b), 110–21. The acclamation of Robert Guiscard as duke by his army at Reggio in 1060, *Malaterra* I.35, p. 25, was probably of only marginal significance, see Hoffmann (1978), 141ff, though for a rather different view, Loud (2000b), 190–1.

[7] Houben (1988a), (1995a), 37ff, 139ff.

the local population prepared the way for the invaders. An important means of integration was marriage into local noble families. The secret of the Normans' success was their ability to adapt rapidly to situations and surroundings.[8]

When Roger I came to the south in about 1055 he helped Robert Guiscard quell a rebellion. However, conflicts soon developed between the two brothers. Roger wanted to build up his own area of rule in Calabria, but his brother was reluctant to allow this. Calabria, like Apulia, had hitherto belonged to the Byzantine empire. The local population tried to use the disunity of the Normans to their own advantage and to drive them out. Robert Guiscard was therefore forced to come to an agreement with his brother and ceded half of Calabria to him. Together the brothers succeeded in consolidating their rule. After the last of the places still in Byzantine hands in the south of the region had fallen, the conquest of Arab-ruled Sicily could be considered.[9]

Under the Romans and the Byzantines, Sicily had only been a peripheral province, which had mainly produced grain. After it was conquered by the Arabs in the ninth century, agriculture there had been intensified. New methods were introduced: terraces and ditches for irrigation, thinning of the soil, and changes in the rotation of crops. The *latifundia*, already reduced under the Byzantines, were shared out further. Apart from grain, rice, cotton, papyrus, citrus fruits, dates and sugar cane were also cultivated. The production of silk and cotton by skilled workers developed. The island, where Muslim Arabs and Berbers lived alongside Jews and Christians, developed into a focus for Mediterranean trade in the tenth and eleventh centuries. The 200-year-old Arab rule had far-reaching consequences for the ethnic and religious composition of the population. The spread of Islam took place via cultural assimilation. Although additional taxes were not particularly high for non-Muslims, they were high enough to encourage the lower classes to convert. A large-scale Arab immigration does not appear to have taken place: Arabs and Berbers were only the ruling class.[10]

'Triangular' Sicily – hence its ancient name of Trinacria – consisted of three regions. The west of Sicily, the Val di Mazara, including Palermo and Agrigento, was virtually entirely Islamic. Muslims formed the greater majority in the southeast, the Val di Noto, including Syracuse and Catania.

---

[8] Benzo of Alba, pp. 286, 316 (for the schism of Cadulus 1061–4, cf. Oldoni (1978), 97ff,
     Loud (2000b), 194–5). Ménager (1975a), Martin (1993), 520ff. Cuozzo (1989b), (1995a),
     Zug Tucci (1995), Settia (1994), 850ff.
[9] *Malaterra* I.19–35, pp. 18ff; II.1, p. 29. Cf. Chalandon (1907), 149ff. The supposition that
     Count Roger was assigned half of Calabria in 1058, based upon *Malaterra* I.29, p. 22,
     would appear to be erroneous, cf. here note 1 above.
[10] Goitein (1967–88), Peri (1978), 64ff.

It was only in the northeast, the Val Demone, including Messina, that Christian – Greek orthodox – communities had been preserved in the countryside, particularly in the inland town of Troina. The towns such as Syracuse, Catania, Taormina and Messina on the east coast declined under Arab rule, although they had played an important role under the Byzantines. Trade with Byzantium also declined sharply. The Straits of Messina, which had represented a bridge to the Byzantine provinces of Calabria and Apulia, became the border between two worlds.

Palermo on the other hand enjoyed a rapid rise and became a centre of Mediterranean trade. Merchants from Arab north Africa and Spain met here with their Christian competitors from Naples and Amalfi, and later from Pisa as well. Pilgrims from Andalucia stopped off there on their way to Mecca. Mazara and Agrigento were medium-sized ports for trade with the Maghreb. The principal export was rock salt, which was important for the preservation of meat, also fish, cheese, grain, fabrics, wood, skins, and fruit, especially almonds. Sicily was the granary for the north African Sahel region. However, the quantity of grain exported was limited. Only the upper class was supplied – for white bread was a luxury item. There were smaller ports in Termini and Partinico, which specialized in the export of pulses and dyes. Dried fruit was exported from Carini. Spices, flax, indigo, gold and precious stones, as well as olive oil were imported into Sicily. There were no towns of any significance in the interior of Sicily. Extensive forests prevented erosion during the heavy winter rain. It was only at the end of the Middle Ages that a greater degree of deforestation occurred which would make a major change to the ecological balance. Many country dwellers lived in caves, a practice that was widespread amongst the Berbers in north Africa. The caves protected them from the heat in summer and the cold in winter.[11]

In the course of the ninth century Sicily had been conquered by an Arab dynasty, the Aglabids, who ruled in Ifrīqiya, present-day Tunisia. In theory they were subject to the Caliph of Baghdad, but in practice they were independent. In the tenth century the Aglabids were driven out by the Shi'ite Fatimids, who in 916 founded the town of Mahdia (al-Mahdīyya) on the coast, south of Monastir. After the conquest of Egypt in 969 and the transfer of the seat of government to the newly founded city of Cairo in 973, Ifrīqiya and Sicily were ruled by Fatimid governors (emirs). The emirate in Sicily became hereditary with the emergence of the Kalbid dynasty, resident in Palermo. The Christian population was accorded the status of 'charges' (*dhimma*), to which followers of monotheistic religions were entitled under Islamic law. Moslem society was exposed to strong internal

[11] Peri (1978), 11–12, 14ff, 23, 25ff. Bresc (1993), 291ff. Gil (1995), 131ff.

tensions, and latent conflicts between Arabs and Berbers, Sunnites and Shi'ites were always breaking out.[12]

When a brother of the Emir of Palermo incited an uprising, the ruler called on the Byzantines for help. The latter had been waiting to reconquer the island for a long time. In 1038 an army led by the famous general George Maniakes landed in Sicily. As we already know, William 'the Iron Arm' and Drogo of Hauteville were amongst his soldiers. Although the enterprise initially met with success, it ultimately failed when the commanding general was called back to Byzantium for domestic political reasons. It is therefore not surprising that the Normans soon turned their attention to the rich island.

Until this point Roger I had been overshadowed by his brother. Now he had an opportunity to take the initiative on his own. This was because Robert had to return to Apulia on a number of occasions in order to quell rebellions. In his 'History of the Normans', written in about 1076–78 (which is unfortunately only preserved in an Old French translation, interspersed with Italianisms, dating from the fourteenth century), the monk Amatus of Montecassino reported that it was Robert Guiscard who took the initiative to conquer Sicily. An emir named Vultimin had called on him for help. However, it was probably a joint venture undertaken by both brothers. Malaterra naturally made his hero, Roger I, appear to have undertaken the venture single-handed.[13]

While he was staying at Reggio with his brother the duke, that most distinguished young man Count Roger of Calabria heard that Sicily was in the hands of the unbelievers. Seeing it from close at hand with only a short stretch of sea lying in between, he was seized by the desire to capture it, for he was always eager for conquest. He perceived two means by which he would profit, one for his soul and the other for his material benefit, if he brought back to Divine worship a country given over to idolatry, and if he himself possessed the temporal fruits and income from this land, thus spending in the service of God things which had been unjustly stolen by a people who knew him not.

The first attempt to erect a bridgehead in Messina failed. Suddenly an unexpected opportunity was presented. An emir called Betumen – according to Malaterra's version – approached Roger I who was staying in Reggio. He appealed to him for help against Prince Belcamedus. The Latin chroniclers mixed up the names of the Arab protagonists, but it has emerged from Arab sources that the emir Vultimin/Betumen was really called Ibn at-Ṭumna; he ruled over the southeast of the island with the towns of Catania and Syracuse. His opponent and brother-in-law, Ibn

[12] Cf. Halm (1987–9), (1991), 163ff, 194ff.
[13] *Amatus* v. 7–8, pp. 229–31: *Malaterra* ii.1, pp. 13–19.

al-Ḥawwās, had in his possession the interior of Sicily with the town of Enna (Castrogiovanni). Robert Guiscard and Roger I did not let the opportunity slip away. The invasion was prepared. They began by capturing Messina. Because of its strategic location on the strait to the Italian peninsula the town was of great importance for guaranteeing supplies.[14]

However, Roger did not choose Messina as his base and 'residence', preferring instead the town of Troina lying in the interior, although its mainly Greek orthodox inhabitants did not exactly react with great enthusiasm. The conquest of Sicily proved to be lengthy. Victories in battles, such as that at Cerami in 1063, did not have any far-reaching implications. Ibn al-Ḥawwās entrenched himself in his mountain lair at Enna, which could not be taken, and an attempt to conquer Palermo in 1064 was unsuccessful. The brothers therefore resolved that they would first bring the conquest of Apulia to an end. After three years of siege, Bari was finally conquered in the spring of 1071. Under Byzantine rule Bari had been important as the capital of the region. The Normans were then able to concentrate all their energy on Sicily. Catania was conquered in July 1071, and Palermo at the beginning of 1072. The Norman fleet, which made the maritime blockade possible, was extremely important here. The town surrendered relatively quickly because capitulation was made easier for the Moslem inhabitants by the offer of favourable conditions; in return for payment of a tribute they could keep their religious beliefs and remain largely self-governing. They were only put under the command of a Norman town commandant. He bore the title *amiratus*, which was derived from the Arabic title of *amīr* (emir).[15]

After the capture of Palermo, the brothers came to an agreement on sharing out Sicily, although only half of the island had yet been conquered. Because of his position as Duke of Apulia, Calabria and Sicily, Robert Guiscard formally ruled the whole island, although in reality Roger I had a free hand to govern it as he wished. In a way very similar to the situation that had been established in Calabria, the duke retained in his possession half of the most important conquests so far (Palermo, Messina and the Val Demone). At the end of 1072 he left the island, which he was never to see again. In Apulia rebellions by Norman nobles needed to be quashed. In the

[14] *Malaterra* II.1–13, pp. 29–33. Cf. Amari (1933–9), II.619ff, Chalandon (1907), 192ff. Rizzitano (1977), 194ff. Loud (2000b), 146–51. Malaterra's dating of the first attack to Messina in 1060–1 conflicts with the Jewish sources, which suggest that Messina was conquered by the Normans before August 1057, for which see above note 1.

[15] *Malaterra* II.13–35, 40–2, 48–50. *Amatus* V.13–18, pp. 235ff; VI.14, pp. 276–8; VI.16–20, pp. 278ff. *Malaterra* II.45, pp. 52–3; *W.Ap*, III lines 255–339, pp. 179ff. Cf. Chalandon (1907), I.191ff. Bennet (1993), 46ff; Ménager (1960), 23ff, 167ff; Falkenhausen (1977), 351ff. Bünemann (1997), 43–78; Loud (2000b), 150–65.

years that followed, Robert Guiscard was preoccupied with other projects. In 1076 Henry IV offered him ducal investiture from his own hands, but the Norman leader refused this. He had greater freedom of action as a vassal of the pope, since Gregory VII was reliant upon his military assistance. In 1076–7 Robert Guiscard successfully conquered Salerno, the last Lombard principality in southern Italy. However, his main interest was now to be directed towards Byzantium, which he dreamt of conquering. It was during a campaign against the Byzantine empire that he met with his death in 1085.[16]

Following the 1072 agreement on the division of Sicily, half of the part of the island still to be conquered should have gone to two important commanders of the Norman army: Serlo, the son of Roger I's brother – also called Serlo – and a certain Arisgot of Pucheuil. These two had distinguished themselves on a number of occasions, notably at the battle of Cerami. It was intended that lordship over Sicily would be divided in this way, but what in fact happened was rather different. Serlo soon fell in battle. Arisgot distinguished himself at the siege of Taormina in 1079; but there is no evidence for him thereafter. Roger I was therefore able to create his own personal region of rule in Sicily. In contrast to his brother in Apulia, he did not have to take into consideration other Normans who had acquired their own counties and lordships. Whilst the sources leave us in no doubt that Roger I was a vassal of Robert Guiscard, in practice the Count of Sicily was in a stronger position than the Duke of Apulia, for unlike the latter he did not need to expend time and resources keeping rebellious vassals under control.[17]

Roger I needed almost twenty more years to conquer the rest of Sicily. He may only have had just over a hundred knights and about as many foot soldiers at his disposal (although, we should remember that Malaterra may have downgraded this figure in order to make the Normans' success appear in a more striking light). A complete territorial conquest or occupation was unthinkable. Since the Muslims greatly outnumbered the Normans, the only possible course of action was to keep them under control from fortified bases. Support from the Christians could not be relied on in the overwhelmingly Muslim south of the island. In addition, the count had to leave Sicily on a number of occasions in order to bring military aid to the Duke of Apulia. Roger I therefore proceeded cautiously, adopting a

---

[16] *Amatus* VI.21, p. 283. *Malaterra* II.46, pp. 53–4; III.1, p. 57. *Amatus* VII.27, pp. 320–1; *W. Ap*, v lines 285ff, pp. 253ff. Cf. Chalandon (1907), I.209ff, 242ff, 265ff. Bünemann (1997), 79–165. Loud (2000b), 137–44, 196–223.

[17] *Malaterra* III.18, IV.46, pp. 54, 67; for Arisgot of Pucheuil (dept. Seine Maritime), see Ménager (1975b), 360–1. For Roger's vassalic dependence on Robert Guiscard, Caravale (1966), 22ff, and (with a different interpretation) D'Alessandro (1975). Cf. also Jahn (1989), 124ff.

policy of wait and see. He offered the towns generous treaties of surrender; and what happened at Palermo became the accepted model for this. The conquered region was rendered safe by the construction of castles in strategically important areas. Thus the castle of Paternò on the slope of Etna dominated the plain of Catania, whilst that of Calascibetta kept the hill town of Enna covered. In Mazara a citadel was built in the town, and it was from here that Roger repelled an attack by Muslims from north Africa in 1075.[18]

A year earlier pirates under the control of the Zirid ruler Tamīm ibn Mu'izz (1061–1108) had launched a successful raid on the town of Nicotera on the coast of Calabria. According to Malaterra's account, the inhabitants had drunk a great deal of wine on the eve of the Feast of St Peter. It was therefore very easy to massacre them. Women and children were taken prisoner in order to be sold as slaves, the town was plundered and set on fire. It was to avoid a repeat of such episodes that Roger I concluded a treaty, effectively an armistice, with Tamīm. In 1087 he therefore rejected a proposal, made by Pisa and Genoa, to undertake a combined attack on the Tunisian port of Mahdia. The Norman leader did not at this point want to risk his good relations with the Zirids. Malaterra's report is only very brief. However, the testimony of the Arab chronicler, Ibn al-Athīr (1160-1233), which is based on older sources, is more detailed. He saw a connection between the Reconquista in Spain, the Norman conquest of Sicily and the First Crusade:[19]

King Baldwin assembled a large army of Franks (i.e. Christians). He sent a messenger to Roger the Frank, who had conquered Sicily and was a relative, in order to inform him: 'I have assembled a large army and am now coming to you in order to set out to conquer the coast of Africa from your bases and so become your neighbour.' At these tidings Roger assembled his companions and asked their advice. All

---

[18] *Malaterra* II.4, p. 30 (Messina 1061, Roger had 160 knights; Ibn Khaldūn, *BAS*, 202, claimed 700 men); *Malaterra*, II.10, p. 32 (1061, Roger had 150 *milites*); *ibid.*, II.17, p. 34 (Enna 1061, the combined forces of Robert Guiscard and Roger totalled 700 men); *ibid*, II.33, pp. 42–4 (at the battle of Cerami in 1063 Roger had 100 knights and his nephew Serlo 36); *ibid.,* II.35, p. 45 (later in 1063 Roger had 200 *milites*, of whom 100 had been sent by Guiscard). *Amatus* V.20, p. 238, claimed that at Messina in 1061 the army of Robert Guiscard and Roger comprised 1,000 *milites* and 1,000 *pedites*. For the capture of various fortified centres, see *Malaterra* II.13, p. 33 (Rometta 1061), III.12, p. 64 (Castronovo 1077); IV.2, p. 86 (Syracuse 1085); IV.6, p. 88 (Enna 1086); IV.15, p. 93 (Noto 1090). On the castles, *ibid.*, III.1, 7, pp. 57, 60–1. Cf. Maurici (1992). On the 1075 attack, *Malaterra* III.9, p. 61.

[19] *Malaterra* III.8, p. 61 (Nicotera); IV.3, pp. 86–7 (correctly 1087 rather than 1086). Ibn-al-Athīr, *BAS* I.450ff (quote). Cowdrey (1977), Abulafia (1983), 5; Abulafia (1985), 29–30; Cantarella (1996), 225ff. Quite when Roger I's treaty with Tamīm was concluded is unknown; the date of 1075 suggested by Wieruszowski (1969), 21, and Hettinger (1993), 236, is only supposition.

replied: 'By the Gospel, this is an excellent plan for us and for him; thus will all the country become Christian.' But Roger lifted his foot and made a great fart, saying 'By my faith, here is far better counsel than you have given.' When his astonished advisors inquired into his reasoning he explained: 'When the Franks are here I shall have to provide a numerous fleet, and much else besides, to transport it across to Africa, both it and my own troops too. If we conquer the country, then it will be theirs; meanwhile we shall have to send them provisions from Sicily and I shall lose the money I draw each year from the sale of my produce. If on the contrary the expedition is unsuccessful, they will return to Sicily and I shall have to suffer their presence. Moreover Tamīm will be able to accuse me of bad faith towards him, claiming that I have broken my word and that I have severed the links of friendship existing between our countries. In addition, Africa is always within our range; when we have become strong enough we will conquer it.' He therefore sent for Baldwin's messenger and informed him: 'If you want to wage war on the Moslems, it would be better to snatch Jerusalem from their hands; that will bring you glory. As far as Africa is concerned, I am bound by treaties with the rulers there.'

Ibn al-Athīr was wrong to attribute the African venture to King Baldwin I of Jerusalem (1100–18) rather than to Pisa and Genoa. The depiction of Roger as a barbarian is typical of the Arabs' contempt for the Europeans. The reasons which persuaded the Count of Sicily to reject the offer of an attack on Mahdia are well known. Norman rule in Sicily was still not fully consolidated. In the summer of 1084 soldiers of the emir, Benavert of Syracuse, had attacked Nicotera and carried the inhabitants away into slavery. They had plundered and desecrated two churches in Reggio Calabria. Finally they had devastated the nunnery of Rocca d'Asino at Squillace, raped the nuns living there, and taken them away as captives. According to Malaterra, when the count heard about this, he was filled 'to a greater extent than usual' with divine wrath. He resolved to adopt a hard line with the Sicilian Muslims who had not yet been conquered. In the years that followed, those towns still in Arab hands – Syracuse, Enna, Butera and Noto – were rapidly overcome.[20]

Even before the completion of the conquest of Sicily in 1091 Roger I had started integrating a considerable contingent of Muslim soldiers, mainly archers, into his army. Archbishop Anselm of Canterbury visited the count during the siege of Capua in 1098 and was horrified. His biographer reported that the Muslims were not only permitted to keep their faith,

---

[20] *Malaterra* IV.1–2, p. 85 (1084). See Amari (1933–9), III.167. Chalandon (1907), I.338, wrote of a '*véritable croisade*', cf. Lopez (1958). Halm (1991), 373 (referring to Ibn 'Idārī = al-Bayān) is in error when he claims that Roger attacked Mahdia in 1088, occupied the suburb of Zawīla and demanded a tribute of 100,000 dinars. This supposed attack was actually that carried out by the Pisans and Genoese in 1087, for which see Cowdrey (1977), Hettinger (1993), 208–26.

but they were even forbidden to convert to Christianity. It is doubtful whether this latter statement is accurate. Roger was probably not interested in converting these soldiers, for as a minority they relied on his protection and therefore submitted to him unconditionally, but this does not mean that the count was at heart favourably disposed towards Islam. Roger only tolerated the Muslims because he needed them. In 1086 he had forced the Emir of Enna, Abū'l-Qāsim ibn Ḥammūd, who had admittedly proved a particularly awkward opponent, not only to capitulate but to convert as well. Furthermore, by calling for the immigration of Christians in Sicily the count was attempting slowly to displace the Muslims from their dominant position. But for practical reasons forced conversion could hardly have been put into effect.[21]

When Roger I conquered Malta in 1090 he freed the Christians who were held prisoner there; these were probably pilgrims and merchants who had fallen into the hands of Muslim pirates. He hoped that they would settle in Sicily. He helped the numerous small Greek monasteries which had become rather run down during the Arabs' rule. He also encouraged the immigration of Italo-Greeks from Calabria. In addition, he founded a few great Latin abbeys such as St Bartholomew on the island of Lipari (before 1085) and the Holy Saviour at Patti on the adjacent north coast of Sicily – these were combined together in 1094. He also founded the monastery of St Agatha at Catania in 1091, which also served as the chapter for the cathedral there, and the nunnery of St Mary at Messina (before 1101). These abbeys lying in the northeast of the island contributed to the Latinization of this hitherto mixed Greek–Arab area. Towards the end of the eleventh century, the Abbot of St Bartholomew on Lipari called on 'Latin-speaking people, wherever they may be' to move to the country. Northern Italians migrated to Sicily in the wake of Roger's third wife Adelaide.[22]

Following the conquest of the island, a new church organization had to be created. It was only in Palermo that a bishop was found, who 'albeit timorous and a Greek' (according to Malaterra) was practising Christian worship as well as he could in a poor church dedicated to St Cyriakus. The cathedral had been turned into a mosque by the Muslims. The Normans reversed this process and gave the cathedral back to the bishop. However, he seems soon to have been replaced by a Latin prelate. In 1080 Roger made his base at Troina the seat of a bishopric, personally appointed the

[21] *The Life of St Anselm, Archbishop of Canterbury, by Eadmer*, ed. R. W. Southern (London 1962), 111–12; Malaterra IV.6, p. 88. Rizzitano (1977), 204ff; Houben (1994a), 166ff; Loud (2000b), 184.

[22] *Malaterra* IV.16, p. 95. Roger II, *Diplomata*, 64–5 no. 23: *homines quicumque sint, latine lingue*. Cf. White (1938), 84–5, Falkenhausen (1987), 47–9, Houben (1995a), 43–5.

new bishop and fixed the boundaries of the new diocese. He considered that he was justified in these actions because he had reconquered the island for Christianity.[23]

The popes were naturally interested in winning back Sicily for the Latin Church; not least because before it was conquered by the Arabs the island's churches had been under the jurisdiction of the Patriarch of Constantinople. In 1050 Leo IX had appointed Humbert of Silva Candida as Archbishop of Sicily; a programmatic act which must have seemed quite utopian at that time, although in reality it was far-sighted. In 1059 Robert Guiscard had in his oath of fealty promised the pope to transfer all the churches in the area under his rule to his jurisdiction. In the first instance this meant only the subordination of the Greek bishoprics to the primacy of Rome, although in the long-term it represented a 'recatholicization' of southern Italy. Sicily, however, first had to be taken away from Islam.[24]

After the victory of Cerami in 1063, Roger gave Pope Alexander II (1061–73) four captured camels. The pope thanked him by sending him a banner which, according to Malaterra, the count had carried at the front of his army during later battles. This could have been the 'Banner of St Peter', which the popes gave to some rulers in order to lend religious legitimacy to military ventures. On some coins Roger is actually depicted as a knight with a banner on his lance. Malaterra reports that through Divine intervention at the battle of Cerami, a banner with a cross suddenly hung from Roger's lance. Just before that, St George had appeared as a knight in shining armour, riding a white horse, holding a white banner with a shining cross on the lance. Was this perhaps an anticipation of a later crusade? Hardly, since the motivation for the conquest of Sicily was not primarily religious; it was not about freeing holy places or combatting Islam. It was just a by-product of the conquest, so to speak, that Sicily was won back for Christianity. However, this was service enough that even a pope as inflexible as Gregory VII had to tolerate Roger's high-handed church policy; he only cautioned him not to disregard the rules of canon law in future.[25]

It was only after he had conquered most of Sicily that 'the count started to become pious'. According to Malaterra, he did not want to be ungrateful

[23] *Malaterra* II.45, pp. 53–4: *quamvis timidus et natione graecus; ibid.*, III.19, pp. 69–70. Cf. *Italia Pontificia* X.337 no. 17. Giunta (1994).

[24] *Italia Pontificia* X. 186 no. 73. *Liber Censuum*, 1.422 c. 163. Cf. Herde (1970), 5–7, Deér (1972), 17–18, 93–5. For the survival of Greek Christianity in Arabicized western Sicily, see most recently Johns (1995b).

[25] *Malaterra* II.33, pp. 44–5. Grierson (1993), 124, Travaini (1995), 42–3, table 11 and illustration 160. Erdmann (1977), 134–6, 185. Taviani-Carozzi (1996), 375–6, and most recently Cantarella (1996), 231–2. *Gregorii VII Registrum*, ed. E. Caspar (*MGH Epistolae Selectae* II, Berlin 1920–3), IX.25, pp. 607–8.

for the favours he had received from God. Around 1086/1090 he founded the bishoprics of Syracuse, Catania, Agrigento and Mazara del Vallo. Pope Urban II (1088–99) sanctioned this action. Urban was in a difficult situation because of the conflict with Henry IV and the antipope Clement III (1080–1100). During the early years of his pontificate he remained under the protection of the Normans mainly in southern Italy. Thanks to his conciliatory stance, he managed to get the count to unite the bishopric of Troina with the old diocesan town of Messina in 1096 and transfer the bishop's residence there. But an attempt by Urban to appoint a legate in order to bring Sicily under the control of the Roman Church failed because of the energetic resistance of Roger I. The pope was forced to bestow on the count and his heirs the practice of apostolic legation. The basis for the construction of a 'national church' under the direct control of the ruler was established. As a result, the Count of Sicily had achieved a position enjoyed by no other prince in Europe.[26]

Towards the end of the eleventh century, Roger I was definitely the dominant personality on the southern Italian stage. It was only with his help that his nephew and overlord, Duke Roger Borsa (1085–1111), was able to assert himself against his half-brother Bohemond I who, even though he was the elder son of Robert Guiscard, had been excluded from the line of succession. Despite this assistance, Roger Borsa had to come to terms with his duchy being reduced to little more than the territory of the earlier principality of Salerno. Bohemond received lordship over a number of areas formerly under Byzantine rule such as the Terra d'Otranto and the Basilicata, as well as Bari and Brindisi. However, Bohemond had to take into consideration the Counts of Conversano and the Lords of Montescaglioso, who soon sought independence from his authority. The Count of Sicily demanded a high price for his help, for Roger Borsa had to cede to him the parts of Calabria and Sicily in his possession. In 1096 he promised Roger I half of Amalfi if he would help him to conquer the town which had risen against his rule. However, the siege had to be abandoned because Bohemond and other Normans preferred to take part in the First Crusade, called for by Urban II. When in 1098 Prince Richard II of Capua, who had come of age after a long minority, appealed to the Count of Sicily for help in order to be able to take up his paternal inheritance, Roger I demanded the right to lordship over Naples. Furthermore, when the Duke of Apulia was not in a position to bring about peace between contending parties, the Count of Sicily intervened.

---

[26] *Malaterra* IV.7, pp. 88–9. Cf. Delogu (1992), 155–6. *Italia Pontificia* X.317–18 no. 70; 290 no. 18; 264 no. 8; 252 no. 1; 337 no. 18. Deér (1972), 166–8. Cf. also Fodale (1977), Fonseca (1977), Becker (1988), 62–4, and most recently Loud (2000b), 174–6, 231–3. For Urban II's itinerary in southern Italy, see Houben (1996a).

Thus Roger mediated in a dispute between the Count of the Principate in the Campania and the abbey of the Holy Trinity in Venosa, in the northeast of the Basilicata, where Robert Guiscard and other brothers were buried.[27]

Roger only enfeoffed close relatives: he gave Syracuse to his illegitimate son Jordan and, after his death, to his nephew Tancred, the son of Count William of the Principate. He granted Ragusa to his son Godfrey, and Troina to another son called Malgerius. He may also have given Paternò, Butera and other places to his brother-in-law Henry del Vasto (although it is possible that this grant was only made by his widow after his death). Roger was more generous towards monasteries and churches, whose territorial lordships could not pose a threat to him. In the administration of Calabria and Sicily he relied on his Norman countrymen such as Robert Borrell, Robert Avenel, William of Hauteville and Josbert of Lucy, and he also used Latin priests. But since the 1080s the count had increasingly relied upon Greek officials from the former Byzantine administration. The most important were the chamberlain and mystolect Nicholas of Mesa (near Reggio), the protonotary John of Troina, the notary Bonos, and the logothete Leo. Scholarios, Roger's Greek court chaplain, came from Reggio. We should note, however, that the functions of these offices were not yet exactly defined. In Calabria and Sicily cadastral surveys and lists of serfs dating back to the previous Byzantine and Arab administrations were still used. The count issued Greek and a few Latin charters, but there was not yet a chancery in the sense of an organized office.[28]

It was through the conquest of Sicily that Roger I was transformed from an impoverished adventurer into one of the most respected princes in Europe. Kings asked him for his daughters' hands in marriage. They were mainly interested in the dowry which was to be expected from the proverbially rich count. For instance, King Philip I of France (1060–1180), having illegally disowned his wife Bertha, was alleged to have asked for the hand in marriage of Roger's daughter Emma. According to Malaterra, the count granted this request because he did not know that the king was still married. The bride was to be given away by the Count of Toulouse, Raymond IV of St-Gilles (1093–1105), who had married one of Emma's

---

[27] *Malaterra* III.42, p. 82; IV.17, 24, 26, pp. 96–7, 102, 104. *Annales Cavenses, MGH SS* III.190. Cf. Chalandon (1907), I.308, Girgensohn (1969), Schwarz (1978), 65–7, Jahn (1989), 237–9, 313–15, Houben (1995a), 307–9.

[28] Cf. Tramontana (1977), 216–39, reprint pp. 226–49. Falkenhausen (1977), 351–4, for Scholarios, *ibid.*, 355–6 note 172, also Scaduto (1982), 116–18, Dölger (1929), Falkenhausen (1985), Takayama (1993), 26–8, 38–40. For the Byzantine character of the mystolect, a post 'which was in practice reserved for jurists', see Falkenhausen (1985), 176 note 12. For Roger's chancery, see most recently, Falkenhausen (1998b), 268–70.

sisters, Matilda, but after he realized that Philip's intentions in the marriage were not genuine and that he only wanted to get his hands on the dowry, he then tried to snatch this dowry for himself. However, the chaperones Roger sent with his daughter saw through this plan and returned to Sicily with the dowry, but not the bride. Finally Raymond had no alternative but marry his sister-in-law to the Count of Clermont.

However, two of Roger's daughters did actually marry kings. When Conrad, the son of the emperor Henry IV, who had been crowned King of Germany in 1087, rebelled against his father in 1093 and had himself crowned as King of Italy in Milan, Urban II and his ally Matilda of Canossa advised him to marry a daughter of Roger I. He would thus gain what he had hitherto lacked for the status of a proper king: a wife and money. In 1095 he was married to Maximilla (this is what we think the bride was called). However, Conrad's plots against his father soon failed. After his death in 1101 the count's daughter returned to the south. Another of Roger's daughters, whose name is unknown, married King Coleman of Hungary (1095–1116) in 1097.[29]

At around this time an Arab coin was minted in Agrigento showing Roger I for the first time as *imām* and *malik*, lord and sovereign (in fact king) of Sicily. The *imām* title is a feature of the coin from Agrigento. The title *malik* had been preserved from the coins of Robert Guiscard minted after the conquest of Palermo, who was also referred to there as 'very great duke'. Roger I had to content himself with the more modest title 'count, brother of the duke'. In the Arab charters he issues, the oldest dating from 1095, Roger called himself 'sultan'. Arab scholars are undecided about the meaning of this title. Albrecht Noth argues that 'in the Arab hierarchy of titles' the title sultan 'stands in second place after caliph, therefore it roughly means king'. However, Jeremy Johns regards it simply as the Arabic translation of the title count. Whichever is true, Roger I never used the title 'gran conte', great count, which is often ascribed to him in modern literature. It was only after his death that in documents of Roger II he was described as *magnus comes* ('great count'), although we should remember that *magnus* can also mean 'the elder' to distinguish Roger I from his son of the same name.[30]

For Malaterra, the Count of Sicily represented the ideal model of a knight: 'He was very handsome, tall, well proportioned, extremely eloquent,

[29] *Malaterra* iv.8, 23, 25, pp. 90, 101–3. Cf. Holtzmann (1963), Houben (1990), as cited in revised version (1996c), 88–90.
[30] Money of 491 from the Hegirah (9 December 1097–27 November 1098), Johns (1986), 37 no. 8, Travaini (1995), 40, 115. Noth, in Brühl (1978), 246; Johns (1986), 16–17; Enzensberger (1977), 20; Brühl (1978), 81. For the Greek documents, see Falkenhausen (1983), 183–4 note 44, and most recently Falkenhausen (1998b), 292ff.

clever in decision-making, far-sighted in his plans, friendly and affable with everyone, very strong, and fierce in battle.' He was married three times. The count had more than ten children by his first two wives, the two Normans Judith of Evreux and Eremburga of Mortain. When he was about fifty in 1089/90 he married Adelaide del Vasto, who was barely fifteen. Two sisters of Adelaide married or were betrothed to two sons of Roger: one to Jordan, who although illegitimate was regarded as Roger's successor, and the other to Godfrey – however, he died before the wedding could take place. Adelaide's brother Henry married a daughter of the count. By this complex set of marriage alliances Roger I closely tied his family with the Aleramici, a powerful noble family from northern Italy, resident in Liguria and Piemont.[31]

The marriage with Adelaide produced two sons, Simon and Roger, and probably at least one daughter as well. The count's young wife understood the importance of having the sons from the earlier marriages excluded from the succession. Roger I died in June 1101 and was buried at Mileto in Calabria, where he had founded a Benedictine abbey which was intended as his burial place. His wife had him buried in an ancient Roman marble sarcophagus, over which was mounted a canopy made of porphyry. This was evidence of high aspirations: the use of porphyry was actually reserved for the Byzantine emperor. A few years later the popes were buried in this material in order to emphasize their universalist claims. Roger II also chose to be buried in a monument of this type.[32]

COUNTESS ADELAIDE AS REGENT

When her husband died in 1101, Adelaide was about twenty-six years old. Since Simon, the intended successor, was only a child she acted as regent for him. Little is known of this period. The Norman monk Orderic Vitalis (1075–1142) reports that Adelaide had entrusted the regency to a son of the Duke of Burgundy. When Roger II came of age she poisoned this regent who was now superfluous. However, there is no evidence for this story in any other source. There is no doubt that Orderic had some excellent information about southern Italy. Norman monks often visited their relatives in the south, and as well as valuable presents they also brought news back with them. However, Orderic's imagination sometimes ran away with him. He also seems to have had a weakness for stories about poisonings

---

[31] *Malaterra* 1.19, pp. 28–9: *militia ferox*. For the Del Vasto family, Bordone (1988), and for Roger's children, Houben (1990), and table 2 above.

[32] Cf. Deér (1959), Faedo (1982), Herklotz (1985), Houben (1996c), 102, De Lachenal (1995), 179–81.

perpetrated by women. A later anonymous chronicler, the so-called Anonymus Vaticanus (named after the place where the manuscript is now kept: the Vatican Library) reports that Simon only lived for a few years and had to face serious problems. However, the reliability of this source is also doubtful. The author largely follows Malaterra for the early Norman period. Whether he also relied on other (now lost) sources must remain in doubt.[33]

What is certain is that the countess suppressed some rebellions by her vassals with great severity. In this connection later Greek charters talk of a 'rebellion of the barons in the whole country of Calabria and Sicily', of rebels being crushed 'like earthenware dishes'. The young regent relied particularly on those who had worked with Roger I. After 1105 the *amiratus* (emir or admiral) Christodoulos took the place of the chamberlain Nicholas, who had previously been the leading official. Christodoulos was a Sicilian, brought up in the Greek–Byzantine culture, and he now became a sort of prime minister. He was also entrusted with the education of young Roger. A sign of his dominant position comes in a later charter, from 1121, in which a document issued in 1109, 'in the time of the *amiratus* Christodoulos', is mentioned. In the same year Christodoulos was decorated with the honorary title of *protonobilissimos* ('most noble') by the Byzantine emperor. Evidence about the others who worked with the countess, such as the notary Bonos, who was also a *protonobilissimos*, and the chaplain John 'the Tuscan' is more scanty.[34]

33 Ordericus Vitalis, *Historia Ecclesiastica*, ed. M. Chibnall, 6 vols. (Oxford 1969–81), VI. 428–32; Anonymus Vaticanus, *Historia Sicula a normannis ad Petrum Aragonensem*, in Muratori, *RIS* VIII.777: 'After this Simon, [his] first-born son, received the rulership; he lived for only a few years, and suffered serious problems from the Apulians'; cf. the version of the Vatican Anonymous in Cod. Vat. Lat. 4936, fol. 24v: 'he lived for only a few years, and suffered serious disturbances from many people [*per paucos vivens annos, graves tamen a plurimis inquietationes substinuit*]'. For this, and for other episodes (including tales of poison) related by Orderic, see Houben (1996c), 93–6, and cf. most recently Falkenhausen (1998c), 96 and note 55.

34 Cusa, *Diplomi*, 471, 532 (Ca. 42, 149; 1123, c. 1140). Cf. Caspar (1904), 27–8, Falkenhausen (1998c), 98, and for the term *terrérios* (baron), Falkenhausen (1980b), 225–6. Takayama (1993), 40–2. For Christodoulos, see Dölger (1929), Ménager (1960), 28–36, Falkenhausen (1985). Roger II, *Diplomata*, 4 no. 1 (1107): *Iohannes Tuscanus comitisse capellanus*. The supposition of Cuozzo (1989a), 627–8, that Robert *de Urbe* (Pirri, *Sicilia Sacra*, II.843), attested in 1110 as chaplain and chancellor of Roger I (!), had under Adelaide attained a position of pre-eminence vis-à-vis the other chaplains, analogous to that of the later chancellor, is unfounded. This document in fact dates from 1093, and its authenticity is anyway dubious, while Brühl (1978), 38 and note 22, has shown that the reference here to *cancellarius* means only an amanuensis, and has no other significance. Falkenhausen (1998c), 105–15, provides a register of Adelaide's documents.

It appears that Graeco-Byzantine culture and religion exerted a great influence on Adelaide, who no longer resided in Troina, but mainly in Messina. Abbot Gregory of St Philip of Fragalà in the Val Demone was particularly close to the regent. When in 1101 young Roger fell ill with ear trouble (he may have had mumps), Adelaide turned to Abbot Gregory, whose efforts brought about his rapid recovery. By way of thanks the countess gave numerous gifts to his monastery. Her 'prime minister' Christodoulos favoured Abbot Bartholomew of Simeri (in Calabria) who between 1101 and 1105 founded the abbey of St Mary of the Patiron at Rossano.[35]

Little is known of Roger's childhood. As a rule, medieval chroniclers pass over this period of a man's life in silence. According to the view prevailing among contemporaries, childhood was not a period of particular significance. Alexander of Telese relates an anecdote which should show how his hero was predestined to rule.[36]

He [Roger] had an older brother called Simon, who on their father's death succeeded him in his lordship of the province. As is the way of children, they were playing at 'coin' [*nummus*] which was their favourite game, and this degenerated into a fight. When they fought, each with a group of other boys whom they had gathered together, the younger, Roger, was the conqueror. As a result he mocked his brother Simon, saying; 'it would be far better that I should have the honour of ruling triumphantly after our father's death than you. However, when I shall be able to do this I shall make you a bishop or even pope at Rome – to which you're far better suited.' And hence I believe that through these insulting words he foretold that he already intended to be truly the ruler after his father, and, as will be shown below, to extend his lands far and wide, as he was to do following his victories.

This is what actually happened, for Simon died aged twelve on 28 September 1105. Adelaide now acted as regent in the name of Roger II. She succeeded in handing on the counties of Calabria and Sicily in an orderly state to her son. Her brother Henry, along with numerous immigrants from northern Italy (whom south Italian sources refer to as 'Lombards'), had settled in the area of Paternò and Butera, which had been given to him by Roger I, or perhaps Adelaide, as a fief. The settlement of these 'Lombards' drove a wedge between the regions of Moslem settlement in the west and the southeast of the island. In the Arabic section of a

[35] Documents redacted at Messina: Ca. 7, 12–14, 20–1, and Collura (1955), 'Appendice', no. 11; at San Marco d'Alunzio (province of Enna), Ca. 1 and 9; at Troina, no. 15; for St Philip of Fragalà: Ca. 1–3, 14–16, 20, 22, cf. Caspar (1904), 26. For the testaments of Gregory (who died after 1108), redacted in 1096–7 and 1105, see Falkenhausen (1983), and Scaduto (1982), 168–9.

[36] *Al. Tel.* I.2, p. 7.

Greek–Arab charter dating from 1109, Adelaide is described as 'the great female ruler, the *malikah* (sovereign or queen) of Sicily and Calabria, the protector of Christian faith'. In a similar fashion, in Greek charters after 1094 Roger I had occasionally added to his title of count that of 'the Protector of Christians'; this additional title would later find its way into the Latin chancery of Roger II.[37]

According to Snorri's 'Book of Kings', the *Heimskringla*, King Sigurd of Norway (1103–30) stopped in Sicily on his way to the Holy Land, probably in 1110.

In the spring King Sigurd came to Sicily, where he stayed for a long time. Rothgeir [Roger] was duke then there, and he greeted the king well and bade him come to a banquet. King Sigurd went and many men were with him. It was a noble welcome, and each day of the feast Duke Rothgeir stood and did service at King Sigurd's table. On the seventh day of the feast, when the men had taken their baths, King Sigurd took the duke [!] by the hand, led him up to the high-seat, and gave him the name of king and the right of being king over the realm of Sicily; before that time there had been jarls over that realm.

Snorri Sturluson wrote his work between 1220 and 1230, using older oral and written sources. The episode mentioned could of course simply belong to the realm of historical legends, having resulted from the author's knowledge of Roger's sensational rise from count to duke and finally to king. Yet, it is possible that Sigurd's visit did actually take place, and perhaps awakened in Roger II the desire for a royal dignity.[38]

The charters issued by Adelaide show the countess was only able to act as ruler effectively in the extreme south of Calabria and the northeast of Sicily. However, at the same time a series of Norman barons settled in the mainly Arab south and west of the island, and thus prepared the way for the transfer of the centre of rule from Messina to Palermo.[39]

Adelaide took this important step shortly before the end of her regency, between March and June 1112. As a result, a large town with a mainly Muslim population became the capital of a Christian kingdom. Ibn Hawqal, a traveller from Baghdad who visited the town in 973, reported that it was surrounded by great gardens and that it had five quarters. Two of those were walled, al-Qaṣr, the merchants' quarter with the principal mosque, and al-Khāliṣah, the government quarter, which contained the

---

[37] For the birth of Simon (1092–3), *Malaterra* IV.19, p. 98. The day of his death is given by the *Necrologia Panormitana*, p. 473. Cf. Bresc (1992), Collura (1955), 556, 'Appendice', no. 6. Cf. Johns (1986), 18, Falkenhausen (1998c), 108 no. 11.

[38] *Heimskringla or the Lives of the Norse Kings by Snorre Sturlasoni*, ed. and trans. E. Monsen and A. H. Smith (Cambridge 1932), 610. Cf. Elze (1964), 104.

[39] Falkenhausen (1998c), 90, lists the recipients of Adelaide's diplomas.

emir's palace. However, there were no fortifications in the harbour quarter, the so-called New Quarter and the mosque quarter, where most of the inhabitants were soldiers, artisans and small traders. The harbour was secured by towers and harbour chains. According to Ibn Ḥawqal there were more than three hundred mosques in Palermo. In the mosque of the butchers' corporation he claimed to have counted more than seven thousand people at Friday prayers. From this it has been estimated that at that time the town numbered over 300,000 inhabitants, in which case it would have been one of the largest towns in the Mediterranean after Baghdad, Córdoba and Constantinople, each of which had approximately 500,000 inhabitants. That is certainly an exaggeration. Ibn al-Athīr reports that when it was conquered by the Arabs in 831 the town had 70,000 inhabitants, of whom only 3,000 survived the siege. In 1277, 11,000 homes were taxed in Palermo, from which we can conclude that there were approximately 50,000 inhabitants. There are, however, no figures for the centuries in between. The estimates of recent research fluctuate between 20,000 and 100,000 inhabitants for the Norman period. After the sixteenth year of his life Roger II, having spent his childhood in the care of his northern Italian mother in a Greek ambiance, therefore grew up in a large town in which Arabic influence predominated.[40]

When Roger II came of age in 1112 Adelaide's mission was at an end. The countess, then about thirty-five, could have retreated into private life. However, she soon had an opportunity to play an important role once again. King Baldwin I of Jerusalem asked for her hand in marriage. He was in dire financial difficulties and needed the generous dowry that he would obtain with Adelaide in order to pay his knights. He was therefore prepared to accept any condition. Adelaide and Roger demanded an assurance that if the marriage did not produce an heir, the succession to the kingdom of Jerusalem would then fall to Roger. Baldwin even agreed to this. It was probably known in Sicily that the king was actually still married; for although he had repudiated his second wife, the Armenian Arda of Edessa, the marriage had not been formally annulled. Clearly it was better to ignore this, for the prospect of a royal crown seemed to be worth the risk. When Adelaide arrived in Jerusalem she brought with her

---

[40] Adelaide was still issuing documents at Messina in March 1112: Cusa, *Diplomi*, 407 (Ca. 20), Falkenhausen (1998c), 113 no. 27, cf. Chalandon (1907), 359–60. Ibn Ḥawqal, *BAS* I.10–11, *Description de Palerme*, trans. M. Amari (Paris 1845), 22ff. Cf. Columba (1910), map after p. 424, De Simone (1971), Johns (1983), 146ff with maps 2–4, 405ff. Ibn al-Athīr, *BAS* I.369, D'Angelo (1978), 73. Estimates of population: Amari (1933–9), II.349 (more than 350,000), Peri (1978), 107ff, especially p. 112 (a maximum of 100,000 c. 1170), Schack (1969), 17ff. (50,000), Johns (1983), 168 (20,000, from a surface area of about 2.5. km²).

ships heavily laden with weapons and soldiers, provisions and gold, and the marriage was celebrated in great splendour in September 1113.[41]

The marriage remained childless. When Baldwin fell seriously ill in the winter of 1116/17 it seemed that the plans made by Adelaide, who by now had turned forty, would come to fruition. However, she had not calculated on the king's vassals and the Patriarch of Jerusalem, who were not prepared to accept the Count of Sicily as Baldwin's successor, for they were afraid that they would have to forfeit their hitherto strong position, acquired at the expense of the weak king. The patriarch therefore raised the argument that Baldwin was still legally married to his second wife. The sick king was as a result forced to repudiate Adelaide. Disappointed, she now left the country as an ex-queen and embarked for Sicily in spring 1117, where she died on 16 April 1118, barely a year after her return. She was buried in the nunnery of the Holy Saviour at Patti.[42]

Roger II did not forget the affront to his mother. This was the only explanation that the chronicler and chancellor of the kingdom of Jerusalem, William of Tyre (d. 1186), could provide for the failure of the Kings of Sicily to support the Crusader states.[43]

Adelaide's son was angered beyond measure, because she had been sent back. He conceived a mortal hatred against the kingdom and its people. Other Christian princes in various parts of the world, either by coming in person or by giving liberal gifts, have amplified and promoted our infant realm. But he and his heirs at the present time have never become reconciled to us to the extent of a single friendly word. Although they could have relieved our necessities by counsel and aid far more easily than any other prince, yet they have always remembered their wrongs and have unjustly avenged upon the whole people the fault of a single individual.

Here one individual attempted a psychological explanation of a more complex situation.

Adelaide's plan to provide her son with the royal crown of Jerusalem had indeed failed. However, in her rise to queen she had nevertheless increased the prestige of the comital house of Sicily. When Roger wanted to become king, he indicated in his charters that he was the son of a queen.[44]

---

[41] Albert of Aachen, *Historia Hierosolymitana* XII.13, *Recueil des Historiens des Croisades, Occidentaux*, IV. 696–7. William of Tyre, *Chronicon*, XI.21, p. 526 [Babcock and Krey, I.496–7]. Cf. Cohn (1910), 16–17, Pontieri (1964), 500–2, Mayer (1984), 59ff, Favreau-Lilie (1989), 89, Houben (1996c), 103.

[42] William of Tyre, *Chronicon*, XI.29, pp. 541–2 [Babcock and Krey, I. 513–14], *Annales Siculi*, in *Malaterra*, 116, *Necrologia Panormitana*, 472. Cf. Mayer (1984), 64 and note 136, Pontieri (1964), 507 and note 194, Siragusa (1910).

[43] William of Tyre, *Chronicon*, XI.29, pp. 542–3 [Babcock and Krey, I.514]. Cf. Loud (1992), 57–9, Hiestand (1993b), 86ff.

[44] Roger II, *Diplomata*, 37 no. 12 (November 1129), 42 no. 14 (30 December 1129).

2

FROM COUNT TO KING

———————— • ————————

When he had become a young man and been made a knight, and was thus in a position to exercise his rights as lord, he showed such activity and demonstrated such admirable firmness, ruling the whole province of Sicily so well and strongly, and exercising such terrible authority over all that no robber, thief, plunderer or other malefactor dared to stir out of his lair. He was most richly endowed with gold, silver and other goods, and this led all to hold him in the greatest awe. Not only his own people but foreigners from faraway lands feared him greatly.

So Alexander of Telese claimed, while celebrating the rise of Roger II from count to duke, and finally to king, as an act of Divine Providence. According to his 'Preface' Roger II carried out the will of God with his sword. The Normans' acts of violence were justifiable punishment for the sins of the southern Italian Lombards: murder, theft, abduction, sacrilege, adultery, perjury, oppression of churches and monasteries, the robbery and murder of pilgrims.

God, greatly offended by these crimes, drew Roger from the sheath of the province of Sicily, so that holding him in His hand as though a sharp sword He might repress those who had committed these crimes, stabbing them by means of Roger, that those whom He had long considered incorrigible should be frightened by fear of Roger and brought back to the path of justice.[1]

In 1112 Roger stepped out from behind the shadow of the regent. In a charter dated 12 June 1112 he is called 'now knight, now Count of Sicily and Calabria'. This was the last time that he and his mother jointly issued a

---

[1] *Al. Tel.* 1.4, p. 8; prologue, p. 4.

document. On his assumption of rulership he confirmed to the church of Palermo its privileges and his father's gifts. The promulgation of the charter took place in the upper citadel of Palermo in the presence of the archbishop of the town and 'many of our own people, clerics, barons, knights'. It is not possible to say with any degree of certainty just how old Roger was at this time. Birthdays were of no great significance in the Middle Ages. The day of someone's death was far more important, signifying the beginning of a new and better life in the next world. In the chronicle of Romuald of Salerno we learn that Roger died aged fifty-eight years, two months and five days. If we calculate backwards from the day of his death (27 February 1154) we arrive at 22 December 1095 as his birthday. As the court doctor and advisor to Roger's successor, William I, Romuald was certainly well informed, although his chronicle does contain a few errors of chronology. We cannot therefore be sure whether his calculation of Roger's age is accurate, but there is no reason why we should not trust him in this case. This would mean that Roger was sixteen years old when he assumed the lordship in 1112. His relative Bohemond II (1108–30) also reached his majority at the same age.[2]

Alexander of Telese's sombre picture of southern Italy, cited at the beginning of this chapter, was written with the intention of making Roger appear in a more positive light. Even so, at the beginning of his lordship there really was a power vacuum in southern Italy. Following the death of Roger I, the Duke of Apulia experienced increasing difficulty in asserting himself. In the course of 1111, Roger Borsa and Bohemond I both died in quick succession, and both left underage successors. Their widows, Adela of Flanders and Constance of France, therefore had to act as regent. Both vassals and towns were constantly in rebellion and tried to make themselves independent. It seemed a favourable opportunity. Opponents of Norman rule, such as Falco of Benevento, hoped that after his first visit to Rome Henry V (1106–1125) would make imperial law valid in southern Italy. Prince Robert I of Capua (1106–20), who was in theory a vassal of the Duke of Apulia, offered his submission to the emperor. Other powerful Normans from Apulia made similar offers, although nothing resulted. In preliminary negotiations with Pope Paschal II (1099–1118), which led to the Treaty of Ponte Mammolo (1111), Henry V had to abandon his claims to southern Italy.[3]

[2] Roger II, *Diplomata*, 7–9 no. 3. *Romuald*, 236. Cf. Hoffmann (1967), 162. Matthew (1981), 267–9. The suggestion of Clementi (1991), 230–1, that Roger's birth should be postdated to 1099, is not convincing. Cf. Houben (1990), 112–13. For Bohemond II, see Ménager (1984).

[3] *Chron. Cas.* IV.40, p. 507. Holtzmann (1933–5), 300–1 (reprint 1957), 122. Deér (1972), 148, 152.

If we eliminate Sicily from the equation, the pope's position in southern Italy was becoming increasingly strong. Although the only representative from Roger II's territory to attend the Lateran council of 1112 was the Bishop of Syracuse, Paschal II achieved great successes in southern Italy. In 1111 he had opened proceedings against Archbishop Walter of Palermo on a charge of simony, although he allowed him to remain in office after he had sworn an oath to his innocence. In 1114 at the synod of Ceprano he deposed Archbishop Landulf of Benevento. Landulf had, against the wishes of the Pope, concluded an armistice with Prince Robert of Capua and Count Jordan of Ariano, who had attacked the town. In doing this, he had exceeded his authority. (Benevento had made itself subject to the pope in 1051, and a year later the emperor Henry III had recognized this *de facto* papal lordship over the town.) At this same synod at Ceprano Paschal granted William, Roger Borsa's son, who had now reached his majority, investiture with the duchy of Apulia. But the young duke seems to have been a weak figurehead. He had little in common with his grandfather Robert Guiscard. The following year Paschal II promulgated a Truce of God at the synod of Troia in an attempt to put a halt to the prevailing anarchy. But the results appear to have been negligible.[4]

While the position of the Duke of Apulia became progressively weaker, Roger was meanwhile working to extend his lordship. He soon had the chance to act as the protector of Christendom in the Mediterranean. The Chronicle of Montecassino testified that in 1114:

As some of our brothers were returning from Sardinia, they were attacked by Saracen pirates who carried them off to Africa as prisoners. When our abbot learned of this, he decided to send money there to ransom them; but those who were carrying it were driven by strong winds to Sicily. Their arrival was brought to the attention of the mighty Count Roger, and because of his love for the most holy Father Benedict he sent envoys to the king of the city of Calama, which is called by the Saracens Alchila, telling him that if he wished to have peace with him and enjoy his friendship, then these monks should be allowed to return to their monastery. The king of Calama immediately granted his request, and sent the brothers back to the count with the latter's envoys. However, Azzo the dean had already ended his life in captivity. The monks went from Africa to Sicily where they were honourably received by the count, who sent them back to the monastery.

The 'King of Calama' from whom Roger secured the monks' liberation was the emir, al-'Azīz, from the Berber dynasty of the Hammadids. The Zirids, the old Berber dynasty who held office from the Fatimids, had granted them part of the territory which had been entrusted to them.

---

[4] *It. Pont.* x.229 no. 22; *ibid.*, viii.28 no. 96; cf. Kamp (1979), 102. *Falco*, 24–5. *Chron. Cas.* IV.49, p. 516. *Romuald*, 207. Cf. Chalandon (1907), I.315–17; Vehse (1930–1), 95–7, 124–5. Deér (1972), 89–90, 99.

The Hammadids had broken with the Zirids in 1015, and during the second half of the eleventh century they had abandoned their former capital, which lay in the mountains of the Qal'at Banī Ḥammād – hence in the chronicle the name 'Calama' – and gone to live in the coastal town of Bougie (Bijāya) in modern Algeria. We may deduce from the chronicle passage cited above that Roger II had concluded a peace treaty with the emir at some stage before 1114.[5]

At about this time a Syrian Christian, George of Antioch, came from north Africa to Palermo, where the *amiratus* Christodoulos remained the most influential personage. George had served as the finance minister at the court of the Zirid lord Tamīm at Mahdia (where the Zirids had exercised independent authority since 1051), but after Tamīm's death in 1108 he had fallen into disfavour. Consequently he had sought new opportunities and had opened contacts with Roger's court. There was rejoicing there at the chance of securing the services of an Arabic financial expert. Under the pretext of bringing foodstuffs, a ship was sent to Mahdia. While the Moslems were busy with the Friday prayer, George and his followers embarked, dressed as sailors. By the time that their flight was discovered they were already well out to sea. In Sicily Christodoulos happily took him on as protégé. He entrusted George with a sensitive mission to Egypt, where the latter proved himself most successful. Soon he also won Roger's favour. So runs the story of at-Tijānī, who lived in Tunis at the beginning of the fourteenth century, and who based his account on older sources.[6]

George's flight did not at first harm the good relations between the count and the Zirid ruler Yaḥyā (1108-16), who can be characterized as no more than a weak figurehead. Hence he permitted the governor (*walī*) of Gabès, Rāfi', to build his own personal trading ship. However, his successor 'Alī was not prepared to tolerate such an affront. He ordered this ship to be seized. The trade in luxury articles was probably a monopoly of Mahdia and Tripoli, with the other ports such as Gabès, Susa and Sfax only being allowed a secondary role. Rāfi' requested Roger to send his fleet

---

5 *Chron. Cas.* IV.50, p. 516. Cf. Amari (1933–9), III.375–6; Chalandon (1907), I.368–9; Wieruszowski (1969), 23; Hettinger (1993), 38–40, 237 n. 5. There (pp. 226–7) the attack of a 'Roman' fleet against Mahdia, mentioned in an Arabic source (al-Bayān) for the year 1104–5, is attributed to the Normans; this probably refers to the Byzantines, cf. Amari (1933–9), III.373.

6 At-Tijānī, *BAS* II.65; Ibn Khaldūn, *BAS* II.206. Cf. Amari (1933–9), III.368–70. Ménager (1960), 44–6. Idris (1962), 306–7. The opinion of Halm (1991), p. 373, that George was an 'Islamic renegade' is untrue. According to al-Maqrīzī (1361–1441) in his *Kitāb al-Muqaffā*, George was born in 1063 and was originally in the service of the Byzantine emperor; he then went to Tamīm's court soon after 1088; see De Simone (1999), 282, who does not rule out that both George and Christodoulos were of Armenian origin. Cf. also Lavagnini (1994), 220.

to help him. 'Ali's councillors sought in vain to prevent him from going to war with the Count of Sicily, but in the conflict between the two fleets (in 1117/18) it was the Arabs who were victorious.[7]

The events described above show that Roger II, in contrast to his father, felt himself strong enough to intervene militarily in north Africa. His African policy came about under the influence of his 'prime ministers' Christodoulos and George of Antioch, who rapidly rose in importance. The count primarily patronized Greek monasteries, but he also had dealings with the Latin Church. In July 1112, immediately after his assumption of rule, he deprived the Latin Archbishop of Reggio Calabria of his jurisdiction over the Greek community in that town and instead placed it under his own authority. The count's involvement in church affairs soon brought him into conflict with the papacy. At the synod of Ceprano in 1114 the Archbishop of Cosenza complained to the pope that Roger had forced him to resign and return to a monastery. What then happened cannot be ascertained. According to the chronicle of Montecassino the pope declined to intervene because this matter came under the jurisdiction of the Abbot of Montecassino, but one can hardly believe the famous, or rather notorious, forger and fantasist Peter the Deacon, who was responsible for this part of the chronicle. Admittedly Abbot Desiderius of Montecassino, (1058–87) had once exercised a sort of vicariate over southern Italy: but this was only with regard to monasteries. The deposition of an archbishop was a matter for the pope. But we cannot really doubt Roger's action.[8]

The fundamental problem was whether the privilege granted by Urban II to Roger I, allowing him to act in place of a papal legate (*legati vice*) in Sicily, also applied to his successors. A letter of Paschal II, dated 1 October 1117, is most informative. From this we can see that the pope had already showered the count with reproaches. The latter had promised to take these exhortations to heart. But now the pope was forced to write to Roger once again. The first part of the letter is a diplomatic masterpiece. First of all the Apostolic legation was confirmed but then in reality annulled through the postscript: 'in such a way that, if we should send a legate or vicar to Sicily, you will carry out his instructions'. In particular, it should never happen that the either laymen or monks should exercise judgement over

---

[7] At-Tijānī, *BAS* II.52–3; an-Nuwairī, *BAS* II.154. Ibn al-Athīr, *BAS* I.454–5. Cf. Chalandon (1907), I.363–4, 370–1; Wieruszowski (1962), 19–21; Idris (1962), 320–1, Goitein (1967–88), I.212; Abulafia (1985), 30.

[8] For the Greek privilege (preserved only in a Latin translation) of Roger II for Peter, *protopapas* of Reggio Calabria, ed. Morisanus (1768), 277–8, see Falkenhausen (1991), 277–8. *Chron. Cas.* IV.49, p. 516; cf. Caspar (1909), 153; *It. Pont.* X.112–13 no. 6. Deér (1972), 170 n. 786 considers this reference credible. Cf. Kamp (1979), 102–3, Servatius (1979), 93–4.

ecclesiastics and their offices. Furthermore, so ran the pope's rhetorical question, has a legate or vicar ever usurped the right to summon bishops to a synod? Paschal behaved as though Urban's privilege for Roger I and his successors had never existed.

The second part of the letter continues this theme:

Hearken, my dearest son, and strike the right balance. Do not use the power [*potestas*] which has been granted you by God against Divine authority. The Roman Church was given its power by God; hence this cannot be taken from it by men. Imitate in your exercise of the comital office the example of the good rulers. Take care to support the Church and not to persecute it; you should not judge or oppress bishops but honour them as the representatives of God. Do not diminish but rather increase what your father, Count Roger of distinguished memory, has given to it. Do not alter your conduct, for then you will secure the light of Everlasting life.

In sum – it is the duty of rulers to support the Church and not to control it. But with Roger II such exhortations fell on deaf ears. He was unwilling to give up the position secured by his father. Perhaps his relations with Paschal were also affected by the latter's role in the annulment of Adelaide's marriage with King Baldwin. Arnulf, the Patriarch of Jerusalem, had been in Rome in 1116, where the illegality of this union was probably pointed out to him.[9]

Roger's high aspirations were also shown in his marriage to a king's daughter. It was probably also in 1117 that the young count married Elvira, a daughter of Alfonso VI, King of Castile and León (1072–1109). The latter had built up a pre-eminent position in the Iberian peninsula among both the Christian lands of the north and the Islamic lordships in the south. He used the title 'Emperor of the whole of Spain' and 'Emperor of the two religions'. Elvira's mother, his fourth wife, was a Moorish woman called Zaida, who at her wedding in 1098/9 had taken the Christian name of Isabella. Given her background, Roger II's wife was also likely to have predisposed her husband towards Christians and Moslems living together in peace. There was a tradition of such *convivencia* (co-existence) in her Spanish homeland, although from the end of the eleventh century this was disrupted by two developments: on the one hand there was the concept of the Crusade, which was introduced by the immigration of foreign nobles and pilgrims, and on the other the idea of the Holy War or *jihād* imported to Spain by the Almoravids of north Africa. By 1118 Elvira had already produced an heir, who was given the name Roger after his father and grandfather. Within the space of a very few years she gave birth to three

---

[9] *Liber Censuum*, II.125–6; JL 6562; *It. Pont.* VIII.30 no. 104. Cf. Deér (1964), 131–2 [reprint (1977), 451–2], Deér (1972), 170–1; Servatius (1979), 94–5.

more sons, called Tancred, after the progenitor of the Hauteville dynasty, Alfonso (after his own father), and William, which was one of the other names favoured by the Hauteville clan. Later there was another son, who was named Henry, after Roger II's maternal uncle, Henry del Vasto.[10]

Meanwhile Popes Gelasius II (1118–19) and Calixtus II (1119–24) were trying to strengthen their influence in southern Italy. A number of the vassals of the Duke of Apulia now entered the direct fealty of the pope. Calixtus II, a Burgundian who before his election as pope had been Archbishop of Vienne, achieved some minor successes. In 1120 he was able to bring about a compromise between the townspeople and the noble party in Benevento, and to secure oaths of fealty from William of Apulia and Jordan II of Capua (1120–7). He promulgated a Truce of God at Troia. At Bari he succeeded in persuading Grimoald Alferanites, who had set himself up as independent 'Lord of Bari', to free Constance of France, whom he was holding prisoner. In return Constance, who as daughter of the King of France claimed the title of queen, had to renounce lordship over the town, to which she was entitled as Bohemond I's heir.[11]

Calixtus was less successful when he sought in late 1121 to arrange a peace between Duke William and Roger. After his envoys had failed to achieve anything, he travelled in person to Calabria. There he was able to hold a synod at Crotone at the beginning of 1122, but he then fell seriously ill, victim of an epidemic which caused the deaths of several of the cardinals in his following. Calixtus's biographer commented laconically that 'in the end Count Roger got what he wanted from the half-dead pope'. The

---

[10] Pelayo of Oviedo, *Crónica del obispo Don Pelayo,* ed. B. Sánchez Alonso (Madrid 1924), 86. *Romuald,* 222. We cannot be certain of the exact dates when Roger's children were born, but some indication is given by *Al. Tel.* III.28, pp. 74–5: in August 1135 his two eldest sons were already old enough to be knighted, that is they must have been about sixteen. The 'boy' (*puer*) Alfonso was not old enough to be knighted, but he received investiture with the principality of Capua. He was probably thus about fourteen or fifteen, although a *puer* might be any age up to twenty-eight, cf. Hofmeister (1926). According to Alexander, two more sons, identified by *Romuald,* 230–1, as William and Henry, were still 'infants', that is under the age of fourteen. However, the former appears to have been in the forty-sixth year of his life when he died on 7 or 15 May 1166, *Romuald,* 253 [*Tyrants,* 138], that is he was born between May 1120 and May 1121. This contradicts Alexander, since if William really was an 'infant', i.e. under fourteen, he cannot have been born before August 1121. See also Cuozzo (1989b), p. 42, who identifies the two younger sons, whose names were not given by Alexander, as William and Simon. However, the latter was actually illegitimate, *Falcandus,* 51 [*Tyrants,* 104]. The *Chronica de Ferraria,* 28, claimed that his mother was a sister of Count Hugh II of Molise, but was in error when suggesting that she and King Roger were married.

[11] *Chron. Cas.* IV.64, p. 526. *Liber Pontificalis,* II.315, 322. *Romuald,* 209–11. Cf. Deér (1972), 153–5; Hoffmann (1978), 170–1. *Falco,* 62. Cf. Vehse (1930–1), 130–1. *Romuald,* 210. *Annales Ceccanenses, MGH SS* XIX.282. Cf. Falkenhausen (1994b), 162; most recently Schilling (1998), 485ff.

appointment of Bishop Peter of Squillace (in Calabria) to the archbishopric of Palermo early in 1123 also took place at Roger's wish. This prelate must have enjoyed the special trust of the count, for he represented Sicily at the Lateran Council of March 1123.[12]

The Duke of Apulia became ever more dependent upon his cousin. In February 1122 the only option that he had left was to travel to Messina and request Roger II's help. Falco of Benevento testified that

Duke William, son of Duke Roger, came to Count Roger, son of Count Roger of the Sicilians, complaining of Count Jordan of Ariano [and asking] that he extend a helping hand to him and be generous with his knights and riches, that by his help he might be revenged on Count Jordan. And when the duke had come to the count he begged him with prayers and tears thus: 'To your power, O distinguished Count, I have recourse, both because of the strength of our blood-relationship and because of the magnitude of your riches in order to make a complaint about Count Jordan, begging humbly that with your support and aid I may be revenged upon him. For when one day I had gone to the town of Nusco, Count Jordan and a band of knights arrived before the gate of that town and brought reproach on me, threatening me with many insults, such as "I shall shorten your cloak for you." Then, raging all around the town of Nusco, he laid everything waste. Since I cannot prevail against him, I have unwillingly sustained this, but I ask for a day when I shall be revenged. And having done this, the count dishonoured me all the times with numerous and varied aggravations.'

Roger did not refuse help to his overlord, but he made him pay dearly for it. He provided William with six or seven hundred knights and placed money at his disposal. But in return the duke handed over to him the half share which he had up to then held of Palermo, Messina and Calabria. Now Roger had the whole of Sicily and Calabria in his own hands.[13]

---

[12] *It. Pont.* x.80–2, nos. 5–10 [Calixtus was at Catanzaro from 21 to 28 December 1121, at Rossano on 6 January 1122, and also at Crotone in January]. *Romuald*, 212. The claim by the *Liber Pontificalis*, II.322–3, that Duke William went to Byzantium in search of a wife, and entrusted the pope with the administration of his duchy in his absence, is not credible. William had already married, in 1114, the daughter of Count Robert of Caiazzo, who survived him, *Romuald*, 207. *Falco*, 84. Cf. Chalandon (1907), I.321–2. Neither Caspar (1904), 54–5, nor Deér (1972), 171–2, is convincing here. Cf. also Falkenhausen (1982b), 63–4, with reference to a fragmentary Troia chronicle, and Schilling (1998), 491–3. For Peter, *It. Pont.* x.60–1 nos. 10–14 (1110–23), *ibid.*, 230 nos. 23–5 (1123–32); cf. Kamp (1979), 103–4.

[13] *Falco*, 66–8: 'The duke conceded to the count his half of the city of Palermo, and Messina and the whole of Calabria, to secure his help in these affairs. He immediately gave him six hundred knights and five hundred ounces of gold.' *Romuald*, 212–13: 'he [Duke William] was first of all forced by necessity to place Calabria in pledge to the count for sixty thousand bezants. Afterwards he sold to him the half of Palermo which belonged to him by hereditary right. Finally, when he was unable to have a son by his wife, he received a great deal of money from the count and at Messina instituted him as his heir to the duchy of Apulia and all his land.' Deér (1972), 176–7.

However, his attention in these years was primarily devoted to north Africa. In retaliation for Roger's attack on Gabès, the Zirid ruler ʿAlī (1116–21) had arrested the Sicilian merchants in Mahdia and confiscated their possessions. The count's threats had soon made him release them and return their goods, and he had renewed the treaty with Roger II. But the latter was still not appeased by this; instead he sent an embassy with further demands which ʿAlī considered to be unacceptable. The count was probably trying to provoke a conflict, which is what happened. The Zirid ruler concluded a treaty with the Almoravids who ruled over Morocco and part of Spain. This Berber dynasty had seized the Balearic Islands from the Genoese and Pisans in 1115. In 1122, a year after ʿAlī's death, an Almoravid naval force attacked the coast of Calabria, stormed the town of Nicotera, killed some of the inhabitants and led the rest off into slavery.[14]

ʿAlī's successor al-Ḥassan (1121–48) was still a minor, and his vassals began to rebel against him; this appeared to Roger to be a situation tailor-made for a decisive attack. According to at-Tijānī, who undoubtedly exaggerated, the Sicilian fleet which left Marsala at the start of July 1123 comprised some three hundred ships, carrying thirty thousand soldiers and a thousand horses. It was commanded by Roger's two leading court officials, Christodoulos and George of Antioch. But the undertaking ended in complete failure. Part of the fleet was destroyed in a storm, and the rest was no match for the well-armed Arab troops. The *ribat* or fortress of ad-Dīmās, on the coast half way between Monastir and Mahdia, which had fallen into the Sicilians' hands through bribery of the local Bedouins, had to be left to its fate. Only a third of the ships which had set out returned to Sicily. The garrison which had been left behind at the *ribat* was wiped out to the last man in a desperate attempt to escape. The Arabs were overjoyed by their success. Al-Ḥassan made it known in letters, which said, among other things: 'the prince of Sicily has committed a grave error if he thinks, all by himself, to insult the majesty of Islam'. However, the Christian chroniclers took no notice of these events. Roger seems to have accepted the disaster without much concern – the two leaders of the expedition, Christodoulos and George of Antioch, remained trusted servants of the count.[15]

In the years which followed Roger turned his attention more and more towards southern Italy. In June 1123 he stormed and destroyed the fortress of San Mauro, near Crotone in Calabria. A year later he advanced into

---

[14] At-Tijānī, *BAS* II.67–8; an-Nuwairī, *BAS* II.155–6; Ibn al-Athīr, *BAS* I.455–6; Al-Bayān, 34; Ibn Khaldūn, *BAS* II.205. Amari (1933–9), III.367–87; Chalandon (1907), I.372–3; Idris (1962), 323–4.

[15] At-Tijānī, *BAS* II.68–74; Ibn al-Athīr, *BAS* I.456–8; Al-Bayān, 35–6; Ibn Khaldūn, *BAS* II.205–7; Ibn Ḥamdīs, *BAS* II.389–400. Amari (1933–9), III.388–95; Chalandon (1907), I.373–5; Cohn (1910), 21–2; Idris (1962), 333–8. For Ibn-Ḥamdīs (1053–1133), see Borruso (1973), De Simone (1997), 67. For ad-Dīmās, Halm (1991), 201.

the Basilicata. At Montescaglioso, near Matera, not far from the Apulian border, he seized the inheritance of his sister Emma, widow of Rodolf (Raoul), Lord of Montescaglioso; she had died a few years earlier, c. 1120. Christodoulos and George of Antioch accompanied him on this expedition. These actions of Roger completely ignored the rights of 'Queen' Constance, who was acting as regent for her minor son Bohemond II. In April 1121, helped by Duke William and Tancred of Conversano, she had seized a fortress on the River Basento, also in the territory of the Montescaglioso lordship.[16]

We know very little about the duke's last years. While Grimoald of Bari was making himself independent, concluding a treaty with Venice in 1122 and assuming the title of prince in 1123, William was busy making donations to the abbey of Cava dei Tirreni, near Salerno. In 1125 he received the investiture of his duchy from Pope Honorius II (1124–30). Although he was only just thirty, in July 1127 the duke took steps to arrange his burial place, perhaps with a premonition that he was soon to die, and like his father he chose Salerno cathedral. Then, on 28 July 1127 he died 'a natural death', according to Romuald of Salerno. The latter described William as 'of middle height, graceful of body, a daring and energetic knight, well-versed in the art of war, generous, humble, kindly and patient, affable to all, pious and merciful, and much loved by his men, greatly honouring the churches of God and their ministers'. This picture is not without inconsistencies, but its predominant features suggest no very strong character. In another place, in fact, the chronicler remarks that while the duke was much loved by his men for his kindness and patience, he was also despised.[17]

A year before William's death in 1126 the relics of St Agatha, which George Maniakes had brought from Catania to Constantinople in 1038 as a sign of his victory over the Arabs, were returned once again to Sicily. The account of the Translation by Bishop Maurice of Catania said that the saint appeared in a dream to a Frankish mercenary in the service of the emperor called Gilbert and gave him instructions to do this. Gilbert undertook the task along with his companion-at-arms Joscelin, a Latin

---

[16] *Romuald*, 211–12. Roger II, *Diplomata*, 16–17 no. 6 (September–December 1124), which is the only surviving document with an autograph signature in Latin of Roger II [see fig. 1; there is a facsimile of the whole document in *Arch. Paleografico Italiano* III (1892–1902), table 45]; cf. Enzensberger (1971), 87, Brühl (1978), 173–4, (1983a), 146–7. Emma called herself countess as the daughter of Count Roger I; however the documents in which her husband (who died c. 1108) is described as 'count' are all outright forgeries, or at best very dubious, Cuozzo (1985), Loud (2000b), 253–5. Jahn (1989), 275ff, is somewhat uncritical in dealing with these documents. For Tancred of Conversano, see Martin (1993), 738–9, and for the date of Constance's death (14 September 1125), Falkenhausen (1994b), 164–5.

[17] *CDB* V, nos. 68–9. De Donato (1974), no. 4; cf. Martin (1993), 746. *Romuald*, 213–14, who gives the date of his death 'at the age of thirty'.

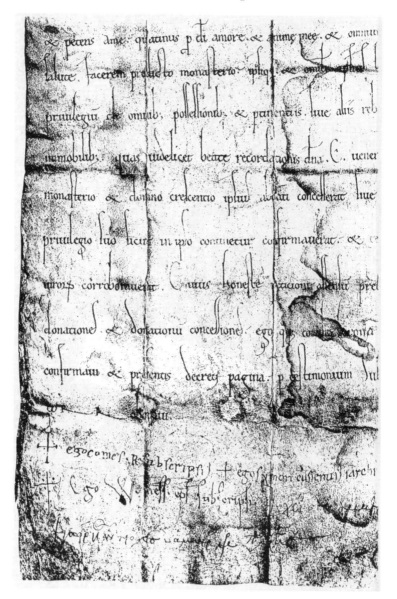

Fig. 1. Signature of Roger II on a charter of 1124 (Roger II, *Diplomata*, no. 6).
Ego comes R. subscripsi ('I Count Roger have signed'). Next to this is the signature
of Archbishop Simon of Cosenza, underneath that of Bishop William of Messina,
and below that, the signature in Greek of the *amiratus* Christodoulos.

from Calabria. The Byzantine emperor sought in vain to apprehend the relic thieves, for this seemed to him 'a sad omen' (*triste praesagium*) for the destiny of the empire. But according to the Bishop of Catania, Man can achieve nothing against Divine Providence. God showed his favour to the Normans who had settled in Sicily and Byzantium was left desolate.[18]

Moslem pirates were a more dangerous threat to Sicily than was Byzantium. In July 1127 they plundered Patti and Syracuse; the inhabitants of Catania were only saved at the very last moment. To limit the pirates' operations, the little islands of Pantelleria and Malta which served them as bases had to be brought under control. A comprehensive defensive policy also required the takeover of the Balearic Islands, from where the Almoravids made the Mediterranean unsafe. Roger established contacts with Count Raymond Berengar III of Barcelona (1097–1131). A joint expedition was prepared, and the Count of Sicily provided fifty ships for the Divinely inspired war against the Moslems. But the sudden death of the Duke of Apulia and the chance that this gave rise to of gaining his inheritance made Roger postpone his Mediterranean plans.[19]

DUKE OF APULIA, CALABRIA AND SICILY

The childless death of Duke William meant that there was a problem over the succession. When Roger II heard of his nephew's demise, he went immediately to Salerno, which under Roger Borsa and William had been the capital of the 'Dukes of Apulia, Calabria and Sicily' – such was their full title. 'He was very upset that he had died without his knowledge,

---

[18] *Historia translationis S. Agathae, Acta Sanctorum* I (Paris 1863), 643: 'two Latins were dwelling at Constantinople, one of whom was called Gilbert, and the other Joscelin. The former was French by birth, the latter a Calabrian. Gilbert, who was one of the guards in the royal hall, claimed in our presence that the most blessed virgin and martyr Agatha appeared to him in a nocturnal vision, not once but two and three times, and ordered him to take her from the church in which she lay and bring her back to Catania, where she had been crowned with martyrdom for the sake of Christ.' Cf. Breccia (1995), 322–4. For the problems which faced the emperor John II Komnenos (1118–43) at the start of his reign, see Angold (1984), 150–5.

[19] At-Tijānī, *BAS* II.74–5; *S. Agathae miracula, Acta Sanctorum* I (Paris 1863), 648–9; William of Tyre, *Chronicon*, XIII.22, p. 615 [Babcock and Krey, II.35]. Sicard of Cremona, *Chronicon, RIS* VII.597. Amari (1933–9), III.385–6; Chalandon (1907), 377–8; Wieruszowski (1962), 25; Luttrell (1975), 47. Roger II, *Diplomata*, 22–4 no. 9 [18 January/March 1128]: *in servicium Dei*. For Raymond Berengar III 'the Great', see Vones (1983), 61ff. The hypothesis that Conrad III, elected anti-king of Germany towards the end of 1127, had, on his return from the Holy Land in 1126–7, 'chosen the road through Sicily' and had then 'concluded an alliance with Roger II' so that 'he and the Normans trapped Honorius II in a pincer movement', Niederkorn (1993), 599–600, is unconvincing and not supported by the sources. Roger's relations with the pope only became difficult late in 1127.

and without, as he had promised in his lifetime he would if he had no son, making him his heir.' Relying on this promise, the count claimed lordship over Salerno 'before all as his inheritance'. Roger announced to the townspeople that the duke had designated him should he die without direct heirs. The chronicler Alexander of Telese ignores the fact that, with Duke William's death and following the legal rules pertaining to fiefs, the duchy reverted to the papacy. He gave a version of events that accorded to Roger's wishes. The Count of Sicily appears as the saviour chosen by God for southern Italy.

> Nobody any longer feared bodily punishment, therefore everyone was more and more inclined to do evil, so that not only were travellers oppressed by fear, but even peasants who wanted to cultivate their fields lacked peace and security. What more is to be said? If God had not preserved a scion of the Guiscard's lineage through whom the ducal power might be quickly relieved, almost the whole country, burdened with unbelievably horrible crimes would have rushed headlong to destruction.[20]

According to Romuald of Salerno, the duke's oral promise had the status of a legal designation:

> Hearing of the death of Duke William, who had instituted him as his heir, Count Roger immediately came with his galleys to Salerno, and was honourably received there by the citizens, to whom he confirmed their teniments, possessions and ancient customs, receiving them as his men. However, he left the citadel in their power. He was anointed as prince in this same city by Bishop Alfanus of Capaccio. Then he went to Reggio where he was acclaimed as duke, and so returned to Sicily.

Romuald indeed described a lawful testamentary agreement. For him Duke William had already, when he sought the count's help in Messina in 1122, not only handed over Calabria but also appointed him as his heir to the duchy of Apulia and 'all his possessions'. Romuald wrote some decades after the event, at a time when the Norman monarchy was universally recognized. In retrospect it appeared that nothing else could have occurred.[21]

However, the contemporary evidence of Falco of Benevento shows that matters were not so simple. Here what happens appears in quite another light. Roger came to Salerno to negotiate the voluntary acceptance of his

---

[20] *Al. Tel.* 1.4–5, pp. 8–9; ibid., 1.1, p. 6. *Falcandus*, 4–5 [*Tyrants*, 56–7], ignored the role of the pope and did not directly mention any hereditary right of Roger, saying rather that on the death of his 'relative' (*consanguineus suus*) William he conquered Apulia, i.e. south Italy, and thus became duke.

[21] *Romuald*, 213–14. Caspar (1904), 58–60, accepted this version and wrote of a 'succession treaty of 1125'; however, cf. Deér (1972), 176–7.

lordship by the town. He was of the family of Robert Guiscard and Duke William, so he explained: thus he was the only man to guarantee Salerno's future. The townspeople had accepted his proposal, after the count had promised them a large measure of self-government. The inhabitants of Benevento had also pledged their goodwill to the count. Afterwards Roger had made the duchy of Amalfi, the towns of Troia and Melfi, and almost all of Apulia subject to him. These successes had led him, after his return to Sicily, to seek the ducal title. 'He ordered all those dwelling in his lands to call him Duke Roger, which was done. Meanwhile he sent presents of gold and silver to Pope Honorius, promising him also the towns of Troia and Montefusco in return for granting him the banner and title of duke. However, at this time the pope absolutely refused to do this.' The position of the pope as overlord of the duchy was emphasized. But there was no mention of any promise by Duke William to make his uncle his heir, nor even of any testamentary agreement. Roger's anointing as prince and formal inauguration as duke were also ignored.[22]

That William had actually designated Roger his heir is unlikely. Alexander of Telese would certainly have described such an act. However, relations between duke and count had been strained in recent years. It is quite possible that the duke had made him a verbal promise, which was not then put into effect. William of Tyre stated that the duke had concluded an agreement about inheritance with Bohemond II, before the latter had set out for Antioch in 1126, that whichever of the two outlived the other should be his heir. But this evidence is contradicted by other chroniclers: according to Alexander of Telese, Bohemond II had appointed the pope as the administrator of his south Italian lordship, while Romuald of Salerno said it was one of his relatives, Count Alexander of Conversano. William appears to have made promises to all and sundry.[23]

According to Walter, Archdeacon of Thérouanne, author of a contemporary biography of Count Charles of Flanders, the duke had 'shortly before his death bequeathed of his own free will all his property to the Blessed Prince of the Apostles Peter and his deputy, the holy Pope Honorius'. This the archdeacon, who had been staying at the Roman Curia, had heard 'often from the mouth of Pope Honorius'. Possibly he had misunderstood the pope. The latter may have been referring to some verbal remark of

---

[22] *Falco*, 88. Immediately after Duke William's death, Count Jordan of Ariano had captured, among other places, the town of Montefusco (province of Avellino), but he was then killed while besieging Fiorentino (in the province of Foggia, now disappeared). See Vehse (1930–1), 133–4. For Montefusco, see Cuozzo (1989b), 85–7.

[23] William of Tyre, *Chronicon* XIII.21, p. 613 [Babcock and Krey, II.32]; *Al. Tel.* I.12, pp. 12–13; *Romuald*, 214. Cf. Deér (1972), 175. For Alexander of Conversano, the grandson of a sister of Robert Guiscard, see Martin (1993), 738.

William's that after his death the duchy would revert to his overlord who had the right to re-assign it. Because of this earlier promises would perhaps be rendered invalid. There was no question of any will to this effect. If there had been such a document, then the popes would certainly have made reference to it in their dealings with Roger.[24]

What one can derive from the sources is this: Roger and Honorius had fundamentally different views of the situation after the death of the Duke of Apulia. The Count of Sicily believed that as the relation of a deceased vassal he had the right to his fief. He had already put this concept into practice in 1124 with his seizure of Montescaglioso. Later on, after the death of Bohemond II in 1130, he based his claim to the principality of Antioch on similar grounds. By contrast, the pope was of the opinion that he need only grant the lapsed fief to Roger if the latter had behaved correctly towards the future overlord. Robert Guiscard had previously promised to Gregory VII in 1080 that 'I shall take this oath to your successors ... who will grant investiture to me, provided that my sin does not remain.' Roger's difficult relations with Calixtus II and the cardinals in the year 1121, as well as his high-handed policy towards the Church, could be viewed as culpable behaviour that brought his investiture as Duke of Apulia into question. Furthermore, after the Treaty of Worms in 1122 the pope's improved relations with the emperor put him in a stronger position vis-à-vis the Normans than his predecessors, and this also made a conflict more likely.[25]

As Alexander of Telese noted, to begin with the Count of Sicily acted cautiously. When the inhabitants of Salerno refused to surrender the town to him, and murdered one of his envoys who had spoken sharply to them, Roger avoided an armed confrontation. He reluctantly granted them control of the upper citadel, the most important part of the town's defences. By doing this he was able to have himself anointed as Prince of Salerno, although only by the hand of the Bishop of Capaccio, since the Archbishop of Salerno, Romuald I, who would normally have conferred this unction, cautiously avoided performing the ceremony. Roger II also made

---

[24] *Vita Karoli Comitis Flandriae, MGH Scriptores* xii.540: 'whatever [property] he seemed to possess in the land, movable or immovable ... he bequethed to be held by perpetual right'. For Walter's credibility, Deér (1972), 178–80, although Loud (1985), 137–8, is sceptical. Charles's mother Adela had married Roger Borsa as her second husband; the count was thus half-brother to Duke William; *Vita Karoli*, 539; *Malaterra* iv.20, pp. 98–9.

[25] William of Tyre, *Chronicon* xiv.9, p. 641 [Babcock and Krey, ii.59–60]: 'Roger ... was claiming Antioch with all its possessions as belonging to him by hereditary right.' Deér (1972), 183–4; Hiestand (1993), 83–4. Cf. *Gregorii VII Registrum*, viii.1a, 515 [English translation in E. Emerton, *The Correspondence of Gregory VII* (New York 1932), 158–9]: 'I shall keep the same faith to your successors ... who shall have confirmed to me, if no fault of mine remains, the investiture granted to me by you.' Cf. Deér (1972), 133–5, 196–8; Hoffmann (1978), 155ff; Loud (1985), 140–3; Loud (2000b), 207–9.

a major concession to his brother-in-law Count Rainulf of Alife, making
the Count of Ariano his vassal. Here he made an exception to the rule that
a count should not be the vassal of someone of equal status, but could only
be the subject to a higher authority. However, according to Alexander of
Telese, Roger II put aside his fundamental beliefs; Rainulf was both his
brother-in-law and a strong personality, whose assistance was necessary for
the conquest of southern Italy. Meanwhile – this was in August 1127 – the
pope went to Benevento so as to frustrate the plans of the Count of Sicily.
He announced Roger's excommunication if he should continue his aspirations for the dukedom. This excommunication would also apply to his supporters. Count Rainulf promptly took this as an excuse to distance himself
from his brother-in-law. Roger sought in vain to change the pope's mind.[26]

Honorius II remained obdurate. He went to Troia in northern Apulia,
which was one of the four 'ducal towns', along with Salerno, Venosa and
Melfi. Its inhabitants wanted to make themselves independent under papal
protection. The pope was in future to receive the fealty of the townspeo-
ple and granted them a wide-ranging autonomy. Under his leadership
the great men of Apulia concluded an alliance, comprising Robert II of
Capua, Rainulf of Alife, Grimoald of Bari, Godfrey of Andria, Tancred of
Conversano and Roger of Ariano. A little bit later on the pope renewed
Roger's excommunication, seeking in vain to deter him. It is possible
that at this time the Count of Sicily did offer to make over the towns of
Troia and Montefusco to the pope, as we are told by Falco of Benevento.
Pandulf's biography of the pope provides further evidence that he offered
Honorius substantial bribes. In any case the parties were firmly established,
and war was inevitable.[27]

Roger went back to Sicily late in the year to collect his forces. On
his return journey, at the end of 1127, he had his army acclaim him
as duke at Reggio Calabria, perhaps influenced by the knowledge that
Robert Guiscard had done the same thing in 1060, although that had
occurred *after* the latter's investiture by the pope. At the beginning of 1128
Honorius II granted investiture to Robert II of Capua – through this
action the principality of Capua was detached from the duchy of Apulia.
The pope was providing himself with allies for the war, which he intended
to undertake in the style of a Crusade. According to Falco of Benevento,

---

[26] *Al. Tel.* 1.5–9, pp. 9–12. *Romuald*, 214. For the unction, see Deér (1972), 168–70; Hoff-
      mann (1978), 148–50; and for Archbishop Romuald I (1121–36), Kamp (1979), 110. For
      the diploma allegedly granted by Roger to Salerno in 1127, see below p. 149 note 97.

[27] *Al. Tel.* 1.10–11, pp. 11–12; *CDP* XXI.182–4 no. 50; *It. Pont.* IX.213 no. 3. Delogu (1979),
      195–7; Martin (1993), 744–5. *Liber Pontificalis prout extat in codice manuscripto Dertusensi*, ed.
      J. M. March (Barcelona 1925), 206–7: 'On the death of William, the illustrious Duke of
      Apulia, he could have had a vast sum of money for the restoration of the ancient churches
      of the City and the rebuilding of the portico of St Paul, offered by Count Roger of Sicily
      so that he might confirm the duchy to him.'

Honorius promised them that those who fell in the war against Roger would receive remission of all penalty for their sins had they confessed in advance. The others would be remitted half. Late in January 1128 the pope went back to Rome to raise troops.[28]

Roger returned to the peninsula in the spring with an army of two thousand knights, three thousand infantry and fifteen hundred archers, along with a considerable baggage train. He had no difficulty in bringing the Basilicata and southern Apulia under his control. The fortress of Oggiano, near Ferrandina on the River Basento, was stormed and destroyed. Taranto was soon forced into submission, while Otranto surrendered without a struggle. Brindisi was captured after a long siege. Mesagne was quickly conquered, as were Oria and various other places. Roger's opponents mustered their troops on the River Bradano in the eastern Basilicata. The Count of Sicily hurried here with his troops and pitched camp on the opposite bank, but he avoided battle. Instead of that he sent an embassy to Honorius to persuade him to give way. The pope however remained obstinate.[29]

Roger relied on delaying tactics. He had the advantage of having a standing army predominantly composed of professional troops. How long the war lasted was irrelevant to him. It was quite the opposite with the forces of his opponent, who was primarily dependent upon the 'feudal' contingents drawn from the vassals of the Apulian and Campanian princes. These were only bound to serve for a limited period (of forty days). The Count of Sicily's calculations soon bore fruit. His opponents ran into supply problems, and the summer heat, for it was July and August, did the rest. The vassals of Robert of Capua in the army started to agitate to be sent home. Furthermore, the prince himself, who according to Falco of Benevento was unfitted for the strains of camp life because of his feeble constitution, began to weaken and make preparations for departure. The pope held out for some forty days, but then realized that he had no other choice but to give way. He secretly sent two cardinals, Haimeric and Cencius Frangipane, to Roger with a peace offer. As soon as his allies were informed of this, they angrily abandoned the campaign.

The Count of Sicily had secured a complete victory without a battle. On 22 August 1128, outside the walls of Benevento, Honorius invested

---

[28] *Romuald*, 214. For the ducal acclamation, Deér (1972), 190–2; Hoffmann (1978), 142; Falkenhausen (1991), 271. For Robert II's investiture, *Falco*, 90–2; Hoffmann (1978), 172–3.

[29] *Al. Tel.* I.12–13, pp. 12–14, and the annotations to *Romuald, ibid.*, 339. Cf. Clementi's *Historical Commentary, ibid.*, 271–3, although the identification there of the place where Roger's army was camped, as the bank of the torrente Bradano near San Fele in the Basilicata, is not convincing.

him with the duchy of Apulia, Calabria and Sicily. Roger promised not to molest the town of Benevento and the principality of Capua. The new duke then marched into Apulia with his army to consolidate his lordship there. His objective was Troia, where he intended to provide an exemplary demonstration of his power. But the strongly fortified town resisted him, and after a few weeks Roger abandoned the operation. It seemed prudent to him to return to Sicily before the onset of winter. On his return journey he received the submission of Melfi and a number of other towns.[30]

Next spring (in 1129) he returned to the mainland with a substantial army. His opponents had been far from idle. Tancred of Conversano had brought Brindisi and other strong points under his control. Roger's first attempt to retake Brindisi failed, but he was more successful with Taranto, Nardò and other less important towns. The duke's army comprised three thousand knights and six thousand infantry, including Muslim archers. These last, in particular, systematically spread terror among the population (or so we are told). They massacred the elderly, tore suckling infants from their mothers' breasts and dashed them to the ground, killed priests at the altar, trod the holy chrism underfoot, and violated women under the eyes of their husbands, while those who were left were dragged off to Sicily in chains. It is questionable whether the Muslims really behaved so appallingly, although a later Christian author who made interpolations to the Chronicle of Romuald of Salerno considered them to be really devils in human form.

Roger's army must in any case have spread fear. With his fleet, comprising forty to sixty galleys, he blockaded Bari by sea. At the beginning of August his opponents gave in. They were granted pardon on condition that they take part in the siege of Troia. The town put up a tenacious resistance, and found support with Count Rainulf of Alife – although the prince of Capua thought it wiser not to take part. But even Rainulf gave up, as soon as Roger threatened to invade his own lands, and Troia was forced to capitulate. Thereafter the remaining ducal towns posed no difficulty. The submission of Apulia and the greater part of southern Italy had been secured.[31]

The pope remained in a very weak position. At Benevento the hitherto-dominant noble party was driven out, and a type of commune was formed. Honorius requested Roger's help, and he proposed an expedition against the town for the next year. At the end of August or early in September the

---

[30] *Al. Tel.* I.14–15, pp. 14–15. *Falco*, 100–2. Cf. Clementi (1991), 274. For military service, see Cuozzo (1989b), 68–9.

[31] *Al. Tel.* I.18–19, pp. 16–18, and the annotations to *Romuald*, *ibid.*, 341–2. Clementi (1991), 276–9.

duke went to Lagopesole, where he encountered Robert de Grandmesnil, the son of one of Robert Guiscard's daughters, who had deserted his army without permission on the pretext that he wished to visit Normandy, the land of his forefathers. The duke took him at his word, confiscated his fief, and gave him permission to go abroad. In September Roger had all the counts, bishops and abbots come to a solemn court at Melfi. The counts had to swear to remain faithful to him and to his two eldest sons. 'At the same time', according to Alexander of Telese, a general peace was promulgated. Those who breached it were to be consigned to the court, which would make arrangements for their punishment. The counts had to swear to leave clerics, peasants, pilgrims and merchants in peace. It was probably at the same time that Roger also issued some laws which were later included in the so-called 'Assizes of Ariano' (c. 1140).[32]

In November 1129 the duke held another high court at Troia. Because of the town's past behaviour, this assembly was intended as an object lesson. From the record of a legal case we know that the Archbishops of Salerno and Palermo, the Archbishop-elect of Siponto, and 'many other bishops' were present. Roger confirmed to the Bishop of Troia, William II (1106–41), the tithes and exemptions formerly granted by Robert Guiscard, 'for the souls of my father Roger, the glorious count, and of my mother Queen Adelaide, and of my predecessors, the Dukes of Apulia, and for our own'. The bishop had been at the head of the 1127 revolt. On the bronze doors of the cathedral which he commissioned, he had himself commemorated as 'the liberator of his homeland', under whose leadership the people of Troia had destroyed the citadel there to safeguard their freedom and fortified their town with walls and towers. Roger's diploma sealed his forgiveness. Now the duke could return peacefully to Sicily where, as was customary, he spent the winter. There he received a visit

---

[32] *Falco*, 104. Vehse (1930–1), 136–7. *Al. Tel.* I.21, pp. 18–20, and the additions to *Romuald*, *ibid.*, 343. Niese (1910), 19ff; Jamison (1913), 237–9; Clementi (1991), 280ff. In the introduction to the Assize 31 of the Vatican text, 'On the violation of the conjugal bed' [*De violatione thori*], ed. Brandileone (1884), 113; Zecchino (1984), 52, 56, there is a reference to a general prohibition of baronial violence by Roger II, which is itself lacking in the so-called 'Assizes of Ariano', and probably refers to the general peace edict of 1129. 'If the providence of our royal majesty refuses in any way to permit one of our barons to invade the *castrum* of another within the bounds of our kingdom, or to plunder it, to make an armed attack on it or to take anything from it by fraud, in order to prevent him by this act depriving him of its property; then by how much more do we hold a person punishable if he should presume to violate the marriage bed of a fellow countryman and neighbour.' See Niese (1910), 19–20. The emendation suggested to this text by Cuozzo (1989b), 90, preferring *militem* to *limitem* makes sense neither in grammar nor in logic. For the Assizes, see below pp. 136–47.

from some monks from Montecassino, a monastery which had extensive property in southern Italy, and on 30 December 1129 this abbey received a wide-ranging privilege of protection and confirmation of its possessions, authenticated by a golden seal. The monks of Montecassino probably hoped that he would support them against the pope, who had sought to lessen the abbey's autonomy.[33]

Next spring (1130) the conquest of southern Italy was completed. Robert de Grandmesnil had broken his promise to leave Italy and fortified Oriolo and Castrovillari in Calabria. But the arrival of Roger's army brought the revolt to a speedy end. It was also time to settle old scores. The concessions made to the inhabitants of Salerno were annulled, and the upper citadel passed under ducal control. Troia and Melfi were also forced to accept garrisons and to rebuild the citadels there which had been destroyed after the death of Duke William. Count Roger of Ariano was made to surrender the strong points of Paduli and Montefusco, near Benevento. When Prince Robert of Capua at last submitted, the new duke's triumph was complete.[34]

Roger's irresistible rise was only explicable to contemporaries as the work of Divine Providence. Shortly before the death of Duke William, a priest had a dream in which he saw a vision of the future:

Duke William [of Apulia], Prince Robert of the Capuans, Count Rainulf and all the barons of Apulia, Calabria, the Capitanata and many other provinces gather together in Apulia to fight against Count Roger of the Sicilians. Hearing this, Roger himself gathered a multitude of soldiers and crossed the sea to fight them. Thus forces of knights and footmen were drawn up in great numbers and battle was joined on each side. Soon the terrified Count Roger took refuge in flight with all his men. When the duke and the rest pursued him as he fled, he tried to escape by throwing himself in the sea. And when he had fled before them through the sea itself for nearly a mile at length, because of the great thirst from which he was suffering, he suddenly drank all the sea. When he had thus drunk his strength returned and soon he charged bravely against those who were following him and immediately made them take flight. Duke William fled and completely disappeared. Prince Robert, Count Rainulf and all the others fell on their faces before him in fear. However, when Count Roger saw that he would be able to kill them all, restrained by his piety he immediately spared them. After he had done this, behold suddenly two men clad in white robes appeared, and rising from the ground said, 'You can for the moment live, but if he had so wished, Count Roger could have killed you all. But since he has spared you and allowed all of you your

---

[33] Roger II, *Diplomata*, 259–61, appendix II, I (November 1129); *ibid.*, 35–8 no. 12. Cf. Chalandon (1907), 1.390n; Magistrale (1992), 50–1; Martin (1993), 744–5. Roger II, *Diplomata*, 40–2 no. 14. *Chron. Cas.* IV.95, p. 556 (July 1127).

[34] *Al. Tel.* I.22–4, 19–21.

lives, now approach and with necks bent low adore him. For you all know that the Divine Will has disposed that whomsoever shall try to resist him shall be struck dead by the sword.' On hearing this, they all came forward without delay, and putting down their weapons adored him and submitted to him by doing homage.

Roger was thus victorious. He then immediately climbed up on a hillock and planted his spear on the top. The spear promptly grew into a most beautiful tree whose topmost part seemed to extend right up to the clouds. It was filled with beautiful foliage and flowers and innumerable fruit, and had a most elegant and excellent appearance on its hillock. Then a broad ladder was placed against the tree, which led up to a marvellous throne. The two men, those who had appeared in their robes, approached and held him by the hand, one on the right and the other on the left, and they led him with them up the ladder by the tree and placed him on the throne. They crowned him and had him sit there like a king.

This is how the vision was described by Alexander of Telese. In another dream it was revealed to the priest that the two men in white robes were St Peter and St Paul; Christ had appointed them as protectors to be at Roger's side. The moral of the dream was that: 'Roger has triumphed by Divine Disposition and received the royal crown by Divine choice. Thus he will never be deprived of it.'[35]

Roger's elevated self-image probably also drew on Byzantine concepts, imparted to him by Greek tutors and collaborators. The arenga (preamble) to one of his Greek charters, issued in 1122 for the abbey of St Mary of the Patiron at Rossano in Calabria, is most instructive, although this only survives in a sixteenth-century Italian translation: 'as the rising sun shines its rays over everything, and lights and warms all those both near and far, so in the same way can I illuminate renowned piety and display it like a shining sun.' The parallel between the sovereign and the sun was often made at Byzantium, and was derived from the Church Father Eusebius. It was no wonder that the young count who had absorbed such ideas should strive after higher status.[36]

KING OF SICILY AND SOUTHERN ITALY

Roger II had been successful in uniting southern Italy and Sicily. The attempts by the popes to play off the various Norman states in the south of the peninsula one against another had failed. They were left only with the feeble consolation of the enclave of Benevento. In February 1130

---

[35] *Al. Tel.* IV.7–9, 84–6, cf. Clementi (1991), 185ff.

[36] Ménager (1957), 336; (1959), 313; Elze (1964), 104n. Cf. Hunger (1964), 75–8, who points to similar *formulae* in documents of Roger I (1097), Cusa, *Diplomi*, 509; Christodoulos (1109), Dölger (1929); and Roger II (1143), Ca. 152; and, more recently Falkenhausen (1998b), 299–300.

schism occurred, caused by the disputes among the various reform groups at the Roman Curia, and that led to the papacy being weakened even further. The College of Cardinals was split. The anti-Norman chancellor, Haimeric, and his supporters, who were in turn aided by the powerful Roman noble family of the Frangipane, elected Cardinal Gregory Papareschi, who took the name of Innocent II. The other cardinals, most of whom came from central and southern Italy, chose a member of a family who were hostile to the Frangipane, Peter Pierleoni, who called himself Pope Anacletus II. The latter, a former monk of Cluny, seemed initially to be the stronger; he was able to establish himself in Rome, while his adversary had to flee from the city and take refuge in France. Both sought to secure recognition from the German king, Lothar III (1125–37), although for the time being he adopted a policy of wait-and-see. However, Bernard of Clairvaux played a decisive role. He declared for Innocent II, and thereafter the latter was soon acknowledged by most of Europe.[37]

Soon after his election, in March, Anacletus sent formal notification of his elevation to Benevento, and asked the townspeople to take an oath of fealty to him. The *comunitas* (the townspeoples' association) was prepared to do this, in the hope that the pope would accept the changes that had taken place in the civic government. However, they had miscalculated here. When Anacletus came to Benevento in September (where he was often to reside in the next few years) he helped the noble fraction to regain power. The leaders of the popular party and their partisans were forced to leave the city, and their property was confiscated. Roger and Anacletus were soon in contact with each other, and they met at Avellino, half way between Benevento and Salerno. The duke could negotiate from a position of strength since he had just consolidated his lordship over southern Italy. He took the oath of fealty to the pope, but in exchange he demanded a royal crown.[38]

A new monarchy could not simply be invented, so there was recourse to the fiction that Sicily had been a kingdom in Antiquity. According to Alexander of Telese, this idea was in particular suggested by Roger's uncle, Henry del Vasto, who argued that since his nephew had subdued Sicily, Calabria, Apulia and the rest of southern Italy 'as far as Rome', he could no longer be satisfied with the dignity of a duke, but ought to be a king. The capital of the new kingdom ought to be Palermo, where it

---

[37] There is a vast literature on the schism: see especially Palumbo (1942), Schmale (1961), Maleczek (1981), Grotz (1983), Reuter (1983), and on its origins Schilling (1998). In English, Stroll (1987), Robinson (1990), 65–78.

[38] *Falco*, 106; *Annales Casinenses, MGH SS* XIX.309; JL 8413; *It. Pont.* VIII.36–7 no. 35. Cf. Vehse (1930–1), 138ff; Deér (1972), 214–15.

was believed that once upon a time kings had ruled, but these had then, through God's inscrutable judgement, disappeared.[39]

Roger had the subject discussed by experts at a court held in Salerno. They came to the conclusion that was expected: 'that kings had once resided in Palermo, who had ruled only over Sicily . . . it is right and just that Roger should be granted the royal crown. Hence not only will this kingdom be restored, but extended to the other lands over which he rules.' Probably there was also some sort of acclamation from the vassals who were present there. But one cannot really describe this as a genuine royal election. Nor is the exact date of this court known. It must have been either shortly before, or just after, the grant by Anacletus II of his privilege of 27 September 1130 which invested Roger with the royal title. If it had already taken place previously, it must have been quite obvious that the pope was acceding to the duke's wishes.[40]

The contents of the document show how extensive the concessions made by Anacletus were. Roger was not only granted the royal title but the right to designate one of his sons as his successor. He was to be free to choose the archbishop from whom he would receive unction and coronation. In addition to Sicily, Calabria and Apulia, he was granted the principality of Capua, overlordship over Naples (*honor Neapolis*) and the help in time of war of the inhabitants of Benevento. Three suffragan bishops (Syracuse, Agrigento and Mazara or Catania) would be made subject to the Archbishop of Palermo; the choice between these last two dioceses would be made later. The new king and his heirs must render homage and fealty to the pope, unless their investiture was prevented through some fault of the pope. The annual census was fixed at six hundred gold pieces (*schifati*). The ruler had obtained everything that he wanted; a good example of this is the stipulation about the failure to renew the investiture. At the time of Robert Guiscard only the fault of the vassal was taken into consideration; now the discussion was rather of the fault of the overlord, something which still ought not to invalidate the vassalic relationship.[41]

---

[39] *Al. Tel.* II.1, p. 23; cf. Elze (1964), 105; Cilento (1981), 166.

[40] *Al. Tel.* II.2, pp. 23–4. Ménager (1959), 446–7, alleged, from the use of the words *laudant, concedunt*, and *decernunt* that there was a real election; for an opposing view, Caravale (1966), 66ff. Cf. also Clementi (1991), 238.

[41] JL 8411; *It. Pont.* VIII.37 no. 137; *ibid.*, X.191–2 no. 106. The best edition is Hoffmann (1978), 173–6. NB the phrase 'to you, your son Roger, and your other sons following you in the kingdom as you shall decree, and to your heirs', discussed therein at pp. 165–6. Cf. also Kehr (1934), 40; Deér (1972), 203–11, who suggests (pp. 205–6), on the basis of the phrase *honor Neapolis* that Duke Sergius VII (d. 1137) had already 'probably in 1130' recognized Roger as his overlord. For the *auxilium* of the Beneventans, *ibid.*, 207–8, and for the phrase *si in nobis vel in nostris successoribus non remanserit* ('if it does not continue in

Under pressure from Roger, the pope granted everything which his predecessors had for a long time refused the Normans. And although he was concluding a fundamental agreement for the future relations of the papacy with its southern neighbour, Anacletus acted without consulting the College of Cardinals, nor did he have it subsequently confirmed by them. The document was drawn up by his chancellor, the cardinal priest Saxo, but (in contrast to other contemporary papal bulls) it had the sig-natures of the pope and of only one other cardinal. This was Matthew of St Eudoxia, who enjoyed Anacletus's particular trust. Instead, there were placed on the document the personal marks (*signa manus*) of six members of the Pierleoni family, and of three other unidentified laymen, reflecting the strong links of the pope with his family, who had traditionally close relations with the Normans. Some years later, in 1134, the Pierleoni were even to enter into a direct vassalic relationship with Roger. Considering how dependent Anacletus was on Roger, it was not surprising that in October 1130 the German king recognized Innocent II. It had been in vain that some months earlier the Romans – including the Frangipane who had meanwhile gone over to Anacletus's side – sent envoys to Lothar III to win him over to the cause of the Pierleoni pope.[42]

After requesting the bishops and abbots of the kingdom to do homage to Roger, Anacletus journeyed from Benevento into Apulia. He convoked a synod for 9 November, to take place in the Bari region. Thereafter he intended to go to Milan. While for the Archbishop of Trani he only renewed an existing privilege of Calixtus II, for the new Archbishop of Bari, whom he consecrated, he not only confirmed the privileges of his predecessors but also gave him, for his lifetime, the exempt church of St Sabinus at Canosa (formerly the cathedral for the diocese of Bari and Canosa) and the monastery of All Saints at Cuti, near Bari: in addition he granted him 'by the authority of the Apostolic See' the right to consecrate Prince Grimoald of Bari and his sons. This permission to consecrate the prince, a rite which probably also included unction, cannot have been conceded without Roger's previous agreement. The king was evidently ready to legitimize Grimoald's promotion from being ruler of the town to be a prince. An agreement concerning this must have been concluded in 1129 when Grimoald submitted to Roger.[43]

---

us or in our successors'), *ibid.*, 210–11, and Hoffmann (1978), 159–61. The suggestion by Matthew (1992), 36, that Anacletus decided 'to offer' Roger the crown, is not convincing.

[42] Deér (1972), 212ff. Roger II, *Diplomata*, no. 35. For the *signa manus* of laymen, Petersohn (1994), 483n, 505ff (18 May 1130).

[43] *Chron. Cas.* IV.97, p. 557: *It. Pont.* VIII.38 no. 138; ix.293 no. 9 [Trani, 30 October 1130]; IX.321 no. 12 [Bari, 5 November]. Full texts of latter two documents in *CDB* IX.40 no. 30; I.80 no. 42. For the monastery of Ognissanti di Cuti, see *It. Pont.* IX.332; *Monasticon Italiae*

Also present at the synod held at Canosa, near Bari, on 9 November
1130 were representatives of the eastern Church, something which
Anacletus was later to announce with pride to the French clergy. But
the plan to go to Milan could not be carried out.[44]

Roger had meanwhile returned to Sicily, inviting his vassals and subjects to his coronation, which was to take place at Christmas in Palermo.
Immediately before his coronation he had himself acclaimed king in some
sort of popular assembly, very similar to the one that had taken place at
Salerno some months previously. He was attempting 'with every means at
his disposal' to legitimize his elevation to the kingship. But there is no evidence that any 'election' of Roger had taken place, 'similar in all essentials
to royal elections in Germany, England and France'. Both at the Salerno
court in September and in the assembly before the coronation the vassals
and people could only confirm what had already been decided.[45]

Roger was concerned to present his monarchy not as something which
he himself had built from scratch, but rather as a legitimate kingdom that
had been 'restored' by the pope with the consent of princes and people.
It was not something created anew, which to the contemporary world

---

III.116. *It.Pont.* VIII.38 no. 140. *Al. Tel.* I.18, pp. 16–17, wrote of 'submission', *Romuald*,
217, of an accord 'agreed with the aforesaid barons and with Prince Robert of Capua'.
For the consecration of both Lombard and Norman princes, Hoffmann (1978), 142ff. He
suggests, *ibid.*, 152, that there was no incompatibility between princely consecration and
vassalic dependence. For Grimoald, see Martin (1993), 745–6. Grimoald was described as
'Prince of Bari by the grace of God and St Nicholas' in a document written in gold letters
on blue-coloured parchment (was this in imitation of the purple documents of Byzantine
emperors?), *CDB* v no. 69, colour reproduction in Cioffari (1984), 140. The recent
attempt by Baaken (1995), 233–4, to assert the validity of a local tradition (recorded in an
inscription of 1614) that Roger was crowned by Anacletus in the church of St Nicholas
at Bari, is unconvincing; this theory had already been refuted by Schulz (1860), 42, and
Caspar (1904), 509. Cf. below, p. 117 n. 37.

44 Baumgarten (1897), 576 [Lateran, 25 February 1131(?)], cf. Palumbo (1942), 666 no.
44; 671, reg. no. 54: 'by the judgement of the Apostolic See and of the whole eastern
Church, in the council at Canosa, which in accordance with the will of God and with
the whole eastern Church we solemnly celebrated there on 9 November'. Cf. *It. Pont.*
VIII.38 no. 140.

45 *Al. Tel.* II.3, p. 25: 'On the day appointed, all they [*the barons*] and a numberless populace
both great and small, flocked together. All were once again solemnly and diligently asked
the same question and answered in the same way as before; and to the glory of God and the
advantage of His Church his promotion [to the kingship] was universally approved by all in
the royal city of Palermo.' Ménager (1959), 446–7, saw three phases of this 'election', i.e.
designatio and *collaudatio* at Salerno, and *acclamatio* at Palermo, cf. Elze (1964), 105–6; but
see Caravale (1966), 66ff, and Cilento (1981), 168–9, for very different interpretations. It
appears unlikely that Christmas Day was chosen for the coronation in deliberate imitation
of the imperial coronation of Charlemagne in 800, as suggested by Marongiu (1955), 218.
Christmas was simply the first important feast day available.

would appear as a revolution, but only the restoration of the former state of affairs. This official line was emphasized in the foundation charter of the Palatine chapel in Palermo in 1140: 'through the authority of our holy mother the Roman Church, and with the unanimous counsel of archbishops, bishops, abbots, princes, counts, nobles, clerics and all the people of our dominions, the kingdom which was for a long time in abeyance has through the Redeemer's benevolence been fully restored to its original state, honourably promoted and exalted'.[46]

We are well informed as to what took place at the coronation thanks to Alexander of Telese. Although the abbot was not actually present, he describes it so vividly that he must have been informed by an eye-witness, perhaps Roger's sister Matilda or her husband, Count Rainulf of Alife.

> The duke was led to the archiepiscopal church in royal manner. There he received unction with the Holy Oil and assumed the royal dignity. One cannot write down nor even imagine quite how glorious he was, how regal in his dignity, how splendid in his richly adorned apparel. For it seemed to the onlookers that all the riches and honours of this world were present. The whole city was decorated in an extraordinary way, and nowhere was there anything but rejoicing and light. Throughout the royal palace the interior walls were gloriously draped. The pavement was bestrewed with multi-coloured carpets and showed a flowing softness to the feet of those who trod there. When the king went to the church for the ceremony he was surrounded by dignitaries, and the huge number of horses which accompanied them had saddles and bridles decorated with gold and silver. Copious amounts of the choicest food and drink were served to the diners at the royal table, and nothing was served except in dishes or cups of gold or silver. There was no servant there who did not wear a silk tunic – the very waiters were clad in silk clothes. The glory and wealth of the royal abode were so spectacular that it caused great wonder and deep stupefaction – so great indeed that it instilled not a little fear in all those who had come from so far away. For many saw there more things than they had even heard rumour of previously.[47]

The coronation, celebrated with oriental magnificence, must have been a striking spectacle, and was a notable demonstration of his almost limitless financial resources. But this account devoted very little attention to the actual ceremony of coronation. According to Falco of Benevento, consecration and unction were given by a cardinal, Comes of St Sabina, who had been sent by the pope, while Prince Robert of Capua placed the crown on the new king's head, 'for which he received no proper reward', as Falco snidely added. Unfortunately he is our only source for this incident, and we have therefore no means of checking his reliability. But the suggestion that the prince of Capua crowned Roger is hard to believe. The king

[46] Roger II, *Diplomata*, 133–7 no. 48.   [47] *Al. Tel.* II.4–6, pp. 25–6.

would scarcely have allowed such a crucial role to one of his vassals, even if the latter was one of the highest rank. Falco may have been seeking an explanation for the later ill-feeling between the two. In Anacletus's privilege creating the kingdom, it was proposed that both the unction and the crowning would be done by an archbishop.[48]

A liturgical source, an *Ordo* (a service book for the coronation), redacted for Roger's coronation on Christmas Day 1130, shows how the ceremony ought to have taken place. The model was the German coronation ritual, with the difference that the King of Sicily received the sceptre and orb rather than the sceptre and staff. One can ignore various minor differences, but one should note that the passage concerning inheritance of the royal dignity from the father was omitted, for Roger was not a king's son. Otherwise the traditional ritual was observed. Unction was provided by the metropolitan 'as once upon a time Samuel anointed King David, so that you are blessed and installed as king over the people, over whom your Lord God has assigned to you lordship and rule'. As symbols of his power, the monarch received from the bishops the sword, bracelet, cloak (*pallium*), and ring, and then sceptre and orb (*regnum*). Once the archbishop had crowned and blessed the king, both he and the bishops accompanied the monarch to the throne where they gave him the kiss of peace. Finally the archbishop celebrated the coronation mass.[49]

Obviously we do not know how strictly Roger's coronation on Christmas Day 1130 followed this *Ordo*, which had perhaps been entrusted to the cardinal by the pope. But, because it deals with a specific liturgical ceremony, it is unlikely that significant variations were introduced. The cardinal whom Falco mentioned may have taken a place among the bishops. Perhaps he also brought the crown with him as a present from

[48] *Falco*, 108: 'Anacletus sent one of his cardinals, named Comes, to the duke; who crowned him as king in the city of Palermo on the day of the Lord's Nativity. Prince Robert of Capua placed the crown on his head, for which he did not receive proper recompense.' For Comes, cardinal priest of St Sabina from 1123, Hüls (1977), 205. Most historians, notably Caspar (1904), 96–7, Elze (1964), 106–7, Brühl (1982), 5 [reprint, 417], accept Falco's version. However, Deér (1959), 11, alleges, without actual proof, that Roger was crowned by Robert of Capua for 'political reasons', while disputing the coronation by the cardinal, on the grounds that this would be in contradiction to Roger's belief that his royal dignity was derived directly from God. Cf. the bull of Anacletus, Hoffmann (1978), 174: 'Furthermore we authorise and concede that you and your heirs shall be anointed as king, and at the appointed times crowned by the hands of those archbishops of your land whom you wish [to do this], assisted if you wish by other bishops of your choice.'

[49] *Romuald*, 218, however, said only that Roger had himself anointed and crowned king at Palermo 'by the advice of the barons and people' (before the death of Honorius II!). The coronation *Ordo*; Elze (1972), 445–52; Elze (1990), 170–8. *Pallium* can mean either a cloak (as here) or the *pallium* or scarf that was the principal sign of archiepiscopal rank.

the pope.[50] But unction and coronation were surely given by Archbishop Peter of Palermo, who had for a long time enjoyed Roger's special trust.

With the creation of the ecclesiastical province of Palermo, the pope was fulfilling another of Roger's wishes. A year later, in 1131, the reorganization of the Church in Sicily was completed. Messina also became the seat of a metropolitan, and received as its suffragan bishoprics Catania, Lipari-Patti and Cefalù. These last two were new foundations. The abbot who ruled the two monasteries of St Bartholomew of Lipari and the Holy Saviour, Patti, in a personal union was promoted to be Bishop of Lipari and Patti. The college of canons at Cefalù was transformed into the cathedral chapter of the new bishopric there, and the canonical church of St Mary at Bagnara in Calabria was made subject to it – the prior of Bagnara became the new bishop. However, these wide-ranging changes were later not to receive the approval of Innocent II and his successors. The king guaranteed the material endowment of these bishoprics through his grant of the 'royal tithes', one tenth of the crown's income from the diocese – church tithes as such were unknown in southern Italy – and through this his control over the clergy was made easier.

The economic security of the Church, freed from the obligation of cultivating its own lands, made the Church on the one hand a sharer in the economic expansion of the state, but on the other reduced it to a dependence, renewed from year to year, if not indeed from day to day, that required more submissive behaviour and greater conformity than would have been required by its endowment with its own fiefs and the military and fiscal obligations attached to them.[51]

This was illustrated by an episode narrated by an anonymous English author, who in his additions to the life of Thomas Becket cited Roger of Sicily as an example not to be followed, of a ruler whose relations with the pope were bad. When the pope summoned the bishops of the kingdom to a council in Rome and they were making preparations for the journey, Roger said, 'I shall not stop you being obedient to God and the pope. But your horses and all your other property in my kingdom belong to me. You can go on foot.' The bishops had been willing to undergo the shame of travelling on foot, indeed they rejoiced to do so, but when they arrived at Benevento and this episode had come to the ears of the pope, he told them not to continue their journey and sent them back to their dioceses.[52]

[50] Deér (1952), 57; Classen (1964), 94 [reprint, 507]. Engelberg (1995), 40, is more cautious. In the privilege of Anacletus, *corona* probably signifies 'kingdom' or 'power' rather than an actual 'crown', cf. Petersohn (1993), 91.

[51] JL 8421–3 (14 September 1131); *It. Pont.* x.339 no. 23; 291 no. 22; 357 no. 4; 364 no. 1. Cf. Kamp (1979), 105 (quote), 110ff.

[52] *Excerpta e codice Lansdowniano 398*, in *Materials for the History of Thomas Becket*, iv.149.

The ruler was not only involved in diocesan organization but also with monastic affairs. It is probably no accident that Roger's earliest surviving Latin charter was issued for a monastery. The Benedictine abbey of Cava, situated on the gulf of Salerno, which already had dependent priories all over the Mezzogiorno, received a church in Sicily along with various landed property and a number of Christian and Muslim serfs. Cava may well have owed this royal favour to the fact that, with its congregation of dependent monasteries, probably structured on the Cluniac pattern, it could represent a force for stable government. Two and a half years later, in 1133, it received a privilege, sealed with a golden bull, in which its rights and properties were confirmed. And when, around 1140, it was decided to reform the abbey of Holy Trinity, Venosa, king and pope decided to entrust this to monks from Cava. Some years later, in 1176, Cava provided the monks to staff the new abbey of Monreale, near Palermo, the burial church of King William II.[53]

Roger also devoted close attention to Greek monasticism. The monastery of the Holy Saviour *in lingua phari*, which he himself founded, after 1122, on a spit of land in the harbour of Messina, became the archimandritate, or head, of a Greek monastic congregation. In its foundation privilege of May 1131 he accorded it a status comparable with a proprietary monastery of the Byzantine emperor. It was exempted from the authority of the Archbishop of Messina, although in return it had to pay the latter an annual census. The archimandrite elected by the monks had to be confirmed by the king, and in any case of dispute was answerable only to the royal court. Lucas, the first archimandrite (d. 1149), came from St Mary of the Patiron, at Rossano in Calabria, whose abbot, Bartholomew of Simeri (d. 1130), was portrayed in the Holy Saviour's monastic tradition as its 'holy founder'. Lucas enjoyed Roger's special trust, and was allowed free access to the royal palace. A privilege of February 1133 listed the monastery's dependencies, subdivided into two groups. Minor houses were ruled by *oikonomoi*, a type of priors, appointed by the archimandrite, while the more important monasteries had a certain amount of independence and their own abbots, although these too were nominated by the archimandrite. There were eighteen monasteries of the first type and thirteen of the second in Sicily, as well as four of each sort in Calabria, making a total of thirty-nine houses, most of which had been founded by members of Roger II's family, above all by his parents.

The king's generosity towards his family's archimandritate, which soon became one of the most important landowners in Sicily, was exceptional.

---

[53] Roger II, *Diplomata*, nos. 16 (February 1131) and 31 (16 October 1133). Cf. Vitolo (1983), Houben (1995a), 55, 60–1, 155. The abbey of St Sophia, Benevento, also enjoyed the favour of the Normans, for which see Loud (1997).

Along with his religious impulses and cultural affinities, strategic considerations may also have played a part. The abbey possessed the port of Catona
(between Villa San Giovanni and Reggio Calabria) which lay opposite
Messina, and controlled the straits. Roger clearly preferred to entrust this
harbour, which was so important for communications between Sicily and
the south Italian mainland, to a religious institution rather than to a lay
noble. The same was probably the case with the subjection of the canonical house at Bagnara, also on the Calabrian coast, to the church of Cefalù.
The fortunes of the archimandritate were closely tied to Roger himself,
and after the king's death its decline was rapid.[54]

The Greek abbey of Grottaferrata, to the south of Rome, also sought
the king's favour. Its provost Leontios travelled to Palermo to seek confirmation of the privileges and properties previously granted by the Dukes
of Apulia. Roger consented to this request, and in April 1131 also gave
the abbey a church in the southern Campania, St Mary of Rofrano. The
diploma detailing this donation was sealed with a golden bull.[55]

Patronage of these great abbeys was an effective means of consolidating
his new royal lordship in the countryside, since monks exercised such a
strong influence over the population.

[54] Falkenhausen (1994a), 44ff, with reference to the thirteen original charters of Roger for
the abbey of the Holy Saviour, Messina, which are preserved in the archive of the Dukes
of Medinaceli at Seville (cf. Brühl (1978)). Caspar (1904), 101ff, is therefore in obvious
need of correction. See also Hofmann (1994), 42ff.

[55] This document survives only in a fifteenth-century Latin translation: Collura (1955),
'Appendice', no. 36; Follieri (1988), Breccia (1991).

3

THE NEW KINGDOM

·

When the king's coronation celebrations had finished, everybody returned to their homes. The king began carefully to consider the problem of how he might strengthen his kingdom in that perpetual peace which was his greatest wish, and how to prevent anybody having the opportunity to resist him. Thus he delivered an ultimatum to the Amalfitans, that they hand over to him all those fortifications which had been left in their hands to guard, for he would in no way consent, nor allow any further agreement, to their holding these while serving him. The Amalfitans unanimously refused this demand, and remained obstinate over this issue, so the king was furious and refused to accept their fealty to him [*a fidei sue consortio dissociavit*].[1]

The chronicler believed that control of the towns was necessary for the enduring domestic peace and security of the kingdom. That Roger was of the same opinion is shown by the fact that early in 1130 Salerno, Troia and Melfi were all forced to receive royal garrisons within their walls. Because Amalfi was unwilling to do this, and hoped to preserve greater autonomy, the king attacked the town. At the beginning of 1131 an army led by the *amiratus* John crossed the Straits of Messina and was reinforced by troops from Apulia and Calabria. At the same time a fleet commanded by George of Antioch blockaded the town by sea and occupied Capri. The land army made rapid progress while Roger, who had up to now remained in Palermo, joined his troops by ship. The last important fortification, the keep of Ravello, on which the Amalfitans had placed great hopes, soon fell, and as a result the citizens decided to surrender. Their capitulation

---

[1] *Al. Tel.* II.7, p. 26.

was by no means unconditional, but they were forced to accept the king's demand for military control of their town.[2]

Roger then went to Salerno, his principal base on the mainland.

And while he dwelt there, the Duke [*magister militum*] of Naples, Sergius, realizing that Roger possessed great power and military might, came to meet him. He submitted to his rule, not indeed because he was constrained by force but simply through fear of him; and so, something which was quite amazing, the city which since the fall of the Roman empire had never submitted to anyone, now was overcome through Roger's word alone.[3]

However, this was not the case with the Campanian and Apulian barons who had already, in 1127, resisted Roger's accession to the duchy. In particular, his brother-in-law Rainulf of Alife and the latter's brother Richard were far from ready to abandon the freedom of action which they had hitherto enjoyed. Roger could not tolerate such behaviour. Rainulf's wife Matilda remained on her brother's side. While her husband was with Prince Robert of Capua supporting Anacletus II in Rome, she went in haste, taking her son with her, to join Roger in Salerno. When Rainulf, after his return from Rome, refused to attend Roger's court, the king returned to Sicily, at the end of May or the beginning of June 1131, and took his sister and his little nephew with him.[4]

Roger's early return to Sicily was probably a consequence of his forces having been in the field or at sea since the end of January. Campaigns of more than four or five months entailed major logistical problems. Thus as a rule the king began his military expeditions to the mainland in the spring and ended them, at the latest, in early autumn. He remained in Sicily in the winter, during which use of the fleet was unfeasible. Rainulf of Alife clearly knew that the next year would see a conflict. He prepared himself for war and strengthened his fortifications. So too did Tancred of Conversano and Grimoald of Bari. The rebels were encouraged by the news that in March 1131 Lothar III had promised Innocent II that he would come to Italy with an army.[5]

Roger and his troops crossed the Straits of Messina in May 1132. He held a court at Taranto where Count Godfrey of Andria, who had taken part in the rebellion, tried in vain to justify himself and lost his fief. The king then marched against Bari which was blockaded by land and sea. The town surrendered after a three-week siege, and the citizens handed over

[2] *Ibid.*, II.8–11, pp. 27–8. Clementi (1991), 288.

[3] *Al. Tel.* II.12, pp. 28–9. For Roger's stays at Salerno, Brühl (1968), 312. For Sergius VII (1123–37), the last Duke of Naples, Vitolo (1994–5).

[4] *Al. Tel.* II.13–16, pp. 29–30. *Falco*, 120. Cf. Clementi (1991), 240ff, 289ff.

[5] *Al. Tel.* II.17, p. 31. Clementi (1991), 291.

Prince Grimoald, who was sent in chains to Sicily. In recompense, Roger allowed the town a measure of self-government. Tancred of Conversano also submitted, surrendering Brindisi and the other towns of which he was lord. In return he received twenty gold *schifati* and permission to emigrate to the Holy Land.[6]

Rainulf of Alife had, on the advice of Robert of Capua, refused to bring help to Grimoald of Bari; probably because Lothar III was still detained in Germany, from which he was able to leave for the south only in the late summer of 1132. But when Roger requested the Prince of Capua to support Anacletus II in Rome with his troops, the prince insisted upon a condition: the king must first of all restore to his vassal Rainulf of Alife the towns of Avellino and Mercogliano, and also his wife and son. Roger refused, and so Robert and Rainulf prepared for war.[7]

The battle took place on 25 July 1132, at Nocera, northwest of Salerno. The king suffered a serious defeat. His tents, chapel and archives, even the charter of investiture from Anacletus, fell into the hands of his enemies. But the latter were unable to exploit their victory – there were too many divisions among them. Roger was able to retreat to Salerno and organize the defence. First of all, he strengthened his strongpoints around Benevento; then he went to Bari, whose townspeople had rebelled against the construction of a royal citadel there. Roger did not want to lose such an important town, and had the work halted. Meanwhile the rebellion was spreading into the Basilicata. Its leader was once again Tancred of Conversano, who had broken his promise to go into exile. He was joined by his brother, Count Alexander of Conversano, and Godfrey of Andria. The king limited himself to fortifying a few strongpoints in Apulia. On his journey back from Apulia he held a court at Melfi, and then returned to Salerno. He installed garrisons in two towns near Benevento, where he had realized that the inhabitants' sympathies lay with the revolt, and he returned to Sicily only at the beginning of December. He had never before remained on the mainland so late into the winter, but this was a case of necessity. However, Roger had lost a battle, not the war.[8]

[6] *Al. Tel.* II.18–21, pp. 31–2; *Falco*, 120; Roger II, *Diplomata*, no. 20. Clementi (1991), 293ff.

[7] *Al. Tel.* II.23–5, pp. 33–4. Clementi (1991), 244ff, 289ff.

[8] *Falco*, 130–42. See the letter of Cardinal Henry of Sant'Agata, *Monumenta Bambergensia*, ed. P. Jaffé (Bibliotheca Rerum Germanicarum v, Berlin 1869), 443–4 no. 259 (July 1132): 'The tents of the duke (*Roger*) and his own chapel, with all its utensils and documents, have been captured. Among these last were the privileges in which Peter Leone granted him Rome itself and all the land from there to Sicily and appointed him advocate of the Roman church, Patrician of the Romans and king.' Clementi (1991), 245ff, 297ff. For the citadel at Bari, see Licinio (1994), 89ff.

Next year hostilities spread further. Robert of Capua and Rainulf of Alife hoped for the support of Lothar III, from whom they sought help at Rome at the beginning of May 1133, but he refused them, because he had come to Italy with only a relatively small force. His goal was to secure his imperial coronation, which Innocent II performed for him on 4 June, exceptionally in the Lateran basilica, because St Peter's was still in the hands of Anacletus and his supporters. Meanwhile Roger had returned to southern Italy with a substantial army. Venosa, which had joined Tancred of Conversano, was stormed and savagely punished. According to the account of Falco of Benevento, the town was burned to the ground and all its inhabitants, even women and children, massacred. Count Alexander of Conversano fled to Dalmatia, Robert of Capua to Pisa. 'Then King Roger, having still not satisfied his thirst for human blood', so Falco angrily reported, marched with his army to Montepeloso (modern-day Irsina, in the Basilicata) where Tancred of Conversano had taken refuge. He was captured and sent to Sicily. Next the town of Acerenza, which dominated the mountainous interior of the Basilicata, was captured; then the Apulian coastal towns of Bisceglie and Trani. Work on the castle at Bari, suspended the year before, was started afresh.[9]

The town of Troia experienced the king's particular fury. He had in 1129 forgiven its original rebellion of 1127, but now it had once again joined his opponents, Roger remained inexorable. For Falco of Benevento this was yet another act of terrorism by the Godless ruler:

He then set his army in motion once again and force marched to the city of Troia. The citizens, who believed his lying assurances of peace, expected him without foreboding. Bishop William summoned all the clergy and monks of the town, clad in white, and went out in procession to meet the king with chants [*laudes*], thinking (as we have heard) to soothe his ferocious spirit by carrying before him relics of the Saints. However, the furious king entered the city, and seeing this glorious procession forgot his promise of security, and being unmindful of the Catholic faith and the enemy of Christian religion, with burning eyes put an end to that procession. 'I do not want', he said, 'honours of this sort, but if life is granted to me, I shall destroy everything, and exile everyone.' [*Nolo, inquit, nolo huiusmodi gloriam, sed vita comite omnes destruam et omnes exulabo.*] The clergy and people who had gone out to meet him were put to flight, and everybody fled as best they could. He immediately arrested many of the citizens of Troia and put their women and children in chains. He ordered a judge named Robert and four other distinguished men to be hanged. Many Troians abandoned their property and fled with their wives and children to Benevento. He then ordered that the houses and property of the Troians to be given over to the sword and consumed by fire. Oh what a wailing of women and children arose over the whole town of

---

[9] *Falco*, 152–3. *Al. Tel.* ɪɪ.36–49, pp. 41–7. Clementi (1991), 248ff, 302ff.

Troia! If my tongue had a hundred voices to narrate everything which happened, then I would still fail to do it justice in writing them down![10]

Roger's anger had probably been provoked by the bishop organizing a ceremonial reception for him, the processional entry of a king according to the ritual of the *adventus regis*, without seeking his permission, probably in the hope of securing an amnesty. If the ruler had accepted this, then his hands would have been tied, but Roger was determined to punish the town for its rebellion.[11]

According to Alexander of Telese, Troia, as well as later the neighbouring town of Ascoli Satriano, was destroyed and its inhabitants scattered among the surrounding villages. However, both towns remained in existence, and so the destruction cannot fully have been put into effect. After brief stops at Melfi and Gravina Roger travelled on to Salerno, where he arrived at the beginning of October. Falco of Benevento claimed that he intended to give Salerno and Amalfi the same treatment as he had given to the towns of Apulia he had discussed:

After King Roger, as we have already said, had depopulated the cities and towns of Apulia and savagely massacred their men and women, he went to Salerno. There he ordered certain nobles [*proceres*] who lived near the town to be summoned, and when they met he discussed with them how he might ruin the citizens of Salerno and Amalfi as he had with his cruel hand those of Apulia. But, since it did not seem to him to be a suitable time for this, he left unrealised what he had conceived in his heart, thinking to put his plan into effect at a more opportune moment. Then a ship was made ready and he set sail for Sicily on 21 October. Furthermore, we have heard that twenty-three ships, loaded with gold, silver and property which he had looted from the cities of Apulia, sank to the bottom of the sea, and in these ships were many men, women and children from all the towns of Apulia who were being taken captive into exile, never to see their homeland or relatives again. They drowned in this shipwreck. Oh what great lamentation and ghastly grief spread through every corner of Apulia! However, the Apulians praised the King of heaven who had saved these people from all sorts of terrible fates and the perils of exile and had in a single moment taken them from the chasm of this world.[12]

In the following year (1134) Rainulf of Alife also surrendered. He had waited in vain for help from Pisa; because Pisa's rival Genoa was friendly towards Roger, Pisa remained loyal to the empire and hostile to the Normans. Roger's reconciliation with his brother-in-law and vassal followed 'feudal' ritual, with the king refusing to have his foot kissed.

[10] *Falco*, 154–8. *Al. Tel.* II.49–53, pp. 47–8. Roger II, *Diplomata*, nos. 27–32. Clementi (1991), 250–1, 306ff.

[11] Kölzer (1977–80), 170–1; and in general for such rituals, Althoff (1993).

[12] *Al. Tel.* II.49, 52, pp. 47–8. Martin (1979), 90. *Falco*, 158–60.

Alexander of Telese, who was quite probably present at the ceremony, which took place not far from his abbey, gives a graphic description:

He [Rainulf] came to the king on bended knee, and wanted to kiss his feet. As he tried to kiss the king's feet, the latter raised him with his own hands and wanted to give him the kiss [of peace] on the mouth. The count first beseeched him to cast all anger out of his heart. The king replied: 'I cast it out of my heart.' Then he said, 'I would also wish that, as I shall henceforth be a servant to you, you shall therefore cherish me.' To this the king said, 'and this too I concede.' Again he said, 'I wish God to be a witness between you and I, of these promises which we have made to each other.' The other then said, 'so be it'. When this had been said, the king immediately gave him the kiss [of peace] and was seen to embrace him for a long time. As a result joyful tears were seen to flow from the eyes of all those who were round about them.[13]

Roger gave the Prince of Capua an ultimatum: if he wished to retain his title, he must submit before the middle of August. But the prince did not do this. By contrast, both Count Hugh of Boiano (in Molise) and Sergius of Naples renewed their vassalage to Roger. If we are to believe Alexander of Telese, this followed the customary ceremonial: 'He [Sergius] came to meet him with his head bowed low, kneeled before him, put his hands between those of the king, did homage to him and swore the oath of fealty.' The king then moved northwards and strengthened his lordship over that region. After obtaining a promise of fealty from the citizens of Benevento, albeit one respecting the rights of the pope over that town, Roger was able to return peacefully to Sicily in early August.[14]

But the extent to which the monarchy was dependent upon the king himself became apparent when towards the end of the year Roger fell sick. His illness was seemingly grave, and perhaps infectious; it was probably what caused the death of his queen, Elvira, early in February 1135, at the age of about thirty-five. Roger took her death very hard, to such an extent that 'he shut himself up in his room for many days, refusing to see anybody except for a few personal servants. As a result the rumour soon spread that he had died, and this was thought true not only by those far away but also by those at court.'[15]

Roger's emotional reaction to the death of his wife was unusual. Marriages in the Middle Ages were in general political affairs, serving to conclude alliances, increase the bounds of lordships, or as a means of social climbing. There was no place for sentiment. For the most part they met for the first time at the betrothal, or at the wedding, without bride and

---

[13] *Al. Tel.* II.63, p. 53. For the significance of the kiss, Schreiner (1990).
[14] *Al. Tel.* II.54–70, pp. 48–57, especially c. 67, p. 56. *Falco*, 166–72. Clementi (1991), 308–16.
[15] *Al. Tel.* III.1–2, pp. 59–60. Houben (1993a), Clementi (1991), 319.

groom having even spoken to each other previously. Roger's despair at the loss of Elvira shows that their marriage must have been unusually happy by contemporary standards – if one may for once express such a modern, and to some extent anachronistic, opinion. However, it is notable that in the years thereafter the king did not remarry, although there was no necessity for that since the five sons whom Elvira had given him seemed to make the dynasty secure. But normally a king required a queen. If Roger was happy to ignore this custom and content himself with mistresses, there must have been some reason for this. It was not until fifteen years after Elvira's death, when only one of his sons was still alive, that the king (as we shall see) contracted a second marriage.

Let us return to the situation in the year 1135. The false news of Roger's death led to the fires of revolt on the mainland being rekindled. Early in April Robert of Capua arrived at Naples from Pisa with twenty ships and 8,000 men. Duke Sergius and Rainulf were waiting for him; the latter had mustered 400 knights. The chancellor Guarin and the *amiratus* John, whom the king had left as governors of the Campania, organized the defence as best they could. They strengthened the fortifications, but were unable to prevent Aversa from surrendering to the Prince of Capua. However, the city of Capua remained in the hands of the royal troops, comprising some 2,000 knights and a corresponding number of infantry. On 5 June 1135 Roger himself arrived at Salerno. He made clear that the town of Aversa, Count Rainulf and Duke Sergius could none of them hope for forgiveness after breaking their oaths of fealty. Only Prince Robert could retain his title, provided that he submitted to him. When the prince refused, Roger's troops attacked Aversa, stormed it and burned it down. The leaders of the rebellion took refuge in Naples, which Roger besieged, in vain. At the beginning of August the Pisans destroyed Amalfi, their commercial rival, and sacked Ischia, but the king surprised them near Ravello and sent them packing. The Pisans did however succeed in conveying a contingent of troops into besieged Naples. Meanwhile Roger had Aversa rebuilt.[16]

Before he returned to Sicily, the king invested his third son, Alfonso, with the principality of Capua. He had previously granted his eldest son Roger the duchy of Apulia, and his second son Tancred the principality of Bari. Hence the tradition of regional principalities was in theory respected, but they were now integral parts of the kingdom and in the hands of members of the royal family. This new structure of the state was also expressed in the royal title. In place of 'King of Sicily and Italy [i.e. southern

---

[16] *Al. Tel.* III.3–28, pp. 60–74; *Falco,* 172–4. 'Chronicon Pisanum', in *Gli Annales Pisani di Bernardo Maragone,* ed. M. Lupo Gentile (*RIS* 2nd edn., Bologna 1936), 102–3. *Romuald,* 221. Clementi (1991), 319–27.

Italy]', from 1136 onwards, Roger II's Latin charters describe him as 'King of Sicily, of the duchy of Apulia and of the principality of Capua', and this title was continued by his successors. The fiefs which had been confiscated from Count Alexander of Conversano were granted to Roger's brother-in-law Robert (I) de Basunvilla (Vassonville). Not long after 1135 Duke Richard II of Gaeta also submitted, did liege homage and swore unconditional fealty (*legium hominium et ligiam fedelitatem*) to the king and his sons, Duke Roger and Prince Alfonso.[17]

Meanwhile the position of Anacletus II grew weaker. After the Council of Pisa in the spring of 1135, at which Peter the Venerable had made a fruitless attempt at mediation, Innocent II had been recognized in northern Italy, even in places such as Milan which had hitherto remained loyal to Anacletus II, largely thanks to the efforts of Bernard of Clairvaux. In Germany Lothar III gained the upper hand against the Staufen anti-king Conrad III, and promised the pope an Italian expedition for July 1136, the aim of which was first to drive Anacletus from Rome and then to wage war against Roger. The Italian expedition began in the autumn of 1136, but remained for some time stalled in northern Italy, for by favouring Milan Lothar drew upon himself the hostility of the traditionally pro-imperial city of Cremona. Only at the beginning of 1137 was he finally able to march against Roger.[18]

Despite being over seventy, the emperor personally led part of his army south towards Bari, sticking for the most part to the Adriatic coast. Only at Ancona did they encounter any resistance, but with Venetian help the port city was soon captured. The emperor's son-in-law, Duke Henry the Proud of Bavaria, went with the rest of the army through Tuscany, where Innocent II joined him. After Benevento had surrendered to them, they joined forces with the emperor's army at Bari towards the end of May 1137. Among their following were many of Roger's south Italian

---

[17] *Al. Tel.* III.28, pp. 74–5. *Romuald*, 221–2, where the principality of Taranto is erroneously mentioned, rather than that of Bari. Cf. Deér (1972), 224–8, Brühl (1983a), 67ff, Zielinski (1982). See below, p. 132. According to *Al. Tel.* III.28, p. 75, Roger had granted the county of Conversano to his son-in-law Adam (not otherwise attested); the charter evidence suggests rather that the county was granted to Robert de Basunvilla, cf. Petrucci (1965a), Martin (1993), 739. On Gaeta, *Codex Diplomaticus Caietanus* II.268–9 no. 334; Deér (1972), 227; Skinner (1995), 201–2. Although after the death of Sergius VII in 1137 Roger invested his son Alfonso with the duchy of Naples, as well as with the principality of Capua which had been granted to him in 1135, when Richard II of Gaeta died c. 1139 his duchy reverted to the crown and Gaeta became a royal city. The principality of Bari was, however, suppressed after the death of Tancred c. 1138, while the principality of Taranto was created c. 1140 for Roger's fourth son William (see Roger II, *Diplomata*, appendix II/3).

[18] *Reg. Imp.* IV(1), nos. 444, 457, 459, 464, 494. Ambrosioni (1993), Zerbi (1993).

opponents, among them Robert of Capua whom the emperor had restored to his principality. The citadel at Bari was taken after a four-week siege. The members of the garrison who had put up such a bitter resistance – most of whom were Roger's Muslim soldiers – were hanged, and the fortress destroyed.[19]

The King of Sicily made no effort to leave the island. He limited himself to having the defences of those towns and fortresses on the mainland which remained in his hands strengthened. He made an offer to Lothar to recognize imperial overlordship over 'Apulia', that is southern Italy with the exception of Calabria and Sicily. The emperor would invest one of Roger's sons with the duchy of Apulia, another son would be handed over as a hostage, as well as a large sum of money. The emperor refused this tempting offer, even though it meant the creation of imperial suzerainty over part of Norman Italy. He may perhaps have doubted whether Roger's offer was serious and suspected that it was only intended to gain time. The decisive factor in his refusal was probably the attitude of the pope, who wanted Roger, and Anacletus whom he supported, to be utterly defeated.[20]

Meanwhile summer had arrived, and as usual the south Italian heat wore down the imperial army. The latent dislike of the pope, who was blamed for the expedition lasting so long, was increased by Roger's bribery. The decision was taken to make a lengthy stay at Lagopesole, in the mountains between Melfi and Potenza, where the temperature was more bearable. Here the pope and emperor argued about the legal standing of the abbey of Montecassino. While this was going on, a contingent of a thousand knights under the command of Henry the Proud was sent out as an advance guard to help Robert of Capua besiege Salerno, where troops from Pisa joined them.[21]

The siege of Naples had lasted since the summer of 1135, but Roger now ordered it to be abandoned so as to concentrate all his forces on

---

[19] *Annalista Saxo, MGH SS* vi.772. *Reg. Imp.* iv(1), no. 567. Leonhard (1983), 26ff. For Lothar's diversion towards Spoleto, *Reg. Imp.* iv(1), nos. 571–3 (April 1137), and for the rest of the expedition, *ibid.*, nos. 575–85.

[20] *Annalista Saxo*, 774: 'Roger sent messengers seeking the emperor's grace, and he promised a huge sum of money and to hand over his son to him as a hostage if the emperor would grant the principality of Apulia to his other son. However, the emperor was more concerned with the peace of the Church than with money, and he flatly refused to hand over that province to a semi-pagan tyrant.' Zielinski (1982), writes of 'a sincere offer to negotiate on the part of Roger II', who had 'with his son's investiture formally renounced lordship over Apulia', and in this way had 'created the preconditions for the offer of negotiations with the emperor'. But with the investiture of his son, Roger had in no way renounced his lordship over Apulia.

[21] *Falco*, 184–6. *Chron. Cas.* iv.108–115, pp. 571–90. *Annales Pisani*, 11. *Romuald*, 223. *Reg. Imp.* iv(1), nos. 586–605.

the defence of Salerno, the capital of the duchy of Apulia. The defence of Salerno was led by his chancellor, the Englishman Robert of Selby. But the town was unable to resist the combined attack from land and sea for very long, and when Lothar III arrived with his troops Salerno surrendered, on Roger's instructions (on 8 August 1137). The terms of the capitulation were reasonable. The townspeople paid over a substantial sum of money, in return for which their city was spared plundering and destruction. Furthermore, the 400 knights who had defended it were permitted to leave. However, this agreement deprived the Pisans of the rich booty to which they had been looking forward. The pope tried in vain to mediate, but the Pisans concluded a peace treaty with the King of Sicily. Without the support of a fleet the papal–imperial expedition was doomed to failure.[22]

Once they had decided on a retreat, the emperor and the pope granted Roger's most determined opponent, Rainulf of Alife, investiture with the duchy of Apulia, but in doing so differences of opinion once again surfaced, both over who had the right to invest him and over the overlordship of southern Italy. The pope cited the position of his predecessors, who had acted as overlords since the original investiture of Robert Guiscard. The emperor insisted on the ancient rights of the empire over the whole of Italy. Finally a compromise was settled whereby they would perform Rainulf's investiture together. The symbol with which this investiture was carried out was a lance with a banner; Innocent II held the upper part of the staff and Lothar III the lower. We do not know to which of them Rainulf swore his oath of fealty.[23]

The new Duke of Apulia could not last long once the papal–imperial army had withdrawn. Roger had up to now remained in Sicily, waiting for his opponent's expedition to come to an end. Indeed, for nearly two years, since the summer of 1135, he had not left the island. Now he marched with his army by the land route to Salerno, which he entered in October 1137. It was probably at this point that Bernard of Clairvaux, under orders from Lothar and Innocent and despite his own ill-health, travelled to southern Italy to negotiate with Roger for a solution to the schism and peace with Rainulf of Alife. It was clear that the king of Sicily could not be defeated by military means.[24]

[22] *Annalista Saxo*, 774–5. *Falco*, 188. *Annales Cavenses*, 192. *Annales Pisani*, 11. *Romuald*, 223. *Reg. Imp.* IV(1), nos. 611–12.

[23] *Romuald*, 223–4. *Falco*, 190. *Annalista Saxo*, 775. Otto of Freising, *Chronica* VII.20, pp. 338–9. For other sources, see *Reg. Imp.* IV(1), no. 615. Deér (1972), 37–8, 42–3.

[24] *Falco*, 200, 202. *Romuald*, 225. Ca. 117 (Tropea), cf. Holtzmann (1963), 152–3. Bernard of Clairvaux, 'Letters', 346 no. 144 [Eng. trans., *The Letters of St Bernard of Clairvaux*, 214–15 no. 146], to be dated before 30 October 1137.

Roger took a bloody revenge on his opponents. Capua was destroyed, Avellino occupied, Naples and Benevento surrendered of their own free will. However, Rainulf of Alife was able to inflict a serious defeat on the king at Rignano, at the foot of Monte Gargano, on 30 October 1137. Roger fled back to Salerno, where he behaved as though nothing had happened. The misfortune on the battlefield seems not to have harmed his reputation. A little while later Bernard of Clairvaux gave him the opportunity to preside over a disputation between the followers of Innocent and Anacletus. The abbot hoped that through such open discussions an end to the schism could be achieved. As might have been predicted, Bernard's eloquence gave Innocent's party the upper hand. But Roger was not swayed by this, postponed a decision, and sought a period of reflection up to Christmas. Before his return to Sicily the king issued the citizens of Salerno a privilege containing extensive fiscal exemptions. This was one of the few charters in which express reference was made to actual political events: 'when, through the faithlessness of our traitors, Lothar and the Germans entered Apulia and almost the whole land was contaminated by the stains of treason, the only town in [southern] Italy to remain true to us was Salerno'.[25]

The death of Anacletus at the end of January 1138 meant that the schism was nearing an end. His supporters did indeed elect a successor, Cardinal Gregory, who took the name Victor IV, but he had little support and abdicated after a few months. In spring 1138 Roger and his army returned to the mainland. He advanced into Apulia to prosecute the war against Rainulf of Alife. Innocent II was ill, and this prevented the planned union of his papal troops with Rainulf's army. Seeing the problems of his opponents Roger turned once again to diplomatic means. He now accorded the pope express recognition, and requested Innocent to grant him investiture, but the latter refused, and so the quarrels were once again to be settled by military means. After his previous experiences, the king avoided open battle and preferred to utilize a type of guerrilla tactics. He returned to Sicily in the autumn without having defeated Rainulf.[26]

Next spring, at the Second Lateran Council of April 1139, Innocent announced the excommunication of Roger and his supporters, but the sudden death of Rainulf of Alife deprived the pope of his most important

[25] *Falco*, 196–204. *Romuald*, 224–5. *Chron. Cas.* IV.126–7, pp. 601–4. Ernald of Bonneval, *Vita Prima S. Bernardi*, II.7; Alan of Auxerre, *Vita Secunda*, c. 22, *PL* 185, cols. 293–5; 506–7. Hueffer (1886), 37ff. Cf. Caspar (1904), 210–20. Roger II, *Diplomata*, no. 46 (22 November 1137).

[26] *Chron. Cas.* IV.130, p. 607. *Falco*, 205–14. Documents from Monte Sant' Angelo (on the Monte Gargano) of June 1138 and Siponto, in March 1139, acknowledge Rainulf as duke, *Regesto di S. Leonardo di Siponto*, ed. F. Camobreco (Rome 1913), 9–10 nos. 12–13.

ally. In the next few months the king succeeded without great difficulty in consolidating his rule over southern Italy. Only a few places such as Bari and Troia continued to resist. The pope could no longer ignore Roger's offers of negotiations, but he insisted upon the revival of the principality of Capua as an independent buffer state between the lands of the papacy and the kingdom. The king would not accept such a demand, and the negotiations remained fruitless.[27]

Roger was well aware of the strength of his position. At San Germano (modern-day Cassino) the papal army ran into a trap. As had happened in 1053 when Leo IX was faced with Robert Guiscard, so now Innocent II was taken prisoner by Roger. He could no longer deny investiture to the king, and on 25 July 1139 the pope enfeoffed Roger with Sicily, and his sons Roger and Alfonso with the duchy of Apulia and the principality of Capua. The use of three banners was a symbol that three separate fiefs were involved, but the bull of investiture was granted solely to the king, and it is probable that he received all three banners from the pope's hand. There can be no doubt that he alone was a direct vassal of the pope: his sons were only rear vassals. The unity of the kingdom was not called into question. On other issues the pope remained inflexible. In the bull of investiture there was no mention of the ecclesiastical reorganization of Sicily that Anacletus had decreed, nor even of such a minor matter as the obligation of the townspeople of Benevento to provide the king with military assistance if needed. Innocent probably obtained confirmation of the privilege, which Roger had granted in 1137, guaranteeing the freedom of the papal enclave of Benevento. To avoid mentioning the anti-pope Anacletus, the bull of investiture alleged, quite untruthfully, that Honorius II had promoted the duke to be King of Sicily. The pope only granted Roger what he could not avoid, but he refused to make further concessions.[28]

From Mignano, to the south of Montecassino, where the peace between the pope and king had been concluded, they travelled together to Benevento. Roger then went on into Apulia to suppress the last rebels at Troia and Bari. Troia surrendered and hoped for mercy. The king demanded that

---

[27] *Annales Ceccanenses*, *MGH SS* xix.283. *Romuald*, 226. *Falco*, 218–20. For the sources for the Lateran Council, Bernhardi (1883), 154–6.

[28] *Falco*, 222. *Chronica de Ferraria*, 25. *Annales Cavenses*, *MGH SS* iii.192. *Romuald*, 225. *Annales Casinenses*, *MGH SS* xix.309. *Annales Herbipolenses* [Würzburg Annales], *MGH SS* xvi.2. *Deeds of John and Manuel Comnenus*, 75. *It. Pont.* viii.42 no. 159, ed. Deér (1969), 74–5. Baaken (1993), 59ff, who suggests that this was the first time that the phrase 'liege homage' was used, probably to accentuate the exclusivity of Roger's vassalage to the papacy, and to obviate rival claims by the emperor. For the Benevento privilege, Roger II, *Diplomata*, no. 47 + , Brühl (1978), 106ff.

the body of his arch-enemy, Rainulf of Alife, who was buried there, be handed over to him. According to the account of Falco of Benevento, he declared that: 'I shall not enter the town as long as that traitor Rainulf lies in your midst.' With heavy hearts the townspeople entrusted four knights with the task of opening the grave and removing the body, 'so that, once the king's anger has been appeased, he can enter the town in peace'.

The duke's enemies ordered one of the knights called Gallicanus, who had been one of his most faithful followers, to break open the tomb and remove with his own hands the putrifying body. They did this both to injure the dead duke and to cause Gallicanus pain. Gallicanus was forced by fear and to avoid incurring the king's wrath to carry the duke's poor bones, as we have described, as though he and the others were happy to do this. Oh horror! The duke's enemies immediately fastened a rope around the corpse's neck and dragged it through the streets up to the town's citadel. They then turned around and went to the charcoal workings outside the town where there was a filthy stagnant ditch, into which they sank the duke's body. What an evil action! Fear and horror straightaway invaded the whole town, and everyone, both friends and enemies of the duke, wished for death. I testify to the Eternal King, Judge of the centuries, that we have never read of such a ghastly deed having happened in previous generations, even among pagans. How could such cruelty as this profit the king's authority? What victory or royal glory did it lead to? But wishing to satisfy his rage against one on whom he could exercise it while he was alive, he did it when he was dead.[29]

Was Roger the black-hearted tyrant that the hostile chronicler from Benevento described? Was he really so 'carried away by his burning hate that he performed the most thoughtless and hateful act of his entire life', as one modern authority claims? Probably not. What we are dealing with was rather an exemplary demonstration of his power to strike fear into rebels. The exhumation of a body and its public mistreatment was nothing new. Some centuries earlier, in 897, Pope Stephen IV had had the remains of his predecessor Formosus exhumed and after the so-called 'corpse's synod' thrown into the Tiber. Paschal II had the body of the anti-pope Clement III cast into the same river in 1106. We are dealing therefore with a ritual gesture for the *damnatio memoriae* ('the obliteration of memory').[30]

After Troia, it was Bari's turn to suffer the king's anger. The town was besieged, and bombarded with the help of movable wooden towers

[29] *Falco*, 224–6. *Romuald*, 226.
[30] Quote from Caspar (1904), 440. For the 'punishment of papal corpses', see Borgolte (1989), 124ff, Servatius (1979), 70n, Ziese (1982), 273. Cf. the Vatican text of King Roger's Assizes, c. 18 [ed. Brandileone, 104, Zecchino, 40]: 'the crime of treason also encompasses those who discuss and attack the reputation of the king after his death'.

wheeled up to the walls. As provisions ran out the inhabitants began to rebel. The Prince of Bari, Jaquintus, offered to capitulate, and Roger accepted this. There was a mutual exchange of prisoners, but this gave the king an excuse once again to show his iron fist. The prince had had one of his prisoners blinded. Roger summoned a commission of inquiry composed of judges from Troia, Trani and Bari, which came to the judgement that was expected: Jaquintus had broken the treaty and should be punished. The king had the prince, his counsellors and ten other men hanged, another ten persons lost their eyes and suffered mutilation. Falco of Benevento alleged that the town's inhabitants shut themselves up in their houses through fear and prayed for the Saviour to have pity upon them and liberate them from their oppressor.[31]

After the Apulian towns had surrendered, Roger's rule was finally secure. Before he returned to Salerno on his way to Sicily, he deprived all those vassals who had revolted against him of their fiefs and exiled them. As a security measure Count Roger of Ariano and his wife were taken as prisoners to Sicily.[32]

Once spring 1140 had come, the king had his sons Roger and Alfonso conquer the Abruzzi, so that his kingdom now comprised the whole of Italy south and to the east of the 'Patrimony of St Peter' (i.e. the papal lands). Roger himself came to the mainland in mid July. He landed at Salerno and went with his army to Benevento where he negotiated with the rector and townspeople about the status of the papal enclave. After a brief stay at Capua he went on to San Germano and requested a meeting with the pope. It was probably at this time that he sent Innocent II, at the latter's request, wooden beams for the repair of the collapsed roof of the Lateran basilica. But nonetheless the pope remained obstinate, because Roger was not prepared to make any territorial concessions. His sons had seized Arce and Sora, places of strategic importance through which the access routes to both the Abruzzi and the Campania could be controlled. They had advanced right up to Ceprano, the most southerly town in papal territory, leading the pope to fear an attack on Rome itself and fortifying the town of Tivoli and the places around it. Roger meanwhile visited the abbey of Montecassino, which was forced to accept an exchange of fortifications which was very much to the crown's advantage. Then, at the beginning of August, the king returned to Capua. A few weeks later he travelled to Pescara and took the opportunity to visit St Clement of Casauria, another former 'imperial' abbey which like Montecassino had supported Lothar in 1137 and thus could expect little favour from Roger. Early in September the king went to Ariano, to the east of Benevento,

[31] *Falco*, 228–30.   [32] *Ibid.*, 230.

where he held a court in which he promulgated an edict for reform of the coinage, and perhaps other legislation as well.[33]

Afterwards he went to Naples where he was accorded a magnificent reception.

The Archbishop of Naples, whose name was Marinus, ordered all the clergy of the city to be summoned, announced the king's arrival to them, and encouraged them and the citizens to greet the king joyfully and in the proper manner. The knights and citizens of the city went out through the Porta Capuana into what they call the Neapolitan Field, welcomed the king with more honour and care than one would have believed possible and escorted him up to the Porta Capuana. The priests and clergy of the city then went out through that gate and led him into the city with hymns and *laudes* rising to the heavens. Four noblemen held the reins of the king's horses and his stirrups, while four more led him to the cathedral. Reader, if you have seen the number of people pouring into the squares, and the widows, married women and virgins leaning out of the windows, you would have been amazed and would have said that no other emperor, king or prince had ever been received with such joy in the city of Naples. What more? After this ecstatic welcome the king dismounted at the cathedral and was entertained in the archbishop's chamber. The next day he rode all through the city and round the outside. While his ship was being prepared the king went to the castle of the Holy Saviour next to the city, and summoning the citizens of Naples there he dealt with various issues to do with the liberty and interests of the city. He gave to every knight five *modia* of land and five villeins, and he promised that if life were granted to him he would reward them with generous gifts.[34]

What the chronicler portrayed as the king's generosity was rather the product of negotiations between the ruler and the city's representatives concerning its autonomy (*libertas*) and interests (*utilitas*). It seems clear that Roger was not inherently hostile to the towns; provided that they remained loyal to him he was prepared to concede them a certain measure of autonomy. But those towns which had repeatedly rebelled, like Troia and Bari, were severely punished.

Some contemporaries justified Roger's actions on the grounds of necessity; they needed to enforce law and order in the political chaos of southern Italy. Otto of Freising commented on this view in his 'world chronicle': 'some people are of the opinion that Roger acted in this way

---

[33] *Ibid.*, 232–4. John the Deacon, *Descriptio Lateranensis Ecclesiae*, 349. *Chronicon de Ferraria*, 29. *Annales Ceccanenses*, 283. For Tivoli, there is an inscription of 4 August 1140, cited by Caspar (1904), 331n. *Annales Casinenses*, 309. *Chronicon Casauriense*, cols. 889–90. Roger II, *Diplomata*, nos. 49–51. Caspar (1904), 330ff. Chalandon (1907), II.95ff. For Arce and Sora, see Sthamer (1995), 6; for the northern boundaries of the kingdom, Clementi (1968); and for Montecassino and Casauria, most recently Houben (1995a), 53–4.

[34] *Falco*, 234–6.

more out of regard for justice than through tyranny. They claim that more than all other princes he loves peace, and so to preserve it he has suppressed rebellion with such sternness.'

This was also the opinion of the so-called 'Hugo Falcandus'.

In short, he made efforts to administer justice in its full rigour on the grounds that it was particularly necessary for a newly established realm, and to exercise the options of peace and war by turns, with the result that he omitted nothing that virtue requires, and had no king or prince as his equal during his lifetime. Now as regards the fact that some writers categorize many of his actions as tyrannical and call him inhuman because he imposed on many men penalties that were severe and not prescribed by the laws, it is my opinion that as a prudent man who was circumspect in all things, he intentionally behaved in this way when his monarchy was only recently established so that wicked men should not be able to wheedle any impunity for their crimes; and that while those who deserved well (to whom he showed himself mild) should not be discouraged by excessive severity, there should nevertheless be no place for contempt as a result of excessive mildness. And if perhaps he seems to have acted somewhat harshly against some, I suppose that he was forced to do it by some necessity. For there was no other way in which the savagery of a rebellious people could have been suppressed, or the daring of traitors restrained.[35]

Monks were also impressed. For the chronicler of the abbey of St Clement of Casauria in the Abruzzi, Roger was 'so terrible that even the mountains trembled before his countenance'. His colleague at Cava quoted from the Bible: 'And the earth is silent before his face.' Typical of Roger's reputation is an addition to the 'world chronicle' of Richard of Cluny, where one reads that after killing or exiling all the nobles of his kingdom, Roger had not hesitated to extort the imperial crown (*diadema imperii*) from the pope.[36]

However, Roger was soon praised as 'the great king', whose rule over southern Italy had provided political stability. An inscription in the cathedral of Brindisi recording the ruler's financial support for its rebuilding in the time of Archbishop Baialardus (1122–44) said: 'May the true glory of God be yours, O great King Roger, with whose help the work of this temple has come to pass' (*Gloria vera Dei/tibi sit rex magne Rogeri/auxilio cuius/templi labor extitit huius*).[37]

---

[35] Otto of Freising, *Chronica*, VII.23, p. 347. *Falcandus*, 6 [*Tyrants*, 58]

[36] *Chronicon Casauriense*, 889. *Annales Cavenses*, 192 (citing I Mac. 1.3). *Ex Richardi Pictaviensis Chronica*, MGH SS XXVI.80–1.

[37] Jurlaro (1968), 246–7; and for Baćalardus (Abelard), Ganzer (1963), 74–5, Kamp (1977), 102. A similar inscription has been found in the citadel at Ostuni (prov. Brindisi), built by Godfrey III of Lecce, Jurlaro (1968), 270 [illustrated] (cf. Poso (1988), 52ff.), and Roger was also hailed as 'great king' in a Greek charter of his son, Duke Roger, from 1142, De Andrés (1983), 384ff. For the bell tower at Melfi, commissioned by Roger II, Todisco (1987), 145ff.

MEDITERRANEAN POLICY

Before the discovery of America the Mediterranean was the centre of the world. In late Antiquity the *mare nostrum* of the Romans lost its political unity, dividing into 'west Roman' and 'east Roman' halves. When the Arabs conquered the whole of its southern coast these two halves became quarters, since the Muslims also saw their half as split into two zones; a western one comprising the Maghreb, Spain and Sicily, and an eastern one of Egypt and the Middle East. Thus three cultures came into contact in the Mediterranean: the western (Roman) Christian, the eastern (Byzantine) Christian, and the Arabic–Islamic one which extended as far as India. The hinge was Sicily, the largest and the central island of this inland sea.[38]

Tunis is no further away from Palermo than Naples. The distance to the Balearic Islands in the west is almost the same as Crete to the east. Messina lies more or less half way between Genoa and Alexandria. Genoa, which controlled the trade of the western Mediterranean, was thus the natural ally of Sicily, just as Venice, which concentrated its attention on the eastern half of the sea, was that of Byzantium. The whole kingdom was surrounded by water – nowhere is more than 80 km away from the sea, and almost all the important towns were ports. The ship was the most comfortable, cheapest and quickest means of communication. This applied especially to the island of Sicily, which possessed only very poor roads. One needed some twenty to thirty days for the land route of 250 km between Palermo and Messina, by ship on average only eight; and if one was lucky, as was the Islamic traveller Ibn Jubayr in December 1184, one could indeed manage the journey in two days. Everything depended upon the winds. From Palermo to Alexandria a ship needed between thirteen and fifty days, from Messina to Damietta in Egypt on average thirty, from Palermo to Mahdia in Tunisia up to thirty-five days.[39]

Relations between Sicily and Tunisia were particularly close. The Sicilian (or Tunisian) straits are at their narrowest point no more than 150 km wide. Whoever rules Sicily ought not to ignore the situation in north Africa. Muslim pirates could come from here, but also immigrants and merchants. From the middle of the eleventh century the incursions of the

[38] Braudel (1972), Goitein (1967–88), I.43.

[39] Peri (1978), 58–9, Goitein (1967–88), I.235, Matthew (1992), 71–6, Bresc (1995), 71, Gil (1995), 132. In 1137 Roger granted the merchants of Salerno equal rights with those of Sicily, who enjoyed a particularly privileged position in the trade with Alexandria, Roger II, *Diplomata*, no. 46: 'Furthermore, we shall have the tithes and other mercantile dues, which the Salernitans have formerly been accustomed to pay in Alexandria, lowered to the manner and level of Sicily, so that the same law and identical custom shall apply to [both] Sicilians and Salernitans.'

nomad tribes of the Banū Hilāl had accelerated the decline of the agrarian economy of the eastern Maghreb. The transfer of the Fatimid power base to Egypt had contributed towards the political fragmentation of this zone from the tenth century. The Zirids, who had been appointed as governors over north Africa and who had made Kairuan (al-Qairawān) their capital, were unable to maintain long-term control over this territory. The Hammadids soon made themselves independent. When they both submitted to the Sunite caliphate of Baghdad, the Shi'ite Fatimids called upon the Banū Hilāl of Upper Egypt to invade, and in 1052 the latter won a major victory over a coalition of the Zirids, Hammadids and other Berbers, and as a result the population fled towards the coast. The Zirids moved their capital to Mahdia in 1057, the Hammadids to Bougie. But while the eastern part of the Maghreb disintegrated politically, the west remained united under the Almoravids, who extended their rule into Spain, and in 1115 to the Balearic Islands.[40]

With the political split of the Maghreb in the eleventh century came the decline of the Muslim fleet which had up to then dominated the Mediterranean. Thus in 1064 the Pisans attacked Palermo (which was at that time still in Muslim hands) and secured a lot of booty. Together with the Genoese they made a successful raid on Mahdia in 1087. Roger I's conquest of Malta in 1090 was indicative of the Muslims' gradual loss of control over the Mediterranean, although this decline was a long drawn-out process. At the beginning of the twelfth century the Arabs were still strong enough to repel Roger II's attack on Mahdia; however, he built up his fleet and was soon more successful. Early in 1128 he was already in a position whereby he could promise the Count of Barcelona fifty galleys to assist him in his struggle against the Muslims in Spain. A few months later, in a treaty with the citizens of Savona, the sea between the Maghreb ('Numidia') and Tripoli was considered to be the Sicilian duke's sphere of influence.[41]

The Zirid emir, al-Ḥassan, who had defeated Roger's attack in 1123, found himself in growing difficulties. The citizens of Mahdia were unhappy with his peace treaty with the Sicilian ruler, and late in 1134 they appealed to the Hammadid Emir of Bougie, Yaḥyā. In the summer of 1135 Yaḥyā's troops closed in on Bougie by both land and sea. However, the siege was raised because the King of Sicily sent his fleet to assist al-Ḥassan. In the autumn of 1135 Roger's forces conquered the strategically important island of Djerba (Jerba) in the Gulf of Gabès, where Berber

---

pirates had their lair. Many of them were killed, and their women and
children taken to Sicily, to be sold as slaves to the Muslims there. The rest
of the population were permitted to remain there. Once the island had
been sacked, it was made subject to a royal governor ('*āmil*). Those pirates
who had survived could continue their operations, but on condition that
this was now to benefit the kingdom of Sicily. Roger sent news of the
capture of Djerba to the Caliph of Egypt, al-Ḥāfiz (1130–49), with whom
he clearly enjoyed good relations.[42]

Meanwhile Roger did not lose sight of the situation in the Near East.
After the death of Prince Bohemond II of Antioch in February 1130
(the son of Roger's first cousin Bohemond I), leaving only one daughter,
Constance, the king advanced a claim to the inheritance, but he was
unable to put this into effect, preoccupied as he was with the subjection
of southern Italy and the vindication of his royal title. When in 1135
Raymond of Poitiers, a son of Duke William X of Aquitaine, went to the
east to marry Constance, Roger sought in vain to prevent this. He may
perhaps have intended to marry one of his sons to the heiress of Antioch,
to strengthen his own claims. In any event, a few years later, in 1139, the
Patriarch of Antioch, Ralph, was accused of making a secret agreement
with Roger. The king's interest in the Holy Land also manifested itself in
his patronage of the Knights of St John; on 10 October 1136 he took the
master and brothers of the hospital at Jerusalem and their dependencies
within the kingdom of Sicily under his special protection and also gave
them permission to found new hospitals.[43]

The repercussions produced by the activity of the Sicilian fleet in the
Mediterranean reached as far as Germany. At a court held in Merseburg in
August 1135, a Byzantine and Venetian delegation pleaded the necessity
for combined action against the usurper Roger, claiming (among other
things) that the latter had seized 'Africa, which is known to be the third
part of the world' from the Byzantine emperor, and also that he had
plundered Venetian merchants. That was, so far as 'Africa' was concerned,
a tremendous exaggeration: Roger had then only just started his north
African campaigns, and furthermore the eastern Roman empire had lost
north Africa to the Arabs many centuries previously. But the embassy to

[42] Al-Idrīsī, *BAS* I.133, Ibn al-Athīr, 459–61, at-Tijānī, 75, an-Nuwairī, 156, Ibn Khaldūn,
      206, Ibn Abī Dīnār, 290ff. Cf. Amari (1933–9), III.406ff, Caspar (1904), 415, Chalandon
      (1907), II.157ff, Canard (1954), 129ff, Idris (1962), 342–6, Abulafia (1985), 32–3, Johns
      (1993), 145ff. For Roger's correspondence with al-Ḥāfiz, see Noth, in Brühl (1978),
      252ff.
[43] William of Tyre, *Chronicon*, XIV.9, 20, XV.12–14, pp. 641, 657, 691–5 [Babcock and
      Krey, II.59–60, 77–9, 113–17]. Cf. Hiestand (1993), 83ff. Roger II, *Diplomata*, no. 43,
      discussed by Wiest (1995).

the court of Lothar III reveals what fears the activities of the Sicilian fleet had caused at Byzantium and Venice.[44]

Famines continued in north Africa, to such an extent that al-Ḥassan became more and more dependent upon the King of Sicily. When the Zirid ruler was unable to pay for any further grain deliveries, Roger dispatched his fleet under the command of George of Antioch and had the ships laying in the harbour of Mahdia seized. Al-Ḥassan was forced to make a formal submission to the king (1141/2). In the following year, 1142/3, Roger started to attack the coastal towns on the western and eastern peripheries of the Zirid kingdom. He tried at first to maintain the appearance of acting in concert with al-Ḥassan. The first attempt was made against Tripoli, which had tried to make itself independent from the Zirids; however, this attack failed in June 1143. Roger's fleet was more successful at Djidjelli (Jījiil), between Bougie and Bône in modern-day Algeria, which was plundered and destroyed. In the following year (1144/5) the port of Bresk, still further west between Ténès (Tinnīs) and Cherchell, was conquered, as was the island of Kerkenna (Qerqenā) off the Tunisian coast.[45]

Tripoli was finally captured in the year 1146. Whereas formerly there had been only plundering raids, there now commenced the legal conquest of towns, in which (at least for a time) garrisons were installed. In Tripoli there had been an armed confrontation between the Arabic ruling group, the Banū Maṭrūḥ, and the general population, the greater part of whom were Berbers. Hence the guard on the town walls was neglected, and it was therefore easy for Roger's soldiers, with the help of ladders, to overcome it. Once the town had been plundered, the commander of the Sicilian army, George of Antioch, granted an *amān*, a general guarantee of security, and as a result those inhabitants who had fled inland returned to the town. For six months a garrison remained in Tripoli. The soldiers then returned to Sicily, taking with them a number of hostages. Most of these were soon set free, and only a few were retained, as guarantee for the trustworthiness of the governor (*walī*) who had been appointed to serve in the town, who came from the Arabic tribe of the Banū Maṭrūḥ. Legal affairs were entrusted to a Berber *qāḍī* or judge. As in Sicily, payment of the head tax (*jizya*) and the land tax (*kharāj*) was demanded from the Muslim population. The town soon flourished, and was visited by merchants from Sicily and other Christian lands – so Ibn al-Athīr testified. From another Arabic source

---

[44] *Annales Erphesfurtenses*, 42. Lilie (1984), 378ff, Hettinger (1990), 250–1. *Reg. Imp.* IV(I), no. 453.

[45] Ibn Abī Dīnār, 292–3, Ibn al-Athīr, 461–3, Abū'l-Fidā, 99–100. Amari (1933–9), 410ff, Chalandon (1907), II.159–60, Idris (1962), 347–50.

we learn that successful appeals were made in Sicily to persuade people to emigrate to Tripoli.[46]

News of the mild treatment of Tripoli spread. In Gabès, after the death of the emir, Rushayd, a freedman named Yūsuf drove out his eldest son, Ma'mar, and installed the latter's brother Mohammed as prince, but the real power remained in Yūsuf's hands. Meanwhile Ma'mar had sought refuge with al-Ḥassan, to whom Gabès was theoretically subject. Fearing his vengeance, Yūsuf offered to submit to Roger, on condition that the latter appoint him as governor (*walī*). The King of Sicily accepted, since by doing so he could bring another north African coastal town under his control without a fight. However, Yūsuf had underestimated the reaction of the local population, who had no wish to live under the rule of an unbeliever, and as a result it proved easy for al-Ḥassan to conquer the city. Yūsuf was executed. Roger sent some ships to take control of Gabès, but their attack failed, probably because the bulk of the Sicilian fleet was busy in Greece at that time, and hence al-Ḥassan's affront remained for a time unpunished.[47]

For the Arabic chronicler Ibn al-Athīr, Yūsuf's career provided a shocking example of a traitor to Islam who had handed over his land to the infidel:

The emir of Gabès, Rushayd ibn Rāfi', had died. One of his freedmen called Yūsuf expelled his eldest son Ma'mar and installed the latter's brother Mohammed as prince. But Yūsuf kept the rule for himself, and did as he wished with Mohammed who was only a child. He was in the habit of dishonouring the wives of his lord [Rushayd], or at least so men said. One of these women came from the tribe of the Banū Qurra. She sent a message to her brothers to inform them of her situation. The brothers arrived and wished to take her away, but Yūsuf refused to hand her over, saying: 'this is my lord's wife'. As a result the Banū Qurra joined with Ma'mar ibn Rushayd and went to al-Ḥassan, the emir of Africa [Mahdia] to complain about Yūsuf's behaviour. Al-Ḥassan wrote to Yūsuf, but received no answer. Yūsuf said that: 'If al-Ḥassan does not leave me in peace, then I shall hand Gabès over to the prince of Sicily.' So al-Ḥassan prepared an army to march against Gabès.

When Yūsuf was informed of this, he sent to Roger the Frank, Prince of Sicily, offering his submission with the words: 'I request of you the uniform and written confirmation as governor (*walī*) of Gabès, and I shall then act as your lieutenant, as do the Banū Maṭrūḥ in Tripoli.' Roger sent him the clothing and the charter,

[46] Ibn al-Athīr, 465–6, Abū'l-Fidā,100, an-Nuwairī, 157–8, at-Tijānī, 60–1, Ibn Khaldūn, 207. *Annales Casinenses*, 310. Robert of Torigny, *MGH SS* vi.497. *Chronica de Ferraria*, 27. Amari (1933–9), 415–7, Idris (1962), 350–2, Abulafia (1985), 33–4, Brett (1991). For the *jizya*, see Johns (1983), 31–4.

[47] Ibn al-Athīr, 466–8, at-Tijānī, 54–5, Ibn Khaldūn, 208–9, Ibn Abī Dīnār, 294. Chalandon (1907), ii.163, Idris (1962), 352–5. Wieruszowski (1969), 28, erroneously identifies Rushayd with his father Rāfi'.

and Yūsuf put on the uniform and had the document read out in an assembly of the leading men. Al-Ḥassan hastened to send his army to Gabès, and the town was besieged. The townspeople immediately rose in revolt against Yūsuf, because he had submitted himself to the Franks, and handed the town over to al-Ḥassan's army. Yūsuf took refuge in the citadel, but this was stormed and he himself was captured. Ma'mar ibn Rushayd and the Banū Qurra condemned him to death. They cut off his male member and stuffed it into his mouth, and then he was put to death with all sorts of tortures. Ma'mar took over the government of Gabès in place of his brother Mohammed. The Banū Qurra took their sister away with them. Yūsuf's brother 'Īsā, together with his son, fled. They took themselves to Roger, King of Sicily, and sought his protection, lamenting the harm that al-Ḥassan had done to them, and thus the king of Sicily was encouraged to exact revenge. That was the reason for the attack on Mahdia, which if it prove pleasing to Almighty God we shall recount in the section for the year 543 [from the Hegira = 1148/9 A D].

In the summer of 1148 Roger prepared for the decisive blow against the Zirid ruler, whose power had been weakened even further by famine and an epidemic. A fleet of 250 to 300 galleys set out under the command of George of Antioch. When it arrived at Mahdia, al-Ḥassan and his family, and many of the inhabitants, fled inland; other people took refuge in the houses and churches of the Christians who still lived there. But once they had realized how mildly the conquered town had been treated, with the soldiers permitted to plunder it for a mere two hours, most of the inhabitants who had fled soon returned. Two other important coastal towns, Susa and Sfax were captured without great difficulty. Only the attempt to seize the fortress of Kélibia (Iqlībiya) on Cap Bon failed. Indeed they were able to make Tunis itself pay tribute, and in addition Gabès was then forced to recognize Roger's lordship.[48]

The conquered towns on the north African coast were all granted a large measure of autonomy, on the model of Tripoli. Muslims could practise their religion unmolested, while at the same time the native Christians were favoured. In September 1148 at Brescia, Pope Eugenius III (1145–53) consecrated an 'Archbishop of Africa' (that is of Ifrīqiya, probably therefore of Mahdia). He went to live in Rome while Mahdia was still under Muslim rule, but Roger then installed him in his see which had, in the meanwhile, been 'liberated' – so ran the account of an anonymous continuator of the chronicle of Sigebert of Gembloux. The Latin sources use the term *Africa* to denote both Ifrīqiya, corresponding to the Roman province of *Africa proconsularis* along with a part of *Numidia*, and also its capital, Mahdia. Here Christian communities had survived the Arab conquest, although

---

[48] Ibn al-Athīr, 469–71, al-Bayān, 37–8, Abū'l-Fidā, 101–2, Ibn Abī Dīnār, 294ff. On Tunisia, see Andrea Dandolo, *Chronica*, 243. Amari (1933–9), 435ff, Idris (1962), 355–60, Abulafia (1985), 34–5.

the lack of bishops created difficulties. In 1053 there were only five for the whole of 'Africa'. Gregory VII had expressed his appreciation of the religious tolerance of the Hammadid prince an-Nāṣir, who was resident in Bougie. Indeed, he appears even to have hoped for his conversion to Christianity, although naturally this proved to be an illusion.[49]

During the course of the twelfth century the advance of the Almohads brought the end of Christianity in north Africa. This movement for the renewal of Islam, coming from the Berbers of Morocco, was far more radical than that of the Almoravids whom it displaced. By 1152 the Almohads were threatening the territory of the Hammadids, which lay to the west of the Zirid kingdom. Roger sought in vain to persuade the Emir of Bougie to ally with him against the Almohads, but the emir refused to fight with an unbeliever against his co-religionists. This decision was fatal for the Hammadids. A year later (in 1153) they were swept away by the Almohad advance.

Seeking to put a brake on the Almohads, Roger decided to capture the town of Bône (Buna), modern-day Annaba in Algeria, a town which they had not yet occupied. His naval commander, Philip of Mahdia, the successor to George of Antioch, secured a speedy victory, in late September or early October 1153. The town was plundered, but then abandoned only ten days after its capture, and its administration was entrusted to a native governor. The islands of Djerba and Kerkenna, which had meanwhile declared themselves independent, were reconquered and severely punished for their rebellion. The expansion of the Almohads could not, however, be contained for very long, and a few years after Roger's death all the Sicilian conquests in north Africa were lost. The expansion of the Christian west, as shown by the First Crusade, the Reconquista in Spain and the recovery of Sicily, came to an end, and Europe was once again forced onto the defensive.[50]

This had already become clear with the fall of Edessa, the oldest of the Crusader states, in December 1144, news of which came to Roger's court.

It is told how the Frankish prince of Sicily had sent a naval expedition against Tripoli and its dependencies, and that the Franks had inflicted death and destruction upon this region. At this time there lived in Sicily a learned Muslim, a virtuous man who was held in great honour and reverence by the prince of Sicily, who hearkened to his words and favoured him above the priests and brothers of his court, and as a result a rumour arose among the people of that country that the king himself was a

---

49 Sigebert of Gembloux, *Continuatio*, 454. Hettinger (1990), 167ff, 244ff, and cf. the review by Houben (1994b). There is also a reference to Christian settlement in 'Africa' in the Commentary on the Apocalypse by Joachim of Fiore, Kedar (1984), 221.

50 Ibn al-Athīr, 478–9, al-Idrīsī, 132–3. Amari (1933–9), 432–3, Idris (1962), 374ff, Wieruszowski (1969), 33, Le Tourneau (1969), 48ff.

Muslim. One day the king was sitting in one of his palaces and he saw a little ship out at sea, on the horizon. It brought the news that the king's forces had entered Muslim territory and plundered it, and with this victory many Muslims had been killed. The Muslim was sitting by the king's side, and showed no emotion. The king turned to him, and asked: 'Have you (calling him by his name) not heard the news?' 'No', the other answered. The king told him what had been announced and inquired: 'Where, therefore, was Mohammed? Has he perhaps forgotten this land and its people?' The Muslim answered: 'If he was far away, it was because he was taking part in the capture of Edessa, which has just been taken by the Muslims.' Some of the Franks who were present mocked him for this answer, but the king told them, 'By God, don't laugh at him! This man always speaks the truth.' A few days later news came from Syria of the conquest of Edessa.[51]

Roger's north African expeditions did not therefore succeed in expanding his dominions, but they did augment the security of the Sicilian coast, because the political instability of north Africa could directly affect the island. They also put a stop to the Arab pirates who, as we have noted above, harassed the trade in the western Mediterranean that was so lucrative for the kingdom of Sicily. At the same time they gave him control over the caravans which brought gold from the Sudan.

Chroniclers like Romuald of Salerno ignored such economic considerations. They could only attribute the military operations in north Africa to Roger being 'great of heart and always full of ambition', and not being content with just Sicily and southern Italy. So he also conquered Africa, and made an advantageous peace treaty with the 'King of Babylon' [or old Cairo], that is the Caliph of Egypt, al-Ḥāfiz. Roger had engraved on his sword the inscription: 'The Apulian and the Calabrian, the Sicilian and the African [all] serve me.' The poetry of an unknown author from Rouen shows that news of Roger's African expeditions had also percolated to Normandy. The Arabic part of a quadrilingual inscription from a gravestone at Palermo of 1148 described Roger as *malik* (lord or king) of Italy, Langobardia, Calabria, Sicily and Ifrīqiya. Similarly, in the introductory clause of a private charter, the provenance and date of which is unknown but which probably comes from the time of Roger II, there is mention of 'the King of Sicily, Italy and the whole of Africa'. However, we are dealing here with isolated examples, which must be interpreted with caution. 'Africa' was never mentioned in the official royal title; hence one ought not to speak of a 'Norman kingdom of Africa'.[52]

---

[51] Ibn al-Athīr, 463–4. The learned Muslim to whom he referred may perhaps have been al-Idrīsī. See below, p. 106.

[52] *Romuald*, 226–7. Similarly *Falcandus*, 5 [*Tyrants*, 57]. *Annales Palidenses*, MGH SS xvi.88. Gervase of Tilbury, *Otia Imperialia*, 943 [or ed. Pauli, *MGH SS* xxvii.381]. Andrea Dandolo, *Chronica*, 243. Kantorowicz (1946), 158n. Krönig (1989). Johns (1987), 90–2,

According to Ibn al-Athīr, Roger would have conquered 'the whole of Africa' if he had not been hampered by a 'great war' with Byzantium. However, this remark both misunderstands the policy the king pursued in north Africa and lays too much emphasis on the conflict with the eastern Roman emperor. The north African bases facilitated the King of Sicily's attacks on Byzantium, but these were only occasional events, which were little more than raids. They were however a demonstration of the battle-readiness of Roger's fleet, especially after attempts to come to an agreement with Byzantium had failed in 1143/4. Once Tripoli had been conquered, the opportunity had come to inflict a salutary lesson on the Byzantine emperor, whose attention was distracted by the Second Crusade.

In the year 1147 the king's ships set sail from Otranto and Brindisi towards Greece. The first conquest was Corfu which surrendered of its own free will since the Byzantines' heavy fiscal demands had made them unpopular there. Cephalonia and the other smaller islands were also taken. They then sailed round the Peleponnese, an unsuccessful attack was made on the fortress of Monemvasia, but other coastal towns such as Nauplion and Modon (Methone) were burned. Next they forced their way into the Gulf of Corinth. The sack of Thebes, a wealthy town which was a centre of silk production, was vividly described by Niketas Choniates:[53]

His [Roger's] army encamped in the land of Kadmos [Boetia], and plundering the towns along the way he came to Thebes of the Seven Gates, which he took by storm, treating her inhabitants savagely. An ancient report that the city spawned wealthy inhabitants sparked an insatiable desire for money within him. His thirst for riches was unquenchable, and his appetite for treasure beyond satisfaction. A measure of his cupidity was his order that all or most of his ships should sink to the third strake from the weight of the monies. He squeezed the artisans dry, and, still inquisitive after filthy lucre, he then subjected the powerful and illustrious of birth, those of venerable age and distinguished in rank, to diverse ill-treatment, indiscriminately and without mercy. He was neither deferential to the reigning

suggests that Roger avoided the title 'King of Africa' so as not to offend the Fatimids. For the document which does use this phrase, see Kehr (1902), 246, although neither the provenance nor the date is given there. William I was described as 'King of Sicily, Italy and Africa' in a number of documents from Molfetta from August 1154 to February 1160, *CDB* VII.37–45, 49, nos. 22, 24–9, 34, and from Cava (October 1157 and January 1158, unpublished, cf. Gregorio (1805), II.84). Both Cerone (1913), 16, and Abulafia (1985), 40ff, argue that Roger intended to integrate his north African conquests into his kingdom; Martin (1994), 115–16, would disagree.

[53] *Romuald*, 227 (Otranto). *Choniates*, 72–3 [Eng. trans. Magoulias, 43–5], (Brindisi). *Annales Cavenses, MGH SS* III.192. *Kinnamos*, 98–100 [Eng. trans. Brand, 80–2]. *Annales Palidenses, MGH SS* XVI.93. Andrea Dandolo, *Chronica*, 242. Otto of Freising, *Gesta Friderici*, I.33, p. 53 [Eng. trans. Mierow, 69–70]. Sigebert of Gembloux, *Continuatio, MGH SS* VI.453. Cf. Caspar (1904), 376–84, Chalandon (1907), 135–8, Lamma (1955–7), I.85ff.

principle of Adrasteia [Divine retribution], nor did he cast a wary glance at his Kadmean victory [i.e. one potentially ruinous to the victor]. Finally, setting out the Sacred Scriptures, he compelled everyone to stand before them and to declare on oath his personal worth, and, after forswearing his rights thereto, to depart. In this fashion he carried off all the gold and silver on the ships, which were also laden with gold-laced textiles. He did not refrain from keeping his hands off the bodies of those whom he had gleaned, but took captive and sailed off with the most eminent according to birth and merit, and chose those women who were comely and well-endowed in form, and who had often bathed in the running waters of Dirce's beautiful spring, and who had styled their tresses and had mastered the weaver's art.

Athens, Chalcis (Eubea) and particularly Corinth fared no better.

As soon as the captain had loaded the riches he had found there onto the triremes, and had taken captive the most comely and deep-bosomed women, he took into his hands the icon of Theodore the Stratelates, the greatest among martyrs, renowned for his miracles, and removed this icon which had been set up in the church of his name . . . One might have said that the Sicilian triremes were not pirate ships but merchantmen of large tonnage, for they were so overloaded with fine merchandise that they were submerged very nearly to the level of the upper rower's bench.

In the spring of 1148 the emperor, Manuel Komnenos (1143–80), prepared a counter-attack. He concluded a truce with the Turkish Sultan of Iconium (Konya) and an alliance with Venice which guaranteed him the support of its fleet in return for confirmation of the city's commercial privileges. The forces involved were impressive – there was talk of a thousand ships and tens of thousands of soldiers. The Sicilian fleet could not match the combined Byzantine and Venetian strength, and was defeated in a battle off Cape Malea, suffering heavy losses. Despite this, a year later, in 1149, Sicilian ships succeeded in forcing an entrance into the harbour of Constantinople; burning the suburbs of the city, firing incendiary projectiles at the imperial palace, and even stealing fruit from the emperor's gardens. On their return journey to Sicily they encountered Byzantine ships carrying tax revenues levied in Crete, and also (probably) the King of France, Louis VII (1137–80), who was returning from the Crusade. The ship carrying the king became caught up in the naval battle, and fell into the hands of Roger's forces, who accorded him honourable treatment, but apart from this episode the Byzantines appear to have had the upper hand. Soon afterwards, in the summer of 1149, they were able to reconquer Corfu, which was strategically important for the control of the Adriatic. There was more at stake for the Byzantine emperor than just defending Greece from Roger. In alliance with the German ruler he sought completely to destroy the 'invader of the empire'

(*invasor imperii*); although for a number of reasons this plan proved to be impracticable.[54]

In contrast to Robert Guiscard, Roger never sought to conquer Constantinople. The war against Byzantium was only of secondary importance for him. The primary goal of his policy was to strengthen the standing of his kingdom among the European powers.

EUROPEAN RELATIONS

The two great powers, the western and eastern empires, regarded the King of Sicily, even after his recognition by Innocent II in 1139, as a parvenu and a usurper of their imperial rights, and they were just waiting for an opportunity to put an end to this state of affairs. To secure entry for his new kingdom into the community of established European monarchies Roger turned to the King of France. Relations with the homeland of his forefathers were still close, and even in the twelfth century knights arrived in search of adventure and booty or churchmen who hoped for posts in the ecclesiastical hierarchy of the new kingdom. Norman monks visited their relatives who had secured their fortune in the south, and then returned to their home abbeys laden with gifts. Pilgrims of course also went there. These contacts were not just from north to south, but also in the other direction. Bohemond I travelled to France in search of reinforcements for his attack on the Byzantine empire, and also found a wife there – a daughter of the King of France. Some Norman nobles who had settled in Sicily came in about 1100 to the Cluniac abbey of St Martial at Limoges, where they had themselves recorded in the commemorative prayers of the monks, and in the early 1130s Roger II's sister Judith founded a Cluniac house at Sciacca, in the modern province of Agrigento. As we have already seen in connection with the schism of 1130, the Abbots of Cluny and Clairvaux, Peter the Venerable and Bernard, did their best, in 1135 and again in 1137, to act as mediators between Roger and Innocent II.[55]

It was therefore logical for the King of Sicily to look to France after the Treaty of Mignano in 1139. The influential Bernard of Clairvaux should have been a suitable go-between for a marriage alliance, for although the

---

[54] *Kinnamos*, 101 [Eng. trans. 82], whose presentation of events is probably to be preferred, assigned victory to the Byzantines; Andrea Dandolo, *Chronica*, 75, to the Venetians. Ibn al-Athīr, 476. See Cohn (1910), 42ff, Rassow (1954), Bernardinello (1975), Lilie (1984), 405ff. *Choniates*, 82–9 [Eng. trans. 48–53], cf. Lilie (1984), 408ff, and for the Byzantine fleet, which in the twelfth century was heavily reliant on mercenaries from the Italian maritime cities, *ibid.*, 613ff. *Romuald*, 227, refers to a Sicilian victory off Cape Malea, but here confused the encounter of 1147 with a later one in 1154, for which see Lilie (1984), 407.

[55] Houben (1992b), 352–4 [reprinted Houben (1996a), 16–18].

chosen bride for Roger's son was not a king's daughter, she was a daughter of a man closely linked with the Cistercian abbot, Count Theobald IV of Blois and Champagne. The latter was a competitor for power and influence with the King of France. He was the son of Adela, the daughter of the first Norman King of England William the Conqueror, who had married Count Stephen I of Blois. After the death of his uncle Henry I (King of England 1100–35), Count Theobald was chosen as his successor, but a coup d'état by his younger brother Stephen deprived him of the throne. On 22 December 1135, two days after Theobald's election, which took place in Normandy, Stephen had himself crowned as King of England in London, with the assistance of his other brother Bishop Henry of Winchester. This fait accompli forced their elder brother to resign his claim. Hence, although the bride chosen for Roger's son was not a king's daughter, she was however the niece of the Norman ruler of England.

To win over Bernard, Roger proposed the foundation of a Cistercian abbey in his kingdom, which would obviously please the abbot. This was the situation in August 1140, as we learn from one of Bernard's letters: Roger's envoys were expected in Montpellier, from whence they would escort the bride, Elizabeth, and some Cistercian monks back to Sicily. The bride's father had received the present of a precious vase (which he would later give to Abbot Suger of St Denis). Three other letters from the correspondence between Bernard and Roger survive, all of which are concerned with the foundation of the first Cistercian house in the kingdom. However, we do not know if Roger went on to found this monastery; nor is it clear whether the house concerned was the abbey of St Mary of Sambucina in Calabria, which later claimed this distinction – for the documents in question have been shown to be forgeries.[56]

It is possible that the marriage was postponed while Roger undertook negotiations with Byzantium, for early in 1143 he was trying to obtain the hand of one of the emperor's daughters for his son. It is probable that for an imperial princess only his heir, Duke Roger, would have been considered. The negotiations soon failed, since the eastern Roman ruler did not consider the King of Sicily sufficiently well born for an alliance.

[56] *The Letters of St Bernard*, pp. 348–51, nos. 276–9; no. 279, probably 1139–40, antedates the others, from c. 1142. Suger, *De Administratione*, ed. Panofsky (1979), 79. This has been identified with a glass vase which is today in the Louvre, see Johns (1995), 28n. Alberic of Trois Fontaines, 841, called the count's third daughter (Elizabeth or Isabelle) 'a certain duchess in remote parts', and recorded that she later married William Gouet, Lord of Montmirail and Perche-Gouet (near Chartres), with whom she had two daughters. See Thompson (1997), 306–7; for Theobald and Stephen, see Davis (1967), 15–17. For the Cistercians, see Dupré Theseider (1956), 207ff, Kölzer (1994), 95–7, Houben (1995a), 76–7.

The marriage between Duke Roger and Elizabeth took place at the latest in 1143, but it was probably childless. The duke had already sired two sons, Tancred and William, who were born around 1140, the products of a liason with a daughter of Accardus, Lord of Lecce, but this was obviously no impediment to a marriage with a spouse of appropriate status. In any event, after Duke Roger's death in 1149 Elizabeth returned to France where she married again.[57]

A new opportunity to consolidate Sicily's position among the European monarchies was presented by the Second Crusade. Pope Eugenius III directed his summons to the Crusade in 1146 primarily to Louis VII of France, and the latter made wide-ranging preparations. He made contact with the German king Conrad III (1137–52) and the Hungarian monarch Géza II (1141–62) to secure a route by land, seeking right of way and provisioning for his army. For a possible sea route he had recourse to the King of Sicily, who immediately took this opportunity not to be outdone by his fellow monarchs. Not only did he promise ships and provisions, but also that either he or his son would take part in the Crusade.

The French Crusaders gathered at Etampes in February 1147, where they held an assembly to decide whether to take the land or the sea route to the Holy Land. The land route was chosen. According to Louis VII's chaplain, Odo of Deuil, who is the most important source for these events (although often highly prejudiced), messengers from King Roger warned in vain of the unreliability of the Byzantines. However, his account of the Second Crusade was written entirely from the perspective of the unhappy ending of the expedition, for which he held the Byzantines to be primarily responsible. Underlying this was the view that Louis would have been better to have allied with Roger against Byzantium; an idea to which the King of France could not be won over, since the Crusade was his primary goal. The Byzantine emperor, Manuel, also discovered this when in October 1147 he suggested in vain to the French king an alliance against Roger.[58]

---

[57] *Kinnamos*, 91–2 [Eng. trans. 75–6]. *Romuald*, 227. Duke Roger only came to Apulia in April/May 1139; Tancred cannot therefore have been conceived before then, nor born before February 1140, and his brother William therefore not before the early months of 1141. *Falcandus*, 51 [*Tyrants*, 105] is therefore probably in error when suggesting that William was almost [*fere*] twenty-two in 1161, and similarly Reisinger (1992), 11, who argues that Tancred was born 'between 1134 and 1138, if not earlier'. A charter of Godfrey III of Lecce of December 1146, preserved only in a sixteenth-century copy, said that Accard, who was attested for the last time in March 1137, was sent into exile by Roger II and died at Jerusalem; see Vallone (1994), 222–3 no. 2. This document is in its present form undoubtedly a forgery, but it is possible that a genuine document lies behind it. Cf. Poso (1996) 47ff.

[58] Odo of Deuil, *De Profectione Ludovici*, 10–11, 13–15. Later on Odo wrote of Louis being advised to write to Roger to request his help in an attack on the Greeks, 'but alas for

The eastern Roman ruler had better luck in his plans against Roger with Conrad III. Manuel's predecessor, John II Komnenos (1118–43), had already dispatched envoys to the German court, late in 1139 or early in 1140. The German–Byzantine alliance was sealed by the marriage between Conrad's sister-in-law, Bertha of Sulzbach, with John's youngest son Manuel. Two of the Staufen envoys were noblemen who had been exiled from the kingdom of Sicily, Count Alexander of Conversano and Prince Robert of Capua. Then, some months after the bride had arrived in Constantinople, escorted by two of Roger's bitterest enemies, Robert of Capua and Count Roger of Ariano, John Komnenos met his death during a military expedition, on 8 April 1143, and the treaty fell into abeyance. Meanwhile both the emperor's eldest sons had died, and Manuel succeeded in displacing his only surviving older brother Isaac and securing the throne for himself. However, this altered the preconditions for the marriage treaty, for since the bride was not a king's daughter, she was no longer of the appropriate status to be Manuel's wife. He therefore demanded Apulia as her dowry, something which Conrad had no wish to hand over.[59]

In an attempt to bring pressure to bear upon the Staufen ruler, Manuel appears to have opened negotiations with Roger. The latter hoped that a treaty with Byzantium might be sealed by the marriage of one of his sons with a Byzantine princess; something which would undoubtedly have put an end to the danger of a combined German–Byzantine attack on his kingdom. However, these negotiations, which on the Byzantine side were unlikely to have been very serious, soon failed because of the scale of the demands made by the King of Sicily. The Byzantine historian Kinnamos reported that Roger had bribed the eastern Roman envoy Basil Cheros to agree to a treaty that, among other things, recognized him as being of equal rank to the Byzantine emperor. The eastern Roman sovereign naturally refused to make such a concession, and his ambassador only escaped punishment because he died on his way home to Constantinople.[60]

---

us . . . their words did not prevail!', *ibid.*, 58–9. Roger had sent his fleet to Greece in 1147 in the hope of conquering Byzantium in alliance with the French crusading army (perhaps anticipating the sort of Frankish empire that was later to be created in 1204). There were certainly some in Louis's army who supported such a concept, notably the Cistercian Bishop Godfrey of Langres, a cousin of Bernard of Clairvaux, Odo, 68–9. Lamma (1955–7) I.73–4.

[59] Otto of Freising, *Chronica*, VII.28, p. 354, *Gesta Friderici*, I.25, pp. 37–43 [Eng. trans. Mierow, 54–9]. For the arrival of Bertha at Constantinople late in 1142, and the continued negotiations with Conrad, see Angold (1984), 162–3, cf. Lamma (1955–7), I.34ff, Magdalino (1993), 46–53, Lilie (1984), 387–95.

[60] *Kinnamos*, 91–2 [Eng. trans. 75–6]. *Romuald*, 227. Caspar (1904), 362–4, Chalandon (1907), II.129, Lilie (1984), 193–5.

The Byzantines' hand was forced by Roger's growing activity in the Mediterranean. In 1145 Conrad III declared Bertha to be his adopted daughter. The question of the dowry was for the moment ignored, and hence nothing now stood in the way of a marriage alliance. The marriage between the emperor Manuel and Bertha (who adopted the Greek name Irene) was celebrated in January 1146. Byzantium and the papacy hoped that Conrad would undertake an expedition to Italy, which would, at the very least, have put a brake on Roger, but the Second Crusade, to which Bernard of Clairvaux recruited Conrad at Christmas 1146, rendered these plans fruitless. For Roger, a serious danger had been removed.

The Crusade ended in a débacle. Conrad III fell ill, and in the winter of 1147–8 had to seek medical care and convalescence in Byzantium. It was probably during this period that he gave verbal consent – written would have compromised him with the pope – to allow Bertha–Irene to have Apulia as her dowry. This was confirmed towards the end of 1148 in the so-called Treaty of Thessalonica. Conrad appears to have later regretted this concession, and to secure the return of Apulia he sought to marry his son Henry to a niece of Manuel, which would in practice have regained Bertha's dowry (as the bride's portion in the new marriage). After Henry's death in 1150, Conrad may even have considered marrying the Byzantine princess himself, but his death in 1152 put an end to this plan.

To reduce the danger of a combined German and Byzantine attack, Roger encouraged the opposition to Conrad within Germany. Welf VI, with whom the king had probably already agreed an alliance in 1145/6, received a friendly welcome in Sicily on his return from the Holy Land in 1148/9. According to a denunciatory letter from Rome (which was included in the letter collection of Guibald of Stavelot), intended to blacken the reputation of Eugenius III at the court of King Conrad, Roger had provided Welf with horses and servants, and given him letters for Dukes Frederick (Barbarossa) of Swabia, Henry the Lion (of Saxony) and Conrad of Zähringen, as well as for the latter's son Berthold, with the intention of stirring up a revolt against Conrad in Germany. Also noteworthy is a rumour reported by Otto of Freising concerning the death of Conrad III: that Italian doctors had been bribed by Roger to cause the German king's demise.[61]

Roger's relations with the papacy remained tense. When in 1142 Innocent II raised objections to the king's appointment of bishops, the

---

[61] *Historia Welforum*, cc. 26–7, p. 52. Godfrey of Viterbo, *Pantheon*, MGH SS XXII.261. *Annales Herbipolenses*, MGH SS XVI.7. For the dating, see Feldmann (1971), 21. Guibald of Stavelot, *Letter* no. 147, *Monumenta Corbeiensia*, 228–9. Reuter (1996), 46–7, is sceptical about the credibility of this letter. Otto of Freising, *Gesta Friderici*, 1.70, p. 98 [Eng. trans. Mierow, 110].

latter's reply rang out loud and clear. 'This has been the practice since the time of Dukes Robert Guiscard, Roger and William, and we have no intention of renouncing this custom – we intend rather to hold fast to it.' It was around this time that the Byzantine theologian and canonist Nilos Doxapatres, who was living in exile in Palermo, composed on Roger's instructions a work in which the Roman primacy and the pope's ecclesiastical jurisdiction over Sicily were called into question. One should therefore hardly be surprised that Innocent's successor Celestine II (1143–4) refused investiture to Roger. The latter responded immediately, as is made clear from the account of Falco of Benevento, which survives only in a later, revised, version in the chronicle of St Mary of Ferraria (a Cistercian abbey near Vairano, in the modern-day province of Caserta):

> The king wanted the pope to confirm the kingdom to him, as had once been conceded by his predecessor. He strove to obtain this, not by requests and persuasion but by giving him no alternative, and he hoped to attain this for himself by the betrayal of the Beneventans. What more? He took away the immunity which he had granted to them in the time of Anacletus and that of Innocent, when he had freed the Beneventans from the exactions, dues and services to which they had been made subject by the Normans. He also got the neighbouring barons to harass the townspeople unmercifully. The Beneventans sent envoys to the king to beg him to observe the immunity which he had given them. The king sent Robert his chancellor to Benevento to inspect his privilege, but the latter not only read it but retained it, nor would he return it before it had been copied and shown to the king [*quod videns tenuit nec reddidit, priusquam illud rescribat et regi ostendat*]. The chancellor then left Benevento, taking the privilege with him without permission [*inlicentiatus*]. The citizens were harassed and made to suffer – indeed they were afraid to go outside the town. The Archbishop of Benevento set off to see the pope, but was arrested while on his journey.

The pope was forced to give ground. Early in 1144 he sent an embassy to Palermo, but at the beginning of March, before anything could be successfully negotiated, Celestine died.[62]

It would appear that Roger placed great hopes in his successor, Cardinal Gerard of Santa Croce, who took the pontifical name of Lucius II (1144–5). So at least claimed Romuald of Salerno, according to whom the latter was a 'good friend' of the king. We do not know on what the chronicler based this assertion. One can only speculate that Roger knew Gerard

---

[62] *Chronica de Ferraria*, 27. Deér (1972), 237ff. Kamp (1979), 121–3. For Nilos Doxapatres, see below p. 102. Brühl (1978), 106ff, (1983), 89ff. Roger II, *Diplomata*, 131–2 no. +47, interprets the account in the sense that the chancellor 'confiscated' the privilege, which he had recognized as an obvious forgery. This document was the one copied by *Falco*, 198–200. For the section of Falco's chronicle known only via the thirteenth-century *Chronica de Ferraria*, see Loud (1993), 178–80, D'Angelo (1994), 174ff.

personally and had gained the impression that the latter was well disposed
towards him. Honorius II had appointed Gerard as Rector of Benevento
in November 1128, but after a rebellion by the citizens in August 1129
both cardinal and pope had left the town. Honorius had then gone to
meet Roger at Leocabante, near Montefusco, to the south of Benevento,
and it may have been then that Gerard had encountered the later king. It
would seem unlikely that he can have had any later contact with Roger,
for in the schism of 1130 he was on the side of Innocent II, and later we
find him in the entourage of Lothar III.[63]

The king and pope met in early June 1144 at Ceprano, on the border
between the papal lands and the kingdom of Sicily. Roger hoped that he
would be able, in a face-to-face interview, to come to an agreement with
Lucius II, but, as soon became clear, the latter was unwilling to make
concessions. Dispute arose over the principality of Capua, which the pope
sought to restore. Roger, however, had no intention of surrendering it.
The negotiations made no progress. The king sought in vain to put Lucius
under pressure by summoning more troops. After fourteen days there was
a complete breach. Roger's soldiers started to invade papal territory, but
neither side wanted a war. The pope was worried about the situation
in Rome, where the communal movement was growing ever stronger,
while the king needed his troops for his north African operations. Hence,
towards the end of 1144, they agreed upon a seven-year truce.[64]

Pope Eugenius III (1145–53), a Cistercian, also had reservations about
Roger, which the efforts of Louis VII did little to alter. The King of
France had become involved in a naval battle between the Byzantines and
Normans during his return journey from the Holy Land. Roger's forces
treated him with respect, and brought him to Calabria where he arrived
on 29 July 1149. Queen Eleanor, who had accompanied her husband on
the Crusade, was carried by unfavourable winds to Palermo, where Roger
welcomed her kindly, and then had her escorted to Calabria to be reunited
with her husband. He himself also left Sicily, anxious not to let the chance
slip for an encounter with the King of France. The two sovereigns met at

---

[63] *Romuald*, 228: 'When King Roger heard of the election of Pope Lucius he greatly rejoiced, because the latter had been his *compater* and friend.' Caspar (1904), 337, interpreted
compater as 'a spiritual relationship, perhaps membership of the confraternity of a Ben-
eventan monastery'; he was therefore thinking of a prayer fraternity. But in that case the
chronicler would have spoken rather of a *confrater*, not *compater*, which here signifies just
'good friend' [see the *Mittellateinisches Wörterbuch*, II.1040. *Falco*, 104. Vehse (1930–1),
137. Hüls (1977), 164].

[64] *Chronica de Ferraria*, 28: 'the king wishing in the meanwhile to acquire the African kingdom and Tripoli in Barbary, conceded and confirmed a truce'. *Romuald*, 228. See also a
letter of Lucius II to Peter the Venerable of 22 September 1144, JL 8653, *It. Pont.* VIII.44
nos. 167–8. Deér (1972), 238–9.

Potenza for three days in late August 1149, although we know nothing of what was discussed at this conference. Roger probably sought to stoke up Louis's resentment of the Byzantines, and since the French ruler was on his way to meet the pope, it is likely that the King of Sicily asked him to act as a mediator with Eugenius III.[65]

Some months earlier, perhaps in the middle of 1149, Roger had placed troops at the pope's disposal to combat the communal movement at Rome. A letter from 'the Senate and People of Rome' to Conrad III claimed that Eugenius responded by granting the King of Sicily the right to use episcopal regalia (staff, ring, dalmatic, mitre and sandals), and also renounced his own right to send legates into the kingdom. This, however, is certainly untrue. The Roman communal movement, which was hostile to the pope, was seeking to discredit him in the eyes of the German ruler. In July 1150 Eugenius and Roger met at Ceprano. They were able to come to an agreement on a number of ecclesiastical issues, as for example the consecration of those bishops who had up until then remained only as 'bishops-elect'; whether they would now receive consecration would depend upon the results of an inquiry into the individual circumstances of their elections. Other problems, such as the recognition of Cefalù as a bishopric and of the metropolitan rights of Palermo remained unsolved, even though the concession of the *pallium* (the lambs' wool scarf that was the sign of archiepiscopal status) to the archbishop and the confirmation of his right to perform the royal coronation left the way open for the latter's future elevation to be the metropolitan of the kingdom. There was, however, no investiture of Roger by the pope, for this act would have signified the formal recognition of his kingdom.[66]

Roger intensified his contacts with France. The king had some time previously gained the goodwill of Peter the Venerable through his favour to Cluniac monasticism, although its diffusion within southern Italy remained

---

[65] *Kinnamos*, II.19, pp. 87–8 [Eng. trans. Brand, 72]. 'Anonymus ad Petrum', c. 28, p. 19. Sigebert of Gembloux, *Continuatio, MGH SS* VI.454. Andrea Dandolo, *Chronica*, 243. *Annales Casinenses, MGH SS* XIX.310. Caspar (1904), 392–3, 403–6. Chalandon (1907), II.143–4. Cohn (1910), 44–5. A number of modern authors suggest that Roger proposed a new Crusade to the French king 'with the intention of turning it against the Greeks', Mayer (1988), 104; but this is mere supposition.

[66] Guibald of Stavelot, *Letter* no. 214, *Monumenta Corbeiensia*, 332–4, also in Otto of Freising, *Gesta Friderici*, I.29, pp. 45–8 [Eng. trans. Mierow, 61–3]. Deér (1964), 136ff [reprinted Deér (1977), 455ff]. Brühl (1983b). Horn (1992), 71ff. The rumour that Roger had been granted the right to use episcopal regalia was perhaps the origin of the story told by the English chronicler Ralph Niger (d. c. 1200), who alleged that, after being imprisoned by Roger, Pope Innocent II had granted him both the royal dignity and his own mitre, *Ex Radulfi Nigri Chronica Universali, MGH SS* XXVII.335. *The Historia Pontificalis of John of Salisbury*, 66–7, c. 32. *It. Pont.* VIII.45 no. 173.

limited. The Abbot of Cluny numbered him among the most important benefactors of his congregation, enrolling him along with the German, French, English and Spanish kings. He considered that, in direct contrast to the chaos of northern and central Italy, the kingdom of Sicily was comparable with that of Solomon, the prince of peace. Around 1150 Peter requested Roger to attack Byzantium, which deserved punishment for its 'betrayal' of the Second Crusade. He hoped for an end to the dispute with Conrad III and the creation of a grand Franco-Sicilian–German alliance:[67]

Furthermore, we make known to your royal majesty that we greatly lament the conflicts that are going on between you and the lord king of the Germans or emperor of the Romans. Both I and many others are strongly of the opinion that this discord is harmful to the Latin kingdoms and to the Christian Faith. For we have heard many times and often how your military power has brought benefits to the Church of God in the lands of his enemies, that is those of the Saracens. Moreover, we believe that greater advantages would accrue if you and the aforesaid king were united in a lasting peace and concord. There is also another matter which has long been of concern to us, and to almost all of our fellow countrymen in France, in seeking such a peace for you; namely the wicked, unheard of and disgraceful betrayal by the Greeks and their miserable king of our pilgrims, that is those in the army of God.

I shall speak of what I have in mind. If it should be necessary, insofar as is appropriate for a monk, I would not refuse to perish, if the justice of God would, through the death of one of his servants, revenge that of so many men, both nobles and commoners, indeed the flower of almost the whole of France and Germany, destroyed by wretched treason. Moreover, I can see no Christian prince under Heaven through whom this work can be carried out who is better, more suitable nor more effective than yourself, nor so acceptable to Heaven and earth. For, by the grace of God, I say this not in flattery but on account of your outstanding deeds and from the general opinion about you. You are wiser of mind, better endowed with riches, and more practised in courage than other princes, and furthermore you are physically closer to this place. So therefore, rise up, good prince, to fulfill what not just I with my voice am saying, but what is the wish both of myself and of everyone else. Rise up to help the people of God, zealously to uphold the law of God like the Machabees, to revenge so many insults, injuries and deaths, and such effusion of blood in the army of God, shed so impiously.

I myself am ready, should an opportunity present itself, to go immediately to the aforesaid emperor, along with anybody else I can recruit, to secure the peace of which I spoke above. I shall try with all my strength and all my care to restore and confirm between you and him a peace that is so pleasing to God.

---

[67] *The Letters of Peter the Venerable*, 231, 330–1 nos. 90 [1139–40] and 131 (c. 1150, written after the death of Duke Roger of Apulia, 2 May 1149). For the contents, see Hehl (1980), 149.

The attempts of the Abbot of Cluny to broker a peace between Conrad III and Roger II were no more successful than those of Bernard of Clairvaux had been. The German king would not abandon his alliance with Byzantium. Roger's attempts to negotiate directly with him also failed. Anti-Byzantine plans were probably the purpose of the letters sent to Roger by Abbot Suger of St Denis, who had acted as regent in France while Louis VII was abroad, and who was the most energetic proponent of a new Crusade. Unfortunately, the only two letters which survive from this correspondence contain nothing more than flowery compliments. 'The rest', as it says at one point, has been entrusted to the messengers to convey by word of mouth.[68]

The pope played no part in these plans for an attack on the eastern emperor. Eugenius III had no wish to jeopardize his good relations with Conrad III, since he expected that the latter would provide him with more effective help against the communal movement at Rome than had Roger, whose expansionist policies he mistrusted. Furthermore, after the experience of the Second Crusade, he had grave doubts as to whether a renewal of the enterprise would succeed. When Bernard of Clairvaux informed him that he had been chosen, at Chartres in 1150, as the leader of a new, anti-Byzantine, Crusade, Eugenius reacted coldly and gave only the most grudging support. In addition, the pope rejected the attempts by Bernard of Clairvaux and Theodwin, Cardinal Bishop of St Rufina, to secure a rapprochement between the Sicilian and the German sovereigns. The pope's opposition cut the ground from under the anti-Byzantine plans of Suger, and the latter finally abandoned them, not least because he found very little support for them in France either.[69]

Roger consolidated his good relations with France by marriage alliances. After the death of his wife Elvira in 1135 he had at first no intention of remarrying. He had five legitimate sons and the succession to the throne was assured. But a few years later he had to face the deaths, one after another, of his sons. Tancred died c. 1138, Alfonso in 1144, Henry probably before 1145, and finally in 1149 also his eldest son Roger, on whom the king had placed great hopes. Only William was left, and he, according to 'Hugo Falcandus' was the least able of all Roger's sons. For 'Falcandus' this was 'the debt due to fate' (*fati debitum*), which the king had to pay as the

---

[68] For Bernard's efforts, aided by Theodwin, Cardinal Bishop of Porto, who had been one of the legates attached to Conrad's crusading expedition, see Guibald of Stavelot, *Letter* no. 252, *Monumenta Corbeiensia*, 377–8; there is also a reference to an embassy from Roger to Conrad in *ibid.*, 480 no. 252. For the exchange of letters with Suger, *PL* 186 cols.1415–17 nos. 143 and 146.

[69] Eugenius III to Suger (19 June 1150), JL 9398 = *PL* 180 col.1419 no. 390. *Monumenta Corbeiensia*, 400–1 no. 273. *Vita Sugerii*, *PL* 186 cols. 1204–6. Hehl (1980), 152ff.

price of his success. Archbishop Romuald of Salerno saw it as the will of God, who punished His son (Roger) in order to prevent him becoming proud.[70]

In any case, the king now had to look for a new wife. About 1149 he married Sibylla, a sister of Duke Odo II of Burgundy (1143–62), but she died while giving birth to a still-born child in 1150. As a result Roger married again in 1151, to Beatrice, a daughter of a Lotharingian count, Gunther of Rethel. She was, through her mother, a daughter of Count Geoffrey of Namur, related to the Zähringen family and the Counts of Hennegau. No sons were born of this union, but only one daughter, Constance, whose birth Roger did not live to see. William, the heir to the throne, was married, round about 1150, to Margaret, daughter of King Garcia IV Ramirez of Navarre (1134–50); her mother was Margaret de l'Aigle, a daughter of the Norman Count Geoffrey of Mortagne (Perche). The sources are silent about the precise circumstances of this marriage. It was, however, the case that all these women came from a western, French or Spanish, background.[71]

At Easter 1151 Roger raised William to be co-ruler, having already designated him as Duke of Apulia, and thus the heir to the throne, after the death of his eldest son. Although William was anointed as king by the Archbishop of Palermo, Roger himself personally carried out the coronation, at least according to the well-informed pseudo-Falcandus. Before this, William had sworn to maintain peace and justice, to honour the Church, and to serve his father 'as his liege lord'. This ceremony, performed without consulting the pope, guaranteed the succession. The king was prepared to accept the resulting deterioration of his relations with Rome – he had anyway consolidated his rule not only without the pope, but despite him. It was probably at this time that Roger invested his illegitimate son Simon with the principality of Taranto, a grant that William later annulled, after his father's death, on the grounds that an illegitimate son could, at most, be made a count.[72]

---

[70] *Falcandus*, 6 [*Tyrants*, 58–9], *Romuald*, 230. For the date of his wife's death, see Houben (1993a). After the death of Alfonso (10 October 1144), William was invested with the principality of Capua and the duchy of Naples, and after his eldest brother Roger's death (2 May 1149), he was also made Duke of Apulia.

[71] *Romuald*, 231. Sibylla died on 16 September 1150, *Necrologio di S. Matteo di Salerno*, ed. Garufi, 136. Hiestand (1993), 53ff. For Margaret of Navarre, see *Tyrants*, 137n and table II. According to *Romuald*, 242 [*Tyrants*, 225–6] the marriage had taken place when William (born 1121/2) had been prince of Capua, hence after 1144, and thus before he became co-king in April 1151, and probably before he acquired the duchy of Apulia in 1149.

[72] *Historia Pontificalis*, 68–9 c. 34: 'without consulting the pope... summoning the archbishops and bishops to Palermo for the Easter celebrations, he had his son consecrated king by the bishop [*sic*] of Palermo. But before consecration he solemnly undertook in a

The pope, meanwhile, came to an agreement with Conrad III who promised that in return for his imperial coronation he would force the submission of the city of Rome and make no territorial concessions in Italy to Byzantium. However, before the final details could be settled, Conrad died on 15 February 1152. His successor, Frederick I Barbarossa, moved quickly to conclude the interrupted negotiations; in March the so-called Treaty of Konstanz was confirmed on oath, and there it was laid down that the Staufen ruler would conclude no peace with the King of Sicily without papal agreement. Eugenius III made no equivalent pledges, but his undertaking to protect the *honor imperii* (the integrity of the empire and imperial office) indirectly excluded an alliance with the Norman monarch. As he was later to demonstrate, Barbarossa considered that the whole of Italy belonged to his empire. He only abandoned his intention to conquer southern Italy and drive out the Norman 'invader of the empire' (*invasor imperii*) when he eventually became convinced that this project was impractical.[73]

public assembly at his father's precept that he would preserve peace and justice all his days, show reverence for the Church of God, and throughout his father's life obey him as lord. This undertaking he confirmed with an oath.' *Falcandus*, 7 [*Tyrants*, 59]: 'his father placed the diadem on his head and made him a partner in sovereignty'. *Romuald*, 231. *Annales Casinenses*, *MGH SS* XIX.310. For William's oath, Ménager (1959), 458ff. But one cannot talk of a royal election, as does Cuozzo (1989a), 657, even if this took place in an assembly of vassals. For Simon, *Falcandus*, 51 [*Tyrants*, 103–4].

[73] Engels (1987), Houben (1992a)

4

BETWEEN EAST AND WEST

CULTURE

Where are you hurrying off to? To where do you wish to return? For the wise man 'everywhere is his home, as the whole world is open to the bird' [Ovid, *Fasti* 1.493]. In Sicily you have the Syracusan and Argolian libraries; there is no lack of Latin philosophy. Theodore of Brindisi, the great authority on Greek literature is available; your Aristippus is here, who even if he is not the cutting edge, you can use as the whetstone. You have the *Mechanica* of the philosopher Hero [of Alexandria] to hand ... the *Optica* of Euclid ... the *Apodictice* of Aristotle on the first principles of knowledge ... the *Philosophica* of Anaxagoras, of Aristotle, of Themistios, of Plutarch and of other famous philosophers are [also] in your hands. But perhaps you [already] have a *summa* of these works; in which case you may consult a good work devoted to the study of medicine, and I can also offer you theological, mathematical and meteorological tracts [*theoreumata*].

Why waste time listing the wonders of these great names? Of course, you can find these texts and others which are comparable in England. Even allowing this to be true, do you admit to a King William? There is not such another one in the world, whose court is a school, whose retinue is a *Gymnasium*, whose own words are philosophical pronouncements, whose questions are unanswerable, whose solutions leave nothing to be discussed, and whose study leaves nothing untried, whose lordship is acclaimed by Sicily, Calabria, Lucania, Campania, Apulia, Libya and Africa, whose victorious hand stretches out to Dalmatia, Thessaly, Greece, Rhodes, Crete, Cyprus, Cyrene and Egypt, whose already glorious deeds are rendered even more glorious and shining by his father, that great [King] Roger. If such advice from your Aristippus does not move you, and you do not abandon the journey you have planned, then fare you well! Be careful that you do not cheat yourself. As recreation for this long journey, take what I can give you, the *Phaedo* of Plato on the immortality of the soul, which I have translated from Greek into Latin [*ab Argivis in Ytalicas translatum litteras*], which I began in the camp as the

aforementioned king besieged the Samnite city of Benevento [1156], and which I completed in Palermo.[1]

This vivid presentation of Sicily as a centre of philosophy and natural science comes in the dedicatory letter of the Latin translation of the *Phaedo* by Henry Aristippus, written in 1160, and lamenting the departure of an English friend. He particularly praised the court of King William I (1154–66) and the monarch's own interest in questions of philosophy and natural science; a lord who dominated the Mediterranean, the birthplace of western culture, as heir of his father, 'that great Roger'.

Aristippus, from c. 1155 archdeacon of Catania cathedral, was not a native Greek speaker but was an excellent translator. He translated from the Greek the *Meno* and *Phaedo* of Plato – the first time in the Middle Ages that the work of this philosopher had been translated into Latin – the fourth book of the 'Meteorology' of Aristotle, and some of the commentaries that related to it. From an embassy to Constantinople in 1158–60 Aristippus brought back various Greek manuscripts as a present from the emperor, Manuel Komnenos, including the *Almagest* of Ptolemy and perhaps also the 'Prophecies of the Eritraen Sibyl'. A translator, whose name is unknown to us, was travelling from Salerno to Sicily to consult this manuscript of Ptolemy when he encountered Aristippus, who was, not without some peril, observing an eruption of Mount Etna. The translator also mentioned the *amiratus* Eugenius, 'a man most learned in Greek and Arabic, and not unskilled in Latin'.[2]

---

[1] *Phaedo, interprete Henrico Aristippo*, ed. L. Minio-Paluelli (London 1950), 89–90, cited also in Giunta (1950), 101–2. Haskins (1927), 168ff, identified the recipient, *Roboratus*, as Robert of Cricklade, prior of St Frideswide, Oxford (pre-1141–post-1171), who visited Catania and Syracuse c. 1155 [Benedict of Peterborough, *Miracula S. Thomae*, II.52, in *Materials for the History of St Thomas Becket*, II.97–8]. Jamison (1938), 39, did not accept this. See also Berschin (1988), 232–3, Wilson (1983), 212–16. Recently, Morpurgo (1997), 131–2, has identified *Roboratus* with Robert of Selby, but this is clearly impossible for the latter had died in 1152.

[2] Franceschini (1962), with discussion of sources, Cavallo (1980), 199–200, Berschin (1988), 233–4. The prologue to the translation of the Almagest is in Haskins (1927), 191–3. For Eugenius (c. 1130–1202), whose mother-tongue was Greek, see Jamison (1957) and Falkenhausen (1993), especially 504 for the Eritraean Sibyl. According to Lemay (1987), 428ff, the translation of the Almagest was made at Roger II's court c. 1150 by Herman of Carinthia. The key argument for this thesis is the date of the manuscript, Vat. Pal. Lat. 1371, and in particular of the rubric on fol. 41r [*Incipit liber Claudii Ptolomei mathematicorum*] and its marginal annotation: 'translated in the city of Palermo in the time of King Roger by Herman from Greek to Latin'. Lemay (1987), 464, 469, dates this to the middle of the twelfth century, but it would appear more likely that the script of the manuscript is no earlier than the 1190s or the first quarter of the thirteenth century, while the rubric was added later on in the thirteenth, or even in the early fourteenth, century, while the marginal annotation is later still.

From the early Middle Ages onwards Salerno had been a centre of medical study, from where Graeco-Arabic knowledge had been spread to the west. Here Archbishop Alfanus I (1058–85), a former monk of Montecassino, had translated Greek medical works into Latin. Alfanus sponsored Constantine *Africanus* (d. 1085), an Arab Christian born in Carthage, who became a monk at Montecassino about 1078 and there translated specialist Arabic medical texts. The English philosopher and translator Adelard of Bath, who travelled widely in the Mediterranean region, also came to Salerno. He dedicated one of his works to Bishop William of Syracuse (c.1105–16), whom he described as 'most learned in all mathematical studies' (*omnium mathematicarum artium eruditissimum*). One may also suspect that natural science manuscripts were available in the library at Syracuse mentioned by Aristippus, and that these were in the main Greek manuscripts.[3]

Given this background, we should not be surprised that the court in Palermo under William I was 'a centre of Greek studies in philosophy and natural science'. His father had laid the foundations for this, and we should stress once more the latter's interest in natural science. Roger was educated by exponents of Graeco-Byzantine culture, heard Greek preachers and used Byzantine symbols of lordship. On his military campaigns he behaved like a Byzantine general, distributing bribes, preferring to use Fabian tactics and to avoid as much as he could the risks of pitched battles. It has been suggested that he had some knowledge of Byzantine writings on warfare, as for example the military manual composed by the Emperor Leo VI the Wise (886–912), which could have been one of the books he studied during his schooling. But we do not know how good Roger's knowledge of Greek really was.[4]

One cannot now reach any definite conclusions concerning the court library of Roger and his successors. It has been suggested that the Greek manuscripts of natural science in the library of Boniface VIII came originally from Palermo, and were given by Charles I of Anjou to Pope Clement IV after the battle of Benevento in 1266.[5] However, this

[3] D'Alverny (1982), 422–6, Falkenhausen (1984), Hettinger (1990), Turner (1986), 43–4, Kamp (1995), 73–4, and on Adelard, see Folkerts (1993), Burnett (1997), 17–32. Adelard, who translated the 'Elements' of Euclid and Arabic writings on astronomy, seems not to have derived his knowledge of Arabic during his stay in Sicily, but rather somewhere else in the Mediterranean during the 1120s. On the other hand, Burnett stresses the influence that the Greek learning of southern Italy had on his work.
[4] Berschin (1988), 232–3, cf. Breccia (1995), 261: 'Roger II is a true model of a Byzantine commander.' By contrast, Falkenhausen (1996), 244, suggests that the Norman rulers were unlikely to have understood complicated Byzantine encomia.
[5] Derenzini (1976), Canart (1978), 50, Cavallo (1980), 201–2, Cavallo (1982), 36–7, Berschin (1988), 263.

hypothesis has been proved to be unfounded. These manuscripts, most of which were written in Byzantium during the ninth and tenth centuries, were probably first brought to the west during the second half of the thirteenth century, perhaps by the Dominican William of Moerbeke (d. before 1286), who, in part through the encouragement of Thomas Aquinas, developed an extensive translation operation.[6]

A commentary on the 'Ethiopian Stories of Theagenes and Charicleia', a romance of Heliodoros (third century AD), has also been cited as proof of a flourishing interest in Greek literature at Roger's court. The author, the philosopher Philip, wrote that he produced his commentary with the encouragement of a group of intellectuals who were extremely fond of such pagan love stories. Since Roger's court preacher Philagathos Keramides was before his conversion called Philip, and in a number of manuscripts containing his sermons was referred to as 'the philosopher Philip', he has been taken to be the same man as the author of the commentary. However, this cannot now be maintained, for it has been shown that the commentary on Heliodoros was compiled in Byzantium during the fifth century by a Neoplatonic philosopher called Philip, who had no connection whatsoever with Roger's court. Only a few Greek poems are known to have been composed there, and anyway knowledge of these appears to have been restricted to a small circle around George of Antioch.[7]

The preacher mentioned above, Philagathos Keramides, did reach a wider audience than these poems, for he preached not only in the cathedral and the palace chapel at Palermo but also in Calabria. For him the King of Sicily was of equal status with the Byzantine emperor. On Palm Sunday

---

[6] Paravicini Bagliani (1983), shows that the sigla *And.* on some of these manuscripts cannot be interpreted as showing their provenance (i.e. as an abbreviation for *Andegavensis* = Anjou); it was more probably written during the cataloguing of Boniface VIII's library in 1295, and was intended as an indication of authorship (*And.* = Andrea) of the Latin title of the codex, necessary for those compiling the catalogue who may not have known Greek. Cuozzo (1995a), 44ff, has a different, but unconvincing, interpretation. In addition neither the Madrid Skylitzes, an illustrated copy of this Byzantine chronicle (for the years 811–1057, with an anonymous continuation 1057–79), cf. Ševčenko (1984), 35–6, nor Cod. Vat. gr. 300, one of the hands of which Cavallo (1980), 35–6, has identified as being that of the scribe of a Greek charter of 1142 written in the royal chancery [Cusa, *Diplomi*, 525ff = Ca. 150], are now believed to be linked with the royal court, but rather with Greek laymen in Calabria, such as the doctor Philip Xeros of Reggio. See Lucà (1993), 36ff.

[7] Canart (1978), 137, 147, writes of 'a circle of enthusiasts at the royal court'; Cavallo (1978), 206, and Falkenhausen (1991), 280, are more cautious. The latter emphasizes that Hunger (1978), 121, has assigned this commentary to the neo-Platonists of the fifth century. This attribution has now been ascertained by Acconcia Longo (1991). For the poetry, Acconcia Longo (1981) and Lavagnini (1982).

(probably in 1131) he addressed him in the cathedral of Palermo as 'the pious emperor' (*basileus*). In a sermon for the feast of St Peter and St Paul (c.1143–1153), preached in the Palace chapel, and to the magnificent decoration of which he referred in his discourse, he stressed the splendour of the rule (βασιλεία) which had been granted to the king by God. It is quite possible that before his conversion Philagathos had taught philosophy and rhetoric in a Greek school at Palermo.[8]

Around 1140 the Byzantine theologian Nilos Doxapatres arrived at Roger's court. He had been a deacon at the church of Hagia Sophia in Constantinople and had risen to be imperial *nomophylax* and patriarchal notary. He had also acquired a reputation as a jurist. When he fell into disgrace – the reasons for this are unknown – he fled to Palermo. In a theological work composed at Constantinople he had defended Greek dogmas and liturgical usages against the Latins. Roger now gave him the task of writing about 'the Orders and Ranks of the Patriarchal thrones' (Τάξις τῶν πατριαρχικῶν θρόνων). In this history of the patriarchates of Antioch, Rome, Alexandria, Jerusalem and Constantinople and of their suffragan bishops Nilos sustained the argument that Rome, with the Gothic invasions and the loss of its role as the imperial city, had surrendered its primacy to Constantinople. The work is an historical geography of the ecclesiastical world, in one sense a companion piece to the geography of al-Idrīsī, but probably also served to show the pope that his primacy was in no sense uncontested. One cannot rule out that Roger had ordered the work to be written as a threat to Rome that he might eventually make the bishoprics of his kingdom subject to the Patriarch of Constantinople, but such a threat was hardly very credible, in that the king's relations with Byzantium were too strained.[9]

Along with Greek culture, Roger was also very much interested in Arabic learning. He especially esteemed the Arabic scholar al-Idrīsī, a descendant of the last Hammadid Prince of Malaga. While older writers believed that al-Idrīsī came from Córdoba in Andalucia, recent studies have shown that this Spanish origin is unlikely and that he was brought up either in north Africa or in Sicily, perhaps at Mazara.[10] Roger commissioned him

---

[8] *PG* 132, col. 541; cf. Caspar (1904), 460–1, Pertusi (1977), 82. Philagathos Keramides, *Omelie*, 174ff no. 27, cf. Kitzinger (1975), Houben (1995b), 267–8 [reprint 349–50]. Falkenhausen (1996), 242–3, suggests that 'the Palermo school of philosophy was in some way linked to the Greek church of S. Maria dell'Ammiraglio (the Martorana)', and that the teaching of Greek philosophy in Sicily continued into the thirteenth century.

[9] Caspar (1904), 346–64, Laurent (1937), Caruso (1973), Falkenhausen (1992), Breccia (1995), 327ff.

[10] Oman (1970) is fundamental. He shows, among other things, that al-Idrīsī also composed a work on pharmacology and poetry, and suggests that one should not entirely discount the claim by the later Arabic author Leo Africanus (1485–1554) that al-Idrīsī was born

to write a description of the world and to prepare a geographic map of the earth. After some fifteen years' work, he began to write this in January 1154, only a few weeks before the king's death. Roger was not merely the patron, but also, according to al-Idrīsī in the preface, took part personally in the research work. Roger is claimed first of all to have consulted the principal Arabic literature, such as that of Ptolemy and Orosius, but had found it unsatisfactory:

But when King Roger had carried out an exhaustive and detailed investigation, he found that these texts had obscured the meaning, and so he summoned to his court learned men well versed in these subjects. However, after discussion with them he discovered that their knowledge was no better than that contained in the aforementioned books. When he realised this, he ordered that men be summoned from all his dominions who knew about these matters and were experienced travellers. He questioned them in groups and also individually, through an intermediary [*wāsita*]. He had written record made only of that part of what they told him on which there was total agreement and seemed credible, excluding what was contradictory.

The king continued this work for about fifteen years, without abandoning for a moment verification, inquiry and research, until he had secured what he wanted. He wished in particular precise confirmation of what the persons selected had told him about the length and breadth of countries. A map was brought to him, and he began to check this bit by bit with the help of an iron compass, consulting also written texts, from which he chose the most likely estimates among the various authors. He examined them carefully until he was certain of the truth. Then he had a great and enormous round disc made from pure silver, which was divided into sections and weighed three hundred pounds. When this was ready, he ordered craftsmen to engrave upon it the figures of the seven climatic regions, with their respective countries and districts, coasts and lands, gulfs and seas, watercourses and river mouths, land which was inhabited and that which was deserted, the roads which had been built to link one place with another, or with several other places, with the distances in miles, the most certain routes and the known harbours. The artisans also had to reproduce, on the basis of the designs which they had seen on the map and without diverging from this in the least, the configurations of the countries as they had been traced.

Meanwhile he arranged for the compilation of a book which would provide an exact reproduction of these forms and geographical figures, to which would be added descriptions of the conditions of these countries and territories, with respect to people, soil, locality, configurations, seas, mountains and rivers, productive and infertile land, crops, types of building and their peculiarities, most common trades, most flourishing industries, import and export trades, wonders which were mentioned in each country or which were attributed to them, in which of the seven

---

at Mazara [see *ibid.*, 138]. Cf. recently De Simone (1995) and (1999), 262–3, who suggests that al-Idrīsī was 'notwithstanding the strong imprint of Andalucian culture, really a "Moroccan", and perhaps one of those north African intellectuals who returned to Sicily during the Norman period'.

climates these lands and territories lay, and then a discussion of their population: their appearance, diet, religion, taste, dress and speech. This book should have the name 'The delight of he who looks to travel throughout the world'. This was in the first ten days of January, corresponding to the Muslim month of Shawwāl of the year 548 [1154].[11]

With 'the intermediary' al-Idrīsī probably described himself. The king's role in the research work, as described in the preface, was probably exaggerated, but one can assume that Roger followed the compilation of the work with interest and here and there collaborated in it. Ibn Khaldūn (1332–1406) recorded that al-Idrīsī had composed the work for the king and given the latter's name to it, and indeed the book was rarely known under its full title, given above, but more usually simply as 'the Book of Roger'.[12]

The testimony of al-Idrīsī about Roger's interest in natural science is also credible, even if it is probably somewhat exaggerated:

His knowledge of mathematics and applied science was boundless. He was deeply grounded in every aspect of these two disciplines, studied them comprehensively and himself made new discoveries and wonderful inventions, as no prince before him had. These discoveries were well known to many witnesses. We could cite and describe them in full, but they are so well known, and their reputation has spread everywhere and to every district, that there is no need to speak of them in detail.[13]

We do not know whether Roger really produced inventions. He had a water-clock constructed in 1142, something which is revealed by a trilingual inscription, Latin, Greek and Arabic, on the wall next to the Palatine chapel. Perhaps this is linked to a device prepared by a 'geometrer of Malta' for a king of Sicily, which dropped balls into a metal box, and by doing so told the time, which was known to the thirteenth-century Arabic cosmographer al-Qazwīnī. A similar clock had earlier been given by the Caliph of Baghdad to Charlemagne. Roger's interest in natural sciences was certainly not divorced from Arabic influence; but it also reflected a general tendency in twelfth-century Europe, which found its origin in the so-called School of Chartres.[14]

---

[11] Al-Idrīsī, *BAS* 1.37–43. Rizzitano (1973), 281ff, Oman (1970), 217–18. Rubinacci (1970), suggests, contrary to general opinion, that on the basis of this preface the work was begun, rather than finished, in January 1154.

[12] Ibn Khaldūn, *BAS* II.203: 'for this king, the *sharīf* Ibn 'Abd Allāh al-Idrīsī compiled the book of the *Nuzhat al-mushtāq* . . . and gave the king's name for its title, so that it is known as "the book of Roger" '.

[13] Al-Idrīsī, *BAS*, 1.35.

[14] Amari (1879), 29–36. Cf. Amari (1933–9), III.702–3, Schack (1969), 131–2. For the School of Chartres and the natural sciences, Stürner (1975), 20–65, Stürner (1992),

Roger's considerable powers of observation and his thirst for knowledge were also attested by the Latin sources. During a stay at Naples in 1140 he had the perimeter of the city walls secretly measured at night. The next morning he asked the inhabitants if they knew how long their walls were. They were astonished and said they did not; the king then told them that the walls were 2,363 paces long. 'As a result the whole city declared that the king was wiser and more learned than his predecessors, and they were amazed by what he had done to ascertain the city's size, since it had never previously been measured.'[15]

Gervase of Tilbury (1140–1220) recounted that Roger had commissioned a diver from Apulia, Nicholas Papa, to investigate the seabed. The latter had informed him that in the depths of the Straits of Messina (the *Pharo*) there was an underwater forest. He thought that the currents which made problems for ships were caused by the existence of the wooded peaks and valleys on the seabed, and he also claimed to have seen fields and acorn-bearing trees there. He had become well acquainted with and almost a friend of the monsters of the deep. Another member of Roger's court was a falconer, 'Master William', who compiled, or rather reworked, a medical/vetinary treatise on falcons ascribed to a mythical king of Armenia, 'Dancus'. He was part of the household of one of the king's sons.[16]

The ruler also had a remarkable sensibility for natural beauty and things of artistic interest. In both Benevento and Naples he took the time to visit churches, palaces and other buildings. During a military expedition in the Campania he made a detour to Alife, in the Volturno valley to the north of Capua, 'saying that he was greatly pleased with the amenity of that place and by the great abundance of water courses round about it'.[17]

The many-sided intellectual interests of the king were also noted by the so-called 'Hugo Falcandus' and by Romuald of Salerno. The former wrote that: 'among the other natural gifts with which Nature herself had endowed this man of great vitality, he had a keen intellect and never lacked confidence in himself, so much so that if he was ever asked about anything

---

27–8, although n.b. the reservations expressed by Southern (1979). The Pöhlde Annals mention Roger's interest in astronomy, *Annales Palidenses*, *MGH SS* xvi.88 [see below, note 28].

[15] *Falco*, 236.

[16] Gervase of Tilbury, *Otia Imperialia*, ed. Liebrecht, 11; ed. Pauli, 376. Jamison (1938), 274. Bresc (1987), 272–3. William the Falconer, *Les plus anciens traités*, 134: 'William the falconer, who was brought up at the court of King Roger, [and] who afterwards dwelt there for a long time with his son'. Reichert (1995), 436, argues that this work suggests 'a certain knowledge of Asian species and medicines'.

[17] *Falco*, 214, 236. *Al. Tel.* iii.18, p. 69.

at all he never made the slightest delay in giving a reply.' The other recorded that he summoned to his court 'men of wisdom of different sorts from the various parts of the earth'. John of Salisbury, no friend himself to the Germans, added: 'he would not readily admit those from the kingdom of the Germans to his following, for that race was suspect to him and he could not abide their barbarism'.[18]

Al-Idrīsī appears to have enjoyed Roger's particular favour. He should probably be identified with the Arabic scholar whom Ibn al-Athīr claimed was preferred by Roger to all others, to such an extent that the rumour arose that the ruler was going to convert to Islam. Further details come from al-Ṣafadī (1297–1362):

Roger, king of the Franks and lord of Sicily, loved learned men of philosophy, and it was he who had al-Sharīf al-Idrīsī brought to him from north Africa. He was the author of the book *Nuzhat*, ... in which he provided for him a description of the world. When he arrived Roger welcomed his guest ceremoniously, making every effort to do him honour. Al-Idrīsī sought from him the metal to build the device he had planned. Roger had silver with a weight of 400,000 drams brought to him, and with this silver al-Idrīsī made spheres like those in the heavens. He then placed them one upon the other, setting them up in a particular way. Roger was full of admiration. For this he had used only a little more than a third of the silver, but the king let him keep the rest as a reward. He added to this a hundred thousand dirhems and a ship filled with 'European' merchandise of royal quality, which hailed from Barcelona. Roger invited him to stay with him. To persuade him to accept [his invitation], he told him [al-Idrīsī]: 'you are from the Caliphal house, and if you were under Muslim rule their lords would seek to kill you, but if you remain with me you will be safe'. After al-Idrīsī had accepted the king's invitation, the latter granted him an income so large as to be princely. Al-Idrīsī was accustomed to ride to the king on a mule, and when he arrived Roger stood up and went to meet him, and then the two sat down together.[19]

In the Islamic world the right to ride a mule inside the palace was a sign of great honour. Even if particular features of the accounts by the Arabic chronicler cannot be verified, the gist of his testimony accords with the evidence from other sources. Al-Idrīsī remained at the royal court after Roger's death, where he wrote for William I a new edition

---

[18] *Falcandus*, 5 [*Tyrants*, 57]. *Romuald*, 233 [*Tyrants*, 219]. The *Historia Pontificalis of John of Salisbury*, 66.

[19] Al-Ṣafadī, *BAS* II.564–5; Arabic text corrected by Oman (1970), 218–19, 229. Oman suggests that, to resolve the contradiction between this author and Leo Africanus, according to whom al-Idrīsī was a native of Mazara [above, note 10], it is possible that when Roger summoned him from north Africa he was only travelling in that region. For the privilege of riding a mule, see Schack (1969), 137–8. For the reference in Ibn al-Athīr, see above p. 83.

of his Geography, a book on medicinal plants and also poetry, as well as a now-lost work with the title 'Gardens of Joy and the Pleasures of the Soul'.[20]

Al-Idrīsī was not the only Muslim at Roger's court. Verses from six Arab poets from Sicily survive, praising the king and his palaces and gardens. Fragments of these works are preserved in the anthology of 'Imād al-Iṣfahānī (1125–1201), in which – so as not to offend the religious susceptibilities of the Muslim public – these poems in praise of the 'infidel Normans' were copied in a severely curtailed form. Abū'd-Ḍaw', who was descended from a noble Arabic family from Palermo, composed an elegy commemorating the death of one of Roger's sons. The Koran reciter 'Abd ar-Raḥmān ibn Muḥammed ibn 'Umar from Butera praised the royal palace and Roger's parks: 'One can only live well in the dear shadow of Sicily, under the rule of a prince who eclipses that of the Caesars!' A collector of poetry from Mahdia, Ibn Bashrūn, added: 'Here (in the palace) Roger, king of imperial kings [*malik al-mulūk al-qayṣarīya*], devotes himself to great undertakings.' However, other Arabic poets, like Ibn Ḥamdīs, had abandoned Sicily after the Norman conquest and lamented the loss of their native land.[21]

Latin culture played a relatively modest role in the court at Palermo under Roger. The historical work of Alexander of Telese, which justified the count's rise to duke and then king, was written in the Campania, and it was commissioned by one of the king's sisters, who was married to Count Rainulf of Alife. It was directed towards a southern audience belonging to the Lombard tradition of the noble world, but also to the king. It is unlikely that the work was read aloud at the court in Palermo, as has been suggested, since under Roger it was rather Greek and Arabic culture that was dominant there.[22]

---

[20] Schack (1969), 139ff.

[21] *Ibid.*, 169ff, and for Roger II's 'Arabic pleasure gardens', *ibid.*, 157ff, and Meier (1994). Abū'd-Ḍaw', in Imād al-Iṣfahānī, *BAS* II.472–3; Abd ar-Raḥmān, *BAS* II.436; Ibn Bashrūn, *BAS* II.438. For the title of *malik al-mulūk al-qayṣarīya*, see Schack (1969), 155, Shahid (1978), Rizzitano (1973), 287ff. For Ibn Ḥamdīs (d. 1133), a native of Syracuse, see Borruso (1973). Another possible member of Roger's court circle was Muḥammed ibn 'Īsā ibn 'Abd al-Mun'im, who studied geometry and astrology in Palermo in the mid twelfth century, for whom see Amari (1933–9), 707–8, De Simone (1997), 79. Al-Maqrīzī claimed that Abū'd-Ḍaw' was the 'secretary of the writing office' of Roger II, and then – after Christodoulos had allegedly been killed on the king's orders – he was named as vizier, but when he would not undertake this position the king invested George of Antioch with the vizierate.

[22] *Al. Tel.*, *alloquium ad Regem Rogerium*, 89: 'Lo, my lord King Roger, we have thought to dedicate this little book to you ... Because we wish therefore something to be made so that while you read over and over [*sepissime*] the story of your most famous victory, you may remember the Lord and Saviour, your Eternal King.' Oldoni (1979), 279, suggests

It is noteworthy that over half, perhaps around 75–80 per cent, of Roger's royal charters were written in Greek, and that the ruler had his signature in Greek placed at the foot of many of the Latin charters.[23] Up to 1127 Latin charters were no more than 'chance products, for which Roger used the services of a chaplain or was even prepared to confirm a document prepared by the recipient'. Under Roger, the Latin chancery remained limited to a single notary, 'a one-man show'. Once he became king, Roger created the office of chancellor, on the model of the other European royal courts, but this was an essentially political post and had almost nothing to do with the actual production of documents. He named as his first chancellor Guarin, his senior chaplain. Later on, the offices of chancellor and master of his chapel (*magister capellanus*) were once again divided. These offices were entrusted to two foreigners, the Englishmen Robert of Selby and Thomas Brown, clearly because suitable indigenous personnel were lacking. After Roger's death, Thomas fell into disgrace and returned to England where he made a second career as a financial expert under King Henry II (1154–89).[24]

According to 'Hugo Falcandus', whose pseudonym probably conceals someone who was a member of the court who had known Roger personally, the king summoned experts from all over to Palermo, but showed a strong preference for *transalpini*, that is French and Anglo-Normans. It would appear that they spoke French at the court. During the regency of Margaret of Navarre (1166–71), her brother Rodrigo (Henry) was refused the office of chancellor on the grounds of his ignorance of that language (*Francorum lingua*). But the significance of Latin culture at the Palermitan court only developed slowly, as a consequence of the growing Latinization of the kingdom.[25]

that 'it must have been possible to have read this in public, perhaps in front of the king and his court'; see also Delogu (1981), 186ff.

[23] The Greek 'signatures' of Roger II were not done in person by him but rather by one of his chancery scribes, see Falkenhausen (1998b), 283–6. However, his signature in Latin on a document of 1124 is probably an autograph, Roger II, *Diplomata*, no. 6 [above, p. 40].

[24] Quote from Kölzer (1986), 23–4. Brühl (1978), 42ff. For Thomas Brown, *Dialogus de Scaccario, The Course of the Exchequer, by Richard Fitz Nigel*, ed. C. Johnson, F. E. L. Carter and D. Greenway (Oxford 1983), 35–6, and Warren (1973), 313–14, Takayama (1993), 12.

[25] *Falcandus*, 6 [*Tyrants*, 58]: 'When he heard that any persons were either effective counsellors or famous warriors, he would honour them with gifts to encourage their virtue. Since he derived his own origins from the Normans and knew that the French race excelled all others in the glory of war, he chose to favour and honour those from north of the Alps particularly.' For Rodrigo/Henry of Navarre, *ibid.*, 127 [*Tyrants*, 179]. Várvaro (1981), 200. The suggestion by Herval (1955), 80–1, that there was a flourishing '*langue d'oil* culture' at Roger's court cannot be sustained.

Under Roger, Palermo was a meeting point for the different cultures of Sicily. Along with the Greek, Latin and Arabic elements one must also cite the Hebraic. A gravestone of 1148 carries inscriptions in Greek, Latin, Arabic and Hebrew scripts. The Hebrew inscription was composed in the Arabic language used by Sicilian Jews. In the text, which shows slight differences from one version to another, mention is made of the burial of Anna, the mother of Grisandus, who in the Arabic and Hebrew inscriptions is described as a royal priest. The content of the inscriptions, which are grouped around a cross with the Greek motto 'Jesus Christ conquers', is Christian. In the Arabic text Roger is described as 'supporter of the pope (the Imām of Rome)' and as 'helper of the Christian religion', while in the Hebrew inscription Mary was recorded as 'Mother of the Messiah'. Those addressed by the text were therefore, probably, Muslims and Jews who had converted to Christianity. The Arabic inscription could also be connected with Mozarabs, Christians who used Arabic as their vernacular and liturgical language, as we know from Spain.

The trilingual gravestone of Grisandus's father Drogo has also survived. To judge by his name, he may have been a Norman, although it is also possible that he could have been an indigenous inhabitant who had been given a Norman name. Grisandus, who was here described as 'a cleric [*clericus*] of the King of Sicily', could have been the son of a Norman and a Sicilian Greek. But it is also possible that the names Anna and/or Drogo concealed Arabic converts who had taken new names after baptism.[26]

The existence of Mozarab Christians is also shown by a surviving trilingual psaltar, written in Greek, Latin and Arabic, probably at Palermo, between 1132 and 1153. Marginal notes in Arabic show that the codex served as a book of hours for a religious community. A German traveller, the priest Ludolf of Sudheim (near Lichtenau in the vicinity of Paderborn), attested the continued survival of a Mozarab community in Sicily as late as 1340.[27]

Despite the value he placed upon Arabic culture and its exponents, Roger did little to limit the effects of the growing Latinization, which was reducing the non-Christian minorities to marginal social groups. Indeed,

---

[26] Houben (1996a), 202–3 (Italian translation of the inscription), 227ff. Krönig (1989), 555. For the role of Jewish culture in southern Italy, Várvaro (1987), 83–4, and the 1992 conference on *L'Ebraismo dell'Italia meridionale peninsulare*.

[27] The psalter is London, BL Harley MS 5786, see Johns (1983), 90, Houben (1996a), 228–9, Johns (1995), 141–2. For the psalter's Greek script, Lucà (1993), 35. Canart (1978), 144, notes also a twelfth-century Gospel book in Greek and Arabic, from either Calabria or Sicily (Venice, Marciana, gr. 539), and a trilingual thirteenth-century manuscript from Sicily in Greek, Latin and Arabic (Marciana, gr. 11). Ludolphus de Suchem, *De Itinere Terrae Sanctae*, 20; cf. Messina (1992), Bresc (1994), and most recently Bresc and Nef (1998).

Romuald of Salerno testified that 'towards the end of his life, allowing secular matters to be delayed, he [the king] laboured in every conceivable way to convert Jews and Saracens to the faith of Christ, and endowed converts with many gifts and resources'.[28]

No other sources say anything about such a conversion of Jews during the period in question; should one therefore doubt Romuald's reliability? Perhaps the archbishop only wanted to say that the king became more pious with age? What is certain is that the conversion of Muslims was growing at the period. A significant episode is revealed in a later marginal addition to Romuald's Chronicle, which was intended to show the reader that Roger was a genuinely catholic (*intencione catholicus*) ruler and 'inflamed with zeal for the Christian religion'.

King Roger had a certain eunuch called Philip, whom the king valued and trusted because of his good service to him. Having found him faithful in deed and reliable in carrying out his business, he gave him precedence over everybody in his palace and appointed him as master of his household. As time went on Philip grew ever more valued and regarded, to such an extent that the king made him admiral of his fleet and sent him with it to Bône, which he took at sword point and sacked, before returning in triumph and glory to Sicily.

But since he showed himself ungrateful to his creator for the benefits he had received, and returned evil for good towards the Celestial King, he rightly incurred the anger and indignation of the temporal monarch. For under the cloak of the Christian name he served as a soldier of the Devil, and while pretending to behave as a Christian he was both by conviction and behaviour completely a Saracen. He hated Christians and greatly loved pagans. He entered Christian churches unwillingly, but more frequently visited the synagogues of the evil doers and provided them with oil to fuel their lights and other things which they needed. He totally rejected Christian traditions; he continued to eat meat on Fridays and in Lent, he sent envoys with gifts to the tomb of Mohammed and commended himself to the prayers of the priests of that place.

These and other of his wicked acts, committed under the shade of the Christian name, came to the ears of King Roger. The latter, filled with zeal for God but acting with his usual wisdom, had Philip summoned to his court [*in sua curia conveniri*] to answer for the aforesaid crimes. Trusting in the grace and love of the king, he replied to his accusers with spirit and claimed that the charges which had been made against him were false. However, thanks to Divine justice, his accusors proved through the testimony of trustworthy witnesses that what had been said was true. Once he realized that he would be found guilty, and fearing the king's justice, Philip began to seek pardon and beg the king for mercy, and promised that in future he would be a genuine Christian. Then the king was lit up by the flame of the faith. He burst into tears and said: 'My faithful subjects, you should know

---

[28] *Romuald*, 236 [*Tyrants*, 220]. This belated piety was also reported by the *Chronica de Ferraria*, 29, and by the Pöhlde annals, which went so far as to allege that he became a monk shortly before his death, *Annales Palidenses*, *MGH SS* XVI.88.

that my heart is filled with deep grief, and racked by anger, in that this servant [*minister*] of mine, whom I raised from boyhood as a catholic, has because of his sins been revealed as a Saracen, and as a Saracen has sheltered under the name of our Faith while he practised the works of the infidel. If he had indeed offended our Majesty in other matters, if he had stolen part, even a large part, of our treasure, then in memory of his past services he would still have merited and obtained grace and pardon. But since by what he has done he has chiefly offended God, and has given to others material and example for sin, I could not pardon either my own son or one of my close relations for such an injury to our Faith and offence to the Christian religion. In this verdict the whole world will come to realize that I am consumed by love for the Christian faith and I will not hesitate to punish even my servants for injuries to it. Let the laws therefore rise up, our government arm itself with the sword of equity, and let them cut down the enemy of the Faith with the sword of justice, and through this the unbelievers shall be struck with terror.' Then the counts, justiciars, barons and judges who were there present, acknowledging the justice of what the king said, gathered together and considered the issue for a long time, and then pronounced this sentence: 'we have decreed that Philip, who has brough the Christian name into disrepute and under a pretence of the Faith has led the life of the infidel shall be burned by the avenging flames. He who has been unwilling to receive the fire of charity shall incur the [actual] fire of burning. Let no relics of this most wicked man remain, but be turned into ashes by temporal fire while he goes to be burned for ever by the eternal fire.' Then, on the orders of the justiciars, his feet were bound to a wild horse and he was violently dragged to a lime pit which was in front of the palace; his feet were freed from the horse and he was thrown into the middle of the flames and immediately burned. All those who were accomplices and sharers in his inquity were also given death sentences.

It was thus most clearly revealed by this affair that King Roger was a most Christian and catholic prince, who to punish an injury to the Faith, did not spare his own chamberlain whom he had brought up, but handed him over to the flames for Its honour and glory.[29]

We do not know who wrote this account. The style makes it unlikely to have been written by Romuald himself. The dating is difficult. Does this come from the twelfth century, or even from the thirteenth? One can provide limits as to when it was produced through the employment of the term *ammiratus stolii* (admiral of the fleet), since this was only in use between 1177 and the first decade of the thirteenth century. It is possible that we have here the reworking of an older text, perhaps the formal judgement of the high court which it mentions. It was undoubtedly based upon a kernel of truth.[30] This is confirmed by the testimony of two other, Islamic, sources, both quite independent of Romuald. One of these is Ibn al-Athīr, who presents these events in a very different light.

---

[29] *Romuald*, 234–6.
[30] Ménager (1960), 66–7, Schack (1969), 145–50, Johns (1983), 106–7.

In this year [1153–4] the fleet of Roger, king of the Franks in Sicily, arrived at the city of Bône, under the command of the king's page Philip of Mahdia. Philip besieged the town, using Arab auxiliary troops, and conquered it in the month of Rajab [22 September – 21 October 1153]. He took the inhabitants prisoner and seized their property; but he closed his eyes towards certain learned and virtuous men who fled with their families and possessions to other places in the neighbourhood. After remaining in Bône for ten days, Philip returned to Mahdia with his prisoners and then went back to Sicily. Roger had him arrested for his mildness towards the Muslims in Bône. It was said at the court of Palermo that he and all the other royal pages were secretly Muslims. Witnesses confirmed that Philip did not fast when the king fasted, and that he was [really] a Muslim. As a result an assembly of bishops, priests and knights was summoned by the king, and sentenced him to be burned. This took place in the month of Ramadan [20 November – 19 December 1153]. This was the first blow that befell the Muslims of Sicily, and God allowed Roger to live for only a short time thereafter.[31]

Thus for the Arab chronicler Philip's condemnation was caused not just by his attachment to Islam, but also because of his mild treatment of the inhabitants of Bône. In any event, Ibn al-Athīr saw in Philip's execution a turning point in the history of the Muslims of Sicily.

In the years beforehand Roger had been the guarantor of the peaceful coexistence of Greek, Arabic and Latin cultures in Palermo. The relatively limited consequences that translation activity in Sicily and mainland southern Italy (in contrast to that in Spain) had on European culture of the twelfth and thirteenth century as a whole can probably be explained by the fact that, if one excepts medical studies in Salerno, it was otherwise limited to the court, and lacked any wider basis. Indeed accusations have been levied of the 'sterility' of Palermitan court culture: 'the court was exclusively a self-sufficient literary circle, without wider ambitions, which was further and further infiltrated and taken over by an imported Western European Latin tradition'.[32]

With the growing Latinization, accentuated after the loss of the North African bases under William I, the scope for Greek and Arabic culture became ever narrower. Bilingual or trilingual figures like Henry Aristippus or Eugenius became the exceptions, and disappeared completely towards the end of the century. But while the Arabic element shrank continuously, Greek culture was able to survive much longer in certain localities, above all

[31] Ibn al-Athīr, *BAS* i.479–80, and similarly Ibn Khaldūn, *BAS* ii.229. Schack (1969), 142–3. Johns (1983), 107, suggests that Ibn Shaddād, who visited Palermo in 1156–7, had informed Ibn al-Athīr of these events.

[32] Kölzer (1986), 32 ff [quote, p. 33, referring to De Stefano (1954), 43]. See also Várvaro (1987), 80–1, and Schipperges (1981). For the greater influence of Arabic science in Spain, Vernet (1984), 125ff, and for the 'irreversible crisis' of Greek culture in southern Italy underway from the second half of the twelfth century, see Lucà (1993), 27.

in southern Apulia. Here there was a certain cultural synthesis. The mosaic pavement of Otranto cathedral, produced only a few years after the death of King Roger (in 1163–5), may be cited. Its iconographic depiction of the story of salvation mixed together Arabic, Greek and western mythology (including the saga of King Arthur).[33]

IMAGES OF RULE

The most celebrated picture of the king is the mosaic in the narthex of the church of S. Maria dell'Ammiraglio, founded by Roger's chief minister, the *amiratus* George of Antioch. Subsequently, in the mid fifteenth century, his church became the property and took the name of the nearby nunnery of S. Maria della Martorana, itself only founded at the end of the twelfth century. George's mother Theodula, who became a nun in old age, lived here, and George and his wife were later buried there.[34] Between 1146 and 1151 the founder had himself depicted in his family church, and also the sovereign in whose service he had made his career. Thus we have, not an official portrait of Roger but an image which shows the way in which George of Antioch, a representative of Greek culture, saw his king. One might, however, believe that the sovereign knew of, and perhaps even saw, how he was depicted in this church. The ideology expressed in the mosaic, of a king crowned by God, was certainly one with which Roger concurred.

The sovereign identified as 'King Roger' ('Ρογέριος ῥήξ) wore the ceremonial costume of a Byzantine emperor, which had evolved from the ancient consular dress (see fig. 2). Its principal element was the loros, a sash wound around the shoulders, waist and left forearm, and which was worn over a magnificent tunic, embroidered with gold and pearls. Underneath, as an undergarment, was another, blue, tunic, threaded with gold. The image is dominated by the very obviously larger figure of Christ, who is placing a Byzantine crown with *pendilia* on the king's head. Roger is caught in an attitude of prayer, with head slightly lowered and hands raised. Like Christ, he is shown with a beard and shoulder-length hair, generating a strong sense of similarity between the two faces. The sovereign resembles God, from whom he is receiving his crown. The monarch belongs to a

---

[33] For the decline of Greek in the royal chancery, which she dates from c. 1145 onwards, see Falkenhausen (1996), 239–40 (1998), 264ff. For the Otranto mosaic, see Settis Frugoni (1970), Haug (1975), and Willemsen (1980) for illustrations. Falkenhausen (1996), 236–7, stresses the presence of both Greek and Latin rites at Otranto, and also points to a fusion between Greek and Latin culture in this area of southern Apulia, *ibid.*, 261–2.

[34] These Greek funerary inscriptions have been transmitted only in manuscripts, Acconcia Longo (1981, 1988), Breccia (1995), 337ff. For the dating of the mosaics, see Kitzinger (1990), 263ff.

Fig. 2. King Roger crowned by Christ, a mosaic from the church of S. Maria dell'Ammiraglio (the Martorana) in Palermo.

sphere half-way between God and mankind. This is therefore the representation of an ideal, very much influenced by Byzantine iconography, an example of the illustration of the eastern Roman emperor as 'one crowned by God'. Clothing and crown, and the style of the beard and hair, were taken from a model. We do not know whether Roger ever in fact wore such a crown and dress.[35]

Another mosaic, in the cathedral of Gerace in southern Calabria, in which the king was shown with a golden crown, sceptre in hand and with a costume which probably resembled that depicted in the Martorana, no longer survives.[36]

A further image of Roger is found in the basilica of San Nicola at Bari. On an enamel plaque, located in the ciborium of the high altar, are depicted both the king and St Nicholas, the patron saint of Bari (see fig. 3). Close inspection reveals that this does not show a 'coronation scene', as one so often reads. The saint is not placing the crown on the head of the king (here described as ROGERIVS REX), but only holding it firmly, although from this the observer might easily gain the impression that a coronation is shown. The iconographic model was derived from Byzantine coins, where a saint, or Christ, holds the crown of an emperor who stands next to him. The act of putting hands upon him shows that the sovereign is placed under Heavenly protection. But in contrast to the Byzantine model, Roger wears a crown with a western-style diadem. In addition, not only does he hold an orb in his hand, but he also leans on a banner with a cross, the Constantinian *labarum*, found in other images of Byzantine emperors. Roger's clothing and beard are similar to those of the mosaic in Palermo, but the Byzantine imperial dress, with the *loros*, the long stole with its complicated folds, is very loosely depicted. The model used here could have been one of Roger's seals. St Nicholas is represented as a western bishop. The variations show that the artist either interpreted his model freely or could not fully understand the details, thereby misinterpreting or simplifying them. Because the enamel plaque was made with a technique used at Limoges, it

[35] Deér (1957), 408ff [reprint, 44ff], Kitzinger (1990), 191ff, with reference to Belting (1970), 75ff. Tramontana (1993), 86–7. Because from the middle of the eleventh century onwards the Byzantine emperors no longer wore the *loros* in the traditional manner, crossed over their shoulders, but rather hanging down in front, Kitzinger has suggested that the mosaic was based upon an older iconographic model, perhaps one similar to the ivory of an Emperor Constantine (probably Constantine VII Porphyrogenitos, 913–59), now in the Pushkin Museum in Moscow, Kitzinger (1990), illustration 190. A similar crown with pendants is depicted in the mosaics of the Palatine chapel: Beck (1970), figs. 33 and 35.

[36] Bishop Ottaviano Pasqua (d. 1591) offered the following description: 'An image in mosaic work of this same Leontios is placed on the right-hand side of the altar of San Salvatore in the cathedral basilic; on the left one of Count [*sic*] Roger can clearly be discerned, in which he seems to be wearing a golden scarf and to be clad in a *pluviale*, with a golden crown placed on his head, holding a royal sceptre in his hand, and with his garment bordered with gold lilies.' Were these lilies in fact golden crosses, as are shown on the king's mantle in the Martorana mosaic? Leontios can be identified with Bishop Leontios II (1124–49), the founder of Gerace cathedral, Zinzi (1986).

Fig. 3. St Nicholas places his hand on King Roger. Enamel plaque, originally on the ciborium of the high altar of the basilica of St Nicholas, Bari. It is now in the church's museum.

was at first thought to be the work of a French artist, but more recent studies have shown that only the figure of the king was made using the western technique of *champlevé*, while that of the saint was done with the Byzantine method of *cloisonné*. The combination of both western and eastern techniques and motifs points to a local workshop, since Apulian medieval art is characterized by a mixture of Byzantine and western motifs.[37]

The image may perhaps derive from the 1130s, when Roger's royal title was still in dispute. St Nicholas's placing of his hands on the king must

---

[37] Bertaux (1898), 70–1, suggests this was modelled on a coin. The image on a gold *solidus* of Romanos III Argyros (1028–34), reproduced by Deér (1961), fig. 16, discussed *ibid.*,

have symbolized, for the citizens of Bari, the legitimacy and the sacrality of the new monarchy. After the city and its prince, Grimoald, who had been entitled 'Prince of Bari by the grace of God and St Nicholas', had been forced to submit in May 1132, Roger guaranteed to the citizens a wide-ranging autonomy which took account of the exceptional position of the basilica of St Nicholas. The king pledged himself not to touch the saint's relics, but rather to protect them, to permit the completion of the basilica (which was still under construction) and to respect the immunity of the the church's enclave. However, it remains uncertain whether the picture was produced after 1132, or following the second surrender of Bari in 1139.[38]

We may therefore conclude that in the only two surviving contemporary representations of Roger – if one excludes the seals and money, which will be discussed later – the ruler was described as a king, but portrayed as an emperor (*basileus*). Both these images are of considerable significance, for although linked to precise iconographic models they maintain a certain 'individual' note. However, they are certainly not sources for those who seek individual characteristics, let alone a portrait, of the king.[39]

Some decades after Roger's death, between 1195 and 1197, some illustrations were drawn and coloured to accompany Peter of Eboli's verses concerning the union of the kingdom of Sicily with the German (Roman) empire under Henry VI. Roger's rise from duke to king was depicted here, not without some errors which show how poorly the author was informed about the events of some time before: thus the royal coronation of 1130 was provided by Pope Calixtus II who died in 1124, and Roger's marriage with Elvira, which actually took place in 1117/18, was placed after he had become king (see fig. 4). The author was though better informed about the premature deaths of the king's sons from his first marriage, and about

296, was of the same iconographic type. For the enamel, also Belli d'Elia, Calò Mariani, Todisco (1990), 301, and for the inscription on the ciborium, Magistrale (1992), 9ff. On the basis of this supposed 'coronation' and of the presence of a votive crown in the treasury of St Nicholas, a local tradition has arisen that Roger II was crowned by Anacletus II at Bari in 1130. The dating of the votive crown is debatable; it has generally been ascribed to the thirteenth century, although in recent exhibition catalogues it has been reassigned to the twelfth, e.g. *I Normanni* (1994), 422, *Federico II* (1995), 538–9.

[38] Roger II, *Diplomata*, no. 20 (22 June 1132). For Grimoald of Bari, see above p. 53 and note 43.

[39] Bertaux (1898), 84: 'the face with its bifurcated beard and long hair on each side, is indeed a faithful portrait of the Norman king'; although Caspar (1904), 435, is more cautious. Kitzinger (1950), 31, argues that the portrait was idealized, while in his 1990 book, 197, he stresses the Christomimesis. For the bishop shown on the Paschal candlestick in the Palatine chapel, who for a long time was identified with Roger II clad as a legate (!), e.g. by Steinberg (1937), 46ff, see Deér (1959), 157ff.

Fig. 4. Scenes from the life of Roger II from the illuminated chronicle-poem of
Peter of Eboli (Bern, Burgerbibliothek Cod. 120 II, fol. 96r, ed. Kölzer-Stähli, 39).
First row, 'Duke Roger', 'the duke receives royal unction from Pope Calixtus', and
'the king took Elvira as his wife'. Second row, 'Elvira is buried with her sons', 'King
Roger married Sibylla as his second wife', 'here Sibylla who died in childbirth
is buried'. Third row, 'King Roger married Beatrice as his third wife', 'Queen
Beatrice gave birth to Constance', 'here the king is buried with his wife'. Fourth
row, 'Queen Constance, King Henry', 'while the king and queen were going to
Germany, Pope Lucius blessed them'.

his second and third marriages. The series of images concerning Roger was intended to emphasize the royal descent of his daughter Constance (1154–98), the wife of Henry VI (d. 1197). One may note that here, as in the images of the sovereign at Palermo and Bari, Roger was shown with a beard. The crown is difficult to identify precisely, but it appears to be a diadem in the western style.[40]

The image of Roger as ruler which was once to be found in the atrium of Cefalù cathedral, but has now been lost with the passage of time, was later still, from the time of Frederick II. In the fresco cycle here, the Staufen emperor had commisioned representations of his predecessors as King of Sicily. Roger II was depicted here crowned and wearing royal robes, and with an inscription identifying him as 'King Roger' (*Rogerius rex*).[41]

Seals and money contain stereotypical images of the sovereign, where the Norman king was shown with Byzantine insignia. The only golden bull of Roger as king to survive is to be found attached to a privilege granted to the abbey of Cava a few weeks after his royal coronation. On the obverse the sovereign is shown wearing the traditional ceremonial costume of a Byzantine emperor, with crown and *pendilia*, orb and cross in the right hand and the *labarum* in the left. The legend proclaims: ρογέριος κραταιὸς εὐσεβής ῥήξ ('Roger, strong and pious king'). On the reverse one can identify Christ on his throne with the Gospel in his right hand. Here too the inscription is in Greek: IC XC ('Jesus Christ'). In the period before he became king, Roger's image was not used on his seals. Hence on the obverse of the golden bull for Montecassino, which dates from the end of his period as duke, in 1129, what was depicted was the Virgin Mary and the baby Jesus, on the model of the seals of the earlier Dukes of Apulia, while on the reverse one finds Roger's ducal title in Greek.[42]

---

[40] Peter of Eboli, *Liber ad honorem Augusti*, fol. 96r, ed. Kölzer and Stähli, 39. The king may well have had a beard, hence the lion-like appearance in the description by *Romuald*, 236 [*Tyrants*, 221]: 'King Roger was large of stature, corpulent, leonine of face, somewhat hoarse of voice.' But to conclude from this that he had 'reddened skin', as does Cantarella (1989), 89n, seems hazardous.

[41] Valenziano and Valenziano (1978), 140n. There is a description of 1329, *Rolleus Rubeus*, ed. C. Mirto, 27: 'King Roger, the founder of this church, offers this same church with his right hand. He is clad in royal vestments and wears a crown. And above the head of the said king is written *Rogerius rex*.' Schaller (1963), 307 [reprint, 17], who suggests a date of between 1226 and 1229.

[42] Roger II, *Diplomata*, no. 16 (February 1131), cf. the illustration in *Archivio paleografico italiano* XIV (1954), plates 18–19. For the form of the *loros*, Kitzinger (1990), 193n. Roger II, *Diplomata*, no. 14 (30 December 1129); there is a drawing of the gold bull which disappeared in the eighteenth century in Gattula, *Ad Historiam Abbatiae Casinensis Accessiones*, fig. VII, Inguanez, (1930), fig. 2. For these gold bulls, Enzensberger (1971), 89ff, Brühl (1978), 75–6, (1987), 63–4.

Fig. 5. Lead seal of Roger II, from a diploma of 3 November 1144 for the monastery of S. Maria di Macchia [Roger II, *Diplomata*, no. 66]. Obverse: Roger II with crown and *pendilia*, *loros*, *labarum* and orb. The legend (which is not completely legible) reads 'Roger, the powerful [and pious king]' (ΡΟΓΕΡΙΟC ΚΡΑΤΑΙΟC...). Reverse: bust of Christ with Greek monogram (IC XC); the legend reads 'Roger by the grace of God, King of Sicily, Calabria and Apulia' (ROGERIVS DEI GRACIA SICILIE CALABRIE APVLIE REX).

A genuine lead seal, which is attached to a forged diploma for Monte-cassino, is similar to the gold bull for Cava, although its poor state of preservation has rendered the inscription virtually illegible. So too is the lead seal of a privilege granted in 1144 to the monastery of St. Maria di Macchia, near Acri, to the north of Cosenza in Calabria. Roger is shown on the obverse with crown and *pendilia*, *loros*, *labarum* and orb (see fig. 5). Only the first two words of the inscription 'Ρογέριος κραταιὸς εὐσεβής ῥήξ' ('Roger, strong and pious king') are still legible. The reverse shows a bust of Christ with the Greek monogram IC XC ('Jesus Christ'), to which is added, in a circle, the king's Latin title: ROGERIVS DEI GRACIA SICILIE CALABRIE APVLIE REX ('Roger by the grace of God King of Sicily, Calabria and Apulia').[43]

These seals confirm that Roger had himself depicted with the symbols of lordship of the Byzantine emperor, but contented himself with the title of king. The same was true for his money, which reached a much wider public than did the seals. Most of this is however so small that the details of the representation can only be identified under very close inspection.

Before Roger became king, the gold *tarì* minted in Sicily had a wholly Arabic appearance: on the obverse a sort of Greek 'tau' with the Arabic legend 'on the order of Roger II' (*bi-amr Rujār al-tānī*), along with the sign of the mint and the date; on the reverse, always in Arabic, the words 'there is no God except Allah'. After 1130 the inscription changed: on the obverse, along with the sign of the mint and the date, there was the legend, in Arabic, 'King Roger, sublime and powerful, by the grace of God [Allah]' (*al-mu'tazz bi-llāh al-malik Rujār al-mu'aẓẓam*), which after 1140 became abbreviated to 'King Roger, powerful through the grace of Allah' (*al-malik Rujār al-mu'tazz bi-llāh*). On the reverse there was a cross with the Greek legend 'Jesus Christ conquers' (IC XC NI KA).[44] This new form of the *tarì* was a compromise between the title of a Muslim sovereign and a Christian motto.

On some of his copper money, the *follari*, Roger is shown on the obverse standing, wearing imperial ceremonial costume: crown with *pendilia*, with the *labarum* (or imperial lance?) in his right hand, and the orb and cross in his left. On the reverse was placed a cross with the Greek inscription 'Jesus

[43] Roger II, *Diplomata*, no. 25†; the seal was previously, up to the nineteenth century, attached to *ibid*. no. 21† (27 July 1132), but belonged originally to another diploma, now lost. There is an illustration in *Archivio paleografico italiano* XIV (1954), plate 25. Roger II, *Diplomata*, no. 66 (3 November 1144), drawing in Engel (1882), plate I, 13, illustration in Garufi, *Catalogo illustrato del tabulario di S. Maria Nuova*, fig. VII.

[44] Travaini (1995), 118, 122ff. For Roger's coinage, see now Grierson and Travaini (1998), 101–25.

Christ conquers' (IC XC NI KA). On other *follari* one can see the ruler seated on his throne with a cross in his right hand, and on the reverse a bust of Christ. Other copper money shows the king on the obverse standing with crown and *pendilia*, lance in his right and orb and cross in his left hand, while on the reverse Christ is seated on a throne (see fig. 6).[45]

The silver ducats introduced after the monetary reform of 1140 are particularly expressive (see fig. 6 again). On the obverse they carry a bust of Christ Pantocrator with the Gospels in His left hand, with the Greek monogram of Christ and Latin legend IC XC RG IN AETRN, which can be expanded to *Jesus Christus regnat in aeternum* ('Jesus Christ rules for [all] eternity'). The reverse is subdivided by a long Byzantine double cross. On the left one sees a frontal view of Roger II in Byzantine ceremonial dress with the *loros* and crown with *pendilia*. His right hand holds the upper part of the cross shaft, while in his left he holds the orb. Next to him stands his son Duke Roger, holding the lower part of the cross shaft with his left hand. He is clad in a short military tunic held together by a belt, his headgear is a princely cap or helm, and he holds a sword in his right hand. The inscription makes clear who the persons depicted are and when the money was struck: R(OGERIVS) R(EX) S(I)C(V)L(V)S, R(OGERIVS) D(V)X AP(VLIE), A(NNO) R(EGNI) X (Roger, King of Sicily, Roger Duke of Apulia, tenth year of the reign).[46]

We do not, in fact, know what sort of crown Roger wore. The iconographic representations show different crowns: one of Byzantine type at Palermo, a western-style one at Bari. Probably the ruler had various crowns at his disposal. He may have worn a different crown during his coronation in 1130 to that worn for later ceremonial crown wearings. An episode of 1160 also suggests that there were several crowns, when 'crowns and other royal regalia' (*diademata quedam aliaque regis insignia*) were discovered in the house of William I's murdered 'prime minister' Maio of Bari, which gave credence to the rumours of royal ambition on Maio's part. However, what this probably described was rather crowns intended to be given as New Year gifts to the king.[47]

---

[45] Engel (1882), plate VI, 28–30. Serafin Petrillo and Travaini (1986), 99–100 and plate 5. The hypothesis of Travaini (1995), 49, 213, 282, that Roger II had himself shown on some copper coins from Messina dressed as a Byzantine ruler before his royal coronation is based on the supposition that the lack of any royal title in the inscription means that these coins must therefore date from pre-1130. However, this is far from convincing: these *follari* are so small that there was simply no room for the royal title.

[46] Engel (1882), plate VI, 24. Serafin Petrillo and Travaini (1986), 101, fig. 2. Travaini (1995), 212–13, fig. 21, and plate 14 no. 241. Cf. Deér (1959), 161.

[47] *Falcandus*, 28 [*Tyrants*, 81]: 'it was broadcast everywhere that the admiral had shown off to many of his associates some sort of diadem and other royal insignia which he had prepared for himself'. Cf. *ibid.*, 48 [*Tyrants*, 101–2]: 'They asserted that everything that

Fig. 6. Coins of Roger II. Above: silver ducat, with on the obverse a bust of Christ Pantocrator with the Gospel in His left hand and Greek monogram in the nimbus. The legend reads *Jesus Christus regnat in aeternum* ('Jesus Christ rules eternally'). Reverse: Roger II (with crown and *pendilia*, *loros* and orb) and his son and heir Roger (with military tunic and sword). The legend reads 'King Roger of Sicily, Duke Roger of Apulia, in the tenth year of the reign' (*Rogerius rex Siculus, Rogerius dux Apuliae, anno regni X*). Below: copper *follaris*: on the obverse Roger II (with crown and *pendilia*, lance and orb – legend 'R[ogerius] II'); on the reverse Christ seated on a throne.

he himself [*Matthew Bonellus*] and his associates had nailed on the admiral was false, and that he had not in fact prepared the crown that had been found in his treasure-chest for his own use, but for the king's, to be handed over to him on the first of January as was the customary New Year's gift.' Deér (1952), 59, argues that 'at the Norman court the crowns were depreciated and their number continually increased by gifts made by the major functionaries'. However, other suggestions by Deér, that the Kings of Sicily used the Byzantine *kamelaukion*, and also a tiara, are unsustainable. See, recently, Engelberg (1995). For the (false) notice of Ralph Niger on the derivation of the royal crown from the papal mitre, see above p. 93 note 66.

The coronation *Ordo* of 1130 mentions the following insignia: the crown (*corona*), sword (*ensis*), bangles (*armillae*), mantel (*pallium*), ring (*anulus*), sceptre (*sceptrum*) and imperial orb (*regnum*). In another *Ordo* for a festival crown wearing, which has been attributed to the reign of Roger II, there appears among the royal regalia (*regalia insignia*), in addition to the crown (indicated by the synonyms *diadema* and *corona*), also the sceptre, orb, sword (*gladium*), shield (*scutum*) and lance (*lancea*). The divergences with the 1130 *Ordo* concern only secondary regalia such as the ring, bangles, shield and lance, but not the principal insignia of lordship – the crown, sceptre and orb. To these was joined as a new element the Byzantine proskynesis, the ritual foot kissing: the great men of the kingdom – the text mentions 'duke, prince, counts and magnates' (*dux, princeps, comites, magnati*), and by 'duke' and 'prince' the king's sons were probably meant – kiss the sovereign's feet. The hymns in honour of the king (*laudes regiae*) were to be sung first in Latin and then in Greek. One must however note that this *Ordo* for a festival crown wearing cannot be securely attributed to the time of Roger II; it may indeed have been redacted under William I. It is though indicative of the penetration of Byzantine elements into the ceremonial of the court in Palermo. Among these was the practice, following eastern Roman precedents, of covered hands, which is attested for the first time in the depiction of the coronation of William II (1166–89) at Monreale, and in the illuminated manuscript of Peter of Eboli, but could have been introduced earlier under Roger II or William I.[48]

In contrast with the iconographic depictions with their Byzantine symbols of rule and with coronation *Ordines*, which are primarily western in inspiration, daily life at the Palermitan court was markedly arabicized. Roger II's cloak, which was later used by the Staufen rulers as their coronation mantel, and hence has ended up in the treasury of the Hofburg in Vienna, is justly famous (see fig. 7). We have no proof that this was used as a coronation garment by Roger II, and indeed this appears rather improbable given that the decorative programme is not Christian. It is more likely that he wore it for audiences and to welcome guests. The cloak has an Arabic inscription in elegant Kufic characters on the lower hem, which tells us that it was produced in the year 528 from the Hegira (that is 1133–4) in the royal workshop (*ṭirāz*) in Palermo. Two camels, each

---

[48] The *Ordo* for the 1130 coronation: Elze (1973), 445–52, (1990), 170–8. The *Ordo* for the festival coronation, Elze (1973), 452–5, (1998), 321–7. For the *laudes regiae*, Kantorowicz (1946), 157ff. Covered hands, Peter of Eboli, fol. 102r, ed. Kölzer and Stähli, 63; Deér (1952), 14n. A ring with the inscription *Rogerius rex* and engraving of a crown, which was once in the Musée Calvet at Avignon, cannot now be found. Information from the Museum authorities via Prof. J-L. Lemaître of Paris, for whose assistance I am most grateful.

Fig. 7. Roger II's cloak or *mantellum*, later used for the coronation of the Staufen rulers. It shows two lions, each attacking a camel. The Arabic inscription on the border reads: 'This was made in the royal factory (*ṭirāz*) for the good fortune, supreme honour, perfection and power, the betterment, capacity, prosperity, sublimity, glory, beauty, the increase of [his] security, fulfillment of his hopes, the goodness of [his] days and nights without end or interruption, for [his] power and guard, [his] defence and protection, good fortune, salvation, victory and excellence. In the capital of Sicily, in the 528 th year [of the Hegira = 1133/4].' Translation by Johns (1986), 40.

being attacked by a lion, are depicted symmetrically (as though on a coat of arms) on a red background. The central axis shows a stylized palm tree, which represents the Arabic 'tree of life'. The lion, which later became the heraldic animal of the Hauteville dynasty, was generally adopted as the symbol of rulership, since it was seen as the king of beasts. Alexander of Telese expressly compared Roger with the lion, 'the strongest of beasts', and Romuald of Salerno described the ruler's face as that of a lion. The camel held in its jaws represented the subject Arabs. The message was clear: his Muslim subjects were in the king's hands, for better or worse. But while the iconographic programme and the inscription of the cloak were Arabic, it was worn as a garment in the western fashion.[49]

The parasol adopted by the court of Palermo, a typically Arab symbol of power, deserves particular mention. Roger had received this insignia as a gift from the Fatimid caliph al-Ḥāfiz (1130–49). It is probable that

[49] Al Samman (1982), Deér (1959), 66ff, Cantarella (1989), 133ff, Tramontana (1993), 91ff. *Al. Tel.*, 90–1, the '*Alloquium*' to King Roger': 'You will be, as Solomon says, as a lion which is strongest among beasts, and turneth not away for any' [Proverbs xxx.30]. For the 'leonine' appearance, see above note 40. For the lions on the bell tower at Melfi, commissioned by Roger II, see above p. 75 note 37, and for lions as the heraldic animals of the Hautevilles, Meier (1994), 182ff.

other elements of the ceremonial of the Palermitan court also drew on the model of Fatimid Egypt. Ibn al-Athīr, who was probably drawing on the testimony of the Zirid prince Ibn Shaddād who had visited Palermo c. 1156/7, wrote that the court of the King of Sicily with its shield and banner carriers (*al-silāḥiyya* and *al-jindariyya*) imitated Arabic models. No image survives of the parasol used in the court at Palermo, but the historian Ibn Ḥammād (c. 1220) has furnished a description:

the sun shade resembled a *daraqah* (a great leather shield) which is placed on the point of a lance. It was so magnificently constructed and elegantly decorated and coloured, studded with rare and precious stones, that its appearance dazzled the beholders and filled them with amazment. It was carried by one of the bravest of the knights, who was given the title of 'lord of the Parasol' (*ṣāḥib al-miẓalla*) . . . The only dynasties which are known to use the parasol are the Banū 'Ubayd (i.e. the Fatimids) and the king of the Europeans (*Rūm*) in Sicily. I believe that the latter received it as a gift [from the Fatimids], so I have heard it said among them.

Later on the parasol also came to be used as a symbol of authority by the popes, as one can see from the celebrated fresco of Constantine and Pope Sylvester in the Roman basilica of Quattro Coronati.[50]

The wooden roof of the Palatine chapel, made by Muslim craftsmen and decorated with stalactites, also shows scenes of arabicized court life. The images revolve around the theme of 'wine, women and song', and the veiled dancers shown there are well known, although in the semi-darkness of the chapel visitors can barely discern them. The same is true for the two images of the ruler which are to be found there, and which may perhaps depict Roger – a bearded figure with an Arabic-pattern crown is seated with a drinking flask in his right hand and a stylized flower in his left. At the sides and behind him are two servants. In one of the scenes these hold a carafe and beaker and a drum respectively, in the other they both hold fly whisks (see fig. 8).[51]

[50] Ibn Ḥammād, *BAS* 1.508–9. Schack (1969), 151ff, Johns (1986), 33, (1993), 146–7, whom I follow. Halm (1991), 312–13, gives an alternative view. See also Peter of Eboli, fol. 102r, ed Kölzer and Stähli, 63, where a parasol is shown among the other symbols of authority around Tancred. Schramm (1955), 717–19, suggests that the popes may have copied this usage from their south Italian vassals. According to al-Maqrīzī, it was George of Antioch who induced Roger II to present himself as an Arabic ruler: 'he kept Roger far away from his subjects, had him assume the exterior appearance of the Muslims [i.e. Muslim rulers], not appear on horseback nor show himself in public except on feast days, had horses with gold and silver saddles and with trappings encrusted with precious stones [led] in front of him . . . and golden vessels, the parasol and on his head the crown'. Cf. De Simone (1999), 278.

[51] Monneret de Villard (1950), figs. 219 (dancers), 189–90 (the sovereign). Very similar to the second representation of the ruler is the image on a medallion that 'Izz ad-Dawla, Emir of Baghdad, had struck in 975 to mark the marriage of his daughter with the caliph at-Ṭā'i', Gelfer-Jørgensen (1986), 31, fig. 13, cf. Johns (1993), 153–5, D'Erme (1995).

Fig. 8. Image of the ruler on the ceiling (decorated with stalactites) of the Palatine chapel at Palermo. He sits with a cup in his right hand and a stylized flower in his left. Behind him stand two servants, one on each side, holding fly whisks.

Furthermore the royal palaces of Palermo and its environs were influenced by Arabic models. Recent research has however shown that there was no simple imitation of Islamic models. What was taken over was only that which responded 'structurally to the architectonic exigencies of the contemporary (medieval Latin) building tradition of the rulers'. Arabic tradition explained the presence of eunuchs, who also played an important role at Byzantium. There was no harem in the strict sense of the term. 'The women's quarters, and those of the girls and eunuchs who served the king and queen' were not absolutely segregated from the other parts of the palace; nor is there any indication that men had no access to them. As for the 'maidens of the palace' (*palacii puellae*), these were serving girls, ladies of the palace and silk spinners from the workshop (*ṭirāz*) located within the palace.[52]

Palermo was both the kingdom's capital and the ruler's residence, and Roger had two castles built there. The sea castle, on the northern side of the harbour, guaranteed the security of the entrance to the port: it can be seen as a 'military building with a major residential capacity'. The 'upper castle' (*castrum superius*) which lay on a dominant position on the ancient Acropolis, became the royal palace. It comprised a number of towers, linked by walled courtyards. The treasure chamber was located on the ground floor of the so-called Pisan tower, while on the second storey above was the tower's hall where, probably, Roger usually spent his time. In the adjoining building on the south side, the *Joharia*, were the king's private appartments. They were richly decorated with mosaics, as is shown by the so-called 'Room of King Roger', although the decorations here were probably only realized under William I.[53]

A lively description of the royal palace survives from an anonymous writer in 1190:

The New Palace sits on the opposite part [of the city], built with amazing effort and astonishing skill out of squared stones; the outer side has walls which wind far and wide, while the inner side is remarkable for its great splendour of gems and gold. On the one side it has the Pisan Tower assigned to the protection of the treasury, on the other side the Greek Tower overlooks that part of the city which is called Kemonia. That part of the palace which is called Joharia glorifies the middle section; it is particularly beautiful, sparkling with the glory of many kinds of adornment, and the king used to spend his time there intimately when he wanted to enjoy peace and quiet. Over the rest of the site there are spread various mansions placed all around for the married ladies, the girls and the eunuchs who are assigned to serve the king and queen. There are some other rooms looking like small palaces there, shining with great beauty, where the king either discusses the

---

[52] Meier (1994), 109. *Epistola ad Petrum* (c. 1190/4), in *Falcandus*, 178 [*Tyrants*, 259]: 'Over the rest of the site there are spread various mansions placed all around for the married ladies, the girls, and the eunuchs who are assigned to serve the king and queen.' Johns (1983), 132–4, Corsi (1991). According to *Falcandus*, 56, some of those involved in the attempted coup of 1161 'thought that the attractions of the concubines [*puellae*] were to be preferred to any material gain'; indeed the chancellor Henry Aristippus was later arrested because 'at the time of the king's capture, this man had also kept some of the palace concubines in his own house for a few days', *ibid.*, 69 [*Tyrants*, 109,120]. *Travels of Ibn Jubayr*, 340–1.

[53] Meier (1994), 36ff, and for the dating of the 'stanza di Ruggero', 115.

state of the realm privately with his *familiares*, or invites the powerful when he is going to talk about the great public affairs of the realm. Nor is it appropriate to pass over in silence the high-quality workshops which belong to the palace, where the threads of silkworms are spun most finely into separate threads of different colours before being knitted together to make multiple strands.[54]

The royal apartments were linked to the upper floor of the Palatine chapel, and hence the ruler and his attendants had direct access to the royal balcony (the so-called 'royal box') in the north choir. Form here they could follow the religious services in the presbytery by the high altar, but were shielded from the view of the lay people in the nave of the church. It is noteworthy that the Transfiguration of Christ, and underneath it the Entry into Jerusalem, were depicted on the wall at the front of the balcony; these can be interpreted as 'a sacral elevation of the ruler'. In the dedicatory inscription of 1143, placed next to the mosaic of Christ Pantocrator in the presbytery, Roger was described as 'king, the ruler who carries the sceptre' ('Ρήξ σκηπτροκράτωρ).

Roger's throne, which no longer survives, was to be found on the western side of the Palatine chapel. The king used this on special occasions such as solemn crown wearings, and perhaps also for holding formal audiences. On the wall above where the throne was there is a mosaic, showing Christ enthroned, flanked by St Peter and St Paul (to the former of whom the church was dedicated) (see fig. 9). The iconographic model may have been the apse of St Peter's in Rome. The princes of the Apostles, and with them the pope, were the guarantors of the legitimacy and sacred character of the monarchy, an aspect which was stressed in the Palatine chapel's foundation privilege of 1140. The porphyry columns and the lions shown in the mosaic on the sides of the throne, and on the mosaic pavement and the bronze doors, symbolized the ruler's power. But in contrast to the Greek inscription in the presbytery, drawing on Byzantine imperial ideology, the west wall shows a western-style monarchy.[55]

Roger had two further palaces built just outside Palermo. The Favara was on the southern limit of the built-up area of the city, and was surrounded by a park with a lake and thermal springs. It was intended as a royal 'holiday retreat' to which the king could retire with a restricted circle of attendants. The palace of Altofonte, situated in the mountains to the south of Palermo,

---

[54] *Falcandus*, 177–80 [*Tyrants*, 258–9]

[55] Beck (1970), Brenk (1990a and b), Meier (1994), 51. For the inscription in the presbytery, and for the dedication inscriptions in S. Maria dell' Ammiraglio and Cefalù (1148), in which Roger was described as king, with no other titles, Cavallo and Magistrale (1995), 297ff. For the foundation privilege, Roger II, *Diplomata*, no. 48, above p. 55. Most recently see Tronzo (1997), who suggests that the original architectonic concept of the Palatine chapel under Roger II was very largely borrowed from Byzantine and Muslim models, and that the western components were only derived from his successors.

Fig. 9. West wall of the Palatine chapel. Above the raised tribune for the throne is a mosaic of Christ in majesty with St Peter and St Paul.

was in a park for wild animals, and was primarily intended for hunting. This was not just a private diversion, but also a privilege reserved for the ruler; but through invitations to important personages it could also be used as a ritual for the creation of alliances. During this period new and improved standards were being demanded for princely residences all over Europe; thus the royal palaces with their parks and gardens in the suburbs of Palermo 'played a formative role in the concept of sovereignty and the princely culture of the new dynasty'. The royal palaces with their mosaics in gold and their water features are testimony to the influence of Arab and Byzantine culture, which the Norman rulers and their architects joined together in 'a new unity'.[56]

Such representations of power included not only iconographic depictions, insignia and the palaces, but also the titles borne by the ruler, which show how he perceived himself. Even in the Arabic inscriptions on his buildings and money, Roger left no doubt that he was a Christian ruler, notwithstanding the tolerance shown towards Muslims and the Arabicized aspects of his court. He described himself expressly as the defender of Christianity and of the pope. On the other hand, he also employed typically Arabic descriptions of a ruler and appeals to the 'one God', which must have made him appear to many of his Muslim subjects as one of their own. We have already discussed the coinage on which Roger was described as 'powerful through the grace of Allah'. One should also consider in this context the good-luck formulae with appeals to Allah used in the Arabic documents and the Arabic motto (*'alāma*). When mentioning his father Roger I, he had recourse to the formula: 'that Allah sanctify his spirit and illuminate his sepulchre'.[57]

In his Latin charters Roger adopted titles which fundamentally followed western models. During the period in which he was count (in an example from 1124), he called himself 'by the grace of God, Count of Sicily and Calabria, son and heir of Count Roger the elder, of happy memory' (*Sicilie atque Calabrie Dei gratia comes, beate memorie magni comitis Rogerii filius et heres*). The reference to his hereditary right is perhaps to be understood with regard to the traditional style of the *intitulatio* of the Dukes of Apulia. In another *intitulatio* clause from his charters as count (in 1126), Roger styled himself, following the Greek formula τῶν χριστιανῶν βοηθός ('protector of the Christians'), as 'by the grace of God, Count of Sicily and Calabria, through the agency of God defender and protector of the Christian religion, son and heir of Count Roger the elder' (*Dei gratia*

---

[56] Cf. Meier (1994), 54ff, 136, 174 (quotes), and for the Scibene palace, which may also have been built under Roger II, *ibid.*, 65ff.

[57] Johns (1986), Noth, in Brühl (1978), 239 (*'alāma*), 245 (good-luck formulae), Johns (1993), 137–8.

Sicilie et Calabrie comes, Christiane religionis auctore Deo defensor et clipeus, Rogerii magni comitis heres et filius). The unction as *princeps* in 1127, and his subsequent acclamation as duke, in 1128, was reflected in his new title 'by the grace of God, Prince and Duke of Apulia, and Count of Sicily and Calabria' (*Dei gratia princeps et dux Apulie, Sicilie et Calabrie comes*). The title of prince was, however, abandoned after his investiture by the pope on 22 August 1128. He was then styled: 'by the grace of God, Duke of Apulia, sustainer and protector of the Christians, son and heir of the magnificent Count Roger' (*Dei gratia dux Apulie, Christianorum adiutor et clipeus, Rogerii magnifici comitis heres et filius*).[58]

The rise to kingship produced a new title 'by the grace of God, King of Sicily, Apulia and Calabria, sustainer and protector of the Christians, son and heir of Count Roger the elder' (*Dei gratia rex Sicilie, Apulie et Calabrie, adiutor Christianorum et clipeus, Rogerii magni comitis heres et filius*). After the 'constitutional reform' of 1135, in which Roger II invested his eldest son Roger with the duchy of Apulia, his second son Tancred with the principate of Bari, and his third son Alfonso with the principality of Capua, the royal title took on its definitive form. Roger thereafter called himself 'through the favour of Divine clemency, King of Sicily, of the duchy of Apulia and of the principality of Capua' (*Rogerius divina favente clementia rex Sicilie, ducatus Apulie et principatus Capue*). In contrast to the contemporary titles of the German, French and English rulers (*rex Romanorum, rex Francorum, rex Anglorum*), Roger's title did not contain any reference to the people over whom he ruled; it was instead territorially based. The kingdom, put together from different parts at various times, was a multi-ethnic state without any one people being dominant (the *Staatsvolk*).[59]

Roger probably took the *rota*, an authentication sign in the form of a circle containing a motto, name and title, from papal documents, although this was also used in some south Italian princely charters. With the motto 'the right hand of God made me strong, the right hand of God raised me up' (Psalm cxviii.16), Roger's chancery underlined the direct link between the monarchy and God. From 1136 onwards a new form of *rota* was developed, which was drawn with red ink, probably following

---

[58] Roger II, *Diplomata*, nos. 6 (1124), 7 (1126), 9 (1128), 14 (1129). Brühl (1978), 80, (1983a), 66–7. For the significance of *magnus*, Kienast (1967). Falkenhausen (1998a), 293–4.

[59] Roger II, *Diplomata*, nos. 16 (1131), 43 (1136). Brühl (1978), 81ff, (1983a), 67ff, Enzensberger (1992), 109ff. For Zielinski (1982) see Brühl (1978), 381n. Kehr (1902) 246n cites the dating clause of a private document, for which he provides neither date nor provenance but which probably refers to either Roger II or William I (see above p. 84 note 52), which uses the formula: 'Our Lord the most serene and invincible King of Sicily, Italy and the whole of Africa, crowned by God, pious, happy, triumphant and *semper augustus*.' This last part of the *intitulatio* reminds one of German imperial documents.

the example of the diplomas of the princes of Capua. Purple diplomas were likely only to have been produced exceptionally, as luxury items for appropriate recipients.[60]

In the Greek diplomas written before he became king, Roger's title was delineated according to territorial criteria, as 'Count of Calabria and Sicily'; from 1124 onwards with the addition of 'Italy' (meaning Apulia). But in Roger's royal documents in Greek there lacked any indications either of the people over whom he ruled or of his territories. In his Greek signatures Roger adopted the style of 'the king, pious and strong in Christ [our] God, and protector of the Christians' (ἐν χριστῷ τῷ θεῷ εὐσεβής κραταιός ῥήξ καί τῶν χριστιανῶν βοηθός). The imperial title (βασιλεύς) was never used in the royal diplomas in Greek, although the adjective 'imperial' (βασιλικός) and the expression 'my imperial sovereignty' (ἡ βασιλεία μου) were. Similar expressions were used by the monk Philagathos Keramides, who did indeed call the king βασιλεύς when preaching in his presence in the Palatine chapel and Palermo cathedral. One thus has the impression that the King of Sicily did claim imperial rank.[61]

Roger's wish to be buried in a porphyry sarcophagus, on the model of the ancient Roman and later Byzantine emperors, can be traced to a papal precedent. Since Innocent II had chosen such a sarcophagus for his burial, in 1143, it is possible that by imitating this practice Roger aspired to 'undermine [his] feudal dependence by means of the appropriation of essential aspects in the representation of the pope'. However, one ought not to exclude the possibility that Byzantium was the direct model. In any event, in the year 1145 Roger had two such sarcophagi set up in the choir of his chosen church, Cefalù cathedral, as an 'eternal reminder' of his death. One was to serve for his burial; the other 'both to signify the memory of our name and for the glory of the same church'. In the event the king's wishes could not be fulfilled: the cathedral had not yet been consecrated, and, notwithstanding the protests of the canons of Cefalù, his remains were interred in another porphyry sarcophagus in the cathedral of Palermo. This sarcophagus, probably constructed a little while after Roger's death, rested on four pairs of kneeling figures, which conferred a triumphal character to the funerary monument[62] (see fig. 10).

---

[60] Enzensberger (1971), 77ff. Brühl (1978), 69ff, and plate XIV, (1977), (1983), 58ff.

[61] Falkenhausen (1998a), 292–7. In the, admittedly rather later, mosaics at Monreale the emperor Nero was given the title of *rex*, suggesting the two terms were interchangeable. For Philagathos, see above p. 101. For the titles used in the Arabic diplomas, Johns (1987), 90ff.

[62] Quote from Deér (1974), 382. Roger II, *Diplomata*, 199 no. 68: 'we instruct that two splendid sarcophagi be placed in the aforesaid church, always to remain there as

Fig. 10. Roger II's tomb in Palermo cathedral. The porphyry sarcophagus rests upon four pairs of kneeling figures and above it there is a baldequin supported by six columns.

a permanent reminder of our death, in one of these, next to the choir where the canons sing, I shall find rest after the day of my death; we decree that the other be suitable both to signify the memory of our name and for the glory of the same church'. See Deér (1959) generally, and especially pp. 85ff for Roger's eventual sarcophagus at Palermo. The sarcophagi at Cefalù were transferred to Palermo by Frederick II who intended them for his own burial and that of his father Henry VI, Deér (1974), 369ff.

We may conclude that the representations of Roger's rulership were intended to show symbolically both the legitimacy and the sacrality of his kingship. The way in which this message was communicated varied depending on to whom it was addressed. For the bulk of the population who were imbued with Byzantine culture the symbols of rule depicted on the coinage, crown, *loros*, *labarum* and orb, were enough. The Martorana mosaic with its Greek inscription was aimed at a restricted, Graecophone, audience which had access to the private church of the *amiratus*, George of Antioch. The enamel plaque in the basilica of St Nicholas was intended for a larger circle of recipients, the Latin/Lombard inhabitants of Bari, the former Byzantine capital of the region. This combined a Latin inscription, and techniques of manufacture which were partly western and partly Byzantine, with an iconography that was essentially Greek. The Muslims living in Sicily were able to see inscriptions in which Roger gave expression to his royal status using Arabic titles, but which left no doubt that he was indeed a Christian king. Those who had access to the court could also marvel over the Arabic embroideries of the cloak and the parasol. The palaces both inside and outside Palermo, with their parks and gardens, underlined the new monarchy's high regard for itself, as did the porphyry tombs, while the architecture stressed the residential character of Palermo as a capital. The titles used by the ruler came from Latin, Byzantine and Arabic models. Roger called himself a king, but he believed his monarchy to be on the same level as that of the Byzantine emperors.

LEGISLATION

'King Roger, however, established peace and good order in his kingdom, and to preserve that peace instituted chamberlains and justiciars throughout the land, promulgated laws which he had newly drafted and removed evil customs from their midst.' So Romuald of Salerno wrote in his chronicle. In the immediately preceding passage he wrote of the death of King Louis VI of France, in 1137, and in the section which followed he discussed the extension of Roger's rule to north Africa. Hence the chronicler did not assign a clear date to the promulgation of these 'new' laws, or connect them with any particular event; all he suggested was that this happened after peace had been re-established in the kingdom, that is after 1139.[63]

This notice has been linked with a passage in the Chronicle of Falco of Benevento, where one reads, under the year 1140, that, after his sons Roger and Alfonso had conquered the region round Pescara on the Adriatic coast,

[63] *Romuald*, 226.

Roger II had in mid July travelled via Salerno and Capua to San Germano in the hope, which turned out to be in vain, of meeting Innocent II. After stops along the way at Montecassino, Capua, Casauria and Pescara, the king went to Ariano, a town in the mountains of Samnium to the east of Benevento. There he held an assembly of 'nobles and bishops' at which 'numerous issues' were discussed. However, of the 'dispositions' which were produced, Falco mentioned only one, a 'terrible edict' for the reform of the coinage.[64]

The view that Roger promulgated his legislation – often called by historians the 'Assizes of Ariano' – in this assembly is merely a hypothesis. It seems rather unlikely that the king would choose such an insignificant place as Ariano from which to promulgate a body of legislation applying to the whole kingdom. The one thing that is certain is that once his kingdom was consolidated Roger issued a series of laws. What we do not know is when and where he did this. As with the peace edict promulgated at Melfi in 1129, the so-called 'Assizes of Ariano' must also have been issued during an assembly, since the foreword to these begins with an address directed towards the great men of the realm. Romuald of Salerno linked them with the introduction of chamberlains and justiciars 'throughout the land'; if this is correct then one may presume that the laws were issued round about 1140, for it was only after this date that such officials can be found all over the kingdom – before then they only appear sporadically.[65]

What took place at Ariano was only an 'assembly of nobles and bishops' (*curia procerum et episcoporum*), not a 'general assembly' in which all free men played a part. The idea that such general assemblies, following the Germanic tradition, took place in the kingdom of Sicily derived from the view that, after the first 'general assembly' of 1140, another of these gatherings, lasting several months, was held in 1142 in the forest of Silva Marca near Ariano, close to the crossroads of the Via Appia and the Via Traiana. Here, it is argued, such important issues were dealt with as the military obligations of vassals and the reorganization of the counties, and legislation was issued. A document from the nunnery of St John the Evangelist at Lecce has been cited in support of this theory. This was issued in July 1142,

---

[64] *Falco*, 234: 'He came to the city of Ariano where he held a court with his nobles and bishops and dealt with numerous issues. Among the other dispositions which he made there he promulgated a terrible edict, hated throughout Italy and leading to death and poverty, namely that nobody dwelling in his kingdom should receive *romesinae* or pay them in any transaction, and on the worst possible advice he introduced his own money, the ducat.' For his conquests in the Abruzzi, above p. 73, and for the monetary reforms below p. 159.

[65] For the background to the 'Assizes of Ariano' theory, see Zecchino (1980), 62–3, and for the *proem* to the Assizes, below p. 141. For Roger's previous legislative activity, see Niese (1910), 15ff.

'in the territory of Ariano at the place called Silva Marca' (*in territorio Ariani in loco, ubi Silva Marca dicitur*), and in its arenga (preamble) Roger declared that 'while we were at Silva Marca along with our son Alfonso, Duke of Naples and Prince of Capua, our counts and other barons, and a very great part of the people of our realm, to put an end to disputes and injustices, there came [to us] Abbess Guimarca . . .'. The view that Roger remained at or near Ariano from July until September 1142 is based upon the conviction that it was here that he issued a diploma, dated 1 September 1142, for the monastery of the Holy Saviour on Monte Majella. However, this document has been shown to be a forgery, and thus the only evidence that remains for Roger's stay at Silva Marca is the document cited above of July 1142. We do not know for how long the king remained there. The next diploma issued by him dates only from April of 1143, when he was once again at Palermo. It remains therefore certain that the king did indeed hold an assembly near Ariano in July 1142, during which, as was customary, he dealt with matters of justice. The formula used in the document with regard to the presence of 'a very great part of the people' signifies simply that in this assembly representatives of different social classes were present. There is nothing in the sources concerning an 'assembly of the people' held at Silva Marca, or of the promulgation of laws, or of any military reorganization or alteration to the counties.[66]

The 'Assizes of Ariano' survive only in two composite juridical manuscripts. Both of these were 'private' collections of laws. The fullest text is that contained in Codice Vaticano latino 8782, which can be dated from its handwriting to the end of the twelfth century, and which contains forty-four assizes, as well as a prologue. Codex 468 of the library of Montecassino appears to be a little later than the Vatican manuscript, and to date from the first half of the thirteenth century. It transmits only an abbreviated version of these laws, although it also contains some additions and another seven assizes which are lacking in the Vatican manuscript. A comparison between the two texts has shown that the Cassinese manuscript is not dependent upon a version of the Vatican one, but that both 'depend upon a fuller third version, the contents of which have as a whole been better transmitted by the Vatican Assizes, but some individual passages of

---

[66] Roger II, *Diplomata*, 149 no. 53. Jamison (1971), 15–16, argued for the general assembly at Silva Marca, and suggested that Roger remained there for several months in the summer and autumn of 1142. Cf. Jamison (1913), 257–8, which pointed to a clause in the *Catalogus Baronum*, art. 509, where a vassal obtained a fief at Silva Marca. This was accepted by Zecchino (1980), 63–72, and Cuozzo (1980), 80ff, (1989b), 105–9, who develops a theory about general assemblies 'on the ancient German model', and that Roger's reforms to the comital structure were established at Silva Marca in 1142. For the problems with the diplomata cited to support the idea of an extended stay there in 1142, Roger II, *Diplomata*, nos. 53–4 (Ca. 146–7), see Brühl (1978), 91, 192.

which are only known thanks to the otherwise very abbreviated Cassinese Assizes'. Only the Montecassino version carries the rubric 'The assizes of the kings of the kingdom of Sicily' (*Assise regum regni Sicilie*). The laws which it alone contains (Cassino Assizes 33–9) were probably for the most part those issued by Roger II after the first publication of his legislative work, hence 'Novels'. One or more probably stem from William I or William II, because the rubric refers to kings (in the plural).[67]

Because no earlier manuscript survives, this has led to the theory that while Roger promulgated individual laws he did not issue any actual legal code. The assizes contained in the two surviving manuscripts would therefore represent private compilations made by monks of Montecassino, produced early in the reign of Frederick II, and may have been used as part of the preparatory work for the Staufen legislation which was brought together in the Constitutions of Melfi in 1231. This argument has not, however, found general agreement. The paleography of the Vatican manuscript suggests that in fact it was written before the end of the twelfth century, and anyway some of the so-called 'Assizes of Ariano' were already known during the second half of that century.[68]

First of all, there was Romuald of Salerno, who was writing in the 1170s. Close similarities between the words that he used and the legislative text lead one to think that he knew of the Assizes. In the proem to the legislative collection it says that God 'has restored peace, and made our kingdom whole again by means of His most gracious tranquillity' (*pacem reddidit, integritatem regni tranquillitate ... reformavit*); in Romuald, that Roger 'established in his kingdom the perfect tranquillity of peace' (*in regno suo perfecte pacis tranquillitate potitus*). At the beginning of the Cassinese version of the Assizes, there is talk of 'the laws newly promulgated by our Majesty' (*leges a nostra maiestate noviter promulgatas*); Romuald writes that 'he [Roger] promulgated laws which he had newly drafted' (*leges a se noviter conditas promulgavit*). Assize 27 of the Vatican redaction uses the expression 'to extirpate evil customs' (*pravas consuetudines extirpare*);

---

[67] For the manuscripts, see Pene Vidari (1994), 206ff, Stürner (ed.), *Die Konstitutionen Friedrichs II.*, 69–71. The most recent edition, with facsimile, is by Zecchino (1984). Here there is some variation with the traditional numbering of the Assizes. Assize 22 of the Vatican text is deemed to be part of Assize 21, and all subsequent sections are therefore renumbered. My discussion retains the traditional numbering. For the Novels, Caspar (1904), 275–83, Niese (1910), 101ff. Stürner, *Die Konstitutionen*, 71 suggests that Ass. Cas. 33–4 and 36 date from pre-1140, while nos. 37–8 were probably promulgated by William II.

[68] Ménager (1969), but n.b. the criticisms raised in the discussion after that paper by H. Enzensberger and A. Marongiu, 601, and Marongiu (1973), Zecchino (1980), 89–104, Trombetti Budriesi (1992), Santini (1994).

in Romuald it says, 'he [Roger] removed evil customs from their midst' (*malas consuetudines de medio abstulit*). Roger's interest in legislative action is also attested by pseudo-Falcandus: 'he also made every effort to find out about the customs of other kings and peoples, in order to adopt any of them that seemed particularly admirable or useful'.[69]

A document of 1167 shows that Roger's Assizes were not only known but also used in the 1160s. A woman from Bari had fallen into penury and wished to sell her house, and in order to do this she had recourse to a royal judge, who gave his consent to the transaction once he was sure that she was acting of her own free will. He made express reference to a prescription of King Roger concerning this, which must have been to his assize concerning the protection of women.[70] The application of this norm does not of course prove that the judge knew and used the entire corpus of the 'Assizes of Ariano'.

The belief that the Bishop of Potenza had 'a copy of the Assizes of King Roger' at his disposal in 1178 is, however, based upon a misunderstanding. The expression contained in the document in question, *assisas et ordinaciones*, means only clerical statutes. The clergy sought the confirmation of the statutes granted to them by King Roger: 'we wish to have those assizes and ordinations which the lord King Roger of happy memory laid down for us'. As a result the bishop had these 'assizes and ordinations' read out and confirmed the various points (*statuta*).[71]

A clear reference showing knowledge of the 'Assizes of Ariano' is contained in a charter of 1180 from Ruvo, near Bari, in which one reads of a marriage celebrated according to 'the sacred constitutions of the lord King

---

[69] Ass. Vat. 27; for which below, note 85. *Falcandus*, 6 [*Tyrants*, 58]. The relationship suggested by Niese (1910), 95–6, between Roger's diploma for the Palatine chapel, Roger II, *Diplomata*, no. 48 (28 April 1140) and the Assizes, which led him to suppose that they were the work of one and the same author, is not convincing. Even less credible is his supposition that the compiler of the Assizes was 'a Sicilian of Norman origin who had studied at Bologna', *ibid.*, 94–7.

[70] *CDB* 1.96 no. 50: 'The said judge, moved by piety and according to the precept and authority which our lord, the most glorious King Roger of most happy memory, grandfather of our aforesaid lord King William, newly promulgated and decreed in his time, gave me permission to do this.' The reference is to Ass. Vat. 15 ('About Wards and Orphans'), ed. Brandileone, 103; ed. Zecchino, 38: 'In addition we settle the equity of the laws on women, who are not less disadvantaged by the fragility of their sex. We order that they should be aided from the depths of piety, both by us and by our officials, as is right and proper.'

[71] Both Schminck (1970), 29 and Enzensberger, in the discussion to Ménager (1969), 606, refer to this charter of 1178, to which they had access only in an abstract in Pedìo (1962), 142 [= Pedìo (1964), 35], who maintains that these 'assizes and ordinances' were those of King Roger. The full text of the document is now edited by Pellettieri (1996–7), 73–4.

Roger'. The reference is undoubtedly to Assize 27: 'About the legitimate celebration of marriages' (*De coniugiis legitime celebrandis*).[72]

A charter of Count Hugh II of Molise of July 1153 presupposes not only knowledge of the 'Assizes of Ariano' but also of two laws of King Roger contained in the Cassinese manuscript. In this document there is a list of the crimes which were reserved to the jurisdiction of the crown: 'murder, arson, theft of cattle, horses and asses, violent burglary, theft of any object worth more than five *romanati*, the cutting down of fruit trees or vines, attacks upon and robbery of travellers, rape, and adultery if this has been publicly proclaimed to our court'. This list is virtually identical with that in two of the assizes preserved only in the Cassinese manuscript, which are thought to be Novels of King Roger. 'Our Majesty has come to know', says Assize 35, 'that within the bounds of the kingdom which has been granted to us by God through the wickedness of certain persons fires have been lit both in town and countryside, and trees and vines have been secretly cut down. Therefore we ordain that . . . .' Those cases which were reserved to the jurisdiction of the royal justiciars were listed in the following assize: 'theft, housebreaking, attacks on travellers, violence towards women, duels, murders, judgements of God, criminal calumnies, and arson'. The parallels are so marked that there is little need for further discussion, for it is clear that Roger's legislation, as laid down in the manuscripts of the 'Assizes', was actually put into practice.[73]

Furthermore, one should also note that all the laws which in the Constitutions of Melfi are designated as deriving from Roger can be found in the Vatican manuscript of the 'Assizes'. Textual examination has, however, shown that while the authors of the Constitutions of 1231 'normally followed with care the versions of the Vatican Assizes, at least with regard to the sequence of the laws', they may have used another version of this Rogerian legislation which 'clearly used some of the alternative readings noted in the Cassino Assizes'. This must therefore have come from the use of a now lost version 'on which both traditions are based'.[74]

The introduction or preamble preserved in the Vatican manuscript[75] gives programmatic expression to the concept of the lawmaker on Roger's

---

[72] *CDB* IX.72 no. 63: 'Our wedding now having been celebrated according to the lawful, solemn and holy ceremonies laid down by the lord King Roger . . .'. Cf. also *CDP* XX.263 no. 125 (Ruvo, July 1171).

[73] Jamison (1929), 557 document no 2. Ass. Cas. 35–6, ed. Brandileone, 134–5; ed. Zecchino, 94–6. Discussion, Jamison (1929), 548–50, Caravale (1966), 306–7.

[74] Stürner, *Die Konstitutionen*, 72, and for discussion of all thirty-eight of Roger's assizes in the Constitutions of Melfi, *ibid.*, 131–2.

[75] Ass. Vat., ed. Brandileone, 94–5; ed. Zecchino, 22–3. Cf. Caravale (1994a), 4ff. for the formulae taken from the legislation of Justinain, Niese (1910), 44ff.

part, laid out in formulae which are very much dependent on those of Justinian – the imperial legislator of the sixth century.

It is right and proper, barons, that we should not be presumptuous either concerning ourselves or about the conditions and deserts of our whole kingdom, and that if we have received anything from the generosity which has resulted from Divine grace, then we should repay these Divine benefits through which we have our strength with humble service, lest we be entirely ungrateful for such great favour. If then holy God has through His mercy laid our enemies low and restored peace, and if He has made our kingdom whole once again by means of His most gracious tranquillity, both in matters temporal and spiritual, we are compelled to renew the paths of both justice and piety, when we see that these have become miserably crooked. This very thing which is called inspiration we have received by a gift from the Giver Himself, when He says: 'By me kings reign, and legislators decree justice' [Proverbs viii.15] . For we consider that nothing is more pleasing to God than if we straightforwardly offer Him that which we have learnt Him to be, namely mercy and justice. In this oblation the office of kingship claims for itself a certain privilege of priesthood; from this a certain wise man skilled in the law calls the interpreters of the law priests. Therefore we who through His grace possess the authority of justice and law ought in part to improve them and in part redraft them, and those of us who have secured mercy should in all matters handle them more mercifully and interpret them in a more kindly way, especially where their severity contains a degree of inhumanity. And we do not claim this on the basis of pride, as if we were more just or more moderate than our predecessors in the establishment or interpretation of laws through our vigilance, but because we have erred in many things and because we are more inclined to err, we take the view that it is appropriate that those who do wrong should be spared in keeping with the moderation that is appropriate to our times. For the Holy One himself has instructed us as follows, saying: 'Be ye also merciful as your Father also is merciful' [Luke vi.36], and the King and Prophet says: 'All the paths of the Lord are mercy and truth' [Psalm xxv.101], and without doubt we shall take the view that the man who has given judgement without mercy shall receive judgement without mercy. We therefore desire and order that you should faithfully and enthusiastically receive the provisions which we make public in the present code, whether they have been promulgated by us or [simply] re-enacted.

With his legislative activity the king thus fulfilled his obligation to give thanks to God. He described himself as a priest of justice, making reference to the first section of the Digest of Justinian in which the jurist Ulpian cites his colleague Celsius: 'Law is the art of Good and Equity', from which it follows that: 'for this reason some call us priests'.[76]

Roman law, which was rediscovered at the end of the eleventh, and more especially in the twelfth century, at Bologna, had never entirely disappeared from the Mezzogiorno. Abbot Desiderius of Montecassino

---

[76] Digest, princ. 1.1.1., para.1.

(1058–87) had had the Institutes and the Novels of Justinian recopied; the latter probably from the extracts in the *Epitome* of Julian. In a legal case between the abbey of Cava and some private individuals, which took place in the archiepiscopal palace at Salerno, in the presence of Duke Roger Borsa, in May 1089, and in which the validity of a will made in favour of the monastery was under dispute, the monks made express appeal to the Institutes of Justinian.[77]

The precepts derived from Roman law which provided the core of the legislative work were not directly taken from the *corpus* of Justinian but from a collection of extracts. More than half of the Assizes were derived from this. The text is briefer and more pointed with regard to the laws redacted *de novo* by Roger, which show similarities with the formulation of the royal diplomas and reflect the basic principle enunciated in the prologue to the Assizes of showing clemency. The influence of Lombard law is relatively slight, as similarly is that of both the local Byzantine law of southern Italy and of Canon law. Thus 'the Assizes of King Roger provide the first example of territorial legislation based upon Roman (Justinaic) law', and indeed the opinion has been expressed that 'they precede, and were actually more important in practice than, the purely academic rediscovery of Roman law on the part of the Bolognese glossators'. However, in this respect one should remember that the Assizes did not exercise any influence outside the frontiers of the Sicilian kingdom.[78]

This legislation was not an organic whole, rather a sort of mosaic work, to which has been imputed 'technical imperfections':

because of the diversity of the extracts and of the original constitutions, the Assizes acquired a seriously chequered aspect, and the composition is far from concise. One long title with many subparagraphs is followed by extremely brief sections, comprising only one phrase. Sometimes a prescription is given in a few words without comment, in other places the legislator speaks clearly and unequivocally in the first person. What is original and what is copied are not in any way blended according to any unifying principle.[79]

---

[77] *Chron. Cas.* III.63, p. 446. Lohrmann (1968), 100. For such legal manuscripts, see most recently Santini (1994), 96ff. For the plea of May 1089, see Perla (1885), 158–61, at p. 160: 'And this document of theirs is invalid according to Roman law, by which this monastery and the brothers live. And since in the Book, the Institutes, the divine Justinian states [that] "one can act in the place of a male up to fourteen years old, and in the place of a woman up to twelve years, and if this time is exceeded, such a right of representation disappears".'

[78] Caspar (1904), 251, suggests that of the forty-four assizes, twenty-seven were derived from Roman law, while seventeen came *ex novo* from King Roger. Dilcher (1994), 38, identifies sixty-five norms, thirty-eight of which 'derive directly from Justinian's laws', eight 'are influenced by Byzantine, canon or lombard law', nineteen were redacted independently.

[79] Caspar (1904), 257. Cf. also Niese (1910), 97–100.

We are therefore undoubtedly dealing with an incomplete legislative work, indeed rather with an attempt to create something of the sort. Roger's recourse to the example of the Roman emperors is indicative of how ambitious his intentions were.

The Assizes touch on only some aspects of the law: ecclesiastical, public, marriage and criminal. Alongside them customary law remained in force, unless it actually contradicted what was in the Assizes. The reason for this was noteworthy: 'because of the variety of different people subject to our rule'.[80] One sees therefore that the legislator was very conscious of ruling over a multi-ethnic state; he respected the individual character of the various groups, although only insofar as this did not conflict with his overriding supervision.

A key point of Roger's legislation was the stress it laid upon the exceptional position of the king. This exalted self-regard and the aspiration to absolute rule showed itself in the declaration that any questioning of the sovereign's orders was equivalent to an offence against God, hence Assize 17 says: 'for to dispute his judgements, decrees, deeds and plans, or if someone whom he has chosen or appointed is worthy, is comparable to sacrilege'. One should not therefore be surprised that the next assize should deal with the crime of treason, and in a manner so pointed that it has been maintained that 'the tenor of Vatican Assize 18 is stamped through with Roman Law concepts in a way that was unprecedented in Europe'.[81]

Whoever should start a plot, whether with one knight or with many, or on his own, or should give an undertaking or oath to a plot, that plans and prepares the murder of one of the illustrious men who are among our councillors or advisors – they have by their wish to commit evil chosen for themselves severe legal punishment. The culprit should be struck down by the sword as guilty of treason and all their property should be confiscated by the state. Their sons should indeed receive no benefit, whether by our generosity or by legal right. Let death be a blessing to them and life a punishment. If however anyone shall have demounced what has been done by the conspirators without delay, he shall promptly receive pardon and grace. The crime of treason also encompasses those who discuss and attack the reputation of the king after his death, so that anyone who should do or be a party to this will from that day on be treated as a criminal and

---

[80] Ass. Vat. 1 ('About the Interpretation of Laws'), ed. Brandileone, 95–6; ed. Zecchino, 26: 'We order that the laws newly promulgated by our majesty, mitigating through piety excessive harshness and thus encouraging benevolent rule, should be fully observed by all. Because of the variety of different people subject to our rule, the usages, customs and laws which have existed among them up to now are not abrogated unless what is observed in them is most clearly in contradiction to our edicts here.'

[81] Ass. Vat. 17 ('About Sacrilege'), ed. Brandileone, 103; ed. Zecchino, 38. Quote from Dilcher (1994), 43. Cf. Hageneder (1996).

have no protection, but everything that they have shall be sold according to the laws of the fisc. He who shall purge a relative of a crime deserves succession to them.

All those by whose advice hostages escape, citizens are armed, plots are fomented, tumults excited, magistrates killed, men desert from the army or flee from the enemy, allies are betrayed, military formations are cloven asunder by wicked tricks, battles lost, fortresses abandoned, help denied to allies, and other things of this type done, shall be considered guilty of this crime, as will anyone who spys on, corrupts or publishes the king's counsels, as well as he who knowingly gives shelter and renders assistance to the enemies of the kingdom.[82]

The last section of this assize reflects Roger's experience of the revolts on the south Italian mainland which had posed him such problems in the previous decade. There follows an assize which has been considered as the earliest evidence for the emergence of a separate and distinct knightly class. This law – not very skilfully formulated – was probably directed only against those breakers of the peace who had arbitrarily arrogated to themselves the rank of knight. Such people were to lose both the title and the 'profession' of knight, unless they were descended from a knightly family. The same was to apply to other professions, such as those of judges and notaries.[83]

Functionaries enjoyed the special protection of the king. Assize 25 said that offences against his officials struck also at the royal dignity. These officials had an exceptional position, but also great responsibilities. If they rendered themselves intentionally guilty of misappropriation or corruption, they ought to face the death penalty. The same fate awaited those who forged charters or counterfeited money. Violation of the rights and property of churches was also equated with treason.[84]

---

[82] Ass. Vat. 18 ('About the Crime of Treason'), ed. Brandileone, 104–5; ed. Zecchino, 38–40. Cf. Schminck (1970), 28–79. For the concept of *consistorium* taken from Justinian's legislation, see Caspar (1904), 269n.

[83] Ass. Vat. 19 ('About New Knighthood'), ed. Brandileone, 105; ed. Zecchino, 40: 'Consenting to Divine justice, we approve what must be approved and reject the contrary. For just as the good must not be exasperated, so the evil should not be benefited. Therefore we order and propose this edict, that if someone should seize new knighthood contrary to the happiness, peace and integrity of our kingdom, he will lose completely the name and profession of knight, unless perhaps he is descended from the stock of a knightly family. We order the same about those who receive the order of any profession, as for example they obtain the authority of a judge or the office of a notary, or others similar.' Ass. Cas. 31, ed. Brandileone, 133; ed. Zecchino, 92. Cf. Niese (1910), 67–8: 'the first evidence that the rank of knight was restricted on grounds of birth', Cuozzo (1989b), 23, Dilcher (1994), 40–1.

[84] Ass. Vat. 25 ('About Public Officials'), ed. Brandileone, 107–8; ed. Zecchino, 44. Cf. also Ass. Vat. 20–1. Falsification of documents had already been viewed as treason in Roger II, *Diplomata*, no. 48 (28 April 1140).

Royal legislation was not limited solely to matters of law, but also dealt with moral and ethical questions. At the beginning of the assize on the celebration of marriage, one reads that the role of the sovereign is not just 'to draft the laws and govern the people', but also 'to instruct them in morals and to extirpate evil customs'.[85]

Along with precepts that were clearly innovative, such as the immunity of children and lunatics from prosecution and the introduction of a state examination for physicians,[86] one also finds norms that were of archaic origin. Thus Assize 31 confirmed the right of a husband to kill his wife and her lover if they were caught *in flagrante*, a principle derived from Lombard law which continued in the Italian penal code right up to the middle of the twentieth century. Something, probably derived from a Byzantine precedent, which appears barbarous was the right given to a cuckolded husband to cut off his wife's nose; a precept which was, along with a number of others, repeated by Frederick II in the Constitutions of Melfi. If the husband renounced this right, then the adulterous woman was to be publicly flogged. What might to us appear to be cruel was seen by the legislator as an amelioration of Roman law, which prescribed the death penalty for adulterers. His concern to take account of the circumstances of the crime was here particularly evident:

Moved by the piety to which we owe our whole being, we decree by the present general law that whenever a charge of adultery or fornication is put before those who, through our foresight and enactment, control our laws, they should pay no attention to status, but should clearsightedly note the conditions and ages, and investigate the state of mind [of the parties] to establish whether it was with premeditation, or from advice received, or because of the perils of youth, that they have rushed into the act, or whether they are fallen women; [to establish] whether the women's financial means are weak or strong, and whether they have been motivated by wilfulness, or by a particularly unhappy marriage. Once all these factors have been investigated, proven and clarified, either a more lenient or a more severe sentence may be passed on the crime committed, not on the basis of the severity of the law but on that of the balance of equity. For if we proceed in

---

[85] Ass. Vat. 27 ('About the Legitimate Celebration of Marriages'), ed. Brandileone, 108–9; ed. Zecchino, 46: 'Since it belongs to the care and solicitude of the kingdom to draft laws, govern the people, instruct them in morals, and extirpate evil customs, it seems right and equitable to our clemency to rescind by the sternness of our edict a certain evil custom which, as though some damage or pestilence, has for a long time and up to the present crept into use by part of our people, to prevent burgeoning vices spreading to the rest. For it is contrary to custom, inconsistent with what is laid down by the holy canons, and unheard of to Christian ears, to contract matrimony, to procreate legitimate progeny and bind oneself indissolubly to a consort, unless seeking the grace and favour of God...'

[86] Ass. Vat. 36 and 39, ed. Brandileone, 115–16; ed. Zecchino, 58. Cf. Dilcher (1994), 56.

this way, justice will tally perfectly with Divine justice; nor will we be departing from that Divine verdict; 'with what measure ye mete, it shall be measured to you once again' [Matthew vii.1].

The harshness of the laws has been softened so that she shall not, as once, be struck down by the sword [i.e. subject to the death penalty], but that the property belonging to her shall be subject to confiscation, if she shall have no legitimate children from this marriage or another. For it is most unjust that those who were born at a time when the law of marriage was legally preserved should be defrauded of their inheritance. And she should certainly not be handed over to her husband whose anger would imperil her life, but rather the punishment for the violation of her marriage should be the slitting of her nose, which [punishment] has been most sternly and cruelly introduced. However, neither her husband nor her relations should be permitted to harm her further. If her husband is unwilling that such a penalty be inflicted upon her, we will not allow a crime of this sort to go unpunished, and we order her to be publicly flogged . . . Those women who through their miserable condition of life [*vilitas vite*] shall not be thought worthy to observe these laws [i.e. known prostitutes] shall stand immune from the judicial punishments for adultery and fornication.[87]

The desire to protect the weakest in the social structure was widely diffused in the Middle Ages; it was shown in the assize on orphans, which also contained a prescription for the protection of women as 'the weaker sex': 'In the same way, we settle the equity of the laws [*legum equitatem*] on women, who are not less disadvantaged by the fragility of their sex. We order that they should be aided from the depths of piety, both by us and by our officials, as is right and proper.'[88]

As was to happen a hundred years later with the Constitutions of Melfi, the 'Assizes of Ariano' were also translated into Greek. Only a tiny part of this Greek version now survives. In addition, a Greek law of King Roger, issued in 1150 and only applicable to Calabria, also survives. It is probable that the edict promulgated in 1144 for the renewal of privileges was also drafted in Greek, and valid only in Calabria and Sicily. This served as the model for similar edicts of revocation issued by Henry VI and Frederick II, which were applied to the whole kingdom.[89]

Roger's legislative activity certainly did not end with the so-called 'Assizes of Ariano', although the only other laws of his which have been found

---

[87] Ass. Vat. 28 ('About Adulteresses'), 31 ('About the Violation of the Marriage Bed'), ed. Brandileone, 109–11, 113; ed. Zecchino, 50, 56. Stürner, *Die Konstitutionen*, III.74, pp. 438–9. Caspar (1904), 253–4.

[88] Ass. Vat. 15 [above note 70].

[89] Burgmann (1982). For the 1150 Novel, see Caspar (1904), 283–4. For the Greek translation of the Constitutions of Melfi, see Stürner, *Die Konstitutionen*, 77ff, who describes this as 'a work for private use'. For the edict of revocation, Niese (1910), 115ff, Brühl (1978), 54–5, (1983a), 44–5. Five diplomas issued as a result of this edict between 18 October and 5 November 1144 now survive, Roger II, *Diplomata*, no. 64A in *Additamentum*.

are those contained in the Montecassino codex. There is a reference to a 'new law' (*nova constitutio*), which can only have emanated from King Roger, in the Chronicle of the abbey of Venosa – although this work itself only survives in fragmentary form thanks to the extracts copied by early modern antiquaries. According to this chronicle, during a judicial hearing in a royal court held at Melfi (probably in June 1147) one of the parties made an appeal to 'a certain new law'. What this actually comprised is uncertain, for this section of the chronicle is only partially comprehensible, and its significance remains unclear. All one can deduce is that it was to do with postponements in legal proceedings.[90]

The Assizes of King Roger were considerably in advance of contemporary legislative activity by other rulers who limited themselves to having the customary laws already in use set down in writing. Far more than, for example, Henry I of England, the Sicilian ruler modified current law to harmonize equity (*aequitas*) and law (*ius*). If, by means of his itinerant justices, the English monarch protected the rights of his free subjects against the claims of his barons, and to some extent contained the centrifugal tendencies of baronial lordship, Roger II tried to reinforce the position of the sovereign by applying the principles expounded in the 'Assizes of Ariano'. However, since, in contrast to England, there was no 'common law' in the kingdom of Sicily, and the customary laws which differed from one ethnic group to another remained in force, the ability of the royal judges to intervene had limited effects.[91]

ADMINISTRATION

The claims expressed by the monarchy in its legislative work were ambitious, but how did things work in practice? The kingdom was indeed politically unified, but as was shown by the complex title of 'King of Sicily, of the duchy of Apulia and of the principality of Capua' it was composed of different regions, each with its own historical and cultural identity. While Sicily and Calabria were directly administered from the royal court, in Apulia and in the northern parts of the kingdom where the king did not have substantial demesne lands at his disposal, royal influence only developed slowly, thanks to the presence of officials who intervened in matters of high justice. We should be clear that such words as administration, offices and functionaries represent modern concepts, which can be used for the time of Roger II only with caution. 'Despite the numerous normative sources, one must remember that duties were often personal and could be directly exchanged between one

---

[90] Houben (1995a), 429.
[91] Caravale (1994a), 18–21 (1994b), 353ff (1998), 395–400.

man and another, that new and sometimes ephemeral functions could
be attached to old offices, and above all note the survival of "informal"
structures.'[92]

In Sicily and Calabria, Roger I had inherited Arabic and Byzantine offices and officials. In Sicily, Arabic registers of land, lists of serfs and even the
administrative districts remained. Senior officials came from the Byzantine
provincial administration; they must also have had a reasonable knowledge of Arabic. Their titles and duties were largely improvised. Alongside
the *amiratus* (from the Arabic *amīr*) we also find protonotaries, derived
from the Byzantine provincial administration. The chamberlain (*camerarius*)
was of Norman origin, while the office of logothete (literally: 'one who
says the word') came from the Byzantine palace administration. Subordinate offices were those of the stratege (*strategus*) – in Byzantium he was a
senior officer in the provincial administration with both civil and military
competence – and the viscount (*vicecomes*) who derived from Normandy.[93]

In Apulia, the Byzantine administrative system broke down after the
Norman conquest, and Robert Guiscard and his successors were unable
to create an overall territorial government. Some of the counties which
had emerged during the conquest were effectively autonomous. Byzantine
offices such as that of the catepan, who had been the provincial governor,
remained in name but assumed quite other functions. The catepans of
the Norman era were ducal or comital officers who administered their
lord's property and collected his revenues within a very limited territory.
Alongside them were various subordinate offices derived from all three traditions, Norman, Byzantine and Lombard: viscounts, strateges, turmarchs
and procurators.[94]

In the Campania, the administrative structures of the Lombard principalities of Capua and Salerno, as well as those of the duchies of Naples and
Gaeta, could still be utilized. Only after the political unification of Sicily
and the mainland had received papal recognition in 1139 with the Treaty
of Mignano, and the resistance among the nobles and towns had ended,
could Roger then think of providing his kingdom with a unified administration and with legislation. It is notable that Romuald of Salerno saw a
direct connection between the establishment of peace, the installation of
chamberlains and justiciars, and the promulgation of legislation.[95]

From 1140 onwards we find these officials throughout the entire kingdom, apart from the island of Sicily which was directly administered from

---

[92] Kölzer (1984–6), 376.

[93] Falkenhausen (1977), 346–57, Takayama (1993), 25–40.

[94] Falkenhausen (1977), 339–46; for the subordinate officers also Jahn (1989), 164–80.

[95] *Romuald*, 226 [above p. 135]. For the individual justiciars and chamberlains after 1135,
see most recently Martin (1994b).

the court. However, under Roger II the justiciars still did not have any precise definition of their districts, and it was only under William II that true justiciarates, with fixed boundaries, can be found. By contrast, in Calabria there was already during Roger's reign a Master Justiciar for the whole region, along with subordinate local justiciars, an arrangement which probably derived from the Byzantine tradition.

The justiciars, recruited for the most part from the nobility, were responsible for higher criminal justice, but could also intervene in disputes between feudatories. Lesser crimes remained within the competence of local judges. The chamberlains were responsible for the administration of crown property and for the collection of revenues both from the royal demesne and from fiefs; they were also charged with civil jurisdiction in the towns. It would appear that under Roger II there were chamberlains only in the principality of Capua and not in Apulia, perhaps in an attempt to respect the wide-ranging administrative autonomy of its towns. With the help of these officers the king sought to intervene in the jurisdiction of vassals, churches and towns, not with the intention of removing their privileges entirely, but certainly to curtail them.[96]

While his rule was still insecure, Roger was prepared to grant some towns, such as Cefalù, Bari, Trani and Gallipoli, a degree of autonomy, but from 1140 onwards the king intervened in the administration of justice in these as in other towns. The competence of the urban officeholders (turmarchs, catepans, strateges and judges) was limited to civil law cases; the *baiuli*, who up to then had been responsible only for the demesne, were now entrusted not only with revenue collection but also with lesser justice in the towns. In those areas which were subject not to the king but to his vassals, Roger tried to transform the judges elected by the communities into royal functionaries, in an attempt to acquire influence over the administration of justice, and in addition to place the officials of territories not belonging directly to the royal demesne under his control.[97]

---

[96] Caravale (1966), 219–83, 305ff. For Ass. Cas. 36 ('What is the Power of the Justiciar'), see above p. 140 and note 73, and Caravale (1966), 230ff. For the chamberlains, see also Jamison (1913), 383ff, Kamp (1974).

[97] Caravale (1966), 338–58. Cefalù: Roger II, *Diplomata*, no. 19 ([March] 1132); Bari, *ibid.*, no. 20 (22 June 1132), discussed by Martin (1979) 91–3; Trani, Roger II, *Diplomata*, no. 83 (1133), *ibid.*, appendix D.I (June 1139, Duke Roger); Gallipoli, *ibid.*, deperditum no. 38. However, *ibid.*, no.†11 (1129) for Messina is a fifteenth-century forgery; also forged is the alleged agreement, up until now unknown to historians of this period, between Roger II and Salerno, which is quoted in a diploma of Alfonso I of 10 December 1442, *Collectio Salernitana* II.787–9. This embodied thirteen *pacta et capitula*, which had allegedly been conceded to the citizens in 1127, after the death of Duke William of Apulia. See Kristeller (1956), 519ff. The privilege presented to the chancellor Stephen of Perche by the citizens of Messina in 1167, 'which King Roger had granted regarding the city's

While the administration of the south Italian mainland remained largely in the hands of the nobility, the royal court was dominated by expert bureaucrats of Greek, Arabic, and soon also Latin provenance. Roger I and Adelaide had governed from Troina and Messina with the aid of indigenous officials. Roger II made Palermo his residence and the capital of the new kingdom, and its lay and religious dignitaries began to acquire houses and property there. A central government, the *curia regis* ('the royal court') gradually developed. The *amiratus*, originally just the governor of Palermo, then the person responsible for financial affairs in Sicily, soon became a sort of prime minister. The first holder of this office, from 1107 until some stage after 1125, was Christodoulos, a Sicilian of Greek–Italian or Arabic origin. His successor was George of Antioch, a Christian from Syria, who had found asylum at the court of Palermo, and received the title of *amiratus* during the time of Christodoulos. In this case, *amiratus* denoted not an office but rather an honorific title, by which senior functionaries were distinguished. Other offices such as those of the logothete and protonotary gradually became less important.[98]

After the creation of the kingdom, George of Antioch assumed the title of 'grand admiral/emir' (*magnus ammiratus*), 'admiral/emir of emirs' (*ammiratus ammiratorum*), or 'greatest of the great' (ἄρχων τῶν ἀρχόντων). In the Arabic sources he was described as 'prime minister' (*wazīr*, vizier). He also commanded the royal fleet, while the army was entrusted to the *amiratus* John, who stemmed from an Italo-Greek family who had moved from Troina to Palermo and who were closely linked to the Norman royal family. His father Eugenius, one of Roger I's notaries, had also held the title of *amiratus*. His brothers, the logothete Philip and the *amiratus* Nicholas, as well as their uncle Basil, were all officials of Roger II. His son Eugenius (c. 1130–1202), a distinguished scholar and translator, later made a splendid career under William II, and survived the transition from the Hautevilles to the Staufen dynasty.[99]

During the 1140s the administration of Sicily and Calabria underwent considerable reform. At the start of the decade a new department was created, expressly for the administration of royal property and the receipt of income from both the demesne and from fiefs. This had the Arabic

---

freedom from taxation', *Falcandus*, 131 [*Tyrants*, 183], would appear also to have been a forgery. For the duties of the *baiuli*, see Ass. Cas. 36. These south Italian 'bailiffs' were subordinate local functionaries, and very different from French *baillis*, whose duties were similar to south Italian justiciars or English sheriffs. See Martin (1993), 820ff, Kamp (1996b), 13–14.

[98] Most recently, Falkenhausen (1985), Takayama (1993), 71. Above, p. 33 note 6.

[99] Jamison (1957), *passim*, Takayama (1993), 67, Falkenhausen (1993), and also above p. 99 note 2.

name of *ad-dīwān al-ma'mūr*, which translates literally as 'the office filled with life'. Lists of serfs, the *jarā'id* (singular *jarīda*), and registers of both of demesne lands and fiefs, the *dafātir* (singular *daftar*), were kept here. A little later, probably around 1145, in connection with the edict of revocation of 1144–5 already mentioned, a new office emerged, the *dīwān at-taḥqīq al-ma'mūr* (the 'office of control' or 'court of accounts'). Its duties were the supervision of the boundaries of demesne property and fiefs, the production of documents concerning donations and exchanges of land, the revision of the land registers and the redaction of lists of serfs. Somewhat later (from about 1166) it also acquired a Latin title, the *duana de secretis* ('the office of secrets').[100]

The royal chamberlains who were active in the *ad-dīwān al-ma'mūr* in the time of Roger II were mainly converts from Islam. At their head, again rather later – from c. 1160, was placed a 'master chamberlain of the royal palace' (*magister camerarius regii palatii*). The 'masters of the office of secrets' (*magistri duane de secretis*), documented only under Roger's successors, were subject to a chamberlain of the royal court. The registers of lands, which served as the basis for taxation, were destroyed during the disorders of 1161, and it was possible to reconstitute them only with the help of an expert, the notary Matthew 'of Aiello'. However, a department for the administration of the mainland (except for Calabria), the *duana baronum* ('office of the barons'), which was located at Salerno, was only created in 1168.[101]

With the growth of the Latin element in the kingdom, the role of the chancellor gained greater importance. Under Roger II, there was no specific chancery office: the chancellor had only a single notary subject to him, even if he might often make use of auxiliary notaries – hence the Latin chancery has been described as a 'one-man operation'. During the time of Guarnerius (1126–9) and Guarin (1131–7), the office of chancellor was still linked to that of chaplain, although with Guarin the chancellorship became more important. In 1135 he was associated with

---

[100] Takayama (1985), (1993), 81–9. Johns (1993), 138–9, gives a different interpretation: with the creation of the *ad-dīwān al-ma'mūr* in 1144/5, and that of the *dīwān at-taḥqīq al-ma'mūr* in 1149, with Fatimid Egypt as a model, and with the redaction and storage of land registers the exclusive concern of the latter, which supervised the activity of the *ad-dīwān al-ma'mūr*. A full solution to these problems, and of the terminology in different languages, may be forthcoming with the publication of Johns's promised monograph, *Duana Regis: Arabic and Norman Kingship in Sicily*. See also Noth, in Brühl (1978), 254ff, Mazzarese Fardella (1994).

[101] Takayama (1985), (1993), 145–57. For Matthew, *Falcandus*, 69 [*Tyrants*, 121], Kamp (1973–82), I.425–7. One should note that the surname 'de Aiello' often attributed to Matthew is an anachronism; it was used for the first time by descendants of his nephew, who had held the title of Count of Aiello.

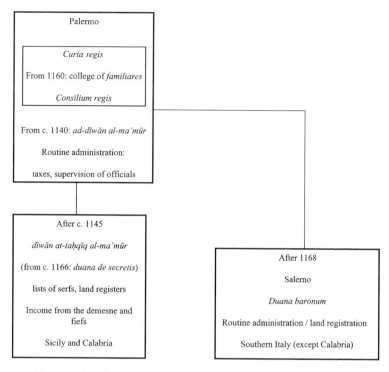

Fig. 11. The administration of the kingdom of Sicily (after Takayama)

the *amiratus* John in directing military operations in the Campania, and at the beginning of 1137 he went to Montecassino to persuade the abbot to come over to Roger II's side in the civil war. After Guarin's death the office of chancellor was separated from that of the supervisor of the royal chapel. Thomas Brown became the *magister capellanus*, another Englishman, Robert of Selby (died 1152), became chancellor.[102]

John of Salisbury, who knew him personally, described Robert as an active and intelligent churchman, with a good, although not exceptional, education, who made an impression above all as a man of generosity and good sense. An episode from 1147 shows the influence that the chancellor had in the royal court. William Fitzherbert, the Archbishop of York, a

---

[102] Enzensberger (1971), 48–77. Brühl (1978), 36–55 [= (1983a), 29–46]. Brühl suggests (1983a), 45–6, that after Guarin's death the chancery may have been entrusted to Henry, Bishop-elect of Messina, a former royal chaplain and Archdeacon of Palermo, and that 'only after Henry died in 1138/9 would it have been possible for Robert of Selby to assume direction of the chancery'.

nephew of King Stephen of England (1135–54), had tried at Rome to obtain his *pallium*, the symbol of his archiepiscopal authority, from Pope Eugenius III, but without success. As a result he had approached the king for help, but not directly. He had rather contacted his compatriot Robert of Selby, who was described as 'the most influential among the king's companions'. However, even the powerful chancellor could not give him any help in obtaining the *pallium*.[103]

Robert of Selby's successor was Maio of Bari, who was to begin with the archivist (*scrinarius*), and then, from 1149, vice-chancellor, an office which was probably specially created for him. After Roger's death, Maio made a splendid career, which came to an abrupt end with his assassination in November 1160.[104]

The importance of the royal chancery grew when, after 1140, the king only rarely left Sicily, and indeed mainly resided in Palermo, although he also occasionally stayed at Messina. We know next to nothing about the Greek chancery of Roger II. Opinions as to what proportion of the total number of documents produced by the whole royal chancery were in Greek vary from 'over 50%' to '75–80%'. Whether or not there was a genuine Arabic chancery at the court of Roger II is also controversial. No documents written solely in Arabic have survived, although they must surely have been produced, for from 1130 onwards Arabic scribes were attached to the chancery, writing a new and elegant script, the so-called 'dīwān script' (*dīwānī*), probably derived from the chancery of the Fatimid caliphs of Egypt, with whom Roger enjoyed good relations. One should also note that Roger had his 'signature' in Arabic placed upon a Greek charter of George of Antioch for the church of St Maria dell'Ammiraglio.[105]

---

[103] John of Salisbury, *Policraticus*, II.19, 173–4. John of Hexham, *MGH SS* XXVII.15: 'Seeing that his efforts were all in vain, Archbishop William went to visit his relation [*cognatus*] King Roger of Sicily, and dwelt for some days with that king's chancellor Robert, who came from England, in fact from Selby. This Robert was the most influential man among the king's companions [*amici*], most wealthy and endowed with great honours.' The relationship was almost certainly not a direct one but through the marriage of the king's eldest son with Elizabeth, from the family of the Counts of Blois and Champagne (above p. 87).

[104] Enzensberger (1971), 75. Brühl (1978), 47–8 [= (1983a), 38–9]. The first evidence for the archive comes in Roger II, *Diplomata*, no. 75 (1148), which mentions a damaged diploma of the Bishop of Messina *in regiis scriniis*.

[105] For Messina as a residence, Enzensberger (1994). For the production of documents, above p. 6 note 11. Both Noth, in Brühl (1978), 251ff and Kölzer (1986), 278, are sceptical on the question of the Arabic chancery (the latter with particular reference to Wansborough (1984)). For the 'dīwān' script and the Arabic 'signature' ('*alāma*) of Roger II, Johns (1993), 136ff. Cusa, *Diplomi*, 68 [= Ca. 153], May 1143, cf. Noth, in Brühl (1978) 220–1, 237–8 (for the script).

The depiction of the chancery in the illustrated chronicle of Peter of Eboli shows pairs of Greek, Arabic and Latin notaries at work. However, one should not necessarily deduce from this that there were separate and equal 'sections' of the chancery. The illustration was probably only intended to show the involvement in the royal administration of the different religious/ethnic groups.[106]

While Sicily and Calabria were governed directly from Palermo, the administration of the other parts of the kingdom depended on the traditional governmental structures. As we have already seen, Roger II invested his eldest son Roger with the duchy of Apulia, his second son Tancred with the principality of Bari, and his third son Alfonso with the principality of Capua, and subsequently also with the duchy of Naples. By contrast, the duchy of Gaeta was taken into the king's hands after the death of its duke, Richard, who had become Roger's vassal around 1135. After the death of Tancred (about 1138), the king suppressed the principality of Bari, and created the principality of Taranto for his fourth son William. Following the death of his other sons, the latter was invested with the principality of Capua and the duchy of Naples, as well as with the duchy of Apulia.

After 1140 the king began to reorganize the mainland counties, except for those in Calabria: some of them disappeared, others were altered in size or had their boundaries redrawn. The new counties were characterized by the fact that their holders were direct vassals of the king, and often related to him. They exercised wide powers within their counties, although the latter were not always coherent territorial units – they could sometimes be made up of a number of scattered lordships. In time of war the counts provided their own military contingents, over which they retained command, and a series of minor vassals were in turn dependent upon them. The royal army comprised both the contingents contributed by the vassals (the *milites* or 'knights') and troops whom they paid (*milites stipendiarii*), who provided service for a limited period, usually forty days. In addition, there were the troops who were directly paid by the king: knights, auxiliary troops (*servientes*) and infantry (*pedites*), among whom were the Muslim archers. The territories which were granted in fief appear to have been relatively restricted in size, at least in Apulia and the Campania.[107]

A detailed picture of the various fief-holders is provided by the so-called 'Catalogue of the Barons' (*catalogus baronum*), which was an inventory of

---

[106] Peter of Eboli, *Liber ad honorem Augusti*, fol. 101r, ed. Kölzer and Stähli, 59. Enzensberger (1981), 123–4, (1992), 51–2.

[107] Cuozzo (1989b), 24, 60ff, 105–52. Cf. *Al. Tel.* IV.4, p. 83: 'He paid on time the military wages or whatever else had been promised or agreed', Loud (1999c), 841. Filangieri (1985), 73, suggests, on the basis of the 'Catalogue of the Barons', that only about a sixth of the territory of Apulia and Campania was held in fief, the remainder being in the hands of towns or other communities (*universitates*). Cf. Vitolo (1990), 23ff.

military obligations in the duchy of Apulia and the principality of Capua, the origin of which goes back to the years 1150–2, but which was then revised round about 1168. The original name, *quaternus magne expeditionis*, shows that the inventory was prepared in case a large-scale defensive levy was required. Roger was probably most of all worried about a combined German and Byzantine attack on his kingdom. In such an emergency, provision of troops, or of financial payment in lieu, would be required not only from lands held in fief, but also from allodial and church properties. It has been suggested that this was linked with Roger's introduction, c. 1150, of the office of *comestabulus* ('military commander' or 'constable'), each of whom had a specific area of jurisdiction. These constables may have been, for a time, subject to the chamberlains, but just before the king's death the office of *magister comestabulus* was created, and the constables were then made subject to him.[108]

Roger also secured his rule by means of castles, both in the towns and in rural areas. In the summer of 1130 he forced the inhabitants of Salerno to surrender their upper tower, a sort of citadel, since according to Alexander of Telese 'he was of the opinion that he could only make the town submit to his lordship if he held the castle in his hand'. Similarly, the king had the castles at Troia and Melfi rebuilt before he returned to Sicily in the autumn of 1130. The citadel at Troia which had originally been had built by Robert Guiscard was destroyed by the citizens after the death of Duke William in 1127, in an attempt to make themselves independent. By contrast, the fortress at Melfi had been demolished on Roger's order, perhaps because he feared that those in rebellion against him might make use of it. In 1132/3 he had a new castle built at Bari, on the outskirts of the town, which was later substantially reconstructed by Frederick II. This location was typical of the Norman castles in south Italian towns; it gave the castle's lord, so to speak, one foot in the town and one outside it, thereby rendering it possible to control the townsmen while obviating the danger of possible siege by them. For the citizens, the castle was the symbol of royal lordship, and its destruction was often quite deliberately their first action if they revolted.[109]

---

[108] Jamison (1971) provides extensive discussion. Cf. Filangieri (1985), 64ff, Cuozzo (1989b), 63ff, 171ff (on the constables). Cuozzo suggests that the districts assigned to the *comestabuli* in the 'Catalogue of the Barons' were derived from diocesan boundaries; both Matthew (1992), 231–4, and Martin (1993), 788ff, are critical of this argument. The first attestation of a 'Master Constable' comes in April 1155, *CDB* v.190 no. 112, which refers to the incumbent, Gilbert of Balvano, having taken part in a court held at Barletta some time earlier; cf. Caravale (1966), 247.

[109] *Al. Tel.* 1.22, p. 20: 'For he realised that he would [be able to] rule the town, so long as that citadel was not under its control'; cf. *ibid.* 1.24, pp. 20–1 (Troia and Melfi), II.34, p. 39 (Bari), II.49, p. 47. Delogu (1979), Licinio (1994), 89ff. The 'most strongly fortified'

These castles in the major towns like Bari were garrisoned by troops belonging to Roger's standing army, much of which was composed of Muslims. Guard over other royal castles was entrusted to vassals. Thus in the summer of 1135 the king had a citadel built at Caiazzo, located in a useful strategic position northeast of Capua, and installed some of his vassals nearby.[110] Roger's efforts to protect his kingdom by means of castles and towers are also shown by a passage from the chronicle of St Mary of Ferraria, although that was only redacted in the thirteenth century.

> The king so fortified the points of entry to his kingdom that it was scarcely possible for anyone to enter it against his will. For the frontiers of this kingdom were barred either by rivers, which could only be crossed by bridges, or by mountains – the valleys through which were defended by walls. The other sides were surrounded by the sea, the coasts of which were furnished with towers and guards, so that if an [enemy] fleet should approach by sea, he would immediately be informed of its size and whereabouts by signals [*fanones*] displayed along the coasts.[111]

It would be going too far to deduce from this isolated testimony from a later chronicler that there was 'a network of castles' through which Roger defended his northern frontiers. We have evidence for a number of castellans, but one cannot therefore speak of a systematic 'castle administration' as was later to be the case under Frederick II, the origins of which go back to the time of Henry VI. Roger was though very much preoccupied with fortifications and their maintenance. That can be seen from the fact that when Frederick II reorganized the defensive system a century later, he had inquiries made as to what 'customs' (*consuetudines*) about castles had been in force in the time of Roger II.[112]

Roger was genuinely interested in administrative matters. Alexander of Telese wrote that the king, in his leisure time, supervised taxes, income

---

(*munitissimum*) citadel at Bari, with a garrison of both knights and Muslim soldiers, held out against Lothar III's army for forty days in 1137, *Annalista Saxo, MGH SS* VI.774.

[110] *Al. Tel.* III.31, p. 76: 'He also arranged that all the barons [*proceres*] who lived in the vicinity, with all the knights who were subject to them who were natives of that area, should build houses in the neighbourhood of Caiazzo and have perpetual residences there, that this *castrum*, which was known to be most strongly fortified both by nature and by man, should be strengthened too by the number of soldiers living there.' Cuozzo (1989b), 84–5, Figliuolo (1991), 59, Houben (1996c), 164.

[111] *Chronica de Ferraria*, 26–7. This section, unlike the preceding part of the chronicle, did not depend on Falco of Benevento.

[112] Cuozzo (1989b), 78, Licinio (1994), 95, go too far in suggesting such a network. Cuozzo (1995c), 42, does however argue that Roger considered these castles as 'watchtowers' rather than as a means of securing his rule; but another suggestion, that King Tancred was the 'inventor' of a new defensive system which was put fully into practice by Frederick II, is unconvincing. Henry VI did make real efforts to secure the effective administration of castles, Kamp (1996a), 152. For Frederick, see Winkelmann, *Acta Imperii Inedita*, I, no. 761, p. 605.

and expenditure, and his accounts; and nothing was spent without good reason.[113] No other twelfth-century ruler showed such a detailed interest in administration. Only Frederick II and then, in particular, Charles I of Anjou (1266–85) were so intensively concerned with the finances of their kingdom.

While Roger II took a personal interest in administrative issues, his successor William I gave his chancellor Maio of Bari a more or less free hand, and only rarely concerned himself with affairs of state.[114] Under Maio, the foundations of a more structured administrative system for the mainland were laid down: at its head was his brother-in-law Simon and his brother Stephen, who received the title of Master Captain (*magister capitaneus*). The chamberlains both in Apulia and in the Campania were made subject to a Master Chamberlain. However, with Maio's assassination in 1160 the period of the great 'prime ministers' like George of Antioch came to an end, and instead of a single all-powerful *ammiratus ammiratorum* – rather inaccurately translated as 'admiral of admirals' or 'emir of emirs' – there was a group of *familiares*, comprising at first three, and later up to ten, persons, comprising both clergy and Latin nobles, in varying proportions, and also Arab administrative experts.[115]

Under Roger and his successors, therefore, the foundations were laid for the formation of a novel type of medieval state official – the civil servant whose role as a public functionary made him quite distinct from aristocratic society. His office was held for a limited period, he had to fulfil a specifically designed role and to provide written accounts. In return he was paid by the state and occupied a special legal position which distanced him from 'feudal' society.[116]

---

[113] *Al. Tel.* IV.3, p. 82: 'He hardly ever gave way to idleness or relaxation, so much so that if and when it should happen that he was not involved with some more profitable occupation, then either he supervised the public exactions or checked what had been or ought to have been given, or ought to be received, with the result that he was always better informed from the accounts of his scribes about the revenues which had to be paid to him, or from where they ought to be drawn. To sum up, there was nothing which was his that was not recorded in a written account.' Falkenhausen (1977), 357, suggests that Roger's interest in administration may have been a result of the influence of the *amiratus* Christodoulos, who was probably one of the young king's tutors.

[114] *Romuald*, 237: 'Afterwards he appointed the chancellor Maio as great admiral and handled almost all the kingdom's business through his advice and foresight.' *Falcandus*, 6: 'This was the man upon whom the greatest honour was bestowed, and to whom the care and government of the whole realm was committed.' [*Tyrants*, 60, 221].

[115] Takayama (1989), (1993), 105–11, 115–23.

[116] Kamp (1977–80), Kölzer (1993), 40–1, who points to 'the enormous growth of written material' in the kingdom of Sicily as 'the most obvious symptom of the creation of a central administration'. Cf. also Kamp (1996b), 5–6.

Admittedly the process whereby such judicial, financial and chancery offices were created was a very slow one, and not necessarily a straight-line progression, but it is nonetheless clear that the kingdom's administration underwent a territorialization and rationalization, which was intended to overcome the centrifugal tendencies of 'feudalism'. However the nobility, especially in Apulia and the northern parts of the kingdom, were able to retain their influence and prerogatives; not least because most of the officials were either themselves of noble origin or developed relationships with the nobility. Later on, Frederick II had to confront this problem, when he attempted to take the rationalization of the kingdom's government a step further.

The Norman rulers achieved a long-term success in their control over the Church, which, in contrast to what happened in Germany, was never able to play any independent role; it remained a 'national' Church (*Landeskirche*) closely tied to the monarchy. Indeed, many of its, in total, 145 bishoprics were economically dependent upon the crown, being assigned the 'royal tithe' by its officials. Robert Guiscard and Roger I had previously exercised a great deal of influence over the organization of the south Italian Church and the election of its bishops, something to which they felt themselves to be entitled because they had restored this region to the jurisdiction of the Roman Church. Although this sort of behaviour was antipathetic to the principles of ecclesiastical reform, it was very largely tolerated by the Roman pontiffs. This royal influence over episcopal elections was recognized in the Treaty of Benevento of 1156: it was enough that a candidate was *odiosus* to the king for him to be rejected. A foreign observer like John of Salisbury could have the impression that in 1150 the King of Sicily could dispose of ecclesiastical offices as though they were positions at his court. Nonetheless, this English cleric had to admit that Roger II did not abuse his rights of intervention, and those whom he appointed to these posts in the Church were men of worth.[117]

In periods of crisis, as after the premature death of William I when his widow Margaret acted as regent for their minor son, William II, the weaknesses of the young state became apparent: the king in person was still necessary to hold it together. On the other hand, one should also note that even in such difficult periods, as again later during the succession

---

[117] *MGH Constitutiones* I.588–90 no. 413, c. 11 [*Tyrants*, 250]. *The Historia Pontificalis of John of Salisbury*, 65, c. 32. See Kamp (1979), Loud (1982), and for royal control over abbeys, Houben (1995a), 53ff. In this latter context, one important case has remained up until now unknown, namely the deposition on Roger's instructions of the Abbot of St Severinus and St Sossius at Naples, probably after 1140 [Hofmeister (1920), 102]. Further investigation is needed here.

dispute after 1190, the administrative apparatus of the kingdom showed a surprising capacity for survival.[118]

ECONOMY

Roger II's administrative reforms were intended not only to consolidate his rule, but also to fill the state's coffers. Alexander of Telese stressed the king's personal supervision of taxes and accounts, and how he was concerned to prevent unnecessary expenditure. This was confirmed by Romuald of Salerno, who characterized the king as 'very concerned to gain money, [but] hardly very prodigal in expending it'.[119] Alongside his administrative reforms, Roger also promulgated, at his assembly at Ariano in 1140, an edict concerning the coinage:

Among the other dispositions which he made there he promulgated a terrible edict, hated throughout Italy, and leading to death and poverty, namely that nobody dwelling in his kingdom should receive *romesinae* or pay them in any transaction, and on the worst possible advice he introduced his own money: the ducat, worth eight *romesinae*, which was reckoned to have been struck far more of copper than of silver. He also introduced copper *follares*, three of which were equivalent to one *romesina*. All the people of Italy suffered and were reduced to poverty and misery by this horrible money, and as a result of these oppressive actions hoped for the king's death or deposition.

The criticism of this monetary reform expressed by the chronicler was probably occasioned by the fact that the *romesinae* had a superior silver content to the new ducats. What happened was therefore a devaluation of the coinage, advantageous for the crown but to the disadvantage of the populace: eight *romesinae* contained round about 2.8 grams of silver whereas a ducat had only about 1.5 grams. The *romesinae* – the name probably derived from *rothomagenses* (from Rouen) – had arrived in the Mezzogiorno in the eleventh century, along with the Normans. Along with these, silver money from Pavia and Lucca, as well as Byzantine and Arab, and locally minted, gold and copper money was also in circulation.[120]

---

[118] Caravale (1987); cf. Martin (1993), 827: 'a quarter of a century of near total anarchy did not affect the bureaucratic structures of the kingdom'; Matthew (1992), 314: 'the speed with which the new policies were implemented [*after 1220*] shows the machinery had not rusted in the meantime'.

[119] *Al. Tel.* IV.3, p. 82 [above, note 113]. *Romuald*, 237; something very similar was said about William I, *ibid.*, 253. *Falcandus*, 6: 'he also made provision for the future and prepared a vast treasure for the defence of the realm, which he stored at Palermo' [*Tyrants*, 58, 221, 238].

[120] *Falco*, 234. Travaini (1995), 295–9. Martin (1986), 89–90, (1993), 460ff, (1994), 324, 329, has a different interpretation, according to which the *romesinae* which Falco mentioned

With this 'terrible edict' of 1140 Roger tried to bring some order to the hitherto rather chaotic monetary situation. Coin hoards have shown that along with the ducat or *ducalis* another smaller silver coin was also introduced, the *tercia ducalis*. The new silver ducat was the same weight as the Fatimid dirhem and the Byzantine miliaresion, although in the twelfth century this last only existed as a money of account. Both these coins had inferior denominations of a third – hence the *tercia ducalis* corresponded to eight *folles*, and a third of a miliaresion had eight *folles*. The smallest of the copper coins introduced by Roger was the Arabic *kharruba*, which was probably valued at half a *follaris*, that is one-sixteenth of the *tercia ducalis*, just as in the Fatimid monetary system it was worth one-sixteenth of a dirhem. The point of reference in the monetary system remained the Arabic gold *tarì* (which equalled a quarter of a dinar). The dinar has been described, along with its Byzantine equivalent, the gold *solidus* or *nomisma*, as the 'dollar' of the Mediterranean world. There were also other types of money, but these were only monies of account, not actual coins; for example the *solidus regalis* which was the equivalent of four Sicilian *tarì* or to twelve ducats, and the *granum* which was worth half of a *tercia ducalis*. Thus after the monetary reform, the actual coins that existed in the kingdom of Sicily were the gold *tarì*, two silver coins – the ducat and the 'third of a ducat' (*tercia ducalis*), and two copper coins, the *follaris* and the *kharruba*. The existence of such a small denomination coin as the *kharruba* (144 to the *tarì*) has been seen as an indication of the efficiency of the fiscal system. However, with the new monetary system, which above all made long-distance trade simpler, not all the local monetary types were eliminated. Salerno and Amalfi retained their own *tarì*, which were worth just over a half of the Sicilian *tarì*. Apart from in these two towns, coins were minted only at Palermo and Messina.[121]

must have been copper *ramesine* or *follari*. The new copper coins introduced by Roger were therefore equivalent to three old *ramesine*. These old *ramesine* were last mentioned in 1145. Cf. here Travaini (1996), 111ff, Grierson and Travaini (1998), 117–18. *Al. Tel.* III.8, pp. 63–4: 'For such was the shortage in that place [*a camp between Capua and Aversa*] one small loaf could scarcely be bought with a penny [*nummus*] of Rouen' (1135), *ibid.*, IV.1, p. 81, where at the siege of Naples in the same year: 'The city was already vexed with such a shortage of bread that a penny of Rouen would scarcely buy two little loaves of millet.' *Falco*, 228, alleged that at the siege of Bari in 1139 the price of bread in the besieged city rose as high as six *romesinae*; cf. Travaini (1995), 55–60, 210–20, Falkenhausen (1986b), 56.

[121] See the table in Travaini (1995), 59, Grierson and Travaini (1998), 118. A *solidus* (called also a *bisantius* or a *schifatus*) = 4 *tarì* = 12 *ducales* = 36 *terciae ducales* = 72 *grana* (a money of account) = 288 *follari* = 576 *kharrube*. A *romanatus* was a *solidus/nomisma* of the emperor Romanos III Argyros (1028–34), although by the twelfth century this was a money of account. In 1180, 1 Sicilian ounce [*uncia*] = 30 Sicilian *tarì* = 50 Amalfitan *tarì*; the same

Roger's monetary reform appears in practice not to have had very significant consequences. The ducats, whose circulation remained almost entirely limited to Apulia, were soon displaced by the gold Sicilian *tarì* and by *provesini*, the silver money coming from the town of Provins in Champagne (one of those where the annual commercial 'fairs' of Champagne took place). By the end of the 1150s the ducat survived only as a money of account, and soon after that it disappeared altogether. Competition from the *provesinus*, which circulated all over Europe, and probably came to Apulia through the grain trade, was just too strong. According to Falco of Benevento, Innocent II asked the Rector (governor) of Benevento to accede to the king's wishes by also introducing the ducat to this papal enclave, although in his letter he also alluded to the fact that this was only an expedient which would not have any long-term consequences.[122]

The crown's income was not only derived from taxes and from military campaigns – we have already discussed the rich booty in gold, silver, hostages and slaves gained in Apulia in 1133 and Greece in 1147 – but also from the renders from the royal patrimony. The extensive royal demesne in Sicily produced above all durum wheat, which was greatly valued for its long life, and other foodstuffs such as cheese and salted meat, some of which were exported to north Africa. The Muslims also sought wood and pitch, which they needed for shipbuilding. Payment was made in gold, which came from the Sudan, and was primarily used for the coining of money. Luxury items were also imported, such as spices, dyestuffs and precious cloths from the east, as well as less valuable textiles from northern Italy. The crown possessed saltmines, and salt could also be extracted from the sea, but there was as yet no monopoly of salt production, which was only introduced by Frederick II. However, in contrast both to Byzantine Italy and to the Staufen period, there were no direct taxes; although there were a good number of indirect ones, levied above all on foodstuffs such as grain, cheese and butter, as well as on commercial traffic.[123]

---

ratio was still applicable in the Amalfitan 'customs' of 1274, Travaini (1995), 58n. The later supposition that either Roger or William I introduced small-denomination leather coins is unfounded, cf. Cuozzo (1989a), 656–60, Enzensberger (1980), 395,Travaini (1995), 69–70.

[122] *Falco*, 238 (*It. Pont.* IX.40 no. 98): 'We have heard from you and from others who have informed us of the truth of what the king has done and of the introduction of his new coins; as a result we order you not to be frightened or upset by such things for they are transitory and they can soon be changed. Besides, we are every day watching out for your interests.' This monetary reform was not very successful, and exchange rates subsequently, in the second half of the century, fluctuated wildly, Falkenhausen (1986), 73–4.

[123] Abulafia (1983a), Martin (1990), 350.

Roger II gave a piece of land in the town of Messina, which was the
stopping point for ships journeying to Alexandria and Syria, to the Genoese consul Ogerius and his brother Amicus in 1116. The close relations
between Genoa and Sicily derived from the marriage between Roger I
and Adelaide del Vasto, a member of the Aleramici family who came from
Liguria. This opened the way for the immigration of people from northern Italy into Sicily. In 1128 Roger concluded a treaty with Savona, a
town not far from Genoa which paid tribute to it. On the request of the
bishop, consuls and citizens of Genoa, Roger released the crew of a ship
from Savona, who had for some time been under arrest on a criminal
charge (probably piracy). The representatives of Savona swore to observe
this treaty, saving their alliance with Genoa and their fealty to their mar-
graves, namely the Aleramici family. Pisa too had commercial interests in
the south, but unlike Genoa, the Arno city was traditionally allied to the
German emperor, thus found itself in open conflict with Roger II, and
took an active part in Lothar III's campaign against the Norman king. Pisa
could not therefore expect to receive favourable treatment in the kingdom
of Sicily; but there was still relatively little hindrance, for the crown had
little interest in disturbing trade, from which it derived a considerable income. The Genoese exported cereals, linen, wool, hides, leather and meat
from Sicily and southern Italy to the north, a trade in which ships from
Gaeta, Naples, Amalfi and Salerno also took part.[124]

Trade in the Adriatic was dominated by Venice, the traditional ally of
Byzantium. To begin with Venice supported the strivings towards independence of the towns of the Apulian coast, and Bari in particular, and
in 1147 it provided help for Byzantium to resist the attacks of Roger's
fleet. Only after Roger's rule was firmly consolidated, probably round
about 1150, did Venice conclude a peace treaty with the Norman kingdom. Among its terms was a reduction in the customary taxes paid by
Venetian merchants whose ships docked at Messina. Some years earlier, in
1144, Roger had allowed some Venetians to rebuild an old Greek church at
Palermo, and in the following decades this became the focus for a Venetian
mercantile colony in the capital.[125]

Roger has been accused of hindering the development of a local en-
trepreneurial class through the advantages that he gave to northern

---

[124] Cusa, *Diplomi*, 359 = Ca. 32 (1116). Abulafia (1977), 62–4, suggests that the Greek
copy of this document was derived from a lost Latin original: the 60 *tarì* here may be
a mistranscription of 60 ounces (i.e. 1,800 *tarì*); see now Falkenhausen (1998c), 104–5.
Roger II, *Diplomata*, 24–8 no. 10 (May/June 1128), cf. on Savona and Genoa, Abulafia
(1977), 65–70, Pavoni (1991) 240–1n., and in general Pistarino (1979).

[125] Abulafia (1977), 76–80. For the date of the lost privilege of Roger II for Venice (1150–4?),
not listed in Roger II, *Diplomata*, which was confirmed by William II in 1175, see
Abulafia (1977), 78n. Ca. 163 (February 1144).

merchants in southern Italy; and that he saw an autonomous, economically active burgess class in the towns as a potential danger to the monarchy. Oppression of the towns led to the stagnation of an economy which had previously been flourishing, and in the long term this led to the formation of 'two Italies': the economically advanced north and the backward south.[126]

One can however raise a number of objections to this hypothesis. In the first place it is based on the premise – one quite anachronistic for the twelfth century – that the king pursued a specific 'economic policy' and was in a position to guide the economic development of his kingdom. It is not to be denied that a ruler of this period could have his own view of economic issues and could therefore take such measures as this implied.[127] With his proclamation protecting merchants as part of his general peace in 1129, and with the relative stabilization of political affairs in the Mezzogiorno, Roger created the conditions for undisturbed internal trade. With the establishment of bases in north Africa, the Mediterranean was made safer for Christian shipping, which had previously been vulnerable to the attacks of Arab pirates. But there was no question of a general suppression of the south Italian towns; rather the king was concerned to bring their customs and local privileges into line with the general administration and legislation of the kingdom.

Furthermore, the favour given to foreign merchants did not necessarily have deleterious consequences for the internal economy of the kingdom; it may rather have had the effect of encouraging production. Hence, the activity of the northern merchants appears to have led to the development of both agriculture and the craft sector. Political unification created a wider internal market for products, and at least in some areas, notably the Campania, led to a specialization of agriculture.[128]

In 1147 Roger had some of the silk workers of Thebes and Corinth, the centres of the Byzantine silk industry, taken away to Palermo, where they were settled in a workshop for making silk which was attached to the royal palace (the *ṭirāz*). This was, however, an isolated measure, which may have led to an improvement in the quality of the silk produced at court, but did not lead to an increase in the quantity of silk production in Sicily. The future of this industry lay rather in the north Italian towns of Lucca and Venice.[129]

---

[126] Abulafia (1977), *passim*. Pistarino (1979).

[127] Thus Fried (1984), 238, who suggests that Frederick Barbarossa had an 'economic policy', albeit one that was 'contradictory and incomplete'. Cf. also Dirlmeier (1992).

[128] See, among others, Del Treppo (1986), 288–9, Vitolo (1987), 178, (1988), 19–20 [reprint 92–3], Caravale (1994), 278–9.

[129] Goitein (1971), Jacoby (1994), 1178–9.

Nor can the long decline of Amalfi as a commercial power be attributed
to the Normans – there were other reasons for this. Amalfitan traders acted
as individuals or as part of a small group; unlike their competitors from
Pisa, Genoa and Venice, they lacked the political and military protection
of a powerful city-state. The decisive factor was probably that during the
course of the twelfth century they were slowly overtaken by new developments in the art of shipbuilding and in banking, while they also failed to
establish links with the markets of Champagne and Flanders. In addition,
the greater availability to the northerners of iron and silver, commodities
which were in particular demand in the east, seems to have played a part.
The Amalfitans were therefore constrained to concentrate upon internal
trade within southern Italy – something in which they had already been
active during the eleventh century. Settlements of 'Amalfitans' (often in
fact merchants from Ravello) were to be found in many of the towns of
the Mezzogiorno; they gradually concentrated their activity in banking,
and later on, with the economic reforms of Frederick II (in 1231–2),
they were to play a crucial role in the administration of the kingdom's
finances.

The beneficiary from the so-called 'decadence' of Amalfi was Salerno,
which during the twelfth century became the most important city of the
south Italian mainland, thanks to the activity of Amalfitan and Calabrian
immigrants, along with the Jews who had already been settled there for a
long time. Gaeta, Bari and Messina, which up to this time had played a
part in the long-distance trade in oil and grain, lost this role during the
course of the century, to the advantage of the always more enterprising
north Italian competition, and finally had to content themselves with the
trade between Sicily and the south Italian mainland.[130]

Under Roger's successors there was an increasing isolation and dis-
placement of the Muslims who lived in the western part of the island of
Sicily, which led to a reduction in the specialist agriculture practised there,
and particularly in sugar production, and to the collapse of the irrigation
system. From the early thirteenth century what developed in its place
were *latifundia*, concentrating on cereal production.[131] But at the time of
Roger II the kingdom's agriculture generally flourished. Cereals, oil, salt,

---

[130] Del Treppo (1977), 166ff, suggests that Amalfitan long-distance trade suffered setbacks
during the course of the twelfth century, and was in full decline in the thirteenth,
and above all the fourteenth, centuries. Abulafia (1983), 231ff, D'Alessandro (1986),
Sangermano (1993), Figliuolo (1993), Cherubini (1993), Pispisa (1993), Martin (1994),
335–43, Kamp (1995b), 14ff, and most recently Falkenhausen (1998a). Rossetti (1986),
316ff, suggests that the economic backwardness of the Mezzogiorno began only in the
sixteenth century after the Reformation had divided Europe into a Protestant north and
a Catholic south.

[131] See especially Epstein (1992); also Cherubini (1987), 205ff, who argues that the scale
of southern exports of agricultural products (especially oil and wine) was more limited

wine and other products were exported to both east and west to meet a growing demand for foodstuffs. The increasing activity of northern merchants and the limited freedom of action allowed to the southern towns did not have, at least in the short and medium term, harmful consequences for the kingdom's economy, for in contrast to the later Staufen, and above all the Angevin, periods it did not suffer from an excessive fiscal burden. The economic decline of many parts of the south Italian mainland and Sicily occurred only in the fourteenth century,[132] and cannot be blamed on Norman rule.

than has been thought, and that it was only in later centuries that this took place on a large scale.

[132] For a wider summary, see Haverkamp (1987), 629ff.

5

EPILOGUE. THE KINGDOM OF SICILY
AFTER ROGER II

•

WILLIAM 'THE BAD' AND WILLIAM 'THE GOOD'

Roger died on 26 or 27 February 1154 at the age of fifty-eight. Romuald of Salerno reported that he died of a fever, while 'Hugo Falcandus' wrote of the king becoming prematurely aged, 'worn down by his immense efforts and more devoted to sexual activity than the body's good health requires'. The government passed smoothly to William I, who had already been co-ruler for some three years. The new king held an assembly at Palermo at Easter 1154, where he received (once again) his solemn coronation.[1]

Roger left his successor a full treasury, some splendid palaces and a developing, and for its time efficient, administration, but also some unresolved problems. In the first place there was the shattered relationship with his overlord, the pope. The successors of Innocent II had denied Roger investiture, and he had been unable to reach agreement with them on either territorial or ecclesiastical problems. The popes hoped, with the help of an expedition from the German emperor, either to drive the king out or at the very least to force him into making concessions. With the accession of Frederick Barbarossa the moment appeared to have arrived to bring this plan to fruition. Pope Adrian IV (1154–9) refused to receive a diplomatic mission sent to him by William I, for he considered the latter's elevation to the kingship in 1151 to have been illegal since it had been done without consultation with his papal overlord. Early in 1155 the pope

---

[1] *Romuald*, 236, with the erroneous date of 1152. *Falcandus*, 7 [*Tyrants*, 59, 220–1]. Both Romuald and most other sources say that he died on 27 February, although the Palatine chapel martyrology lists the day of his burial (*depositio*) as 26 February; Houben (1984), 130–1, *Necrologia Panormitana*, 472, Rocco (1977), 142.

sent a cardinal to the king with a letter, in which William was addressed as 'lord of Sicily', and not as 'king'. Because of this insult the king refused to accept the letter.[2]

Furthermore the Byzantine emperor Manuel Komnenos, who was negotiating with Barbarossa and hoped to forge a great anti-Norman coalition, felt that the moment had come to put an end to the kingdom of Sicily. He refused William's peace offers, although the king declared himself ready to make concessions such as the restoration of the booty and prisoners taken at the capture of Thebes in 1147. He ordered an immediate attack upon the Sicilian fleet, although this resulted in a defeat for the Byzantines.[3]

William had meanwhile succeeded in concluding a treaty with the Venetians, whose relations with Byzantium had been tense after various incidents which had occurred at the time of the Byzantine reconquest, with Venetian help, of Corfu in 1149. William was also negotiating with King Géza II of Hungary, another opponent of the Byzantine emperor, although when he realized how difficult the situation of the Sicilian king was the Hungarian ruler preferred to make peace with Byzantium (in 1155). This intense diplomatic activity shows how afraid King William was of a combined German and Byzantine attack on southern Italy. Early in 1155 the king went to Salerno, to lead the defence in person.[4]

It was predictable that the news that Barbarossa was going to lead an expedition to Italy would stimulate the latent dissatisfaction among both nobles and townsmen against the monarchy that Roger had created and led to rebellion. At the head of the rebels was the king's cousin, Robert II of Basunvilla. This was despite the fact that at Easter 1154 he had been granted the extensive county of Loritello in the Abruzzi, to be held along with the county of Conversano which he had inherited; and had thus become the most important noble on the south Italian mainland.[5]

The king returned to Palermo just after Easter 1155, while his chancellor Asclettin, to whom command of the army had been entrusted, attacked the papal enclave of Benevento. Many of the vassals rebelled, abandoning the army and changing sides, and the siege had to be abandoned. With the troops who were left, most of whom were probably mercenaries, in

[2] *Romuald*, 237–8 [*Tyrants*, 221–2]. Deér (1972), 239–47.

[3] Kinnamos, III.12–13 = *Deeds of John and Manuel Comnenus*, 95–6. Chalandon (1907), II.188–9. Magdalino (1993), 53–4.

[4] Chalandon (1907), 192–3, 199, Mákk (1989), 60ff, Magdalino (1993), 54–5.

[5] *Romuald*, 237. It is difficult to believe the rumour, which according to *Falcandus*, 11, was put about by Maio, that Roger II had said in his will that if his son William proved manifestly incapable, the government of the kingdom should pass to Count Robert [*Tyrants*, 63–4, 222]. Cf. Petrucci (1965b).

late May and early June the chancellor ravaged a number of the smaller towns in the south of the patrimony of St Peter, such as Ceprano, while all but twelve of the monks abandoned Montecassino. As a result Adrian IV excommunicated the king.[6]

The revolt spread more widely and soon convulsed almost the whole of the mainland. But the hopes that the rebels had placed in Barbarossa, who according to the Treaty of Konstanz was supposed to attack the King of Sicily, were disappointed. After his imperial coronation on 18 June 1155 his German vassals refused to follow him to southern Italy. Robert of Basunvilla was willing to assist the emperor's south Italian expedition, but this offer fell on deaf ears. The rebels obtained much more efficacious assistance from the Byzantine emperor, who sent them both troops and money. The pope also supported the rebels. On the feast of St Michael (29 September) Pope Adrian received the fealty and homage of the former Prince of Capua, Robert II, who had spent most of the last fifteen years in exile in Germany, and of a number of other nobles who had gone with him to Benevento.[7]

The Byzantine troops and the supporters of Robert of Basunvilla had brought almost all of southern Italy under their control. When, at the end of 1155, King William fell ill and remained unwell for some months, a rumour spread that he had died, which gave the rebellion further encouragement. Only Naples, Amalfi, Salerno, Troia, Melfi and a few other fortified places remained in the king's hands. The situation became more and more menacing, and there was a rebellion in Sicily itself, which had never occurred under Roger II. The Byzantine emperor concluded an alliance with the Genoese, and opened negotiations with the pope, to whom he sent money to employ soldiers. William's situation was desperate. Late in 1155 or at the very beginning of 1156 he sent an embassy to the pope with a generous offer. In return for the lifting of his excommunication and his receipt of papal investiture, the king was prepared to restore the Church's freedom within his kingdom, and in particular not to interfere any more in ecclesiastical elections. Furthermore, he promised Adrian an extension of the papal enclave of Benevento to encompass three places in the vicinity (Paduli, Montefusco and Morcone), as well as to provide him with money and military support against the communal movement in Rome. The pope was ready to accept this tempting offer, but was prevented from doing so by the cardinals who felt that it would be wiser

---

[6] *Romuald*, 238, *Liber Pontificalis*, II.389 [*Tyrants*, 222, 244]. *Annales Ceccanenses, Annales Casinenses, MGH SS* XIX.284, 311. Chalandon (1907), II.202ff.

[7] *Kinnamos*, IV.2 = *Deeds of John and Manuel Comnenus*, 115. *Liber Pontificalis*, II.393–4 [*Tyrants*, 245].

to abandon William to his fate, since it seemed that his downfall was inevitable.[8]

During the king's illness government had remained in the hands of Maio of Bari, who in June 1154 had been appointed as *ammiratus ammiratorum* or chief minister. Our principal source for this period is the contemporary 'History of the Kingdom of Sicily', authorship of which was attributed by the editor of the first printed edition of 1550 (which was based on a now-lost manuscript) to a certain 'Hugo Falcandus'. Since the author's name does not appear in this work and up to now his identity has never been established, it seems probable that this was a pseudonym or an attribution made by the Renaissance editor, or perhaps by the amanuensis of the manuscript – hence the general tendency to speak of the 'pseudo' Hugo Falcandus. In this work the intrigues at court are described by one whom knew them well. The author portrayed the king as an incompetent and his minister as a monster in human form. This brilliant but extremely partisan chronicler has had a great influence upon the historical verdict upon William I, from the late Middle Ages up to the present day. However, the epithet 'the Bad' – as opposed to William II 'the Good' – was only applied to the king in the fourteenth century.[9]

William was by no means as incapable as the so-called 'Hugo Falcandus' suggested. After recovering from his illness he gathered his army and fleet at Messina, and in the spring of 1156 he launched a combined land and sea attack on Brindisi, where the citadel was still holding out against the rebels. He won a speedy victory and took a bloody revenge on the insurgents. Bari, the most important town in Apulia, was razed to the ground and its inhabitants dispersed to nearby villages; only the church of St Nicholas was spared. Then it was the turn of the Campania, where Prince Robert of Capua was captured. Tradition would have suggested that he should have been condemned to death; instead he was 'only' sent as a prisoner to Palermo, where according to 'Falcandus' he was then blinded. Count Robert of Basunvilla and other noble rebels got away lightly by being exiled from the kingdom.[10]

---

[8] *Romuald*, 238–9, *Kinnamos*, IV.3–5 = *Deeds of John and Manuel Comnenus*, 116–8. For William's illness, *Annales Pisani*, ed. Gentile, 15, *Annales Palidenses*, *MGH SS* XVI.89. Robert of Torigny, *Chronica*, *MGH SS* VI.505. *Annales Casinenses*, *MGH SS* XVI.311. *Falcandus*, 13, who notes that 'for a long period of time he appeared to no one at all, apart from the admiral Maio and Archbishop Hugh'. *Liber Pontificalis*, II. 393–4 [English trans. in *Tyrants*, 65–6 and note 19, 223, 245–6]. For discussion, Chalandon (1907), 225, Lamma (1955–7), I.149–52, Magdalino (1993), 53–61.

[9] For assessment of William I, see especially Loud (1996), Pio (1996). For the nicknames, Enzensberger (1980), 386–94, Cuozzo (1989a), 656ff.

[10] *Falcandus*, 20–3, *Romuald*, 240 [*Tyrants*, 73–5, 223–4]. William of Tyre, XVIII.8, pp. 821–2 [English trans. Babcock and Krey, II.249–50]. *Kinnamos*, IV.11–13 = *Deeds of John and*

Pope Adrian soon realized that everyone had abandoned him. The cardinals who opposed a rapprochement with the Normans had left. After William had laid siege to Benevento and provisions within the town were exhausted, the pope sent out intermediaries to conclude an agreement. A joint commission under the leadership of Maio of Bari and Cardinal Roland (the future Pope Alexander III) drew up a bilateral treaty which was concluded on 18 June 1156. William did homage and swore fealty to Adrian, and received investiture with the three banners, as Roger had previously been invested by Innocent II in 1139. The pope confirmed to him the right to arrange the succession as he saw fit, the full territorial extent of the kingdom (including the Abruzzi and Marsia, for which he was to pay a supplementary census), as well as control over the Church within his kingdom. However, with regard to the Church a distinction was made between the mainland, where appeals to Rome, ecclesiastical synods and papal legations were to be permitted, and the island of Sicily where they would not be allowed unless expressly sanctioned by the king. Crucially, the king retained control over ecclesiastical elections throughout his kingdom. Palermo became the seat of a metropolitan archbishop, with Agrigento, Mazara and Malta as its suffragan sees. Adrian had thus granted William everything that his predecessors had refused to Roger.[11]

The King of Sicily was able further to strengthen his position by treaties with Genoa, in 1156, and Byzantium in 1158. The loss in the next few years of the bases that Roger had established on the north African coast, which fell to the attacks of the Almohads, was not particularly significant. Minor revolts in the Abruzzi and Campania were speedily suppressed.[12]

The one serious threat to the kingdom that remained was from Frederick Barbarossa, who considered the Treaty of Benevento as the annulment of the papal–imperial alliance that had been established at Konstanz. The double election of Alexander III and of the imperial antipope Victor IV in 1159 strengthened Barbarossa's determination to attack the King of Sicily, who became the principal protector of Alexander III. In addition, a fresh revolt occurred after the murder of Maio of Bari, on 10 November

---

Manuel Comnenus, 124–30. Niketas Koniates, *Historia*, II.7, p. 125 [English trans. Magoulias, 55]. Magdalino (1993), 59–61. One may note that the twelfth-century citadel at Brindisi was on a different site to the (still-existing) Staufen-period castle: the earlier citadel was probably on the site where the later Franciscan church of St Paul was built.

[11] *Liber Pontificalis*, II.395, *MGH Constitutiones* I.588–90 no. 513 [English trans. *Tyrants*, 246–52]. The *Annales Casinenses*, *MGH SS* XIX.311, claimed that Adrian crowned William at Benevento; this is not otherwise attested. Deér (1972), 247–53, Enzensberger (1980), 396–401, and *ibid.*, 401–32 for William I's church policy. For Marsia and the northern borders of the kingdom, see Clementi (1968), 191–7, Sennis (1994), 70–1.

[12] *Codice diplomatico della Repubblica di Genova*, nos. 279–80, 282, 338–42, 344–9. *Annales Casinenses*, 311. Chalandon (1907), II.246–53, Lamma (1955–7), I.275ff.

1160, for Maio's attempts to centralize the administration had alienated both the nobles and the towns. During this revolt the king and his family were taken prisoner, in March 1161, and the heir to the throne, Roger, was killed. However, the disunity of the rebels allowed the king to suppress this rebellion too.[13]

That the state created by Roger II had finally been consolidated was shown after the sudden death of King William I in 1166, at the early age of forty-five. During the regency of his widow Margaret, who showed herself ready to make concessions to the nobility, there were, it is true, disorders at court which forced the regent to agree to the exile of her cousin Stephen of Perche, who had been appointed chancellor and archbishop-elect of Palermo, in the spring of 1168. But from the beginning of the personal rule of William II, late in 1171, there was no longer any serious threat to the existence of the monarchy.[14]

Frederick Barbarossa was forced to abandon his plans for the conquest of southern Italy after the catastrophe at Rome in 1167, when an epidemic ravaged his army, and after the foundation of the Lombard League of north Italian towns hostile to him. The result was a fundamental reversal of imperial policy towards the kingdom of Sicily. When a proposal for a matrimonial alliance between the Norman dynasty and the Byzantine imperial family fell through, in 1172, Barbarossa suggested that William II should marry one of his daughters. The king however refused, in view of the emperor's continued conflict with Alexander III. Some years later, in 1177, and with papal mediation, William II married Joanna, a daughter of King Henry II of England. Hence he became the brother-in-law of Henry the Lion, Duke of Saxony, and of King Alfonso VIII of Castile.

The emperor, the pope and the King of Sicily finally reached agreement at the peace of Venice in 1177, and this left the way open for a solution to the conflict between the Norman dynasty and the Staufen. When Constance, Roger II's posthumous daughter, married Barbarossa's son Henry (later the emperor Henry VI) in 1186, an alliance was secured that was advantageous to both parties. William II was able to devote his attention to a seemingly promising Mediterranean policy, for the Christian states of the Holy Land were becoming increasingly dependant on the help of the Sicilian fleet, and after its defeat at Myriokephalon in 1176 Byzantium was so weakened that its eventual conquest no longer seemed utopian. Thanks to his alliance with the king of Sicily, Barbarossa was free to pursue other plans, above all for a crusade. Furthermore, at the time when the marriage was agreed, in 1184, the fact that William II did not have a son can hardly

---

[13] Houben (1992a), Cuozzo (1994).
[14] Cuozzo (1989a), 656–74.

be seen as definitive – he was thirty-one, his wife only nineteen – although it was of course possible that he might be childless. But it must have been difficult to foresee that such a possibility would come to pass in a mere five years.[15]

THE END OF THE DYNASTY

William II did indeed die without children, on 18 November 1189 at the age of thirty-six. The union of the kingdom of Sicily with the German empire, which had in 1184 been only a theoretical possibility, now became a reality. The group in power in Palermo, above all the *familiares* in whose hands power had lain under William II, were not however in favour of this, fearing that the personal union of the Sicilian kingdom with the Staufen empire would lead to the loss of their pre-eminence. Contacts were opened with the pope, to whom the union of these two kingdoms was equally unwelcome, for it would lead to a pincer-like encirclement of the Church's state in central Italy. As a result Tancred of Lecce, an illegitimate son of Duke Roger, Roger II's eldest son who died young, was elected as king, or rather 'anti-king'. This action was unlawful, for the kingdom of Sicily was not an elective monarchy, rather the king had the right to designate his own successor – something which up to then had always been the case, and a right which the papacy had recognized, the last time as recently as 1188. Assemblies of nobles served merely to ratify decisions which had already been taken. There had simply been no case up to then of female succession. To avoid any possible difficulties which might arise, William II had arranged for the great men of the kingdom to confirm on oath his designation of Constance as the heir, should he die without children, during an assembly held at Troia in 1185. Hence, legal right undoubtedly rested with her.[16]

Tancred had probably been born at Lecce c. 1138, and had been raised at the court of his grandfather Roger after his father's death in 1149. He had been exiled because of his involvement with the plot against William I in 1161, but pardoned by Queen Margaret, who had sought to reach agreement with the rebel nobles, and invested with the county of

---

[15] Kölzer (1990), Houben (1992c). Fröhlich (1993) is less convincing.

[16] The most convincing among the sources seems to me to be the *Annales Casinenses*, *MGH SS* XIX.314: 'Count Tancred of Lecce, who had (amongst others) sworn fealty to Constance, the wife of King Henry of the Germans and daughter of the late King Roger, at Troia, was summoned to Palermo by the magnates of the court, and was crowned as king in the month of January with the assent and favour of the Roman Curia.' See most recently Reisinger (1992), although I would differ from this on points of detail (see my review in *Studi Medievali* 36 (1995), 872–8).

Lecce in 1169. Tancred had proved himself in the service of William II as commander of the fleet and as 'viceroy' for the mainland, the latter with the title of 'Great Constable and Master Justiciar of the whole of Apulia and Terra di Lavoro' (*magnus comestabulus et magister iustitiarius totius Apulie et Terre Laboris*). After his coronation as king, at Palermo on 18 January 1190, it seemed at first that fortune was on his side.[17]

Henry VI was at that time preoccupied with internal problems in Germany, while Barbarossa had already departed on his crusade, in which he met his death on 10 June 1190. Once the news of this trickled back to Germany some months later, this meant a further delay to the proposed expedition to Italy. Only in January 1191 could Henry at last set off for the south. In Rome, where he planned to receive his imperial coronation, a new problem emerged, for on 29 March, shortly before the Staufen ruler arrived, Pope Clement III died. Further precious time was lost before the latter's successor, Celestine III (1191–8) was elected and enthroned. Henry and Constance finally received their coronation on Easter Monday (15 April) 1191; and only then, and in defiance of the pope's wishes, could they set foot in the kingdom of Sicily, to which Henry wished to vindicate his claim derived both from 'the ancient right of the empire' (*antiquum ius imperii*) and, above all, from the hereditary right of his wife. However, the attempt collapsed at the first serious obstacle, the siege of Naples, following an epidemic brought on by the summer heat, and in which the emperor himself fell ill. Henry sought a cure in the mountains at Montecassino, and while he was there Constance, who had gone to Salerno, fell into the hands of the supporters of Tancred of Lecce.[18]

Tancred had in the meanwhile concluded an alliance with the English king Richard the Lionheart who was taking his army on crusade and, along with the French king Philip II (1180–1223), was spending the winter of 1190–1 at Messina. In the following year Tancred succeeded in making his kingship accepted in most of southern Italy, although a party among the nobility remained obstinately hostile. These people expected to have greater freedom of action under the rule of Henry VI than they had from the strict control exercised by the 'bureaucrats' in Palermo. Tancred was forced to make considerable concessions both to the towns and to the pope – the latter is clear from the Treaty of Gravina of 1192, which effectively marked the end of the 'Norman' control over the kingdom's Church. Constance was handed over to the pope, but along the way was set free and escaped back to Germany. But one undoubted success for

---

[17] Reisinger (1992), 8–40; however, for Tancred's date of birth see the review cited in previous note, pp. 873–4.

[18] Baaken (1972). For the date of Clement III's death, Houben (1988b), and for Constance, Kölzer (1983), 8–30, (1990), Stürner (1992), 55–6, and recently Maleczek (1996), 33ff.

Tancred was the marriage of his son Roger, the heir to the throne who had already been crowned king, to Irene, the daughter of the Byzantine emperor.[19]

Henry VI was always preoccupied with affairs in Germany, but only a little while later a series of lucky accidents made the conquest of the kingdom of Sicily possible. Relations between the Kings of England and France had always been strained. The former possessed extensive lands within the French kingdom; the latter claimed rights of overlordship over those lands and that the King of England ought therefore to be his vassal. There had been periodic conflicts between the two since the accession of Henry II to the English throne in 1154. While he was in the Holy Land, Richard I had once again been in dispute with King Philip of France. When Philip and Henry VI renewed the traditional alliance between the Capetian and the Staufen families in December 1191 they agreed that Henry should imprison Philip's rebellious vassal. This rapidly came to pass, for Richard's arrogant behaviour had made him other enemies as well. One of these, Duke Leopold V of Austria (1177–94), made him prisoner, and then sent him to the emperor, who proceeded not only to make him take an oath of fealty, subjecting his kingdom to him, but also to extort a huge ransom from his prisoner. The emperor's opponents inside Germany thus lost support, while he acquired new financial resources to aid his preparations for a further Italian expedition.

Fortune also favoured the Staufen ruler in that first Tancred's son and co-ruler Roger died on 24 December 1193, and then Tancred himself on 20 February 1194. The only survivors of his family were his younger son William [III] whom Tancred had had crowned as co-ruler after Roger's death, but who was still a minor, three of his sisters, and his widow Sibylla, who acted as regent for the young king. In the spring and early summer of 1194 the imperial army, supported by a combined Pisan and Genoese fleet advanced quickly into the south. After they had been promised the county of Lecce and the principality of Taranto in compensation, Sibylla and her son surrendered. On Christmas Day 1194 Henry was crowned as King of Sicily; the next day Constance, who had been left behind, gave birth to a son at Jesi, in the March of Ancona, who to begin with carried a double name, Roger Frederick, after his two grandfathers, but who was probably baptised with the name of Frederick alone.[20]

A few days later a conspiracy was discovered in Palermo – although it is possible that this was just an excuse that was fabricated – but it gave Henry

---

[19] Reisinger (1992), 131–60.

[20] *Annales Casinenses, MGH SS* XIX.317. For the birth and naming of Frederick II, Stürner (1992), 41–9; for his baptism, Schaller (1995).

the chance to rid himself of Tancred's family, who were arrested and deported to Germany. William III was blinded and castrated, and then taken to the castle of Hohenems in the Voralberg (in modern-day Austria), where he died a few years later. Sibylla and her daughters were more fortunate; they were shut up in the nunnery of Hohenberg in Alsace, from where they were later able to escape and flee to France. Irene, Roger's young widow, was betrothed to Henry's youngest brother, Philip of Swabia, whom she married in 1197 (when she took the new name of Maria).[21]

To mend his relations with the pope, but also perhaps to revive earlier Norman plans for expansion in the Mediterranean, the emperor pledged himself, in March 1195, to lead a crusade. He entrusted the Sicilian regency to Constance while he returned to Germany. He tried in vain to persuade the German princes and the pope to accept the so-called 'hereditary reign plan' [*Erbreichsplan*] by which the German royal crown would become hereditary just as were those of the other European monarchies. He was, however, only successful in having the baby Frederick II elected as King of Germany in December 1196. Relations with the pope remained tense because Henry refused to render him homage and fealty for the kingdom of Sicily, since he considered that this was incompatible with his imperial dignity.[22]

Henry VI died young on 28 September 1197: he was just short of his thirty-second birthday. Fourteen months later Constance also died, on 28 November 1198. Their disappearance caused a fundamental alteration in the political situation in both Germany and Italy. Constance had had Frederick crowned as co-ruler of Sicily at Pentecost 1198, but he was only three and a half and a gap of some years inevitably elapsed before he could take over his Norman inheritance. During this period Pope Innocent III (1198–1216) played a dominant role within the kingdom. However, the existence of that kingdom, created by Roger II, was no longer in any doubt.

[21] Csendes (1993), 155–6.
[22] Naumann (1994), Maleczek (1996), 34ff, and most recently Jericke (1997).

6

CONCLUSION. A MULTICULTURAL RULER

The modern observer who knows how matters turned out easily falls into the temptation of interpreting historical evolution as an inevitable process.[1] Another risk is to ascribe to the protagonists long-term strategies or modern ideas which they certainly never envisaged. One must therefore pose the question whether Roger II really was the deliberate 'founder of a state', or if he was rather simply intent on strengthening and extending his own rule, and utilizing whatever opportunities that presented themselves to him.

The means which he used to do this were not as unconventional as they seemed to be to many observers, both contemporary and later. His Fabian tactics in warfare, the recourse to bribery, the firm line taken towards the Church, his interest in administration and finance, were all things that he probably learned from the Byzantines, to whose culture and mentality he had been introduced by his Greek tutors. However, the Arab world which exercised such a strong influence at Palermo also played its part, while the Latin element was reinforced by the extension of his rule into the mainland provinces with their Lombard tradition.

The picture of Roger's personality which we derive from the sources is significantly different from that of other contemporary European rulers. He lacked the courtesy and generosity, the fear of God and chivalric spirit of a Frederick Barbarossa; nor did he have much in common with a (for the most part) good-tempered soldier like Louis VI of France. The one who most resembled him was the Norman King of England Henry I, who like Roger was described by his opponents as cruel and avaricious,

---

[1] See in general, Esch (1994), 7–8

who paid little attention to the archetypal chivalric virtues, and who did his best to be an efficient administrator.[2]

Abbot Alexander of Telese was the product of a traditional Benedictine background, and his work, commissioned to be in praise of the king, and preserve his memory for posterity, was written in terms which represented Roger as a 'normal' European Christian sovereign. Nonetheless, he suggested some interesting aspects of the king's character which were far from conventional:

He was a lover and defender of justice and a most stern judge of evildoers. He had above all a great dislike for liars, and if somebody who ought to have spoken the truth instead told a lie, then ever after he could scarcely if ever bring himself to believe them. He was a generous benefactor and protector to churches and monasteries. He hardly ever gave way to idleness and recreation, so much so that if and when it should happen that he was not involved with some more profitable occupation, then either he supervised the public exactions or checked what had been or ought to have been given, or ought to be received, with the result that he always understood better in the accounts of his scribes the revenues which had to be paid to him, or from where they ought to be drawn. To sum up, there was nothing which was his that was not recorded in written account, neither did he squander anything in empty generosity; hence he never lacked means for any enterprise, for he looked after his property with great care and diligence, fearing to fall into that state which is commonly described thus, 'he who does not live within his means shall live to shame' (*Qui non vixit ad numerum, victurus erit ad dedecus*).

He paid on time military salaries or whatever it had been agreed or promised should be paid. He was never willing to promise what he could not or ought not to pay. In doing things he was not headlong, but before he did anything he was careful to study it with the eye of prudence. Nor did he seek to punish anybody or to exact any due without proper hearing. If he promised anyone any benefit, or threatened them with any ill, according to their merits, that was settled and ratified. But, and this was most admirable in him, when he was campaigning against an enemy he laid his military plans with such foresight that wherever possible he overcame him without bloodshed, and thus always tried to avoid risk to his army. In speaking he was quick, in prudence mighty, endowed with gravity of counsel, clear of speech, and always prepared to reply wisely and with ready answers. But, since familiarity generally breeds contempt, he himself was both in public and in private restrained in familiarity, affability and in mirth, so that he never ceased to be feared. For fear of him grew so much that with the help of God evildoing was almost entirely eliminated from every part of his kingdom and only justice and peace still prevailed, thus the words of the Psalmist seemed to be fulfilled in him, 'justice and peace shall be kissed' [Psalm 84.11].[3]

---

[2] Douglas (1976), 2, 17–19, 61. Warren (1984) provides a timely warning against the over-estimation of the Norman administration in England.

[3] *Al. Tel.* IV.3–4, pp. 82–3.

The description of Roger's qualities as a ruler given by 'Hugo Falcandus', probably written a few years after the king's death, is similar, but adds various nuances:

Among the other natural gifts with which Nature herself had endowed this man of great vitality, he had a keen intellect and never lacked confidence in himself, so much so that if he was ever asked about anything at all he never made the slightest delay in giving a reply. Whenever there was a discussion of more important matters, he was not embarrassed to call his court together and first hear the opinion of each person in order to choose the one that was best. And if there was any point that he had considered more deeply and carefully concerning the matter in hand, he would give his own opinion last of all, and immediately explain the reason why that seemed to him to be the best course of action. Although the man's spirit was always awake and on the lookout for greater things, leaving him no time for inactivity or idle leisure, he never undertook anything thoughtlessly or on the spur of the moment, and the application of discretion restrained the impulses of his great spirit, so that nothing at all trivial should be present in the works of this wisest of kings; and it was not easy to judge whether he was wisest in speech or action. He took enormous care both to sort out present problems and to make careful provision for the future out of present conditions, and he made certain that he would use wisdom not less than power both in destroying his enemies and in increasing his kingdom by extending its territories. For he subjugated Tripoli in Barbary, Africa [i.e. Mahdia], Sfax, Gabès and numerous other barbarian cities through many personal efforts and dangers.

He also made every effort to find out about the customs of other kings and peoples, in order to adopt any of them that seemed particularly admirable or useful. When he heard that any persons were either effective counsellors or famous warriors, he would honour them with gifts to encourage their virtue. Since he derived his own origin from the Normans and he knew that the French race excelled all others in the glory of war, he chose to favour and honour those from north of the Alps particularly. In short, he made efforts to administer justice in its full rigour on the grounds that it was particularly necessary for a newly established realm, and to exercise the options of peace and war by turns, with the result that he omitted nothing that virtue requires, and had no king nor prince as his equal during his lifetime. Now as regards the fact that some writers categorize many of his actions as tyrannical and call him inhuman because he imposed on many men penalties that were severe and not prescribed by the laws, it is my opinion that as a prudent man who was circumspect in all things, he intentionally behaved in this way when his monarchy was only recently established so that wicked men should not be able to wheedle any impunity for their crimes; and that while those who deserved well (to whom he showed himself mild) should not be discouraged by excessive severity, there should nevertheless be no place for contempt as a result of excessive mildness. And if perhaps he seemed to have acted somewhat harshly against some, I suppose that he was forced to it by some necessity. For there was no other way in which the savagery of a rebellious people could have been suppressed, or the daring of traitors restrained.

When after many efforts and dangers he had brought a peace to his kingdom that remained unshaken for as long as he lived, he also made provision for the future and prepared a vast treasure for the defence of the realm, which he stored at Palermo . . . He himself surrendered to fate, overcome by early old age, both worn down by his immense efforts and more devoted to sexual activity than the body's good health requires.[4]

This last observation may perhaps have been an allusion to the ladies of the court who lived in the royal palace and to the women who worked in the silk factory there, and gave credence to the rumour that the king possessed a harem. Similar reproaches must later have been cast at Frederick II. The doctor-archbishop, Romuald of Salerno, who may have been writing a decade or so later than 'Falcandus', was silent about such matters. However, although his description of King Roger is somewhat colourless, it contains the only information that we have about his appearance:

King Roger was large of stature, corpulent, leonine of face, somewhat hoarse of voice; wise, far-seeing, careful, subtle of mind, great in counsel, preferring to use his intelligence rather than force. He was very concerned to gain money, hardly very prodigal in expending it, fierce in public but in private kindly, generous with honours and rewards to those faithful to him, but inflicting injuries and punishments on those disloyal. He was more feared than loved by his subjects, dreaded and feared by the Greeks and Muslims . . . Although the king himself was possessed of great wisdom, intelligence and judgement, he also gathered men of good sense of different classes from the various parts of the earth and made them partners in his decisions . . . And if he could find honest and wise men, whether from his own land or born elsewhere, laymen or clerics, he ordered them to be at his side, and promoted them to honours and riches as each man's status suggested.[5]

Finally, a very idealized portrait of the ruler which allows very few individual traits to appear comes from al-Idrīsī, who inserted it into the introduction to his book, redacted only a few weeks before Roger's death:

The nobility of the king's outward appearance is equalled by the excellence of his character, and his noble actions are accompanied by the best of dispositions, composed of an intrepid spirit, a clear mind, deep thought and a notable helping of magnanimity. He exercises great judgement in observation and foresight, and the wisdom with which he manages public affairs is rooted in a sharp mind. He always achieves what he sets out to do, makes light of solving the most difficult questions, and all the burden of affairs of state falls on him: in short he is such a man that his dreams are worth more than the waking thoughts of ordinary mortals. The verdicts of the royal courts are most just, the gifts given through his royal generosity are as deep as the sea and fall like snow.[6]

[4] *Falcandus*, 5–7 [*Tyrants*, 58–9].
[5] *Romuald*, 233–4, 236–7 [*Tyrants*, 221].
[6] Al-Idrīsī, *BAS* I.34–5.

The differences between these accounts are hardly surprising given the different origins and outlook of the authors, but the descriptions of Roger's character nonetheless have certain features in common, which argues in favour of their credibility, and also agrees with the analysis of the king's actions which we have made from other sources – a ruler who was intensely preoccupied with legislation and administration, and especially with financial matters, who was successful in war not through fighting battles but thanks to adroit strategy, who suppressed rebellion with a heavy hand, and who instilled respect in his subjects thanks to a court ceremonial in which western, Byzantine and Arabic elements were intermingled.

This picture is confirmed by Greek authors such as Nilos Doxapatres and Philagathos Keramides, who compared the king to the Byzantine emperor, and by the Arab poets and scholars who praised his interest in the natural sciences and his sumptuous palaces and gardens. However, this view is decidedly one-sided since it depends upon the opinion of the king's courtiers, while only a very little of the criticism by his enemies has survived. And to the Byzantines and from the point of view of the German emperor, Roger remained a parvenu; it was only under his grandson, William II, that Sicily was fully integrated into the ranks of the European monarchies. Roger's achievement was to have created the basis which made that possible.

It is quite anachronistic to attribute to him the intention of creating a 'model state' or even of founding a 'state'. He seized the opportunities which presented themselves to create a kingdom, in which elements of the three cultures which intersected in the Mediterranean were combined. Inevitably there were contradictions. The Byzantine concept of the absolute freedom of action of a ruler who was accountable only to God was incompatible with western elements such as the respect shown to the nobility which was expressed in the formal acclamation of the ruler and in his assemblies. Above all it was at odds with papal overlordship. The king's public image was also ambiguous; the way in which this was presented differed depending upon for which audience – Latin (western), Byzantine or Arab – it was intended. Nor – from a modern point of view – were his efforts to promulgate legislation and create a unitary administration entirely consistent or fully realized. The creation of an effective territorial government and the organization of the kingdom could not be completed in the space of a single generation. Such measures were however brought to fruition under Roger's successors; thus showing that the king's efforts to create a more effective judicial and administrative system had not been in vain.

Roger tried to safeguard the Arabic and Greek sections of his society, alongside the Latin element which became more and more dominant, although the Greeks and Arabs were slowly reduced to a minority, dependent for good or ill on royal protection, and their culture became progressively impoverished. A decisive role in this decline was played by the long-term standardizing influence of the Latin Church, which covered the entire kingdom with a network of bishoprics and monasteries.

Roger had commenced his career as Count of Sicily, therefore as a vassal of the Duke of Apulia, and through this also a sub-vassal of the pope. At the end of his life he was a king who may have been technically a papal vassal but who was in practice the stronger of the two parties thanks to his military power, his material resources and to his influence over the Church within his kingdom. But when Roger died the survival of his kingdom was by no means certain. Concerted action by the two emperors of east and west and by the pope, supported by the mainland nobility and the towns, could undoubtedly have destroyed it. That this did not happen was primarily because of the divergent interests of the king's enemies.

The creation of a new kingdom was hardly unique, even in the twelfth century. The kingdom of Jerusalem was founded in the Holy Land, the Portuguese monarchy in the Iberian peninsula. But the Crusader kingdom did not last long, while that of Portugal always remained on the periphery of European events. By contrast, the kingdom of Sicily not only survived until the nineteenth century but played a central role in Europe, especially in the Staufen period, and under Roger's grandson Frederick II – who in many ways resembled his ancestor – the multicultural kingdom flowered once again.

MEDIEVAL AUTHORS

———————————— • ————————————

1. ARAB AUTHORS

Abū 'l-Fidā' (Abulfeda) (1273–1331), Damascus-born emir and chronicler (compiler), later in Egypt and Syria

al-Bayān, *see* Ibn 'Idārī

Ibn Abī Dīnār, seventeenth-century Arab chronicler (compiler)

Ibn al-Athīr (1160–1233), Mesopotamian-born chronicler (compiler)

Ibn 'Idārī, native of Marrakesh, compiler of a history of Islamic Spain and north Africa (al-Bayān) written in 1312

Ibn Khaldūn (1332–1406), chronicler and compiler, native of Tunis

al-Maqrīzī (1364–1441), Egyptian chronicler

an-Nuwairī (d. 1322), Egyptian chronicler

al-Ṣafadī (1297–1362), author of a biographical encyclopaedia

at-Tijānī, native of Tunis, author of travellers' tales which appeared 1306–9.

2. GREEK AUTHORS

John Kinnamos (approx. 1143–1203), Byzantine chronicler; in his historical work he gives an overview of the government of John II Kommenos (1118–43) and then deals in rather more detail with the government of his son, Manuel I (1143–80). The work ends in 1176.

Niketas Choniates (mid twelfth century–1213), Byzantine chronicler. His historical work follows on from earlier works, including that of Kinnamos, and deals with the Byzantine empire from 1118 to 1206.

3. LATIN AUTHORS

Alexander of Telese, abbot of the Benedictine monastery of St Salvatore in Telese (northwest of Benevento), died before 1143; commissioned by Countess Matilda, wife of Rainulf of Alife and sister of Roger II, he wrote a history of Roger II's rise from count to king. The work ends at the beginning of 1136.

Falco of Benevento (died around 1144–5), notary and judge. Only those parts of his chronicle from 1102 to 1140 remain; the beginning and end are lost. The section from 1140 to 1144 was included in the chronicle of the Cistercian monastery of St Mary of Ferraria (near Vairano) in the early thirteenth century and has therefore only been transmitted indirectly.

Geoffrey Malaterra, monk at the cathedral monastery of St Agatha in Catania, of Norman origin, but not from the abbey of Saint-Evroult as is often erroneously assumed. He was commissioned by Count Roger I of Sicily (died 1101) and wrote a history of the conquest of southern Italy, with Roger I as a central figure. The work ends in 1098.

'Hugo Falcandus'. The first edition of the 'History of the Kingdom of Sicily', which appeared in 1550, covering the years from the death of Roger II in 1154 to the spring of 1169, is attributed to this author. However, it remains doubtful whether this name originates from a now-lost manuscript and/or whether this is a pseudonym. We therefore usually talk about the 'so-called Hugo Falcandus'. Nothing certain is known about the identity of this author who was so well informed about the inner workings of the royal court in Palermo. A number of possible candidates have been suggested, but none of these theories carries much conviction.

Malaterra, see Geoffrey Malaterra.

Orderic Vitalis (1075–1141/2), monk of the abbey of Saint-Evroult in Normandy, author of a 'church history'. Began writing this work before 1114; the definitive edition of the last section (books 7–13), containing a number of reports relating to Norman southern Italy, appeared around 1137, but Orderic continued writing until his death.

Romuald of Salerno, Archbishop of Salerno from 1153 to 1181, at the royal court from 1161 at the latest and personal physician to King William I (died 1166), crowned William II and represented him in 1177 at the peace negotiations in Venice. Presumed author of a world chronicle, which becomes more detailed from 1125 and ends in 1178. This earlier sections of this work may have been written by others.

BIBLIOGRAPHY

———————— • ————————

MANUSCRIPTS

Bern, Burgerbibliothek Cod. 120 II: plate 4 (p. 118).
London, British Library, Harley MS 5786.
Montecassino, Abbey, Cod. Lat. 468.
Rome, Vatican Library, Cod. Barb. Lat. 283.
    Cod. Vat. graec. 300.
    Cod. Vat. lat. 4936
    Cod. Vat. lat. 8782.
    Cod. Vat. Pal. lat. 1371.
Venice, Biblioteca Marciana, Cod. Graec. 11.
    Cod. Graec. 539.

PRIMARY SOURCES

Abū 'l-Fidā' (Abulfeda): *BAS* I.249–52.
Additamentum ad Rogerii II. regis Diplomata latina, ed. C. Brühl, in *Wilhelmi I. regis Diplomata latina*, ed. H. Enzensberger (Codex Diplomaticus Regni Siciliae, ser. I.ii(2)), Cologne–Vienna 1996, 133–55.
Alberic of Trois-Fontaines: *Ex chronica Alberici Trium Fontanium monachi*, ed. P. Scheffer-Boichorst, *MGH SS* XXIII, Hanover 1874, 631–950.
Albert of Aachen, *Historia Hierosolymitana*, in *Recueil des historiens des croisades, Historiens occidentaux* IV, Paris 1879, 256–713.
Alexander of Telese: *Alexandri Telesini abbatis Ystoria Rogerii regis Sicilie Calabrie atque Apulie*, ed. L. De Nava, Historical Commentary by D. Clementi (*FSI* 112), Rome 1991.

Amari, Michele (ed.), *Le epigrafi arabiche di Sicilia, parte 2: Iscrizioni sepolcrali* (Documenti per servire alla storia di Sicilia, III,i), Palermo 1879. New edition by F. Gabrieli, Palermo 1971.

Biblioteca arabo-sicula. Versione italiana, Turin 1880–1881 [reprint Sala Bolognese 1982].

Amatus of Montecassino, *Storia de' Normanni volgarizzata in antico francese*, ed. V. De Bartholomaeis (*FSI* 76), Rome 1935.

Andrea Dandolo: Andreas Dandulus, *Chronica per extensum descripta a. 46–1280 d. C.*, ed. E. Pastorello (*RIS²* 12, 1), Bologna 1937–58.

Annales Casinenses a. 1000–1212, ed. G. H. Pertz, *MGH SS* XIX, Hanover 1866, 303–20.

Annales Cavenses a. 569–1315, ed. G. H. Pertz, *MGH SS* III, Hanover 1839, 185–97.

Annales Ceccanenses (Chronicon Fossae Novae), ed. G. H. Pertz, *MGH SS* XIX, Hanover 1866, 275–302.

Annales Erphesfurtenses: S. Petri Erphesfurtensis continuatio Ekkehardi, in *Monumenta Erphesfurtensia saec. XII., XIII., XIV.*, ed. O. Holder-Egger, *MGH SRG* 42, Hanover–Leipzig 1899, 34–44.

Annales Herbipolenses, ed. G. H. Pertz, *MGH SS* XVI, Hanover 1859, 1–12.

Annales Magdeburgenses, ed. G. H. Pertz, *MGH SS* XVI, Hanover 1859, 105–96.

Annales Palidenses, ed. G. H. Pertz, *MGH SS* XVI, Hanover 1859, 48–98.

Annales Pisani: Gli Annales Pisani di Bernardo Maragone, ed. M. L. Gentile (*RIS²* 6, 2), Bologna 1936.

Annales Siculi, ed. E. Pontieri, in *Malaterra*, 109–20.

Annalista Saxo, ed. G. Waitz, *MGH SS* VI, Hanover 1844, 542–777.

Anonymus ad Petrum, ed. B. Kugler, *Studien zur Geschichte des zweiten Kreuzzugs*, Stuttgart 1886, 13–20.

Anonymus Vaticanus, *Historia Sicula a Normannis ad Petrum Aragonensem*, in L. A. Muratori, *Rerum Italicarum Scriptores* VIII, Milan 1726, 741–80.

The *'Assizes of Ariano'*, ed. F. Brandileone, *Il diritto romano nelle leggi normanne e sveve del regno di Sicilia*, Rome–Turin–Florence 1884, 89–138; or ed. O. Zecchino, *Le Assise di Ariano*, Cava dei Tirreni 1984.

Baumgarten, Paul Maria (1897), 'Ein Brief des Gegenpapstes Anaclet (II.)', *NA* XXII. 576–78.

al-Bayān: Ibn Idāri, Al-Bayān, *BAS* II. 1–40.

Benedict of Petersborough, *Miracula S. Thomae Cantuariensis*, in *Materials for the History of Thomas Becket, Archbishop of Canterbury*, ed. J. C. Robertson, II (Rolls Series), London 1876, 21–281.

Benzo of Alba: *Benzo von Alba, Sieben Bücher an Kaiser Heinrich IV.*, ed. H. Seyffert, *MGH SRG* 65, Hanover 1996.

Bernard of Clairvaux, *Letters*: San Bernardo, 'Lettere', *Opere di S. Bernardo*, ed. F. Gastaldelli, VI, 1–2, Milan 1986–7 [English trans. B. Scott James, *The Letters of St Bernard of Clairvaux*, London 1953].

Boso, *Vita Adriani IV*, in *Liber Pontificalis* II.388–97 [partial English trans. in *Tyrants*, 243–7].

Camobreco, F. (ed.), *Regesto di S. Leonardo di Siponto* (Regesta Chartarum Italiae 10), Rome 1913.

Catalogus Baronum, ed. E. M. Jamison (*FSI* 101), Rome 1972.

CDB I: *Le pergamene del Duomo di Bari (952–1264)*, ed. G. B. Nitto de Rossi and F. Nitti di Vito (*Codice Diplomatico Barese* I), Bari 1897.

CDB V: *Le pergamene di S. Nicola di Bari. Periodo normanno (1075–1194)*, ed. F. Nitti di Vito (*Codice Diplomatico Barese* V), Bari 1902.

CDB VII: *Le carte di Molfetta (1076–1309)*, ed. F. Carabellese (*Codice Diplomatico Barese* VII), Bari 1912.

CDB IX: *I documenti storici di Corato (1046–1327)*, ed. G. Beltrani (*Codice Diplomatico Barese* IX), Bari 1923.

CDCaiet. II = *Codex Diplomaticus Caietanus* II (Tabularium Casinense 2), Monte Cassino 1891.

CDP XX: *Le pergamene di Conversano, 1 (901–1265)*, ed. G. Coniglio (*Codice Diplomatico Pugliese, continuazione del Codice Diplomatico Barese* XX), Bari 1975.

CDP XXI: *Les chartes de Troia. Édition et étude critique des plus anciens documents conservés à l'Archivio Capitolare, 1 (1024–1266)*, ed. Jean-Marie Martin (*Codice Diplomatico Pugliese, continuazione del Codice Diplomatico Barese* XXI), Bari 1976.

Chronica de Ferraria: Chronica ignoti monachi S. Mariae de Ferraria, ed. A. Gaudenzi (Società Napoletana di Storia Patria. Monumenti Storici, ser. 1: Cronache), Naples 1888.

Chronica monasterii Casinensis, ed. H. Hoffmann, *MGH SS* XXXIV, Hanover 1980.

Chronicon Casauriense auctore Johannes Berardi, ed. L. A. Muratori [*RIS* II (2), Milan 1726, 775–1018]. Facsimile edition, *Liber instrumentorum seu chronicorum monasterii Casauriensis. Codicem Parisinum Latinum 5411 quam simillime expressum edidimus*, ed. A. Pratesi, L'Aquila 1982.

Chronicon Pisanum: Chronicon Pisanum seu fragmentum auctoris incerti, in *Annales Pisani*, ed. M. L. Gentile, appendix 2, pp. 99–103.

Cinnamus see Kinnamos

Codex Diplomaticus Caietanus see *CDCaiet*.

Codice diplomatico della Repubblica di Genova 1 958–1163, ed. C. Imperiale di Sant' Angelo (*FSI* 77), Rome 1936.

Collectio Salernitana, ed. S. De Renzi, vol. II, Naples 1853.

Cusa, Salvatore (ed.), *I diplomi greci ed arabi di Sicilia*, 2 vols., Palermo 1868–82 [reprint Cologne–Vienna 1982].

De Donato, Vittorio, 'Aggiunte al Codice Diplomatico Barese. Pergamene dell'Archivio della cattedrale', in *Archivio storico pugliese* 27 (1974), 191–232.

Deér, Josef (ed.), *Das Papsttum und die süditalienischen Normannenstaaten 1053–1212* (Historische Texte / Mittelalter 12), Göttingen 1969.

Dialogus de Scaccario, The Course of the Exchequer, by Richard Fitz Nigel, ed. C. Johnson, F. E. L. Carter and D. Greenway, Oxford 1983.

Delogu, Paolo, *I normanni in Italia. Cronache della conquista e del regno*, Naples 1984.

Digesta Iustiniani Augusti, ed. T. Mommsen and P. Krüger, Berlin 1868–1870 [reprint Berlin 1962–3].

Eadmer: *The Life of St Anselm, Archbishop of Canterbury, by Eadmer*, ed. and trans. R. W. Southern, London 1962.

Epistola ad Petrum Panormitane ecclesie thesaurarium de calamitate Sicilie, ed. Siragusa, in *Falcandus*, 169–86 [English trans. *Tyrants*, 252–63].

Ernaldus of Bonneval, *Vita prima S. Bernhardi* II, *PL* 185, coll. 267–302; *ex libro II. auctore Ernaldo*, ed. G. Waitz, *MGH SS* XXVI, Hanover 1845, 99–109.

Excerpta e codice manuscripto Lansdowniano 398, in *Materials for the History of Thomas Becket, Archbishop of Canterbury*, ed. J. C. Robertson, 4: *Anonymous Lives, Quadrilogus, etc.* (Rolls Series), London 1879, 145–85.

Falcandus, see Hugo Falcandus

Falcone di Benevento, *Chronicon Beneventanum*, ed. E. D'Angelo, Florence 1998 [also edited (very badly) by G. Del Re, *Cronisti e scrittori sincroni napoletani*, I (Naples 1845), 161–252].

Filagato da Cerami, *Omelie per i vangeli domenicali e le feste di tutto l'anno*, ed. G. Rossi Taibbi, I (Istituto Siciliano di studi bizantini e neoellenici, Testi 11), Palermo 1969.

Gabrieli, Francesco (ed.), *Arab Historians of the Crusades*, London 1969.

Garufi, Carlo Alberto (ed.), *I documenti inediti dell'epoca normanna in Sicilia* (Documenti per servire alla storia di Sicilia, ser. I, 18), Palermo 1899.

  Catalogo illustrato del Tabulario di S. Maria Nuova in Palermo (Documenti per servire alla storia di Sicilia, ser. I, 19), Palermo 1902.

  Necrologio del Liber Confratrum di S. Matteo di Salerno (*FSI* 56), Rome 1922.

Gattula, Erasmo, *Ad Historiam Abbatiae Cassinensis Accessiones*, Venice 1734.

Geoffrey Malaterra: Gaufredus Malaterra, *De rebus gestis Rogerii Calabriae et Siciliae comitis et Roberti ducis fratris eius*, ed. E. Pontieri (*RIS²*), Bologna 1925–8.

Gervase of Tilbury, *Otia imperialia*, ed. G.W. Leibniz, *Scriptores rerum Brunsvicensium*, 2 vols., Hanover 1707–10, I.881–1004; II.751–84; extracts ed. R. Pauli, *MGH SS* XXVII, Hanover 1885, 359–94 [a new edition by J. Binns, for the Oxford Medieval Texts, is in preparation].

Godfrey of Viterbo, *Pantheon: Gotefridi Viterbiensis Pantheon*, ed. G. Waitz, *MGH SS* XXII, Hanover 1872, 107–307.

Gregorii VII Registrum: Das Register Gregors VII., ed. E. Caspar, 2 vols., *MGH Epistolae Selectae* 2, Berlin 1920 [partial English trans. E. Emerton, *The Correspondence of Gregory VII. Selected Letters from the Registrum*, New York 1932].

Guibald of Stavelot, *Letters: Epistolae Wibaldi*, in *Monumenta Corbeiensia*, ed. P. Jaffé (Bibliotheca Rerum Germanicarum I), Berlin 1864, 76–616.

Historia translationis corporis S. Agathae virginis martyris Constantinopoli Catanam auctore Mauritio episcopo Catanensi, *Acta Sanctorum* I, Paris 1863, 637–48.

Historia Welforum, ed. E. König (Schwäbische Chroniken der Stauferzeit I), Stuttgart–Berlin 1938.

Hugo Falcandus: *La historia o liber de regno Sicilie e la epistola ad Petrum Panormitane urbis thesaurarium di Ugo Falcando*, ed. G. B. Siragusa (*FSI* 22), Rome 1897 [English trans. G. A. Loud and T. Wiedemann, *The History of the Tyrants of Sicily by 'Hugo Falcandus' 1154–1169*, Manchester 1998].

Ibn abī Dīnār, *BAS* II.273–97.

Ibn al-Athīr, *BAS* I.353–507.

Ibn Ḥamdīs, *BAS* II.308–413.

Ibn Ḥammād, *BAS* I.508–509.

Ibn Ḥawqal, *BAS* I.10–27, or *Description de Palerme au milieu du Xe siècle de l'ère vulgaire, par Ebn-Haucal, traduit par M. Amari*, Paris 1845 [offprint from *Journal Asiatique* (1845)].

Ibn ʿIḍārī, see al-Bayān

Ibn Jubayr, *BAS* I.137–80 [English trans. R. J. C. Broadhurst, *The Travels of Ibn Jubayr*, London 1951].

Ibn Khaldūn, *BAS* II.163–243.

al-Idrīsī, *BAS* I.31–133; or Idrisi, *Il libro di Ruggero. Il diletto di chi è appassionato per le peregrinazioni attraverso il mondo*, Italian trans. U. Rizzitano (Siciliana 1), Palermo 1994.

ʿImād al-Iṣfahānī, *BAS* II.429–90.

John the Deacon, *Descriptio Lateranensis ecclesiae*, in *Codice topografico della città di Roma*, ed. R. Valentini and G. Zucchetti, III (*FSI* 90), Rome 1946, 319–49.

John Kinnamos, see Kinnamos

John of Hexham: *Ex Historia Iohannis prioris Haugustaldensis*, ed. F. Liebermann, *MGH SS* XXVII, Hanover 1885, 14–16 [also edited in *Symeoni Monachi Opera Omnia* II, ed. T. Arnold (Rolls Series 1885), 284–332].

John of Salisbury: *The Historia Pontificalis of John of Salisbury*, trans. M. Chibnall, London 1956, repr. Oxford 1986.

John of Salisbury, *Policraticus sive De nugis curialium et vestigiis philosophorum*, ed. C. C. J. Webb, 2 vols., Oxford 1909.

Kinnamos: Johannes Cinnamus, *Epitome rerum ab Joanne et Alexio Comnenis gestarum*, ed. A. Meineke (Corpus scriptorum historiae byzantinae 15), Bonn 1836 [English trans. C. M. Brand, *Deeds of John and Manuel Comnenus by John Kinnamos*, New York 1986].

Liber Censuum: *Le Liber censuum de l'Eglise romaine* I–III, ed. P. Fabre and L. Duchesne, Paris 1889–1952.

Liber Pontificalis: *Le Liber pontificalis* I–III, ed. L. Duchesne and C. Vogel, Paris 1866–1957.

Ludolphus de Suchem: *De itinere Terrae Sanctae liber*, ed. F. Deycks (Bibliothek des Literarischen Vereins in Stuttgart 25), Stuttgart 1851.

Malaterra see Geoffrey Malaterra

Marginal Notes to Romuald of Salerno: Clementi (1991), appendix 1, pp. 337–44.

Migne, J.-P. (ed.), *Patrologia Graeca*, 161 vols., 2nd edn, Paris 1857–66.

Migne, J-P. (ed.), *Patrologia Latina*, 226 vols., 2nd edn, Paris 1878–90.

Monumenta Bambergensia, ed. P. Jaffé (Bibliotheca rerum Germanicarum 5), Berlin 1869.

Necrologia Panormitana, ed. Winkelmann, 'Reisefrüchte', 471–5.

Niketas Choniates, *Historia*, ed. J. A. van Dieten (Corpus fontium historiae Byzantinae 11), Berlin–New York 1975 [English trans. H. P. Magoulias, *O City of Byzantium! Annals of Niketas Choniates*, Detroit 1984].

Notae sepulcrales Babenbergenses, ed. P. Jaffé, *MGH SS* xvII, Hanover 1861, 640–2.

an-Nuwairī, *BAS* II.110–60.

Odo of Deuil, *De Profectione Ludovici VII in Orientem*, ed. and trans. V. G. Berry, New York 1948.

Ordericus Vitalis, *Historia ecclesiastica*, ed. M. Chibnall, 6 vols., Oxford 1969–81.

Otto of Freising, *Chronica: Ottonis episcopi Frisingensis Chronica sive Historia de duabus civitatibus*, ed. A. Hofmeister, *MGH SRG* 45, Hanover 1912.

Gesta Friderici: Ottonis et Rahewini Gesta Friderici I. Imperatoris, ed. G. Waitz, *MGH SRG*, Hanover–Leipzig 1912 [English trans. C. C. Mierow, *The Deeds of Frederick Barbarossa*, New York 1953].

Pandulfi Vita Honorii, Liber Pontificalis prout extat in codice manuscripto Dertusensi, ed. J. M. March, Barcelona 1925.

Pelagius of Oviedo: *Crónica del obispo Don Pelayo*, ed. B. Sánchez Alonso (Textos latinos de la edad media española, ser. 1, 3), Madrid 1924.

Peter of Eboli: Petrus de Ebulo, *Liber ad honorem Augusti sive de rebus Siculis. Codex 120 II der Burgerbibliothek Bern. Eine Bilderchronik der Stauferzeit*, ed. T. Kölzer and M. Stähli, with G. Becht-Jördens, Sigmaringen 1994.

The Letters of Peter the Venerable, ed. G. Constable, 2 vols., Cambridge, Mass., 1967.

Philagatos Keramides see Filagato

Phaedo, interprete Henrico Aristippo, ed. L. Minio-Paluelli and H. J. Drossaart Lulofs (Corpus Platonicum Medii Aevi), London 1950 [reprint Nendeln–Liechtenstein 1979].

Pirri, Rocco: *Sicilia sacra disquisitionibus et notitiis illustrata*, 3rd edn by A. Mongitore, 2 vols., Palermo 1733.

Prodromos see Theodoros Prodromos

Radulf Niger: *Chronica: Ex Radulfi Nigri Chronica universali*, ed. R. Pauli, *MGH SS* 27 (1885), pp. 331–41.

Regesta Imperii IV 1, Die Regesten des Kaiserreichs unter Lothar III. und Konrad III. 1. Teil: Lothar III. 1125 (1075)–1137. Nach J. F. Böhmer neubearbeitet von W. Petke, Cologne–Weimar–Vienna 1994.

Regesta pontificum Romanorum ab condita ecclesia ad annum post Christum natum MCXCVIII, ed. P. Jaffé, S. Loewenfeld, F. Kaltenbrunner and P. Ewald, 2 vols., Leipzig 1888 (reprint 1956).

Richard of Cluny (Pictaviensis): *Ex Richardi Pictaviensis Chronica*, ed. G. Waitz, *MGH SS* xxvI (1882), 74–86.

Robert of Torigny: *Roberti de Monte Cronica a. 1100–1186*, ed. L. C. Bethmann, *MGH* ss 6, Hanover 1844, 475–535 [also *Chronicles of the Reigns of Stephen, Henry II and Richard I* iv, ed. R. Howlett (Rolls Series 1889), 81–315].

Rogerii II. regis Diplomata latina, ed. C. Brühl (Codex diplomaticus regni Siciliae, ser. 1. ii, 1), Cologne–Vienna 1987. See also above: *Additamentum ad Rogerii II. regis Diplomata latina*.

Rolleus Rubeus. Privilegia ecclesie Cephaleditane, a diversis regibus et imperatoribus concessis, recollecta et in hoc volumine scripta, ed. C. Mirto (Documenti per servire alla storia di Sicilia, ser. 1, 29), Palermo 1972.

Romuald of Salerno, *Chronicon*, ed. C. A. Garufi (*RIS*²), Città di Castello 1909–35 [Eng. trans. of annals for 1153–69 in *Tyrants*, 219–43].

al-Ṣafadī, *BAS* II.563–7.

S. *Agathae miracula descripta a Blandino monacho*, *Acta Sanctorum* I, Paris 1863, 648–51.

Sicardo di Cremona: *Sicardi episcopi Cremonensis Chronicon*, ed. L. A. Muratori, *Rerum italicarum scriptores* VII, Milan 1725, 521–654.

Sigebert of Gembloux: *Continuatio: Sigeberti Gemblacensis Chronica. Continuatio Praemonstratensis*, ed. L. C. Bethmann, *MGH SS* VI, Hanover 1844, 477–56.

Snorri Sturluson: *Heimskringla or the Lives of the Norse Kings by Snore Sturlusoni*, ed. and trans. E. Monsen and A. H. Smith, Cambridge 1932.

Stürner, W. (ed.), *Die Konstitutionen Friedrichs II. für das Königreich Sizilien*, *MGH Constitutiones et acta publica imperatorum et regum 2 Supplementum*, Hanover 1996 [English trans. J. M. Powell, *The Liber Augustalis or Constitutions of Melfi promulgated by the Emperor Frederick II for the Kingdom of Sicily in 1231*, Syracuse, NY, 1971].

Suger of Saint-Denis, *Liber de rebus in administratione sua gestis*, ed. L. Delisle (Recueil des historiens des Gaules et de la France, 12), Paris 1877, pp. 96–102; also ed. with English trans. E. Panofsky, *Abbot Suger on the Abbey Church of St Denis and its Treasures*, 2nd edn, Princeton 1979, 40–81.

Theodoros Prodromos, *Historische Gedichte*, ed. W. Hörandner (Wiener Byzantinistische Studien 11), Vienna 1974.

at-Tijānī, *BAS* II. 41–81.

Vita Karoli comitis Flandriae auctore Waltero archidiacono Tervanensi, ed. R. Köpke, *MGH SS* XII, Hanover 1856, 537–61.

Vita Leonis IX, in *Pontificum Romanorum Vitae*, ed. J. M. Watterich, I, Leipzig 1862.

William of Apulia: *La geste de Robert Guiscard de Guillaume de Pouille*, ed. M. Mathieu, Palermo 1961.

William of Tyre, *Chronicon*, ed. R. B. C. Huygens (Corpus Christianorum, Continuatio mediaevalis 63–63A), Turnhout 1986 [English trans. E. Babcock and A. C. Krey, *A History of Deeds Done beyond the Sea*, New York 1941].

William *falconarius*: Dancus Rex, Guillelmus falconarius, Gerardus falconarius. *Les plus anciens traités de fauconnerie de l'Occident publiés d'après tous les manuscrits connus*, ed. G. Tilander (Cynegetica 9), Lund 1963.

Winkelmann, E. (ed.), *Acta imperii inedita saeculi XIII et XIV*, Innsbruck 1880 [reprint 1964].

SECONDARY SOURCES

Abulafia, David (1977), *The Two Italies: Economic Relations between the Norman Kingdom of Sicily and the Northern Communes*, Cambridge.

(1983a), 'The Crown and the Economy under Roger II and his Successors', *Dumbarton Oaks Papers* 37, 1–14; reprinted in Abulafia (1987a).

(1983b), 'Maometto e Carlo Magno: le due aree monetarie italiane dell'oro e dell'argento', in *Storia d'Italia. Annali*, 6: *Economia naturale, economia monetaria*, Turin, 223–70; reprinted in Abulafia (1987a).

(1985), 'The Norman Kingdom of Africa and the Norman Expeditions to Majorca and the Muslim Mediterranean', *Anglo-Norman Studies* 7, 26–49; reprinted in Abulafia (1987a).

(1987a), *Italy, Sicily and the Mediterranean, 1100–1400*, London.

(1987b), 'Asia, Africa and the Trade of Medieval Europe', in *The Cambridge Economic History of Europe* II, *Trade and Industry in the Middle Ages*, ed. M. M. Postan and E. Miller, 402–73.

(1993), *Commerce and Conquest in the Mediterranean, 1100–1500*, Aldershot.

Acconcia Longo, Augusta (1981), 'Gli epitaffi giambici per Giorgio di Antiochia, per la madre e per la moglie', *QFIAB* 61, 25–59.

(1988), 'S. Maria Chrysè e S. Maria dell'Ammiraglio a Palermo', *Rivista di studi bizantini e neoellenici*, n.s. 25, 165–83.

(1991), 'Filippo il filosofo a Costantinopoli', *Rivista di studi bizantini e neoellenici*, n.s. 28, 3–21.

Al Samman, see Samman

Althoff, Gerd (1993), 'Demonstration und Inszenierung. Spielregeln der Kommunikation in mittelalterlicher Öffentlichkeit', *Frühmittelalterliche Studien* 27, 27–50.

Amari, Michele (1933–9), *Storia dei Musulmani di Sicilia*, 2nd edn by C. A. Nallino, 3 vols., Catania.

Ambrosioni, Annamaria (1993), 'San Bernardo, il papato e l'Italia', in *San Bernardo e l'Italia*, 25–49.

Angold, Michael (1984), *The Byzantine Empire 1025–1204*, Harlow.

Le Assise di Ariano 1140–1990. Atti del convegno internazionale di studio ad 850 anni dalla promulgazione (Ariano Irpino, 26–28 ottobre 1990), ed. O. Zecchino (Centro Europeo di Studi Normanni, Fonti e Studi I), Ariano Irpino 1994; reprinted as *Alle origini del costituzionalismo europeo. Le Assise di Ariano 1140–1990*, ed. O. Zecchino (Centro Europeo di Studi Normanni Ariano Irpino, Collana di Fonti e Studi I), Rome–Bari 1996.

Atti del Congresso Internazionale di Studi sulla Sicilia Normanna (Palermo, 4–8 dicembre 1972) Palermo 1973.

Atti del Convegno Internazionale di Studi Ruggeriani. VIII Centenario della morte di Ruggero II (21–25 aprile 1954), 2 vols., Palermo 1955.

Aubé, Pierre (1991), *Les empires normands d'Orient, XIe-XIIIe siècle*, Paris.

Baaken, Gerhard (1972), 'Unio regni ad imperium. Die Verhandlungen von Verona 1184 und die Eheabredung zwischen König Heinrich VI. und Konstanze von Sizilien', *QFIAB* 59, 219–97; reprinted in Baaken (1997), 81–142.

(1993), *Ius imperii ad regnum. Königreich Sizilien, Imperium Romanum und Römisches Papsttum vom Tode Kaiser Heinrichs VI. bis zu den Verzichterklärungen Rudolfs von Habsburg*, Cologne–Weimar–Vienna 1993.

(1995), 'Das sizilische Königtum Heinrichs VI.', *Zeitschrift der Savigny-Stiftung für Rechtsgeschichte, Germanistische Abteilung* 112, 202–44; reprinted in Baaken (1997), 307–43.

(1997), *Imperium und Papsttum. Zur Geschichte des 12. und 13. Jahrhunderts. Festschrift zum 70. Geburtstag*, ed. K.-A. Frech and U. Schmidt, Cologne–Weimar–Vienna.

Baumgärtel-Fleischmann, Renate (1990), 'Der Sternenmantel Kaiser Heinrichs II. und seine Inschriften', in *Epigraphik 1988. Fachtagung für mittelalterliche und neuzeitliche Epigraphik, Graz, 10–14. Mai 1988. Referate und Round-Table-Gespräche*, ed. W. Koch, (Österreichische Akademie der Wissenschaften, Philosoph.-Hist. Kl., Denkschriften 213 = Veröffentl. der Kommission für die Herausgabe der Inschriften des Deutschen Mittelalters 2), Vienna, 105–25.

Baumgarten, see Primary sources

Beck, Ingamaj (1970), 'The First Mosaics of the Cappella Palatina in Palermo', *Byzantion* 40, 119–64.

Becker, Alfons (1988), *Papst Urban II. (1088–1099), Teil 2: Der Papst, die griechische Christenheit und der Kreuzzug*, Stuttgart.

Belli D'Elia, Pina, Maria Stella Calò Mariani and Luigi Todisco (1990), *Architettura e arti figurative: dai Bizantini agli Svevi*, in *Storia di Bari. Dalla conquista normanna al ducato sforzesco*, ed. G. Musca and F. Tateo, Rome–Bari 1990, 277–370.

Belting, Hans (1970), *Das illuminierte Buch in der spätbyzantinischen Gesellschaft*, Heidelberg.

Bennet, Matthew (1993), 'Norman Naval Activity in the Mediterranean c. 1060 – c. 1080', *Anglo-Norman Studies* 15, 41–58.

Bernardinello, Silvio (1975), 'Sicilia e Normanni in Teodoro Prodromo', in *Byzantino-Sicula* II, 51–72.

Bernhardi, Wilhelm (1883), *Konrad III.*, Leipzig (Jahrbücher der Deutschen Geschichte).

Berschin, Walter (1988), *Greek Letters and the Latin Middle Ages. From Jerome to Nicholas of Cusa*, trans. J. C. Frakes, Washington DC.

Bertaux, Emile (1898), 'L'émail de Saint-Nicolas de Bari', *Monuments et Mémoires* 4, 61–90.

Beumann, Helmut, ed. (1985), *Kaisergestalten des Mittelalters*, Munich.

Bianca Lancia d'Agliano. Fra il Piemonte e il Regno di Sicilia. Atti del Convegno (Asti-Agliano, 28–29 aprile 1990), ed. R. Bordone, Alessandria 1992.

Bisanzio e l'Italia. Raccolta di studi in memoria di Agostino Pertusi, Milan 1982.

Bordone, Renato (1988), 'Affermazione personale e sviluppi dinastici del gruppo parentale aleramico: il marchese Bonifacio "del Vasto" (sec. XI–XII)', in *Formazione e strutture*, 29–44.

Borgolte, Michael (1989), *Petrusnachfolge und Kaiserimitation. Die Grablegen der Päpste, ihre Genese und Traditionsbildung*, Göttingen.

Borruso, Andreino (1973), 'La nostalgia della Sicilia nel dīwān di Ibn Hamdīs', *Bollettino del Centro di studi filologici e linguistici siciliani* 12, 38–54.

Borsook, Eve (1990), *Messages in Mosaic. The Royal Programmes of Norman Sicily (1130–1187)*, Oxford.

Braudel, Fernand (1972), *The Mediterranean and the Mediterranean World in the Age of Philip II*, trans S. Reynolds, London.

Breccia, Gastone (1991), 'Il monastero di S. Maria di Rofrano grangia cistercense. Note storiche', *Bollettino della badia greca di Grottaferrata*, n.s. 45, 213–28.

(1995), 'Ultima grecità d'Occidente. Greci e Normanni nel Mezzogiorno d'Italia. I. Dalla conquista alla morte di Ruggero II (c. 1050–1154)', D. Phil. thesis, Scuola Superiore di Studi Storici, Università di San Marino, II ciclo di dottorato (1991–3), [supervisor G. Cavallo] unpublished.

Brenk, Beat (1990a), 'La parete occidentale della Cappella Palatina a Palermo', *Arte medievale* 4 (2), 135–50.

(1990b), 'Il concetto progettuale degli edifici reali in epoca normanna in Sicilia', *Quaderni dell'Accademia delle arti del Disegno* 2, 5–21.

Bresc, Henri (1987), 'La pêche dans l'espace économique normand', in *Terra e uomini nel Mezzogiorno normanno-svevo*, 271–91.

(1990), *Politique et société en Sicile, XIIe-XVe siècles* (Variorum Collected Studies Series 329), Aldershot.

(1992), 'Gli Aleramici in Sicilia: alcune nuove prospettive', in *Bianca Lancia d'Agliano*, 147–63.

(1993), 'Le marchand, le marché et le palais dans la Sicile des xe–xiie siècles', in *Mercati e mercanti nell'alto Medioevo: l'area euroasiatica e l'area mediterranea* (Settimane di studio del Centro italiano di studi sull'alto medioevo 40), Spoleto, 285–321.

(1994), 'Arab Christians in the Western Mediterranean (XIth–XIIIth Centuries)', in *Library of Mediterranean History*, ed. V. Mallia-Milanes, Malta, 1.3–45.

(1995), 'Messagers et postes', in *Strumenti, tempi e luoghi di communicazione*, 67–87.

Bresc, Henri and Annelise Nef (1998), *Les Mozarabes de Sicile (1100–1300)*, in Cuozzo and Martin (1998), 134–56.

Brett, Michael (1991), 'Muslim Justice under Infidel Rule. The Normans in Ifrīqija 517–555 H/1123–1160 AD', *Les Cahiers de Tunisie* 43 (= *Le Maghreb et les pays de la Méditerranée: échanges et contactes. Actes du Ve Congrès d'Histoire et de Civilisation du Maghreb. octobre 1989*), 325–68.

Brown, R. Allen (1984), *The Normans*, Woodbridge.

Brückner, W. (1978), 'Leichenbestrafung', in *Handwörterbuch zur deutschen Rechtsgeschichte* 2, 1810–14.

Brühl, Carlrichard (1968), *Fodrum, gistum, servitium regis. Studien zu den wirtschaftlichen Grundlagen des Königtums im Frankenreich und in den fränkischen Nachfolgestaaten Deutschland, Frankreich und Italien vom 6. bis zur Mitte des 14. Jahrhunderts*, Cologne–Graz.

(1977), 'Purpururkunden', in *Festschrift für Helmut Beumann*, ed. K.-U. Jäschke and R. Wenskus, Sigmaringen 1977, 3–21 [reprinted in Brühl (1989), II.601–19].

(1978), *Urkunden und Kanzlei König Rogers II. von Sizilien*. Mit einem Beitrag: *Die arabischen Dokumente Rogers II.* von A. Noth, Cologne–Vienna (Studien zu den normannisch-staufischen Herrscherurkunden Siziliens. Beihefte zum Codex diplomaticus regni Sicilae 1); revised Italian translation A. Noth, *Diplomi e cancelleria di Ruggero II.* Con un contributo sui diplomi arabi di A. Noth, Palermo 1983 = Brühl (1983a).

(1982), 'Kronen und Krönungsbrauch im frühen und hohen Mittelalter', *Historische Zeitschrift* 234, 1–31 [reprinted in Brühl (1989), I.413–43].

(1983a): see Brühl (1978).

(1983b), *Das sogenannte Gründungsprivileg Rogers II. für die Abtei S. Giovanni degli Eremiti in Palermo*, in *Aus Kirche und Reich*, 265–73 [reprinted in Brühl (1989), II.785–93].

(1984), 'Das Archiv der Stadt Messina in Sevilla', *DA* 34, 560–7 [revised version in Brühl (1989), II.777–84].

(1989), *Aus Mittelalter und Diplomatik. Gesammelte Aufsätze*, 2 vols., Hildesheim.

(1994), 'Die normannische Königsurkunde', in *Civiltà del Mezzogiorno*, 369–82.

Bünemann, Richard (1997), *Robert Guiskard 1015–1085. Ein Normanne erobert Süditalien*, Cologne–Weimar–Vienna.

Burgmann, Ludwig (1982), 'Eine griechische Fassung der "Assisen von Ariano"', *Fontes Minores* V = *Forschungen zur byzantinischen Rechtsgeschichte* 8, ed. D. Simon, Frankfurt am Main, 179–92.

Burnett, Charles (1997), *The Introduction of Arabic Learning into England*, London.

Byzantino-Sicula II. Miscellanea di scritti in memoria di Giuseppe Rossi Taibbi (Istituto siciliano di studi bizantini e neoellenici, Quaderno 8), Palermo 1975.

Canard, Marius (1955), *Une lettre du calife fâtimite al-Hâfiz (524–544/1130–1149) à Roger II*, in *Atti Ruggeriani*, 125–146; reprinted M. Canard, *Miscellanea Orientalia*, London 1973 (Variorum Collected Studies 19), no. VI.

Canart, Paul (1978), 'Le livre grec en Italie méridionale sous les règnes normand et souabe: aspects matériels et sociaux', *Scrittura e civiltà* 2, 103–62.

Cantarella, Glauco Maria (1989), *La Sicilia e i Normanni. Le fonti del mito*, Bologna.

(1994), 'Falcando, Ugo', *DBI* 44, 240–7.

(1996), 'La frontiera della crociata: i Normanni del Sud', in *Il Concilio di Piacenza e le Crociate*, Piacenza, 225–46.

(1997), *Principi e corti. L'Europa del XII secolo*, Turin.

Caravale, Mario (1966), *Il regno normanno di Sicilia*, Milan.

(1984), 'La legislazione statutaria dell'Italia meridionale e della Sicilia', *Storia e Politica* 23, 497–528; reprinted in Caravale (1998b), 167–200.

(1987), 'Le istituzioni del Regno di Sicilia tra l'età normanna e l'età sveva', *Clio* 23, 373–422; reprinted in Caravale (1998b), 71–135.

(1994a), 'Giustizia e legislazione nelle Assise di Ariano', in *Le Assise di Ariano*, 3–21; reprinted in Caravale (1998b), 3–23.

(1994b), *Ordinamenti giuridici dell'Europa medievale*, Bologna.

(1998a), 'Giustizia regia nel secolo XII in Inghilterra e in Sicilia', in Cuozzo and Martin (1998), 363–400; reprinted in Caravale (1998b), 25–69.

(1998b), *La monarchia meridionale. Istituzioni e dottrina giuridica dai Normanni ai Borboni* (Centro Europeo di Studi Normanni, Fonti e Studi 6), Rome–Bari.

Caruso, Stefano (1973), 'Echi della polemica bizantina antilatina dell'XI–XII sec. nel De oeconomia Dei di Nilo Doxapatres', in *Atti del Congresso . . . sulla Sicilia Normanna*, 403–32.

Caspar, Erich (1904), *Roger II. (1101–1154) und die Gründung der normannisch-sicilischen Monarchie*, Innsbruck [reprint Darmstadt 1965; Italian trans., *Ruggero II e la fondazione della monarchia normanna di Sicilia*, introduction by

O. Zecchino, Rome–Bari 1999 (Centro Europeo di Studi Normanni, Fonti e Studi 7)].

(1909), *Petrus Diaconus und die Monte Cassineser Fälschungen. Ein Beitrag zur Geschichte des italienischen Geisteslebens im Mittelalter*, Berlin.

Cavallo, Guglielmo (1980), 'La trasmissione scritta della cultura greca antica in Calabria e in Sicilia tra i secoli X–XV. Consistenza, tipologia, fruizione', *Scrittura e civiltà* 4, 158–245.

(1982), 'Scritture italo-greche librarie e documentarie. Note introduttive ad uno studio correlato', in *Bisanzio e l'Italia. Raccolta di studi in memoria di Agostino Pertusi*, Milan, 29–38.

Cavallo, Guglielmo and Francesco Magistrale (1995), 'Mezzogiorno normanno e scritture esposte', in *Epigrafia medievale greca e latina. Ideologia e funzione*, ed. G. Cavallo and C. Mango (Biblioteca del Centro per il collegamento degli studi medievali e umanistici 11), Spoleto, 293–328.

Centenario della nascità di Michele Amari, 2 vols., Palermo 1910.

Centri di produzione della cultura nel Mezzogiorno normanno-svevo. Atti delle dodicesime giornate normanno-sveve. Bari, 17–20 ottobre 1995 (Università degli Studi di Bari, Centro di studi normanno-svevi, Atti 12), ed. G. Musca, Bari 1997.

Cerone, Francesco (1913), *L'opera politica e militare di Ruggiero II in Africa ed in Oriente*, Catania.

Chalandon, Ferdinand (1907), *Histoire de la domination normande en Italie et en Sicile*, 2 vols., Paris (reprint New York 1960).

Cherubini, Giovanni (1987), *I prodotti della terra: olio e vino*, in *Terra e uomini nel Mezzogiorno normanno-svevo*, 187–234.

(1993), 'Gaeta', in *Itinerari e centri urbani nel Mezzogiorno normanno-svevo*, 249–67.

Chiesa e società in Sicilia. L'età normanna. Atti del I Convegno internazionale organizzato dall'arcidiocesi di Catania (25–27 novembre 1992), ed. G. Zito, Turin 1995.

Cilento, Nicola (1981), 'La "coscienza del Regno" nei cronisti meridionali', in *Potere, società e popolo nell'età dei due Guglielmi*, 165–84.

Cioffari, Gerardo (1984), *Storia della basilica di S. Nicola di Bari, 1: L'epoca normanno-sveva*, Bari.

Civiltà del Mezzogiorno d'Italia. Libro, scrittura, documento in età normanno-sveva. Atti del Convegno dell'associazione italiana dei paleografi e diplomatisti (Napoli – Badia di Cava dei Tirreni, 14–18 ottobre 1991) (Cultura scritta e memoria storica. Studi di Paleografia, Diplomatistica, Archivistica 1), ed. F. D'Oria, Salerno 1994.

Classen, Peter (1964), 'Corona Imperii: Die Krone als Inbegriff des römisch-deutschen Reiches im 12. Jahrhundert', in *Festschrift für Percy Ernst Schramm zu seinem siebzigsten Geburtstag*, 1, Wiesbaden, 90–101; reprinted in Classen, *Ausgewählte Aufsätze*, Sigmaringen 1983 (Vorträge und Forschungen 28), 503–14.

Clementi, Dione (1968), 'The Relations between the Papacy, the Western Roman Empire and the Emergent Kingdom of Sicily and South Italy, 1056–1156', *Bollettino dell'Istituto Storico Italiano per il Medio Evo e Arch. Muratoriano* 88, 191–212.

(1991), 'Historical Commentary on the "Libellus" of Alessandro di Telese, previously known as "De rebus gestis Rogerii Siciliae regis" or as "Ystoria Rogerii regis Siciliae, Calabrie atque Apulie"', in *Al. Tel.*, 175–364.

Cohn, Willy (1910), *Die Geschichte der normannisch-sizilischen Flotte unter der Regierung Rogers I. und Rogers II. (1060–1154)*, Breslau.

Collura, Paolo (1955), 'Appendice al Regesto dei diplomi di Re Ruggero compilato da Erich Caspar', in *Atti... di Studi Ruggeriani* II.545–625.

Columba, Gaetano Maria (1910), 'Per la topografia antica di Palermo', in *Centenario della nascità di Michele Amari* II.395–426.

Condizione umana e ruoli sociali nel Mezzogiorno normanno-svevo. Atti delle none giornate normanno-sveve (Bari, 17–20 ottobre 1989) (Centro di studi normanno-svevi, Università degli Studi di Bari, Atti 9) ed. G. Musca, Bari 1991.

Constable, Giles (1953), 'The Second Crusade as Seen by Contemporaries', *Traditio* 9, 213–79.

Corsi, Pasquale (1991), 'L'eunuco', in *Condizione umana*, 251–77.

Cowdrey, H. E. J. (1977), 'The Mahdia Expedition of 1087', *English Historical Review* 92, 1–29.

Csendes, Peter (1993), *Heinrich VI.*, Darmstadt.

Cuozzo, Errico (1980), 'Prosopografia di una famiglia feudale normanna: i Balvano', *Archivio storico per le provincie napoletane* 98, 61–87 [actually appeared in 1982].

(1985), 'La contea di Montescaglioso nei secoli XI–XIII', *Archivio storico per le provincie napoletane* 103, 7–37 [actually appeared in 1987].

(1989a), *L'unificazione normanna e il Regno normanno-svevo*, in *Storia del Mezzogiorno*, ed. G. Galasso, II(2), Napoli, 593–825.

(1989b), *'Quei maledetti normanni'. Cavalieri e organizzazione militare nel Mezzogiorno normanno*, Naples.

(1992), 'Drengot, Rainulfo', *DBI* 41, 689–92.

(1994), 'Salerno e la ribellione contro re Guglielmo d'Altavilla nel 1160/62. La versione delle fonti narrative e la testimonianza di quelle documentarie', in *Civiltà del Mezzogiorno*, 29–40.

(1995a), 'Trasporti terrestri militari', in *Strumenti, tempi e luoghi di communicazione*, 31–66.

(1995b), *Normanni: Nobiltà e cavalleria*, Salerno.

(1995c), 'L'incastellamento nel Mezzogiorno altomedievale ed i castelli normanno-svevi della Calabria', in *Federico II: cultura, istituzioni, arti*, ed. E. Bentivoglio, Reggio Calabria, 35–48.

(1996), 'L'annessione del ducato di Gaeta al Regno di Sicilia', in Cuozzo, *Normanni. Feudi e feudatari*, Salerno, 217–33.

Cuozzo, Errico and Edoardo D'Angelo (1994), 'Falcone da Benevento', *DBI* 44, 321–5.

Cuozzo, Errico and Jean-Marie Martin (eds.) (1998), *Cavalieri alla conquista del Sud. Studi sull'Italia normanna in memoria di Léon-Robert Ménager* (Centro Europeo di Studi Normanni Ariano Irpino, Collana di Fonti e Studi 4), Rome–Bari.

Ćurčić, Slobodan (1987), 'Some Palatine Aspects of the Cappella Palatina in Palermo', *Dumbarton Oaks Papers* 41 (= *Studies on Art and Archeology in Honor of Ernst Kitzinger on His Seventy-Fifth Birthday*, ed. W. Tronzo and I. Lavin), 125–44.

Curtis, Edmund (1912), *Roger of Sicily and the Normans in Lower Italy (1016–1154)*, New York–London.

D'Alessandro, Vincenzo (1975), 'Il problema dei rapporti fra Roberto il Guiscardo e Ruggero I', in *Roberto il Guiscardo e il suo tempo*, 91–105 [reprint 1991, 101–15].

—— (1986), 'Amalfi in età normanna', in *Istituzioni civili e organizzazione ecclesiastica nello Stato medievale amalfitano. Atti del Congresso internazionale di studi amalfitani (Amalfi, 3–5 luglio 1981)*, Amalfi, 33–52.

D'Alverny, Marie-Thérèse (1982), 'Translations and Translators', in *Renaissance and Renewal in the Twelfth Century*, ed. R. L. Benson and G. Constable, Oxford, 421–62.

D'Angelo, Edoardo (1994), 'Studi sulla tradizione del testo di Falcone Beneventano', *Filologia mediolatina. Rivista della Fondazione Ezio Franceschini* 1, 129–81.

D'Angelo, Franco (1978), 'Terra e uomini della Sicilia medievale (secoli XI–XIII)', *Quaderni medievali* 6, 51–94.

De Andrés, Gregorio (1983), 'Un diploma griego del duque normando Roger, príncipe de Sicilia (a. 1142)', in *Archivos Leoneses* 37, 379–86.

Davis, Ralph H. C. (1967), *King Stephen 1135–1154*, London.

Deér, Josef (1952), *Der Kaiserornat Friedrichs II.*, Bern.

—— (1957), 'Byzanz und die Herrschaftszeichen des Abendlandes', *Byzantinische Zeitschrift* 50, 405–36; reprinted in Deér (1977), 42–69.

—— (1959), *The Dynastic Porphyry Tombs of the Norman Period in Sicily*, Cambridge, Mass.

—— (1961), 'Der Globus des spätrömischen und des byzantinischen Kaisers. Symbol oder Insigne?', *Byzantinische Zeitschrift* 54, 53–85, 291–318; reprinted in Deér (1977), 70–124.

—— (1964), 'Der Anspruch der Herrscher des 12. Jahrhunderts auf die apostolische Legation', *Archivum Historiae Pontificiae* 2, 117–86; reprinted in Deér (1977), 439–94.

—— (1972), *Papsttum und Normannen. Untersuchungen zu ihren lehnsrechtlichen und kirchenpolitischen Beziehungen*, Cologne–Vienna.

—— (1974), 'Das Grab Friedrichs II', in *Probleme um Friedrich II.*, 361–83.

—— (1977), *Byzanz und das abendländische Herrschertum. Ausgewählte Aufsätze*, ed. P. Classen (Vorträge und Forschungen 21), Sigmaringen.

De Lachenal, Lucilla (1995), *Spolia. Uso e reimpiego dell'antico dal III al XIV secolo*, Milan.

Del nuovo sulla Sicilia musulmana. Giornata di studio (Roma, 3 maggio 1993) (Accademia Nazionale dei Lincei, Fondazione Leone Caetani 26), Rome.

Delogu, Paolo (1979), 'I Normanni in città. Schemi politici ed urbanistici', in *Società, potere e popolo nell'età di Ruggero II*, 173–205.

(1981), 'Idee sulla regalità: l'eredità normanna', in *Potere, società e popolo nell'età dei due Guglielmi*, 185–214.

(1992), 'La "militia Christi" nelle fonti normanne dell'Italia meridionale', in *'Militia Christi' e Crociata nei secoli XI–XIII (Atti della undecima Settimana internazionale di studio)* (Miscellanea del Centro di studi medioevali 13) Milan, 145–65.

Del Treppo, Mario (1977), *Amalfi: una città del Mezzogiorno nei secoli IX–XIV*, in Mario Del Treppo and Alfonso Leone, *Amalfi medioevale*, Naples, 1–175.

(1986), 'Il re e il banchiere', in *Spazio, società, potere nell'Italia del Comuni*, 229–304.

Derenzini, Giovanna (1976), 'All'origine della tradizione di opere scientifiche classiche: vicende di testi e di codici tra Bisanzio e Palermo', *Physis* 18, 87–103.

D'Erme, Giovanni M. (1995), 'Contesto architettonico e aspetti culturali dei dipinti del soffitto della Cappella Palatina di Palermo', *Bollettino d'Arte* 92, 1–32.

De Simone, Adalgisa (1971), 'Palermo nei geografi e viaggiatori arabi del Medioevo', *Studi Maghrebini* 2, 129–89.

(1995), 'Un'ipotesi su al-Idrīsī geografo e poeta', in *Azhàr. Studi arabo-islamici in memoria di Umberto Rizzitano (1913–1980)*, ed. A. Pellitteri and G. Montaina, Palermo, 111–23.

(1997), 'I luoghi della cultura arabo-islamica', in *Centri di produzione della cultura*, 55–87.

(1999), 'Il Mezzogiorno normanno-svevo visto dall'Islam africano', in *Il Mezzogiorno normanno-svevo visto dall'Europa e dal mondo mediterraneo*, 261–93.

De Stefano, Antonino (1954), *La cultura in Sicilia nel periodo normanno*, 2nd edn, Bologna.

Dilcher, Hermann (1966), 'Normannische Assisen und römisches Recht im sizilischen Stauferreich', in *Aktuelle Fragen aus modernem Recht und Rechtsgeschichte. Gedächtnisschrift für Rudolf Schmidt*, ed. E. Seidl, Berlin, 463–81.

(1994), *Die historische Bedeutung der Assisen von Ariano für Süditalien und Europa*, in *Le Assise di Ariano 1140–1990*, 23–59 [Italian trans., 1996 reprint, 21–53].

Di Meo, Alessandro (1805), *Annali critico-diplomatici del Regno di Napoli della mezzana età*, vol. x, Naples.

Dirlmeier, Ulf (1992), 'Friedrich Barbarossa – auch ein Wirtschaftspolitiker?', in Haverkamp (1992), 501–18.

Dölger, Franz (1929), 'Der Kodikellos des Christodulos von Palermo', *Archiv für Urkundenforschung* 1, 1–24; reprinted in Dölger, *Byzantinische Diplomatik*, Ettal 1956, 1–26.

Douglas, David C. (1969), *The Norman Achievement*, London.

(1976), *The Norman Fate 1100–1154*, London.

Dupré Theseider, Eugenio (1956), 'Sugli inizi dello stanziamento cisterciense nel regno di Sicilia', in *Studi medievali in onore di Antonino De Stefano*, Palermo, 203–18.

L'Ebraismo dell'Italia meridionale peninsulare dalle origini al 1541. Società, economia, cultura. IX Congresso Internazionale dell'Associazione Italiana per lo Studio del Giudaismo (Potenza–Venosa, 20–24 settembre 1992), ed. C. D. Fonseca, M. Luzzati, G. Tamani and C. Colafemmina, Galatina 1996.

Eickhoff, Ekkehard (1966), *Seekrieg und Seepolitik zwischen Islam und Abendland. Das Mittelmeer unter byzantinischer und arabischer Hegemonie (650–1040)*, Berlin.

Elze, Reinhard (1964), 'Zum Königtum Rogers II. von Sizilien', in *Festschrift für Percy Ernst Schramm zu seinem siebzigsten Geburtstag*, Wiesbaden 1964, I.102–16; reprinted in Elze, *Päpste – Kaiser – Könige und die mittelalterliche Herrschaftssymbolik. Ausgewählte Aufsätze*, ed. B. Schimmelpfennig and L. Schmugge, London 1982, no. IX.

— (1973), 'Tre ordines per l'incoronazione di un re e di una regina del regno normanno di Sicilia', in *Atti . . . Sicilia Normanna*, 438–59.

— (1990), 'The Ordo for the Coronation of King Roger II of Sicily: An Example of Dating from Internal Evidence', in *Coronations. Medieval and Modern Monarchic Ritual*, ed. J. M. Bak, Berkeley–Los Angeles–Oxford, 165–78.

— (1998), 'Der normannische Festkrönungsordo aus Sizilien', in Cuozzo and Martin (1998), 316–27.

Engel, Arthur (1882), *Recherches sur la numismatique et la sigillographie des Normands de Sicile et d'Italie*, Paris.

Engelberg, Meinrad von (1995), 'Friedrich II. und die Krone von Palermo', MA Thesis, University of Bonn (unpublished).

Engels, Odilo (1987), 'Der Konstanzer Vertrag von 1153', in *Deus qui mutat tempora. Festschrift für Alfons Becker zu seinem fünfundsechzigsten Geburtstag*, ed. E.-D. Hehl, H. Seibert and F. Staab, Sigmaringen, 235–58.

Enzensberger, Horst (1971), *Beiträge zum Kanzlei- und Urkundenwesen der normannischen Herrscher Unteritaliens und Siziliens*, Kallmünz.

— (1977), 'Cancelleria e documentazione sotto Ruggero I di Sicilia', in *Ruggero il Gran Conte*, 15–23.

— (1980), 'Der "böse" und der "gute" Wilhelm. Zur Kirchenpolitik der normannischen Könige von Sizilien nach dem Vertrag von Benevent (1156)', *DA* 36, 385–432.

— (1981), 'Il documento regio come strumento del potere', in *Potere, società e popolo nell'età dei due Guglielmi*, 103–38.

— (1992), 'La cancelleria normanno-sveva tra unità monarchica e tendenze regionali', in *Unità politica e differenze regionali nel Regno di Sicilia*, 105–18.

— (1994), 'Messina e i re', in *Messina. Il ritorno della memoria*, 331–6.

— (1995a), 'Le cancellerie normanne: materiali per la storia della Sicilia musulmana', in *Del nuovo sulla Sicilia musulmana*, 51–67.

— (1995b), 'Fondazione o "rifondazione"? Alcune osservazioni sulla politica ecclesiastica del Conte Ruggero', in *Chiesa e società in Sicilia*, 21–49.

Epstein, Stephan R. (1992), *An Island for Itself: Economic Development and Social Change in Late Medieval Sicily*, Cambridge.

Erdmann, Carl (1977), *The Origin of the Idea of the Crusade*, trans. W. Goffart, Princeton [German edition first published 1935].

Esch, Arnold (1994), *Zeitalter und Menschenalter. Der Historiker und die Erfahrung vergangener Gegenwart*, Munich.

Esch, Arnold and Norbert Kamp (eds.) (1996), *Friedrich II. Tagung des Deutschen Historischen Instituts in Rom im Gedenkjahr 1994*, Tübingen.

Faedo, Lucia (1982), 'La sepoltura di Ruggero, conte di Calabria', in *AΠAPXAI. Nuove ricerche e studi sulla Magna Grecia e la Sicilia antica in onore di Paolo Enrico Arias*, Pisa, 691–706.

Falkenhausen, Vera von (1977), 'I ceti dirigenti prenormanni al tempo della costituzione degli stati normanni nell'Italia meridionale e in Sicilia', in *Forme di potere e struttura sociale in Italia nel Medioevo*, ed. G. Rossetti, Bologna, 321–77.

(1979), 'I gruppi etnici nel regno di Ruggero II e la loro partecipazione al potere', in *Società, potere e popolo nell'età di Ruggero II*, 133–56.

(1980a), review of Brühl (1978), *Studi medievali* 21, 256–63.

(1980b), 'L'incidenza della conquista normanna sulla terminologia giuridica e agraria nell'Italia meridionale e in Sicilia', in *Medioevo rurale. Sulle tracce della civiltà contadina*, ed. V. Fumagalli and G. Rossetti, Bologna, 221–45.

(1982a), 'I Bizantini in Italia', in *I Bizantini in Italia*, ed. G. Cavallo *et al.*, Milan, 1–136.

(1982b), 'Olympias, eine normannische Prinzessin in Konstantinopel', in *Bisanzio e l'Italia. Raccolti . . . Pertusi*, 56–72.

(1983), 'Die Testamente des Abtes Gregor von San Filippo di Fragalà', *Harvard Ukrainian Studies* 7 [*OKEANOS. Essays presented to Ihor Ševčenko on his Sixtieth Birthday by his Colleagues and Students*], 174–95.

(1984), 'Costantino Africano', *DBI* 30, 320–24.

(1985), 'Cristodulo', *DBI* 31, 49–51.

(1986a), 'Bari bizantina: profilo di un capoluogo di provincia (secoli IX–XI)', in *Spazio, società, potere nell'Italia dei Comuni*, ed. G. Rossetti, Naples, 195–227.

(1986b), 'La circolazione monetaria nell'Italia meridionale e nella Sicilia in epoca normanna secondo la documentazione di archivio', *Bollettino di numismatica* 6–7, 55–79.

(1987), 'Il popolamento: etnie, fedi, insediamenti', in *Terra e uomini nel Mezzogiorno normanno-svevo*, 39–73.

(1991), 'Reggio bizantina e normanna', in *Calabria bizantina. Testimonianze d'arte e strutture di territori*, Soveria Mannelli, 249–82.

(1992), 'Doxapatres, Nilo', *DBI* 41, 610–13.

(1993), 'Eugenio da Palermo', *DBI* 43, 502–5.

(1994a), 'I rapporti con Bisanzio', in *I Normanni, Popolo d'Europa*, 350–55.

(1994b), 'Constantia oppure Constantinopolis? Sui presunti viaggi in Oriente della vedova di Boemondo I', in *ΣYNΔEΣMOΣ. Studi . . . Anastasi*, 153–67.

(1994c), 'L'Archimandritato del S. Salvatore in lingua phari di Messina e il monachesimo italo-greco nel regno normanno-svevo (secoli XI–XIII)', in *Messina. Il ritorno della memoria*, 41–52.

(1996), 'Friedrich II. und die Griechen im Königreich Sizilien', in Esch and Kamp (1996), 235–62.

(1998a), 'Il commercio di Amalfi con Costantinopoli e il Levante nel secolo XII', in *Amalfi, Genova, Pisa e Venezia. Il commercio con Costantinopoli e il vicino Oriente nel secolo XII*, ed. O. Banti, Pisa, 10–38.

(1998b), 'I diplomi dei re normanni in lingua greca', in *Documenti medievali greci e latini. Studi comparativi. Atti del seminario di Erice (23–29 ottobre 1995)*, ed. G. De Gregorio and O. Kresten, Spoleto, 253–308.

(1998c), 'Zur Regentschaft der Gräfin Adelasia del Vasto in Kalabrien und Sizilien (1101–1112)', in *ΑΕΤΟΣ. Studies in honor of Cyril Mango presented to him on April 14, 1998*, ed. I. Ševčenko and I. Hutter, Stuttgart–Leipzig, 87–115.

Favreau-Lilie, Marie-Luise (1989), *Die Italiener im Heiligen Land vom ersten Kreuzzug bis zum Tode Heinrichs von Champagne (1098–1197)*, Amsterdam.

Federico II. Immagine e potere (Catalogo della mostra Bari 1995), ed. M. S. Calò Mariani and R. Cassano, Venice 1995.

Feldmann, Karin (1971), *Herzog Welf VI. und sein Sohn. Das Ende des süddeutschen Welfenhauses (mit Regesten)*, Tübingen [Phil. Diss. 1967].

Figliuolo, Bruno (1991), 'Morfologia dell'insediamento nell'Italia meridionale età normanna', *Studi Storici*, n. s. 1, 25–68.

(1993), 'Salerno', in *Itinerari e centri urbani nel Mezzogiorno*, 195–224.

Filangieri, Angerio (1985), 'La struttura degli insediamenti in Campania e in Puglia nei secoli XII–XIV', *Archivio storico per le province Napoletane* 103, 61–86.

Fodale, Salvatore (1977), 'Il Gran Conte e la Sede apostolica', in *Ruggero il Gran Conte*, 25–42 [revised version Fodale (1991), 51–117].

(1991), *L'Apostolica Legazia e altri studi su Stato e Chiesa*, Messina.

Folkerts, Menso (1993), 'Adelard v. Bath', *Lexikon für Theologie und Kirche*, 2nd edn, 1 (1993) 151.

Follieri, Enrica (1988), 'Il crisobollo di Ruggero II re di Sicilia per la badia di Grottaferrata (aprile 1131)', *Bollettino della badia greca di Grottaferrata*, n. s. 42, 49–81; reprinted in Follieri, *Byzantina et Italograeca. Studi di filologia e paleografia*, ed. A. Acconcia Longo, L. Perria and A. Luzzi, Rome 1997, 433–61.

Fonseca, Cosimo Damiano (1977), *Le istituzioni ecclesiastiche dell'Italia meridionale e Ruggero il Gran Conte*, in *Ruggero il Gran Conte*, 43–66; reprinted in Fonseca (1987), 105–33.

(1979), 'Ruggero II e la storiografia del potere', in *Società, potere e popolo nell'età di Ruggero II*, 9–26; reprinted in Fonseca (1987), 283–300.

(1987), *Particolarismo istituzionale e organizzazione ecclesiastica del Mezzogiorno medioevale*, Galatina.

Formazione e strutture dei ceti dominanti del medioevo: marchesi, conti e visconti nel regno italico (sec. IX-XII). Atti del primo convegno di Pisa (10–11 maggio 1983), Rome 1988.

France, John (1991), 'The Occasion of the Coming of the Normans to Southern Italy', *Journal of Medieval History* 17, 185–205.

Franceschini, Ezio (1962), 'Aristippo, Enrico', *DBI* 5, 201–6.

Fried, Johannes (1984), 'Die Wirtschaftspolitik Friedrich Barbarossas in Deutschland', *Blätter für Deutsche Landesgeschichte* 120, 195–239.

Fröhlich, Walter (1993), 'The Marriage of Henry VI and Constance of Sicily: Prelude and Consequences', *Anglo-Norman Studies* 15, 99–115.

Fuhrmann, Horst (1986), *Germany in The High Middle Ages, C.1050–1200*, trans. T. Reuter, Cambridge.

Gallina, Mario (1999), 'Il Mezzogiorno normanno-svevo visto da Bisanzio', in *Il Mezzogiorno normanno-svevo visto dell'Europa e del mondo mediterraneo*, 197–223.

Gandolfo, Francesco (1993), 'Le tombe e gli arredi liturgici medievali', in *La cattedrale di Palermo. Studi per l'ottavo centenario della fondazione*, ed. L. Urbani, Palermo, 231–53, 468–71.

Ganzer, Klaus (1963), *Die Entwicklung des auswärtigen Kardinalats im hohen Mittelalter. Ein Beitrag zur Geschichte des Kardinalkollegiums vom 11. bis zum 13. Jahrhundert*, Tübingen.

Garufi see Primary sources

Gattula see Primary sources

Gelfer-Jørgensen, Mirjam (1986), *Medieval Islam, Symbolism and the Paintings in the Cefalù Cathedral*, Leiden.

Gil, Moshe (1995), 'Sicily 827–1072, in Light of the Geniza Documents and Parallel Sources', in *Italia Judaica. Gli ebrei in Sicilia sino all'espulsione del 1492. Atti del V convegno internazionale Palermo, 15–19 giugno 1992* (Pubblicazioni degli Archivi di Stato, Saggi 32), Rome, 96–171.

Girgensohn, Dieter (1969), 'Boemondo', *DBI* 11, 117–24.

Giunta, Francesco (1950), *Bizantini e bizantinismo nella Sicilia normanna*, Palermo [2nd edn 1974].

    (1982), 'Per una biografia di Ruggero II', in Giunta, *Medioevo normanno*, Palermo, 71–103.

    (1994), '"Donaria ecclesie Traianensis"', in *Società, istituzioni. Studi . . . Violante*, I.445–50.

    (1995), 'Il fondo Sicilia dell'Archivio della Fondazione Medinaceli di Siviglia', in *Del nuovo sulla Sicilia musulmana*, 153–65.

Goitein, Shelomo Dov (1967–88), *A Mediterranean Society. The Jewish Communities of the Arab World as Portrayed in the Documents of the Cairo Geniza*, 5 vols., Berkeley–Los Angeles–London.

    (1971), 'Sicily and Southern Italy in the Cairo Genizah Documents', *Archivio storico per la Sicilia orientale* 67, 9–33.

Gregorio, Rosario (1805), *Considerazioni sopra la storia di Sicilia dai tempi normanni sino ai presenti*, II, Palermo.

Grierson, Philip (1976), *Münzen des Mittelalters*, Munich.

    (1993), 'The Coinages of Norman Apulia and Sicily in their International Setting', *Anglo-Norman Studies* 15, 117–32.

Grierson, Philip, and Lucia Travaini (1998), *Medieval European Coinage. With a Catalogue of the Coins in the Fitzwilliam Museum Cambridge, 14: Italy (III) (South Italy, Sicily, Sardinia)*, Cambridge.

Grotz, Hans (1983), 'Kriterien auf dem Prüfstand: Bernhard von Clairvaux angesichts zweier kanonisch strittiger Wahlen', in *Aus Kirche und Reich. Festschrift . . . Kempf*, 237–63.

Hageneder, Othmar (1996), 'Der Zweifel an Regierungsmaßnahmen als Sakrileg. Römisches und kanonisches Recht bei der Ausbildung des päpstlichen und fürstlichen Absolutismus', *Zeitschrift für Katholische Theologie* 118, 126–37.

Halm, Heinz (1987–9), 'Fatimiden', *LdM* IV. 318–19.

(1991), *Das Reich des Mahdi. Der Aufstieg der Fatimiden (875–973)*, Munich.

Haskins, Charles Homer (1927) *Studies in the History of Mediaeval Science*, Cambridge, Mass., 2nd edn.

Haug, Walter (1975), 'Artussage und Heilsgeschichte. Zum Programm des Fuß-bodenmosaiks von Otranto', *Deutsche Vierteljahresschrift für Literaturwissenschaft und Geistesgeschichte* 49, 577–606.

Haverkamp, Alfred (1987), 'Italien im hohen und späten Mittelalter 1056–1454', in *Handbuch der europäischen Geschichte* II, ed. T. Schieder, Stuttgart, 546–681.

(ed.) (1992), *Friedrich Barbarossa. Handlungsspielräume und Wirkungsweisen des staufischen Kaisers* (Vorträge und Forschungen 40), Sigmaringen.

Hehl, Ernst-Dieter (1980), *Kirche und Krieg im 12. Jahrhundert. Studien zu kanonischem Recht und politischer Wirklichkeit*, Stuttgart.

Herde, Peter (1970), 'Das Papsttum und die griechische Kirche in Süditalien vom 11. bis zum 13. Jahrhundert', *DA* 26, 1–46 [revised version in English in Loud and Metcalfe (2002)].

Herklotz, Ingo (1985), *'Sepulcra' e 'Monumenta' del Medioevo. Studi sull'arte sepolcrale in Italia*, Rome.

Herval, René (1955), 'Eclectisme intellectuel à la cour de Roger II de Sicile', in *Atti . . . Studi Ruggeriani*, 73–104.

Hettinger, Anette (1990), 'Zur Lebensgeschichte und zum Todesdatum des Constantinus Africanus', *DA* 46, 517–29.

(1993), *Die Beziehungen des Papsttums zu Afrika von der Mitte des 11. bis zum Ende des 12. Jahrhunderts*, Cologne–Weimar–Vienna.

Hiestand, Rudolf (1993a), 'Zur Geschichte des Königreichs Sizilien im 12. Jahrhundert', *QFIAB* 63, 52–69.

(1993b), 'Antiochia, Sizilien und das Reich am Ende des 12. Jahrhunderts', *QFIAB* 63, 70–121.

(1993c), '*Neptis tua* und *fastus Graecorum*. Zu den deutsch-byzantinischen Verhandlungenum 1150', *DA* 49, 501–55.

Hoffmann, Hartmut (1967), 'Hugo Falcandus und Romuald von Salerno', *DA* 23, 116–70.

(1969), 'Die Anfänge der Normannen in Süditalien', *QFIAB* 49, 95–144.

(1978), 'Langobarden, Normannen, Päpste. Zum Legitimationsproblem in Unteritalien', *QFIAB* 58, 137–80.

Hofmann, Thomas (1994), *Papsttum und griechische Kirche in Süditalien in nachnor-mannischer Zeit (13–15. Jahrhundert). Ein Beitrag zur Geschichte Süditaliens im Hoch- und Spätmittelalter* (Phil. Diss.), Würzburg.

Hofmeister, Adolf (1920), 'Der Sermo de inventione sancti Kataldi. Zur Geschichte Tarents am Ende des 11. Jahrhunderts', *Münchner Museum für Philologie des Mittelalters und der Renaissance* 4, 101–14.

(1926), '*Puer, iuvenis, senex*. Zum Verständnis der mittelalterlichen Altersbezei-chnungen', in *Papsttum und Kaisertum. Forschungen zur politischen Geschichte und Geisteskultur des Mittelalters. Paul Kehr zum 65. Geburtstag dargebracht*, ed. A. Brackmann, Munich, 287–316.

Holtzmann, Walther (1933–5), 'Zur Geschichte des Investiturstreites. (Englische Analekten II.)', *NA* 50, 246–319, part 3. 'England, Unteritalien und der Vertrag von Ponte Mammolo', 282–301 [reprinted in Holtzmann (1957), 107–22].

(1957), *Beiträge zur Reichs- und Papstgeschichte des Mittelalters. Ausgewählte Aufsätze*, Bonn.

(1961), 'Papsttum, Normannen und griechische Kirche', in *Miscellanea Bibliothecae Hertzianae*, Munich 1961, 69–76.

(1963), ' Maximilla regina, soror Rogerii regis', *DA* 19, 149–67.

Hood, Gwenyth E. (1999), 'Falcandus and Fulcaudus, "Epistola ad Petrum, Liber de Regno Sicilie". Literary Form and Author's Identity', *Studi medievali*, 3rd series, 40, 1–41.

Horn, Michael (1992), *Studien zur Geschichte Papst Eugens III. (1145–1153)*, Frankfurt am Main.

Houben, Hubert (1984), *Il 'libro del capitolo' del monastero della SS. Trinità di Venosa (Cod. Casin. 334): una testimonianza del Mezzogiorno normanno*, Galatina.

(1987), 'Il principato di Salerno e la politica meridionale dell'Impero d'Occidente', *Rassegna storica Salernitana*, 4, 59–83; reprinted in Houben (1989), 31–54.

(1988a), 'Malfattori e benefattori, protettori e sfruttatori: i Normanni e Montecassino', *Benedictina* 35, 343–71; reprinted in Houben (1989), 67–92, and in *L'età dell'abate Desiderio, III, 1: Storia arte e cultura. Atti del IV Convegno di studi sul Medioevo meridionale*, ed. F. Avagliano and O. Pecere (Miscellanea Cassinese 67), Montecassino 1992 [actually published in 1994], 123–51.

(1988b), 'Philipp von Heinsberg, Heinrich VI. und Montecassino. Mit einem Exkurs zum Todesdatum Papst Clemens' III', *QFIAB* 68, 52–73.

(1989), *Tra Roma e Palermo. Aspetti e momenti del Mezzogiorno medioevale*, Galatina.

(1990), 'Adelaide "del Vasto" nella storia del Regno di Sicilia', *Itinerari di ricerca storica* 4, 9–40; reprinted in *Bianca Lancia d'Agliano*, 121–45; revised version in Houben (1996a), 81–113.

(1992a), 'Barbarossa und die Normannen. Traditionelle Züge und neue Perspektiven imperialer Süditalienpolitik', in Haverkamp (1992), 109–28.

(1992b), 'Il monachesimo cluniacense e i monasteri normanni dell'Italia meridionale', *Benedictina* 39, 341–61; reprinted in Houben (1996a), 7–22.

(1992c), 'Tra vocazione mediterranea e destino europeo: la politica estera di re Guglielmo II di Sicilia', in *Unità politica e differenze regionali*, 119–133; reprinted in Houben (1996a), 145–57.

(1993a), 'Elvira, regina di Sicilia', *DBI* 42, 532–3.

(1993b), 'Melfi, Venosa', in *Itinerari e centri urbani nel Mezzogiorno*, 311–31; reprinted in Houben (1996a), 319–36.

(1994a), 'Möglichkeiten und Grenzen religiöser Toleranz im normannisch-staufischen Königreich Sizilien', *DA* 50, 159–98; Italian trans. 'Possibilità e limiti della tolleranza religiosa nel Mezzogiorno normanno-svevo', in Houben (1996a), 213–42 [revised version in English in Loud and Metcalfe (2002)].

(1994b), review of Hettinger (1993), in *Quaderni medievali* 38, 214–15.

(1995a), *Die Abtei Venosa und das Mönchtum im normannisch-staufischen Süditalien*, Tübingen.

(1995b), 'La predicazione', in *Strumenti, tempi e luoghi di communicazione*, 253–73; reprinted in Houben (1996a), 337–54.

(1996a), *Mezzogiorno normanno-svevo. Monasteri e castelli, ebrei e musulmani*, Naples.

(1996b), 'Urbano II e i Normanni (con un'appendice sull'itinerario del papa nel Sud)', in Houben (1996a), 115–43.

(1996c), 'I castelli del Mezzogiorno normanno-svevo nelle fonti scritte', in Houben (1996a), 159–76.

Hueffer, Georg (1886), *Der heilige Bernhard von Clairvaux. Eine Darstellung seines Lebens und Wirkens, 1: Vorstudien*, Münster.

Hüls, Rudolf (1977), *Kardinäle, Klerus und Kirchen Roms 1049–1130*, Tübingen.

Hunger, Herbert (1964), *Prooimion. Elemente der byzantinischen Kaiseridee in den Arengen der Urkunden*, Vienna.

(1978), *Die hochsprachliche profane Literatur der Byzantiner*, vol. II (Byzantinisches Handbuch V, 2), Munich.

Idris, Hady Roger (1962), *La Berbérie orientale sous les Zīrīdes, X^e-XIIe siècles*, 2 vols., Paris.

Inguanez, Mauro (1930), *Diplomi cassinesi con sigillo d'oro* (Miscellanea Cassinese 7), Montecassino.

Italia Pontificia 8: Regnum Normannorum – Campania, ed. P. F. Kehr, Berlin 1935; reprint 1961.

Italia Pontificia 9: Samnium – Apulia – Lucania, ed. W. Holtzmann, Berlin 1962.

Italia Pontificia 10: Calabria – Insulae, ed. D. Girgensohn, Zürich 1975.

Itinerari e centri urbani nel Mezzogiorno normanno-svevo. Atti delle decime giornate normanno-sveve (Bari, 21–24 ottobre 1991) (Centro di Studi normanno-svevi, Università degli Studi di Bari, Atti 10), ed. G. Musca, Bari 1993.

Jacoby, David (1994), 'Nuovi e mutevoli orizzonti: verso ed oltre l'Oriente mediterraneo', in *Storia d'Europa, 3: Il Medioevo. Secoli V–XV*, ed. G. Ortalli, Turin, 1143–92.

Jäschke, Kurt-Ulrich (1981), *Die Anglonormannen*, Stuttgart.

Jahn, Wolfgang (1989), *Untersuchungen zur normannischen Herrschaft in Süditalien (1040–1100)*, Frankfurt am Main.

Jamison, Evelyn M. (1913), 'The Norman Administration of Apulia and Capua More Especially under Roger II and William I 1127–1166', *Papers of the British School at Rome* 6, 211–481 [reprinted as a separate volume, Aalen 1987].

(1929–30), 'The Administration of the County of Molise in the Twelfth and Thirteenth Centuries', *English Historical Review* 44 (1929), 529–59; 45 (1930), 1–34; reprinted in Jamison (1992), 1–65.

(1938), 'The Sicilian Norman Kingdom in the Mind of Anglo-Norman Contemporaries', *Proceedings of the British Academy* 24, 237–85; reprinted in Jamison (1992), 159–207.

(1957), *Admiral Eugenius of Sicily, his Life and Work and the Authorship of the Epistola ad Petrum and the Historia Hugonis Falcandi Siculi*, London.

(1971), 'Additional Work on the Catalogus Baronum', *Bullettino dell'Istituto Storico Italiano per il Medio Evo e Arch. Muratoriano* 83, 1–63; reprinted in Jamison (1992), 523–85.

(1992), *Studies on the History of Medieval Sicily and South Italy*, ed. D. Clementi and T. Kölzer, Aalen.

Jericke, Hartmut (1997), *Imperator Romanorum et Rex Siciliae. Kaiser Heinrich VI. und sein Ringen um das normannisch-sizilische Königreich*, Frankfurt am Main.

Johns, Jeremy (1983), 'The Muslims of Norman Sicily c. 1060–c. 1194', D. Phil. thesis, University of Oxford [unpublished].

(1986), 'I titoli arabi dei sovrani normanni di Sicilia', *Bollettino di Numismatica* 6–7, 11–54.

(1987), 'Malik Ifrīqiya: The Norman Kingdom of Africa and the Fāṭimids', *Libyan Studies* 18, 89–101.

(1993), 'The Norman Kings of Sicily and the Fāṭimid Caliphate', *Anglo-Norman Studies* 15, 133–59.

(1995a), 'I re normanni e i califfi fatimiti. Nuove prospettive su vecchi materiali', in *Del nuovo sulla Sicilia musulmani*, 9–50.

(1995b), 'The Greek Church and the Conversion of Muslims in Norman Sicily?', *Byzantinische Forschungen* 21 (=*Bosphorus. Essays in Honour of Cyril Mango*), 133–57.

Jurlaro, Rosario (1968), 'Epigrafi medievali brindisine I', *Studi salentini* 29–30, 231–77.

Kamp, Norbert (1973–82), *Kirche und Monarchie im staufischen Königreich Sizilien. I: Prosopographische Grundlegung. Bistümer und Bischöfe des Königreichs 1194–1266, 1: Abruzzen und Kampanien, 2: Apulien und Kalabrien, 3: Sizilien, 4: Nachträge und Berichtigungen, Register und Verzeichnisse*, 4 vols., Munich.

(1974), 'Vom Kämmerer zum Sekreten. Wirtschaftsreformen und Finanzverwaltung im staufischen Königreich Sizilien', in *Probleme um Friedrich II.*, 43–92.

(1977), 'Soziale Herkunft und geistlicher Bildungsweg der unteritalienischen Bischöfe in normannisch-staufischer Zeit', in *Le istituzioni ecclesiastiche della 'societas christiana' dei secoli XI–XII, Diocesi, pievi e parrocchie. Atti della sesta Settimana internazionale di studio (Milano 1–7 settembre 1974)* (Pubblicazioni dell'Università Cattolica del Sacro Cuore, Miscellanea del Centro di Studi medioevali 8), Milan, 89–116 [revised version in English in Loud and Metcalfe (2002)].

(1979), 'Der unteritalienische Episkopat im Spannungsfeld zwischen monarchischer Kontrolle und römischer "libertas" von der Reichsgründung bis zum Konkordat von Benevent', in *Società, potere, e popolo nell'età di Ruggero II*, 99–132.

(1977–80), 'Beamtenwesen, VI. Königreich Sizilien', *LdM* I.1728–31.

(1987–9), 'Gaeta', *LdM* IV.1075–7.

(1995a), 'I vescovi siciliani nel periodo normanno: origine sociale e formazioni spirituali', in *Chiesa e società in Sicilia*, 63–89.

(1995b), 'Gli Amalfitani al servizio della monarchia nel periodo svevo del Regno di Sicilia', in *Documenti e realtà nel Mezzogiorno italiano in età medievale e moderna*. *Atti delle giornate di studio in memoria di Jole Mazzoleni (Amalfi, 10–12 dicembre 1993)* (Centro di cultura e storia amalfitana, Atti 6), Amalfi, 9–37.

(1996a), 'Die deutsche Präsenz im Königreich Sizilien (1194–1266)', in Kölzer (1996), 141–85.

(1996b), 'Friedrich II. im europäischen Zeithorizont', in Esch and Kamp (1996), 1–22.

Kantorowicz, Ernst H. (1946), *Laudes Regiae. A Study in Liturgical Acclamations and Mediaeval Ruler Worship*, Berkeley–Los Angeles.

Kedar, Benjamin Z. (1984), *Crusade and Mission. European Approaches toward the Muslims*, Princeton.

Kehr, Karl Andreas (1902) *Die Urkunden der normannisch-sicilischen Könige*, Innsbruck.

Kehr, Paul Fridolin (1934), *Die Belehnungen der süditalienischen Normannenfürsten durch die Päpste (1059–1192)* (Abhandlungen der Preußischen Akademie der Wissenschaften 1934, Phil.-Hist. Kl. Nr. 1), Berlin.

Kienast, Walther (1967), 'Magnus = der Ältere', *Historische Zeitschrift* 205, 1–14.

[*Aus*]*Kirche und Reich. Studien zu Theologie, Politik und Recht im Mittelalter. Festschrift für Friedrich Kempf*, ed. H. Mordek, Sigmaringen 1983.

Kitzinger, Ernst (1949), 'The Mosaics of the Cappella Palatina in Palermo. An essay on the choice and arrangement of subjects', *Art Bulletin* 31, 269–92; reprinted in Kitzinger (1976), 290–319.

(1950), 'On the Portrait of Roger II in the Martorana in Palermo', *Proporzioni* 3, 30–5; reprinted in Kitzinger (1976), 320–26.

(1975), 'The Date of Philagathos' Homily for the Feast of Sts. Peter and Paul', in *Byzantino-Sicula II*, 301–6.

(1976), *The Art of Byzantium and the Medieval West: Selected Studies*, ed. W. E. Kleinbauer, Bloomington–London.

(1990), *I mosaici di Santa Maria dell'Ammiraglio a Palermo* [with a chapter on the architecture of the church by S. Čurčić] (Istituto Siciliano di studi bizantini e neoellenici, Monumenti 3 [= *Dumbarton Oaks Papers* 27]), Palermo.

Kölzer, Theo (1977–80), 'Adventus regis', *LdM* 1.170–1.

(1983), *Urkunden und Kanzlei der Kaiserin Konstanze, Königin von Sizilien (1195–1198)* (Studien zu den normannisch-staufischen Herrscherurkunden Siziliens, Beihefte zum Codex diplomaticus regni Siciliae 2), Cologne–Vienna.

(1984), 'Costanza d'Altavilla', *DBI* 30, 346–56.

(1984–6), 'Curia regis, III. Königreich Sizilien', *LdM* III.376–8.

(1986), 'Kanzlei und Kultur im Königreich Sizilien 1130–1198', *QFIAB* 66, 20–39.

(1990), 'Sizilien und das Reich im ausgehenden 12. Jahrhundert', *Historisches Jahrbuch* 110, 3–22.

(1993), 'Herrschen aus der Ferne. Die Staufer in Italien', in *Die Hauptstädte der Deutschen. Von der Kaiserpfalz in Aachen zum Regierungssitz Berlin*, ed. U. Schultz, Munich, 33–43, 241–4.

(1994), 'La monarchia normanno-sveva e l'Ordine cistercense', in *I Cistercensi nel Mezzogiorno medioevale. Atti del Convegno internazionale di studio in occasione del IX centenario della nascita di Bernardo di Clairvaux (Martano-Latiano-Lecce, 25–27 febbraio 1991)*, ed. H. Houben and B. Vetere, Galatina, 91–116.

(1995), 'Die normannisch-staufische Kanzlei (1130–1198)', *Archiv für Diplomatik* 41, 273–89.

(ed.) (1996), *Die Staufer im Süden. Sizilien und das Reich*, Sigmaringen.

Koller, Walter (1998), 'Toleranz im Königreich Sizilien zur Zeit der Normannen', in *Toleranz im Mittelalter*, ed. A. Patschovsky and H. Zimmermann, Sigmaringen, 159–85.

Kristeller, Paul Otto (1956), *Studies in Renaissance Thought and Letters*, Rome.

(1986), *Studi sulla Scuola medica salernitana*, Naples.

Krönig, Wolfgang (1989), 'Der viersprachige Grabstein von 1148 in Palermo', in *Zeitschrift für Kunstgeschichte* 52, 550–8.

Lamma, Paolo (1955–7), *Comneni e Staufer. Ricerche sui rapporti fra Bisanzio e l'Occidente nel secolo XII*, 2 vols., Rome.

Laurent, Vitalien (1937), 'L'œuvre géographique du moine sicilienne Nil Doxapatris', *Echos d'Orient* 36, 5–30.

Lavagnini, Bruno (1974), 'Filippo-Filagato promotore degli studi di greco in Calabria', *Bollettino della Badia greca di Grottaferrata*, n.s. 28, 3–12; reprinted in Bruno Lavagnini, *ATAKTA. Scritti minori di filologia classica, bizantina e neogreca*, Palermo 1978, 760–9.

(1982), ' "Versi dal carcere" di un anonimo poeta italo-bizantino di età normanna (1135–1151)', *Rivista di Studi bizantini e slavi* 2 (=*Miscellanea Agostino Pertusi* 2), 323–31.

(1994), 'Giorgio di Antiochia e il titolo ΑΡΧΩΝ ΤΩΝ ΑΡΧΟΝΤΩΝ', in ΣΥΝΔΕΣΜΟΣ, 215–20.

Lemay, Richard (1987), 'De la scolastique à l'histoire par le truchement de la philologie: itinéraire d'un médiéviste entre Europe et Islam', in *La diffusione delle scienze islamiche nel Medio Evo europeo. Convegno internazionale promosso dall'Accademia Nazionale dei Lincei . . . (Roma, 2–4 ottobre 1984)*, Rome, 399–535.

Leonhard, Joachim-Felix (1983), *Die Seestadt Ancona im Spätmittelalter. Politik und Handel*, Tübingen.

Le Tourneau, Roger (1969), *The Almohad Movement in North Africa in the Twelfth and Thirteenth Centuries*, Princeton.

Licinio, Raffaele (1994), *Castelli medievali. Puglia e Basilicata: Dai Normanni a Federico II e Carlo I d'Angiò*, Bari.

Lilie, Ralph-Johannes (1984), *Handel und Politik zwischen dem byzantinischen Reich und den italienischen Kommunen Venedig, Pisa und Genua in der Epoche der Komnenen und der Angeloi (1081–1204)*, Amsterdam.

Lohrmann, Dietrich (1968), *Das Register Papst Johannes VIII. (872–882)*, Tübingen 1968.

Lopez, Roberto Sabatino (1958), 'The Norman Conquest of Sicily', in *A History of the Crusades*, ed. K. M. Setton, i, Philadelphia, 54–67.

Loud, G. A. (1982), 'Royal Control of the Church in the Twelfth-Century Kingdom of Sicily, in Religion and National Identity', *Studies in Church History* 18, 147–59; reprinted in Loud (1999).

(1985), *Church and Society in the Norman Principality of Capua, 1058–1197*, Oxford.

(1992), 'Norman Italy and the Holy Land', in *The Horns of Hattin*, ed. B. Z. Kedar, Jerusalem–London, 49–62; reprinted in Loud (1999).

(1993), 'The Genesis and Context of the Chronicle of Falco of Benevento', *Anglo-Norman Studies* 15, 177–98; reprinted in Loud (2000a).

(1996), 'William the Bad or William the Unlucky?', *The Haskins Society Journal* 8, 99–113 [actually published 1999].

(1997), 'A Lombard Abbey in a Norman World: St Sophia, Benevento, 1050–1200', *Anglo-Norman Studies* 19, 273–306.

(1999a), 'Coinage, Wealth and Plunder in the Age of Robert Guiscard', *English Historical Review* 114, 815–43.

(1999b), *Conquerors and Churchmen in Norman Italy*, Aldershot.

(2000a), *Montecassino and Benevento in the Middle Ages*, Aldershot.

(2000b), *The Age of Robert Guiscard: Southern Italy and the Norman Conquest*, Harlow.

Loud, G. A. and A. Metcalfe (eds.) (2002), *The Society of Norman Italy*, Leiden [to appear].

Lucà, Santo (1993), 'I Normanni e la "rinascita" del sec. XII', *Arch. Storico per la Calabria e la Lucania* 60 [actually 1995], 1–91.

Luttrell, Anthony T. (1975), *Approaches to Medieval Malta*, in Luttrell (ed.), *Medieval Malta. Studies on Malta before the Knights*, London, 1–70.

Magdalino, Paul (1993), *The Empire of Manuel I Komnenos, 1143–1180*, Cambridge.

Magistrale, Francesco (1992), 'Forme e funzioni delle scritte esposte nella Puglia normanna', *Scrittura e civiltà* 16, 5–75.

Mákk, Ferenc (1989), *The Árpáds and the Comneni. Political Relations between Hungary and Byzantium in the 12th Century*, Budapest.

Maleczek, Werner (1981), 'Das Kardinalskollegium unter Innocenz II. und Anaklet. II', *Archivum Historiae Pontificiae* 19, 27–78.

(1992), 'Rombeherrschung und Romerneuerung durch das Papsttum', in B. Schimmelpfennig and L. Schmugge (eds.), *Rom im hohen Mittelalter. Studien zu den Romvorstellungen und zur Rompolitik vom 10. bis zum 12. Jahrhundert*, Sigmaringen, 15–27.

(1996), 'Ecclesiae patrimonium speciale. Sizilien in der päpstlichen Politik des ausgehenden 12. Jahrhunderts', in Kölzer (1996), 29–42.

Marongiu, Antonio (1955), 'Concezione della sovranità di Ruggero II', in *Atti . . . di Studi Ruggeriani*, 213–33; reprinted in Marongiu (1972), no. III.

(1964), 'A Model State in the Middle Ages: the Norman-Hohenstaufen kingdom of Sicily', *Comparative Studies in Society and History* 6, 307–24; reprinted in Marongiu (1972), no. XI.

(1972), *Byzantine, Norman, Swabian and Later Institutions in Southern Italy*, London.

(1973), 'La legislazione normanna', in *Atti . . . Sicilia Normanna*, 195–212.

Martin, Jean-Marie (1979), 'Les communautés d'habitants de la Pouille et leur rapports avec Roger II', in *Società, potere e popolo nell'età di Ruggero II*, 73–98.

(1986), 'Le monete d'argento nell'Italia meridionale del secolo XII secondo i documenti d'archivio', *Bollettino di numismatica* 6–7, 85–96.

(1990), 'Città e campagne: economia e società (sec. VII–XIII)', in *Storia del Mezzogiorno* III, Napoli, 257–382.

(1993), *La Pouille du VIe au XIIe siècle*, Rome.

(1994a), *Italies normandes. XIe–XIIe siècles*, Paris [Italian edition, *La vita quotidiana nell'Italia meridionale al tempo dei normanni*, Milan 1997].

(1994b), 'Législation royale, coutumes locales, procédure: la haute justice en Apulie et Terre de Labour au XIIe siècle', in *Le Assise di Ariano 1140–1990*, 137–63 [Italian translation in 1996 reprint, 127–51].

(1996), 'L'administration du Royaume entre Normands et Souabes', in Kölzer (1996), 113–40.

Mathieu, Marguerite (1954), 'La Sicile normande dans la poésie byzantine', *Bollettino del Centro di studi filologici e linguistici siciliani 2*, 52–84.

Matthew, Donald J. A. (1981), 'The Chronicle of Romuald of Salerno', in *The Writing of History in the Middle Ages. Essays Presented to R. W. Southern*, ed. R. H. C. Davis and J. M. Wallace-Hadrill, Oxford, 239–74.

(1988), *L'Europa normanna*, Rome.

(1992), *The Norman Kingdom of Sicily*, Cambridge.

Maurici, Ferdinando (1992), *Castelli medievali in Sicilia. Dai bizantini ai normanni*, Palermo.

Mayer, Hans Eberhard (1984), *Mélanges sur l'histoire du royaume latin de Jérusalem* (Mémoires de l'Académie des Inscriptions et belles lettres n.s. 5), Paris.

(1988), *The Crusades*, trans. J. Gillingham, 2nd edn, Oxford.

Mazzarese Fardella, Enrico (1966), *Aspetti dell'organizzazione amministrativa nello Stato normanno e svevo*, Milan.

(1994), 'Note sull'amministrazione normanna al tempo di Ruggero II', in *Le Assise di Ariano 1140–1990*, 125–36 [reprint, 115–25].

Meier, Hans-Rudolf (1994), *Die normannischen Königspaläste in Palermo. Studien zur hochmittelalterlichen Residenzbaukunst*, Worms.

Ménager, Léon-Robert (1957), 'Notes et documents sur quelques monastères de Calabre à l'époque normande', in *Byzantinische Zeitschrift 50*, 7–30, 321–61.

(1958), 'Notes sur les codifications byzantines et l'Occident', in *Varia. Etudes de Droit Romain 3*, Paris, 239–303.

(1959), 'L'institution monarchique dans les Etats normands d'Italie. Contribution à l'étude du pouvoir royal dans les principautés occidentales, aux XIe–XIIe siècles', *Cahiers de civilisations médiévale 2*, 303–31, 445–68.

(1960), *Ammiratus–Ἀμηρᾶς. L'émirat et les origines de l'amirauté (XIe-XIIIe siècles)*, Paris.

(1969), 'La législation sud-italienne sous la domination normande', in *I Normanni e la loro espansione in Europa nell'alto Medioevo* (Settimane di studio del Centro italiano di studi sull'alto medievo 16), Spoleto, 439–96.

(1975a), 'Pesanteur et étiologie de la colonisation normande de l'Italie', in *Roberto il Guiscardo e il suo tempo*, 189–215; reprinted in Ménager (1981), no. IV.

(1975b), 'Inventaire des familles normandes et franques émigrées en Italie méridionale et en Sicile (XIe–XIIe siècles)', in *Roberto il Guiscardo e il suo tempo*, 259–390; reprinted with additions in Ménager (1981), no. v.

(1981), *Hommes et institutions de l'Italie normande*, London.

(1984), 'Costanza di Francia', *DBI* 30, 361–3.

Merores, Margarete (1911), *Gaeta im frühen Mittelalter (8. bis 12. Jahrhundert). Beiträge zur Geschichte der Stadt*, Gotha.

Messina, Aldo (1992), 'Gli arabi cristiani della Sicilia normanna', *Rivista di Storia della Chiesa in Italia* 46, 483–8.

(1993), 'Uomini e mestieri della Sicilia normanna', *QFIAB* 73, 19–51.

Messina. Il ritorno della memoria, Catalogo della mostra Messina, Palazzo Zanca 1 marzo–28 aprile 1994, Palermo 1994.

Il Mezzogiorno normanno-svevo visto dall'Europa e dal mondo mediterraneo. Atti delle tredicesime giornate normanno-sveve, Bari 21–24 ottobre 1997 (Centro di studi normanno-svevi, Università degli Studi di Bari, Atti 13), ed. G. Musca, Bari 1999.

Mittellateinisches Wörterbuch bis zum ausgehenden 13. Jahrhundert, Bayerischen Akademie der Wissenschaften et al., 2nd edn, Munich 1968–94.

Monasticon Italiae III: Puglia e Basilicata, ed. G. Lunardi, H. Houben and G. Spinelli, Cesena 1986.

Monneret de Villard, Ugo (1950), *Le pitture musulmane al soffitto della Cappella Palatina in Palermo*, Rome.

Morisanus, Josephus (1768), *De protopapis et deutereis Graecorum et catholicis eorum ecclesiis diatriba*, Naples.

Morpurgo, Piero (1989), '"Nos vero physicae rationis sectatores". La scuola medica salernitana nel secolo XII tra le invettive di Gerardo da Cremona e l'intervento di Federico II', *Quaderni medievali* 28, 37–61.

(1993), *L'idea di natura nell'Italia normannosveva*, Bologna.

(1997), 'I centri di cultura scientifica', in *Centri di produzione della cultura*, 119–44.

Musca, Giosué and Raffaele Iorio (eds.) (1997), *Ruggero II d'Altavilla*, Rome.

Naumann, Claudia (1994), *Der Kreuzzug Kaiser Heinrichs VI.*, Frankfurt am Main.

Neitmann, Klaus (1990), 'Was ist eine Residenz? Methodische Überlegungen zur Erforschung der spätmittelalterlichen Residenzbildung', in *Vorträge und Forschungen zur Residenzenfrage*, ed. P. Johanek, Sigmaringen, 11–43.

Niederkorn, Jan Paul (1986), 'Die Mitgift der Kaiserin Irene. Anmerkungen zur byzantinischen Politik König Konrads III', *Römische Historische Mitteilungen* 28, 125–39.

(1993), 'Konrad III. als Gegenkönig in Italien', *DA* 49, 589–600.

Niese, Hans (1910), *Die Gesetzgebung der normannischen Dynastie im Regnum Siciliae*, Halle.

I Normanni. Popolo d'Europa, 1030–1200 (Catalogo della mostra Roma 1994), ed. M. D'Onofrio, Venezia 1994.

Norwich, John Julius (1967), *The Normans in the South 1016–1130*, London.

(1970), *The Kingdom in the Sun 1130–1194*, London.

Noth, Albrecht, see Brühl (1978)

Oexle, Otto Gerhard (1983), 'Die Gegenwart der Toten', in *Death in the Middle Ages*, ed. H. Braet and W. Verbeke, Louvain, 19–77.

Oldoni, Massimo (1978), 'Intellettuali cassinesi di fronte ai Normanni (secoli XI–XII)', in *Miscellanea di storia italiana e mediterranea per Nino Lamboglia*, Genoa, 93–153.

—— (1979), 'Realismo e dissidenza nella storiografia su Ruggero II: Falcone da Benevento e Alessandro di Telese', in *Società, potere e popolo nell'età di Ruggero II*, 259–83.

Oman, Giovanni (1970), 'Osservazioni sulle notizie biografiche comunemente diffuse sullo scrittore arabo al-Šarīf al-Idrīsī (VI–XII sec.)', *Annali dell'Istituto Orientale di Napoli* 30, 209–38.

Palumbo, Pier Fausto (1942), *Lo scisma del MCXXX. I precedenti, la vicenda romana e le ripercussioni europee della lotta tra Anacleto e Innocenzo II*, Rome.

Paravicini Bagliani, Agostino (1983), 'La provenienza "angioina" dei codici greci della biblioteca di Bonifacio VIII. Una revisione critica', in *Italia medioevale e umanistica* 26, 27–69.

Pasqua, Ottaviano (1755), 'Vitae episcoporum Ecclesiae Hieraciensis', in *Constitutiones et acta sinodi Hieraciensis ab illustriss(imo) et reverendiss(imo) domino Caesare Rossi episcopo celebratae diebus 10, 11 & 12 Novembris 1754*, Naples.

Pavoni, Romeo (1991), 'Il mercante', in *Condizione umana e ruola sociale*, 215–50.

Pedìo, Tommaso (1962), 'La vita a Potenza dai Normanni agli Aragonesi attraverso una inedita cronaca del sec. XVII ed un inedito Codice diplomatico', *Archivio storico pugliese* 15, 119–74; separately Tommaso, *Potenza dai Normanni agli Aragonesi. Note ed appunti*, Bari 1964.

Pellettieri, Antonella (1996/7), 'Le pergamene di Potenza di età normanno-sveva (1178–1257)', *Tarsia* [Melfi] 20, 69–92.

Pene Vidari, Gian Savino (1994), '"Assise", consuetudini, statuti: note comparative', in *Le Assise di Ariano 1140–1990*, 203–31; reprint, 191–217.

Peri, Illuminato (1978), *Uomini, città e campagne in Sicilia dall'XI al XIII secolo*, Rome–Bari.

Perla, Raffaele (1885), 'Del diritto romano giustinianeo nelle province meridionali d'Italia prima delle Assise Normanne', in *Archivio storico per le provincie napoletane* 10, 130–85.

Pertusi, Agostino (1977), 'Aspetti letterari: continuità e sviluppi della tradizione greca, in Il passaggio dal dominio bizantino allo Stato normanno nell'Italia meridionale', in *Atti del secondo Convegno di studio sulla civiltà rupestre*, ed. C. D. Fonseca, Taranto, 63–101.

Petersohn, Jürgen (1993), 'Echte und falsche Insignien im deutschen Krönungsbrauch des Mittelalters? Kritik eines Forschungsstereotyps', in *Sitzungsberichte der wissenschaftlichen Gesellschaft an der Johann-Wolfgang Goethe-Universität, Frankfurt am Main* 30 (3), Stuttgart, 72–119.

—— (1994), 'Der Brief der Römer an König Lothar III. vom Jahre 1130. Überlieferung – Text – Absenderschaft', *DA* 50, 461–507.

Petrucci, Armando (1965a), 'Basunvilla, Roberto (I)', *DBI* 7, 185–6.

(1965b), 'Basunvilla, Roberto (II)', *DBI* 7, 186–8.

Piltz, Elisabeth (1977), *Kamelaukion et mitra. Insignes byzantins impériaux et ecclésiastiques*, Stockholm.

Pio, Bernardo (1996), *Guglielmo I d'Altavilla. Gestione del potere e lotta politica nell'Italia normanna (1154–1169)*, Bologna.

Pispisa, Enrico (1993), 'Messina', in *Itinerari e centri urbani nel Mezzogiorno*, 147–94.

Pistarino, Geo (1979), 'Commercio e vie marittime di comunicazione all'epoca di Ruggero II', in *Società, potere e popolo nell'età di Ruggero II*, 239–58.

(1981), 'Commercio e comunicazioni tra Genova e il Regno normanno-svevo', in *Potere, società e popolo nell'età di due Guglielmi*, 231–90.

Pontieri, Ernesto (1955), 'La madre di re Ruggero: Adelaide del Vasto contessa di Sicilia, regina di Gerusalemme (?–1118)', in *Atti...di Studi Ruggeriani* II.327–432; reprinted E. Pontieri, *Tra i Normanni nell'Italia meridionale*, 2nd edn, Naples 1964, 409–509.

Poso, Cosimo Damiano (1988), *Il Salento normanno. Territorio, istituzioni, società*, Galatina 1988.

(1996), 'Lecce normanna e sveva. Dalla signoria alla contea', *Università degli Studi di Lecce, Annali del Dipartimento di Scienze Storiche, Filosofiche e Geografiche* 9–12 (1992–3/1995–6) (=*Studi in onore di Domenico Novembre*), 39–64.

Potere, società e popolo nell'età dei due Guglielmi. Atti delle quarte giornate normanno-sveve (Bari–Gioia del Colle, 8–10 ottobre 1979) (Centro di studi normanno-svevi, Università degli Studi di Bari, Atti 4), Bari 1981.

Potere, società e popolo tra età normanna ed età sveva (1189–1210). Atti delle quinte giornate normanno-sveve (Bari–Conversano, 26–28 ottobre 1981) (Centro di studi normanno-svevi, Università degli Studi di Bari, Atti 5), Bari 1983.

Probleme um Friedrich II., ed. J. Fleckenstein (Vorträge und Forschungen 16), Sigmaringen 1974.

Pryor, John (1988), *Geography, Technology and War. Studies in the Maritime History of the Mediterranean, 649–1571*, Cambridge.

Rassow, Peter (1954), 'Zum byzantinisch-normannischen Krieg 1147–1149', *Mitteilungen des Instituts für Österreichische Geschichtsforschung* 62, 213–18.

Reichert, Folker (1995), 'Geographie und Weltbild am Hofe Friedrichs II.', *DA* 51, 433–91.

Reisinger, Christoph (1992), *Tankred von Lecce. Normannischer König von Sizilien 1190–1194*, Cologne–Weimar–Vienna.

Reuter, Timothy (1983), 'Die Anerkennung Papst Innozenz' II. Eine neue Quelle', *DA* 39, 395–416.

(1996), 'Vom Parvenü zum Bündnispartner: das Königreich Sizilien in der abendländischen Politik des 12. Jahrhunderts', in Kölzer (1996), 43–56.

Rizzitano, Umberto (1973), 'La cultura araba nella Sicilia normanna', in *Atti... Sicilia Normanna*, 279–97.

(1977), 'Ruggero il Gran Conte e gli Arabi di Sicilia', in *Ruggero il Gran Conte e l'inizio dello stato normanno*, 189–212 [reprint, 199–222].

Roberto il Guiscardo e il suo tempo. Relazioni e comunicazioni nelle prime giornate normanno-sveve (Bari, maggio 1973) (Fonti e studi del Corpus membranarum italicarum 11), Rome 1975 [reprint Centro di studi normanno-svevi, Università degli Studi di Bari, Atti 1, Bari 1991].

Roberto il Guiscardo tra Europa, Oriente e Mezzogiorno. Atti del Convegno internazionale di studio in occasione del IX centenario della morte di Roberto il Guiscardo (Potenza–Melfi–Potenza, 19–23 ottobre 1985), ed. C. D. Fonseca, Galatina 1990.

Robinson, I. S. (1990), *The Papacy 1073–1198. Continuity and Innovation,* Cambridge.

Rocco, Benedetto (1977), 'Il tabulario della Cappella Palatina di Palermo e il martirologio di epoca Ruggeriana', *Ho Theologos* 14, 131–44.

Rossetti, Gabriella (1986), 'Civiltà urbana e sistema dei rapporti nell'Europa del Medioevo e della prima età moderna: una proposta di ricerca', in *Spazio, società, potere nell'Italia dei comuni,* 307–19.

Rubinacci, Roberto (1970), 'La data della geografia di al-Idrīsī', *Studi Magrebini* 3, 73–7.

Ruggero il Gran Conte e l'inizio dello Stato normanno (Fonti e studi del Corpus membranarum italicarum 12), Rome 1977 [reprint, Università degli Studi di Bari, Centro di studi normanno-svevi. Atti 2, Bari 1991].

Salvati, Catello (1970), *Misure e pesi nella documentazione storica dell'Italia del Mezzogiorno,* Naples.

Samman, Tarif al (1982), 'Arabische Inschriften auf den Krönungsgewändern des Heiligen Römischen Reiches', *Jahrbuch der Kunsthistorischen Sammlungen in Wien* 78, 7–34.

San Bernardo e l'Italia. Atti del Convegno di studi Milano, 24–26 maggio 1990, ed. P. Zerbi, Milan 1993.

Sangermano, Gerardo (1993), 'Amalfi', in *Itinerari e centri urbani nel Mezzogiorno,* 225–48.

Santini, Giovanni (1994), 'Problemi relativi alle Assise di Ariano: gli uomini di legge', in *Le Assise di Ariano 1140–1990,* 89–123 [reprint, 81–113].

Scaduto, Mario (1982), *Il monachesimo basiliano nella Sicilia medievale. Rinascita e decadenza (sec. XI–XIV),* 2nd edn, Rome.

Scalia, Giuseppe (1980), 'Contributi pisani alla lotta anti-islamica nel Mediterraneo centro-occidentale durante il secolo XI e nei primi decenni del XII', *Anuario de Estudios Medievales* 10, 135–44.

Schack, Dietlind (1969), 'Die Araber im Reich Rogers II.' (Ph. Dissertation, Freie Universität Berlin [in MS]).

Schaller, Hans Martin (1963), 'Das Relief an der Kanzel der Kathedrale von Bitonto. Ein Denkmal der Kaiseridee Friedrichs II.', *Archiv für Kulturgeschichte* 45, 295–312; reprinted in Schaller, *Stauferzeit. Ausgewählte Aufsätze,* Hanover 1993, 1–23.

— (1995), 'Wann und wo wurde Friedrich II. getauft?', in *Regensburg, Bayern und Europa. Festschrift für Kurt Reindel zum 70. Geburtstag,* ed. L. Kolmar and P. Segl, Regensburg, 301–6.

Schilling, Beate (1998), *Guido von Vienne–Papst Calixt II.,* Hanover.

Schipperges, Heinrich (1981), 'Die Rezeption arabisch-griechischer Medizin und ihr Einfluss auf die abendländische Heilkunde', in *Die Renaissance der Wissenschaften im 12. Jahrhundert*, Zürich, ed. P. Weimar, 173–96.

Schmale, Franz-Josef (1961), *Studien zum Schisma des Jahres 1130*, Cologne–Graz.

(1978), 'Arnold von Berge und Nienburg', in *Die deutsche Literatur des Mittelalters. Verfasserlexikon*, 2nd edn, ed. K. Ruh *et al.*, 1.462–4.

Schminck, Christoph Ulrich (1970), *Crimen laesae maiestatis. Das politische Strafrecht Siziliens nach den Assissen von Ariano (1140) und den Konstitutionen von Melfi (1231)*, Aalen.

Schramm, Percy Ernst, Josef Deér *et al.* (1955), *Herrschaftszeichen und Staatssymbolik. Beiträge zu ihrer Geschichte vom dritten bis zum sechzehnten Jahrhundert*, 3 vols., Stuttgart.

Schreiner, Klaus (1990), '"Er küsse mich mit dem Kuß seines Mundes" (Osculetur me osculo oris sui, Cant 1, 1). Metaphorik, kommunikative und herrschaftliche Funktion einer symbolischen Handlung', in *Höfische Repräsentation. Das Zeremoniell und die Zeichen*, ed. H. Ragotzky and H. Wenzel, Tübingen, 171–208.

Schreiner, Peter (1992), 'Byzanz und der Westen: die gegenseitige Betrachtungsweise in der Literatur des 12. Jahrhunderts', in Haverkamp (1992), 551–80.

Schulz, Heinrich Wilhelm (1860), *Denkmäler der Kunst des Mittelalters in Unteritalien*, ed. F. von Quast, 1, Dresden.

Schütz, Walter (1995), *Catalogus comitum. Versuch einer Territorialgliederung Kampaniens unter den Normannen von 1000 bis 1140 von Benevent bis Salerno*, Frankfurt am Main.

Schwarz, Ulrich (1978), *Amalfi im frühen Mittelalter (9–11. Jahrhundert). Untersuchungen zur Amalfitaner Überlieferung*, Tübingen.

Sennis, Antonio (1994), 'Potere centrale e forze locali in un territorio di frontiera: la Marsica tra i secoli VIII e XII', *Bollettino dell'Istituto Storico Italiano per il Medio Evo e Arch. Muratoriano* 99, 1–77.

Serafin Petrillo, Patrizia and Lucia Travaini (1986), 'Le monete argentee dei Normanni di Sicilia nella collezione di Vittorio Emanuele III di Savoia', *Bullettino di Numismatica* 6–7, 97–126.

Servatius, Carlo (1979), *Paschalis II. (1099–1118). Studien zu seiner Person und seiner Politik*, Stuttgart.

Settia, Aldo A. (1994), 'Un "Lombardo" alla prima crociata. Tecnologie militari fra Occidente e Oriente', in *Società, istituzioni, spiritualità*, II.843–55 [Also published in Settia, *Comuni in guerra. Armi ed eserciti nell'Italia delle città*, Bologna 1993, 249–60].

Settis Frugoni, Chiara (1968), 'Per una lettura del mosaico pavimentale della cattedrale di Otranto', *Bullettino dell'Istituto Storico Italiano per il Medio Evo e Archivio Muratoriano* 80, 213–56.

(1970), 'Il mosaico di Otranto: modelli culturali e scelte iconografiche', *Bullettino dell'Istituto Storico Italiano per il Medio Evo e Archivio Muratoriano* 82, 243–70.

Ševčenko, Ihor (1984), 'The Madrid Manuscript of the Chronicle of Skylitzes in the Light of its New Dating', in *Byzanz und der Westen. Studien zur Kunst des europäischen Mittelalters*, ed. I. Hutter (Österreichische Akademie der Wissenschaften, Phil.-hist. K1., SB 432), Vienna, 117–30.

Shahīd, Irfan (1978), 'Ḳayṣar', in *Encyclopédie de l'Islam* 4², 872–3.

Siragusa, Giovan Battista (1910), 'La tomba di Sibilla regina', in *Centenario della nascita di Michele Amari* II.252–61.

Skinner, Patricia (1995), *Family Power in Southern Italy. The Duchy of Gaeta and its Neighbours 850–1139*, Cambridge.

Società, istituzioni, spiritualità. Studi in onore di Cinzio Violante, 2 vols., Spoleto 1994.

Società, potere e popolo nell'età di Ruggero II (Università degli Studi di Bari, Centro di studi normanno-svevi. Atti 3), Bari 1979.

Southern, R. W. (1979), *Platonism, Scholastic Method and the School of Chartres. The Stenton Lecture for 1978*, Reading.

Spazio, società, potere nell'Italia dei Comuni, ed. G. Rossetti, Naples 1986.

Steinberg, Sigfrid H. (1937), 'I ritratti dei re normanni di Sicilia', *La Bibliofilia* 39, 29–57.

Sthamer, Eduard (1995), *L'amministrazione dei castelli nel Regno di Sicilia sotto Federico II e Carlo I d'Angiò*, ed. H. Houben, Bari; originally published as *Die Verwaltung der Kastelle im Königreich Sizilien unter Kaiser Friedrich II. und Karl I. von Anjou*, Leipzig 1914; reprinted Tübingen 1997.

Störmer, Wilhelm (1992), 'Königtum und Kaisertum in der mittelhochdeutschen Literatur der Zeit Friedrich Barbarossas', in Haverkamp (1992), 581–601.

Stroll, Mary (1987), *The Jewish Pope. Ideology and Politics in the Papal Schism of 1130*, Leiden.

Strumenti, tempi e luoghi di comunicazione nel Mezzogiorno normanno-svevo. Atti delle undecime giornate normanno-sveve (Bari, 26–29 ottobre 1993), (Università degli Studi di Bari, Centro di studi normanno-svevi, Atti 11), ed. G. Musca and V. Sivo, Bari 1995.

Stürner, Wolfgang (1975), *Natur und Gesellschaft im Denken des Hoch- und Spätmittelalters. Naturwissenschaftliche Kraftvorstellungen und die Motivierung politischen Handelns in Texten des 12. bis 14. Jahrhunderts*, Stuttgart.

—— (1992), *Friedrich II., Teil 1: Die Königsherrschaft in Sizilien und Deutschland 1194–1220*, Darmstadt.

ΣΥΝΔΕΣΜΟΣ. *Studi in onore di Rosario Anastasi*, 2 vols., Catania 1994.

Takayama, Hiroshi (1985), 'The Financial and Administrative Organization of the Norman Kingdom of Sicily', *Viator* 16, 129–57.

—— (1989), 'Familiares regis and the Royal Inner Council in Twelfth-Century Sicily', *English Historical Review* 104, 357–72.

—— (1990), 'The Great Administrative Officials of the Norman Kingdom of Sicily', *Papers of the British School at Rome* 58, 317–35.

—— (1993), *The Administration of the Norman Kingdom of Sicily*, Leiden.

Tangheroni, Marco (1996), *Commercio e navigazione nel Medioevo*, Rome–Bari.

Taviani-Carozzi, Huguette (1991), *La principauté lombarde de Salerne (IXᵉ-XIᵉ siècle). Pouvoir et société en Italie lombarde méridionale*, Rome.

(1996), *La terreur du monde. Robert Guiscard et la conquête normande en Italie. Mythe et histoire*, Paris.

Terra e uomini nel Mezzogiorno normanno-svevo. Atti delle settime giornate normanno-sveve (Bari, 15–17 ottobre 1985) (Università degli Studi di Bari, Centro di studi normanno-svevi, Atti 7), ed. G. Musca, Bari 1987.

Tessitore, Giovanni (1995), *Ruggero II*, Palermo.

Thompson, Kathleen (1997), 'The Formation of the County of Perche: the Rise and Fall of the House of Gouet', *Family Trees and the Roots of Power*, ed. K. S. B. Keats-Rohan, Woodbridge, 299–314.

Todisco, Luigi (1987), 'L'antico nel campanile normanno di Melfi', *Mélanges de l'Ecole Française de Rome, Moyen Age–Temps Modernes* 99, 123–58.

Toubert, Pierre (1979), 'La terre et les hommes dans l'Italie normande au temps de Roger II: l'exemple campanien', in *Società, potere e popolo nell'età di Ruggero II*, 55–71.

Tramontana, Salvatore (1977), 'Popolazione, distribuzione della terra e classe sociali nella Sicilia di Ruggero il Gran Conte', in *Ruggero il Gran Conte e l'inizio dello stato normanno*, 213–70 [reprint, 223–80].

(1983), 'La monarchia normanna e sveva, in A. Guillou e. a., Il Mezzogiorno dai Bizantini a Federico II', *Storia d'Italia*, ed. G. Galasso, III, Turin, 435–810 [also as a separate volume, Turin 1986].

(1993), *Vestirsi e travestirsi in Sicilia. Abbigliamento, feste e spettacoli nel Medioevo*, Palermo.

Trasselli, Carmelo (1992), *I privilegi di Messina e di Trapani (1160–1355). Con un'appendice sui consolati trapanesi nel sec. XV*, 2nd edn, Messina.

Travaini, Lucia (1995), *La monetazione nell'Italia normanna*, Rome.

(1996), 'The Monetary Reforms of William II (1166–1189): Oriental and Western Patterns in Norman Sicilian Coinage', *Schweizer Münzblätter* 46, 109–23.

Trombetti Budriesi, Anna Laura (1992), 'Sulle Assise di Ruggero II', in *Unità politica e differenze regionali*, 63–83.

(1994), 'Il testo latino delle "Assise" di Ruggero II nella tradizione del "Liber Augustalis"', in *Le Assise di Ariano 1140–1990*, 245–305 [reprint, 231–90].

Tronzo, William (1997), *The Cultures of His Kingdom. Roger II and the Cappella Palatina in Palermo*, Princeton.

Turner, Ralph V. (1986), 'Les contacts entre l'Angleterre normanno-angevine et la Sicile normande. Un réexamen du "Mythe Normand" de Davis', *Etudes normandes* 55, 39–60.

Unità politica e differenze regionali nel Regno di Sicilia. Atti del Convegno internazionale di studio in occasione dell'VIII centenario della morte di Guglielmo II, re di Sicilia (Lecce–Potenza, 19–22 aprile 1989), ed. C. D. Fonseca, H. Houben and B. Vetere, Galatina 1992.

Valenziano, Maria and Crispino Valenziano (1978), 'La supplique des chanoines de la cathédrale de Cefalù pour la sépolture du roi Roger', *Cahiers de civilisation médiévale* 21, 3–30, 137–50.

Vallone, Giancarlo (1994), 'Lecce normanna e quattro documenti della sua storia medievale', *Bollettino storico di Terra d'Otranto* 4, 215–26.

Varga, Livia (1993), 'A New Aspect of the Porphyry Tombs of Roger II, First King of Sicily, in Cefalù', *Anglo-Norman Studies* 15, 307–15.

Várvaro, Alberto (1981), *Lingua e storia in Sicilia (Dalle guerre puniche alla conquista normanna)*, i, Palermo.

　(1987), 'Il regno normanno-svevo', in *Letteratura italiana. Storia e geografia, i: L'età medievale*, Turin, 79–99.

Vehse, Otto (1930–1), 'Benevent als Territorium des Kirchenstaates bis zum Beginn der Avignonesischen Epoche, i. Bis zum Ausgang der normännischen Dynastie', *QFIAB* 22, 87–160.

Vernet, Juan (1984), *Die spanisch-arabische Kultur in Orient und Okzident*, Zürich–Munich.

Violante, Cinzio and Johannes Fried (eds.) 1993, *Il secolo XI: una svolta?*, Bologna.

Vitolo, Giovanni (1983), 'Cava e Cluny', in Simeone Leone and Giovanni Vitolo, *Minima Cavensia. Studi in margine al IX volume del Codex Diplomaticus Cavensis*, Salerno, 19–44 [also published in *L'Italia nel quadro dell'espansione europea del monachesimo cluniacense. Atti del Convegno internazionale di Storia medioevale (Pescia, 26–28 novembre 1981)*, ed. C. Violante, A. Spicciani and G. Spinelli, Cesena 1985, 199–220].

　(1987), 'I prodotti della terra: orti e frutteti', in *Terra e uomini nel Mezzogiorno normanno-svevo*, 159–85.

　(1988), 'La conquista normanna nel contesto economico del Mezzogiorno', *Rassegna Storica Salernitana* 9, 7–21; reprinted in *Roberto il Guiscardo tra Europa, Oriente e Mezzogiorno*, 83–94.

　(1990), *Città e coscienza cittadina nel Mezzogiorno medioevale (secc. IX–XIII)*, Salerno 1990.

　(1994–5), 'Sergius VII.', *LdM* vii.1788.

Vollrath, Hanna (1977), 'Konrad III. und Byzanz', *Archiv für Kulturgeschichte* 59, 321–65.

Vones, Ludwig (1983), *Geschichte der Iberischen Halbinsel im Mittelalter 711–1480. Reiche–Kronen–Regionen*, Sigmaringen.

Walter, Ingeborg (1965), 'Beatrice di Rethel', *DBI* 7, 369.

Wansbrough, John (1984), 'Diplomatica Siciliana', *Bulletin of the School of Oriental and African Studies* 47, 10–21.

Warren, W. L. (1973), *Henry II*, Berkeley.

　(1984), 'The Myth of Norman Administrative Efficiency', *Transactions of the Royal Historical Society* 5th series 34, 113–32.

White, Lynn Townsend jr. (1938), *Latin Monasticism in Norman Sicily*, Cambridge, Mass.

Wieruszowski, Helene (1963), 'Roger II of Sicily, Rex-Tyrannus, in Twelfth-Century Political Thought', *Speculum* 38, 46–78; reprinted in Wieruszowski (1971), 51–97.

　(1969), 'The Norman Kingdom of Sicily and the Crusades', in K. M. Setton, *A History of the Crusades*, ii *The Later Crusades, 1189–1311*, ed. R. L. Wolff and H. W. Hazard, Madison–Milwaukee–London 1969, 3–42; reprinted in Wieruszowski (1971), 3–49.

(1971), *Politics and Culture in Medieval Spain and Italy*, Rome.

Wiest, Elisabeth (1995), 'Die Anfänge der Johanniter im Königreich Sizilien bis 1200', in *Von Schwaben bis Jerusalem. Facetten staufischer Geschichte*, ed. S. Lorenz and U. Schmidt, Sigmaringen, 167–86.

Willemsen, Carl Arnold (1980), *L'enigma di Otranto. il mosaico pavimentale del presbitero Pantaleone nella Cattedrale*, Galatina.

Wilson, Nigel G. (1983), *Scholars of Byzantium*, London.

Winkelmann, Eduard (1878), 'Reisefrüchte aus Italien und anderes zur deutsch-italischen Geschichte', *Forschungen zur Deutschen Geschichte* 18 (1878), 469–92.

Zecchino, Ortensio (1980), *Le Assise di Ruggiero II. Problemi di storia delle fonti e di diritto penale*, Naples.

(1994), 'I Parlamenti nel Regno di Ruggero II', in *Le Assise di Ariano 1140–1990*, 61–88 [reprint, 55–80].

Zeitler, B. (1996), '"Urbs felix dotata populo trilingui": Some Thoughts about a Twelfth-Century Funerary Memorial from Palermo', *Medieval Encounters* 2(2), 114–39.

Zerbi, Pietro (1993), 'San Bernardo di Clairvaux e Milano', in *San Bernardo e l'Italia*, 51–68.

Zielinski, Herbert (1982), 'Zum Königstitel Rogers II. von Sizilien (1130–1154)', in *Politik, Gesellschaft, Geschichtsschreibung. Giessener Festgabe für František Graus zum 60. Geburtstag*, ed. H. Ludat and R. C. Schwinges, Cologne–Vienna, 165–82.

Ziese, Jürgen (1982), *Wibert von Ravenna: der Gegenpapst Clemens III. (1084–1100)*, Stuttgart.

Zinzi, Emilia (1986), 'L'immagine tramandata', in *La cattedrale di Gerace. Il monumento, le funzioni, i corredi*, ed. S. Gemelli, Genoa, 56–83.

Zug Tucci, Hannelore (1995), 'Armi e armature', in *Strumenti, tempi e luoghi di communicazione*, 131–51.

INDEX

Cambridge Medieval Textbooks

Already published

Germany in the High Middle Ages c. 1050–1200
HORST FUHRMANN

The Hundred Years War
England and France at War c. 1300–c. 1450
CHRISTOPHER ALLMAND

Standards of Living in the Later Middle Ages:
Social Change in England, c. 1200–1520
CHRISTOPHER DYER

Magic in the Middle Ages
RICHARD KIECKHEFER

The Papacy 1073–1198: Continuity and Innovation
I. S. ROBINSON

Medieval Wales
DAVID WALKER

England in the Reign of Edward III
SCOTT L. WAUGH

The Norman Kingdom of Sicily
DONALD MATTHEW

Political Thought in Europe 1250–1450
ANTONY BLACK

The Church in Western Europe from the Tenth to the Early Twelfth
Century
GERD TELLENBACH
Translated by Timothy Reuter

The Medieval Spains
BERNARD F. REILLY

England in the Thirteenth Century
ALAN HARDING

Monastic and Religious Orders in Britain 1000–1300
JANET BURTON